CH00616529

DATE 6-7.

SIGNATURE:

ELEMENTARY, MY DEAR WATSON

Bevis Colmer

MINERVA PRESS
LONDON
MIAMI   RIO DE JANEIRO   DELHI

ELEMENTARY, MY DEAR WATSON
Copyright © Bevis Colmer 2000

ISBN 0 75411 000 1

First Published 2000 by
MINERVA PRESS
315–317 Regent Street
London W1R 7YB

Printed in Great Britain for Minerva Press

ELEMENTARY, MY DEAR WATSON

Dedicated to Barbara, my wife

About the Author

Before the Second World War, Bevis Colmer assisted his father, Francis Colmer, with his research into the history and archaeology of Buckinghamshire. He assisted in the excavation of a Bronze Age crouching burial, an Iron Age pit-dwelling and two Roman villas; he also collected rubbings of church monumental brasses.

On the day that France capitulated, 17 June 1940, the author was drafted into RAF Signals, being stationed at Northolt, and in Egypt, Iraq and Bahrain in the Persian Gulf. He was awarded the Africa Star, the 1939–1945 Star and the Defence Medal.

After the war, he became a cartographical draughtsman for the Ordnance Survey, then a recorder in the Archaeology Branch of the O.S. and, later, he worked as a cartographical draughtsman in the Ministry of Defence, London, until 1981. He has written a history of Shere School, 1842, and of Shere Bowling Club. He was a folk dancer and musician.

He married Barbara, a school teacher, in 1951. They have two children, Robin and Sally, and now have three grandchildren, Tom, Lucy and Laura.

Acknowledgements

The author acknowledges kind permission from Wordsworth Editions to quote from *The Original Illustrated 'Strand' Sherlock Holmes*.

Preface

It does not appear, that Holmes ever uttered the words of my title, *Elementary, My Dear Watson*, as such. As an excellent biographer, Watson did record Holmes as saying 'elementary' as he explained his deductions, which appeared to Watson so wonderful, and to Jabez Wilson as 'nothing in it after all', while 'my dear Watson' personified the affection and deep warmth that Holmes had for his only friend, oft-times belied by his cold, calculating exterior.

Watson wrote his accounts from notes he made in his journal, and from memory, and might well, unconsciously, have forgotten that the two expressions together slipped from the lips of the world-famous, unofficial consulting detective. All the information contained in the following pages, is to be found in the sixty stories of Holmes and Watson, written by Sir Arthur Conan Doyle between the years 1887 to 1927.

Contents

Early Years

Sherlock Holmes was sixty years old in August 1914, so that he was born in late 1853 or in 1854.[1] He was most reticent where his early life and family were concerned. His ancestors[2] were county squires, but which county is unknown.[3] Perhaps there had been nothing of exceptional moment to recall, nothing of note to be handed down verbally over the years; his artistic temperament he thought might have been derived from his grandmother, the sister of Vernet, the French artist; he was distantly related to a young Dr Verner. As Holmes said, 'Art in the blood is liable to take the strangest forms.' His brother Mycroft, seven years his senior, had powers of observation that were better than his own. He thought that his faculty of observation and facility for deduction were due mainly to his hereditary aptitudes, and to some extent to his own systematic training.

Were there any more children? Holmes did say once, speaking of Miss Violet Hunter, who had taken a post as governess with Jephro Rucastle, that 'no sister of his should ever have accepted such a situation'.[4] So perhaps Sherlock had a sister, or did he mean if he had had a sister? It certainly showed a tenderness and feeling for the fair sex.

We do not know anything of Holmes' parents. Even in the Baker Street days Watson makes no mention of family photographs gracing their sitting room in an age when family photographs abounded in their silver and velvet frames. Could his mother maybe have been American, for he was attracted to America and Americans – maybe a Miss Altamont, for it was quite

[1]Mention of Dr Sherlock, Captain and Mrs Watson in Daniel Defoe (1660–1731), *The True Relation of the Apparition of one Mrs Veal*, 1706.

[2]There was an Irish lawyer, Robert Holmes (1765–1859).

[3]Dr A C Donnelly of Dublin thought that Holmes' ancestral seat may have been Sherlockstown Castle, Sherlockstown, County Kildare (*Daily Telegraph*, 31 December 1987).

[4]Jephro. Used in ACD, *Lot 249*.

likely that Holmes chose a family name for his bogus American of the First World War. His parents must have been well-to-do as he was able to keep rooms in Montague Street, London, where he carried out experiments in organic chemistry during many weeks of the long college vacation and afterwards. We do not know which college; it might have been St Luke's; but Holmes visited this college with Watson, and upon his departure, called the Greek tutor Mr Hilton Soames just 'Soames'. Hardly such familiarity if he had been a former undergraduate!

At college Holmes was not a very sociable person, for he was always rather fond of staying in his rooms, working out his own little methods of thought, so that he never mixed very much with the men of his year. He restricted his fitness to boxing and fencing. His line of study was quite distinct from the others, so that there was no point of contact at all, and yet Holmes must have stirred up some interest as he and his methods were duly talked about. He had a slight acquaintance with Reginald Musgrave but his only friend was Victor Trevor during his two years' study.[5] Holmes learnt to swim, but whether here or during earlier grammar school holidays, we do not know.

Sherlock Holmes Meets James Armitage

Sherlock Holmes was first and foremost an organic chemist, his hobby the study of crime and criminals. He continued this study in his rooms in Montague Street and at Bart's Hospital. How then you might well ask, did he become the world's unofficial consulting detective? The answer is simple, even if a little unusual – a dog, a bull terrier, bit Holmes on the ankle when he one day went down to the college chapel. A strange reason, one might say; the dog happened to belong to an undergraduate called Victor Trevor. As Holmes related to Watson, later on:

'It was a prosaic way of forming a friendship, but it was effective. I was laid by the heels for ten days, and Trevor used to come in to inquire after me. At first it was only a minute's chat, but soon his visits lengthened, and before the end of the term we were close friends. He was a hearty, full-blooded fellow, full of

---

[5]Musgrove family (a for o) mentioned in Jane Austen, *Persuasion,* 1815.

spirits and energy, the very opposite to me in most respects, but we found we had some subjects in common, and it was a bond of union when I found he was as friendless as I. Finally, he invited me down to his father's place at Donnithorpe, in Norfolk, and I accepted his hospitality for a month of the long vacation.

'Old Trevor was evidently a man of some wealth and consideration, a Justice of the Peace and a landed proprietor. Donnithorpe is a little hamlet just to the north of Langmere, in the country of the Broads. The house was an old-fashioned, widespread, oak-beamed brick building, with a fine lime-lined avenue leading up to it. There was excellent wild-duck shooting in the fens, remarkably good fishing, a small but select library, taken over, as I understood, from a former occupant, and a tolerable cook, so that it would be a fastidious man who could not put in a pleasant month there.

'Trevor senior was a widower, and my friend was his only son. There had been a daughter, I heard, but she died of diphtheria while on a visit to Birmingham. The father interested me extremely. He was a man of little culture, but with a considerable amount of rude strength, both physically and mentally. He knew hardly any books, but he had travelled far, had seen much of the world, and had remembered all that he had learned. In person he was a thick-set, burly man with a shock of grizzled hair, a brown, weather-beaten face, and blue eyes which were keen to the verge of fierceness. Yet he had a reputation for kindness and charity on the country side, and was noted for the leniency of his sentences from the bench.

'One evening, shortly after my arrival, we were sitting over a glass of port after dinner, when young Trevor began to talk about those habits of observation and inference which I had already formed into a system, although I had not yet appreciated the part which they were to play in my life. The old man evidently thought that his son was exaggerating in his description of one or two trivial feats which I had performed.'

Laughing good-humouredly, he asked Holmes if he could deduce anything from him, for he thought himself an excellent subject.

'I fear there is not very much... I might suggest that you have gone about in fear of some personal attack within the last twelve months.' This caused the laugh to fade away from his host's lips as he stared in great surprise; he admitted that what Holmes said was true as he had been threatened by a poaching gang, that they would knife him. Holmes had observed Trevor's very handsome stick, perhaps only a year old, the head of which had been bored and filled with melted lead, making it a most formidable weapon.

Holmes also told him correctly that he had boxed a good deal in his youth, his ears having the peculiar flattening and thickening of the boxing man; that he had done a great deal of digging by his callosities, which Trevor told him had taken place in the gold-fields; that he had been in New Zealand and Japan.

But the most telling shot came when Holmes told Trevor that he had been most intimately associated with someone with the initials J A and whom he wanted to forget, whereupon Trevor stood up, fixed his eyes upon Holmes with a wild strange stare and then pitched forward in a dead faint with his face among the nutshells which strewed the tablecloth. The attack did not last long, he being revived by water sprinkled upon his face from one of the finger glasses.

Upon coming to, Trevor forced a smile as he said, 'I hope I haven't frightened you. Strong as I look, there is a weak place in my heart, and it does not take much to knock me over… Might I ask how you know, and how much you know?' he asked in a half-jesting fashion, trying to cover up the look of terror at the back of his eyes. Holmes explained: 'It is simplicity itself… When you bared your arm to draw that fish into the boat I saw that J A had been tattooed in the bend of the elbow. The letters were still legible, but it was perfectly clear from their blurred appearance, and from the staining of the skin round them, that efforts had been made to obliterate them. It was obvious, then, that those initials had once been very familiar to you, and that you had afterwards wished to forget them.' Trevor was relieved, thinking that much more had been read there. 'What an eye you have! …It is just as you say. But we won't talk of it. Of all ghosts the ghosts of our old loves are the worst. Come into the billiard-room and have a quiet cigar.' Earlier, coming round from his attack he commented: 'I don't know how you manage this, Mr Holmes, but it seems to me that all the detectives of fact and of fancy would be children in your hands. That's your line of life, sir, and you may take the word of a man who has seen something of the world.'

Just before Holmes curtailed his visit, Mr Trevor received a visitor, 'a little wizened fellow with a cringing manner and a shambling style of walking'. This was Hudson, who had sailed with Trevor in the convict ship the *Gloria Scott*, and witnessed the mutiny in 1855; he said that it was thirty years and more, since they had met.

Mr Trevor died of a stroke, following the receipt of a letter with the Fordingham postmark, just before Holmes arrived upon his second visit, seven weeks later, following a telegram from the son. Holmes was shown the short note scribbled upon a single sheet of grey paper, which had so seriously affected Mr Trevor. It read:

> THE SUPPLY OF GAME FOR LONDON IS GOING STEADILY UP. HEAD-KEEPER HUDSON, WE BELIEVE, HAS BEEN NOW TOLD TO RECEIVE ALL ORDERS FOR FLY-PAPER AND FOR PRESERVATION OF YOUR HEN-PHEASANT'S LIFE.

Holmes found the answer, that every third word beginning with the first, gave the message. In a letter to his son, Victor, James Armitage recalled his voyage with Hudson as thirty years ago so that Holmes visit was in 1885.[6]

The papers of James Armitage (found in a Japanese cabinet), were given to Holmes upon his returning to his London rooms, where he spent the rest of his vacation working out a few experiments in organic chemistry. Victor Trevor, heartbroken, went out to the Terai tea planting, where Holmes heard that he was doing very well.

Perhaps Holmes did not fully realise at the time just how much he owed to James Armitage, who set him upon the road to world acclaim; for the recommendation and the exaggerated estimate of his detection ability was the very first thing which ever made Holmes feel that a living might be made out of what was,

---

[6]Helen Stoner intended to marry Percy Armitage, ACD, *The Speckled Band*.

until then, a mere hobby. The extra ingredient was that danger attracted him.

Holmes now realised that he could bring about a most convenient marriage; that of his first love, chemistry, with the detection of crime; there would be a new approach to the subject, a new factor, the evidence of hard fact, gilded by chemistry, which would revolutionise the profession.

His chemical experiments at Baker Street gave his mind a necessary rest from the detective work; when he dissolved the hydrocarbon, concurring with one of our greatest statesmen, who said that a change of work is the best rest, he was then able, his mind being refreshed, to return to the problems of the Sholtos, and to rethink the whole matter. Similarly, when working upon the analysis of the acetones, which normally he would have continued through the night until completion, he thought better to postpone it, so that he and Watson could both get a good night's sleep before their journey on the morrow.

As late as 24 April 1891, Holmes was looking forward to the demise of Professor Moriarty, for that would be the zenith of his detective work, and his sound financial position would permit him to live in a quiet, congenial fashion, and he could then concentrate upon his first love, chemical research.

Did Holmes collate all his notes upon his various chemical experiments, with a view to publishing a textbook? If Watson knew, he made no mention of it, only recording that 'Science lost an acute reasoner, when he became a specialist in crime.'

Holmes remembered Cuvier, who could correctly describe a whole animal by the contemplation of a single bone.[7] So, thought Holmes, could he, having thoroughly understood one link in a series of incidents, be able accurately to state all the other ones, both before and after. He knew that he had not yet grasped the results which the reason alone could attain to. Problems might be solved in the study which had baffled all those who had sought a solution by the aid of their senses. To carry the art, however, to its highest pitch, it was necessary that the reasoner should be able to utilise all the facts which had come to his knowledge; this in itself

---

[7] Dupin quoted Cuvier in Edgar Allan Poe (1809–1849), *Murders in the Rue Morgue*.

implied a possession of all knowledge, a rare accomplishment, even with free education and the use of encyclopaedias. But it was not so impossible for a man to gain the knowledge likely to be useful to him in his work, and this is what Holmes set himself to accomplish.

There is nothing published about the second case of Sherlock Holmes – perhaps it hinged upon too delicate a matter in an exalted place.

The third of Holmes' early cases, while he still lived in Montague Street, just around the corner from the British Museum, was first written down by himself, and later embellished by Watson and published as 'The Musgrave Ritual'.

Although Reginald Musgrave had only a slight acquaintance with Holmes, while at college he had been very impressed with the nature of Holmes' work. After the lapse of some four years, he paid a visit to him in his rooms. He was now heir to the family home of the sixteenth-century Hurlstone Manor House, in Sussex, and he now sought help, as he understood that Holmes was now turning to practical ends those powers which had amazed the undergraduates. 'Yes,' said Holmes, 'I have taken to living by my wits.'

After long months of inaction, Holmes sensed that here was another chance to put his methods to the test and unravel the strange goings-on down in Sussex. First he would have to unravel the strange ritual ceremony, peculiar to the family; then solve the disappearance of Brunton, the ex-schoolmaster butler of some twenty years' service – a man of many gifts who spoke several languages and played nearly every instrument. He was a widower engaged to Rachel Howells, the second housemaid, but who was thrown over for Janet Tregellis, the head gamekeeper's daughter.

Holmes was convinced that all things were interconnected, and that there was only one mystery to solve, if only he could understand the meaning of the Musgrave Ritual. With a wooden peg and two lengths of a three-foot fishing rod, and using Reginald Musgrave's knowledge that the extinct elm was sixty-four feet high, Holmes made his calculations; these brought him almost to the wall of the house, where he found a peg mark, possibly Brunton's. Here he erroneously thought he should dig, having overlooked the words 'and under' (very un-Holmes-like!). Luckily Reginald was more alert, and suspected a cellar; they proceeded down a winding stone stairway and there in the middle of the floor lay a large and heavy flagstone with a rusted ring in the centre, to which was attached Brunton's thick shepherd's check muffler. With the added help of a constable, the flagstone was at last removed, revealing a small chamber some four feet square and seven deep. A squat brass-bound wooden box was disclosed, showing the ravages of damp and worms upon it; but more startling was the body of Brunton, dead some days, but with no wound upon him. But Holmes was still far from knowing what the Musgrave family had concealed with such elaborate precautions. He placed himself in Brunton's shoes and considered what he would have done. He needed help, and with charm probably engaged the help of the girl who had been devoted to him – Rachel Howells. They used the billets of wood lying there, as levers, until Brunton was able to get below. Holmes then assumed that the spurned lover, Rachel, seeing a chance for revenge, shut the stone lid, entombing the butler.

Reginald Musgrave dragged the nearby lake, but only found a linen bag containing old rusted and discoloured metal, and several dull coloured pieces of pebble or glass; coins of Charles I had been found in the chest. The metalwork was in the form of a double ring, but bent and twisted; the pebbles, when rubbed, glowed in Holmes' hand. 'My ancestor, Sir Ralph Musgrave, was a prominent cavalier and the right-hand man of Charles the Second in his wanderings,' explained Reginald to Holmes. This was the last piece in the jigsaw that Holmes required; he explained that the metalwork was the ancient crown of the kings of England, possibly held in trust by the Musgrave family, and, for reasons unknown, never returned to the king.

Holmes was unable to trace the maid, Rachel Howells, the suspected murderess, who had probably escaped overseas. The crown was allowed to remain at Hurlstone Manor, after a lot of legal bother and payment of a considerable sum of money by the family. Holmes kept all these records in his large tin box, which was a third full of bundles of paper tied up into separate packages with red tape. This singular chain of events, and the large issues which proved to be at stake, aroused such interest that Holmes traced his first stride towards the position he gradually held at home and abroad.

From these early beginnings, Holmes gradually built up a great reputation, his practice extending to the Continent, where he was consulted by François le Villard, one of the foremost of French detectives, with the Celtic power of quick intuition but lacking in a wide range of exact knowledge. The case concerned a will, and Holmes was able to refer him to two parallel cases, at Riga in 1857 and at St Louis in 1871. The Frenchman in his letter was full of admiration, as if he had been the pupil. Holmes thought he rated his assistance too highly, for the Frenchman had considerable gifts himself – the power of observation and deduction – but lacked for the moment, knowledge.

Another early case of Holmes while still living in rooms in Montague Street, at the time that he had done a good deal of business in Germany, concerned Von Bork's mother's elder brother. This was Count Von und Zu Grafenstein, whom he saved from being murdered by the nihilist Klopman. (Holmes must have been very surprised to find himself working for, and against, Von Bork, in the years up to 1914.)

Among the cases of which Holmes had knowledge, both unfinished and unpublished, we know of the following:

Abergavenny murders. Abernetty family, brought to Holmes' notice by the depth which the parsley had sunk into the butter on a hot day.[8] Addleton tragedy. *Alicia*, a cutter which sailed one spring morning into a small patch of mist, from where she never again emerged. Aluminium Crutch. Amateur Mendicant Society, 1887 – the club was in the lower vault of a furniture warehouse. Ancient British Barrow, 1877. Anderson Murders in North Carolina. Archie Stamford, forger, taken by Holmes and Watson near Farnham, Surrey. Arnsworth Castle business – Holmes used false alarm of fire. Atkinson Brothers of Trincomalee. Alec MacDonald. Adams and the Manor House case. Baron Maupertuis, involved in colossal schemes of abominable memory. Black Pearl of the Borgias – Holmes was consulted upon this case,

---

[8]Abernetty. Edgar Allan Poe, *The Purloined Letter*.

but only when he was involved with the busts of Napoleon, did he solve it. Bogus Laundry Affair – Holmes and Lestrade were helped by a man called Aldridge. Brooks and Woodhouse – two of fifty men who had good reasons for taking Holmes' life. Case of the Bishopgate Jewel. Camberwell Poisoning – solved by winding up the dead man's watch. Con Singleton Forgery. Crosby the Banker, death of Bert Stevens, 1887 – terrible murderer, seemingly a mild-mannered Sunday School young man. Culverton Smith, who murdered Victor Savage. Count Sylvius – Holmes noted all his vile actions in his squat notebook. Cardinal Tosca: the Pope expressly asked Holmes to investigate his sudden death. Colonel Upwood, card scandal and atrocious conduct of the Nonpareil Club. Darlington Substitution Scandal: Holmes used false alarm of fire. Dolsky in Odessa, forcible administration of poison. Dundas Separation Case, Holmes engaged – husband hurled his false teeth at his wife after every meal. Ex-President Murillo. Fairdale Hobbs. Fashionably dressed girl. Ferrers Documents. Forgery case, Lestrade. Godno in Little Russia, 1866. Grice Patterson, Island of Uffa. Grosvenor Square Furniture Van. Hammerford Will Case – Sir James Damery's negotiations with Sir George Lewis. Henry Staunton – Holmes helped to hang him. Holland's Royal Family. Huret the Boulevard Assassin. Isadora Persano – well known journalist and dualist. James Phillimore – he stepped back into his house to get his umbrella and was never seen again. John Clay – Holmes had previous skirmishes with him, although he had never seen him. Harden – tobacco millionaire. Jewish Pedlar. King of Scandinavia. Leturier in Montpellier, forcible administration of poison. Mrs Farintosh of Margate, who had no powder on her nose. Mrs Cecil Forrester. Mrs Stewart of Lander, 1887, her death thought due to Colonel Moran. Mathews. Mortimer Maberley, twice helped by Holmes. Madame Montpensier, suspected of murdering her stepdaughter, Mademoiselle Carere, although found married in New York. Morgan – poisoner. Merridew, of abominable memory. Netherlands Sumatra Company. Old Baron Dowson. Old White-haired Gentleman. Old Russian Woman. Palmer and Pritchard, criminal physicians of whom Holmes said, 'When a doctor does go wrong he is the first of criminals.' Parodol Chamber. Mrs

Etheridge – although presumed dead, found alive by Holmes. Red Leech, repulsive story. Ricoletti of the club foot and his abominable wife. Railway Porter in his velveteen uniform. 'Matilda Briggs' and the Giant Rat of Sumatra. Slipshod Elderly Woman. Service to French Government. Sir James Saunders – professional services by Holmes to the great dermatologist. Smith-Mortimer Succession. 'Sophy Anderson', 1887. St Pancras – Holmes asked by Inspector Merryvale to look into this case. Selden, the Notting Hill murderer – Holmes was interested in the peculiar ferocity of the crime. Sultan of Turkey, 1903, asked for Holmes' immediate action as political consequences of the gravest kind might arise if neglected. Trained Cormorant. Tankerville Club Scandal – Major Prendergast saved.[9] Tarlton Murders. The Tired Captain. Trepoff Murder in Odessa. Two Coptic Patriarchs – Holmes preoccupied with the case in 1899. Vamberry, Wine Merchant. Vanderbuilt and the Yeggman. Vatican Cameos – this small affair to oblige the Pope caused Holmes to lose touch with several English cases. Venomous Lizard or gila. Victor Lynch, forger. Vigor, Hammersmith wonder. Victoria, circus belle. Van Jansen, Utrecht, 1834, Holmes reminded of this case by similar circumstances surrounding the murdered body of Enoch J Drebber of Cleveland, where there was no apparent wound, but gouts and splashes of blood which were around the body. Wilson, notorious canary trainer of the East End of London. Von Bischoff – he would have been hung had Holmes' reliable test for bloodstains been known. Woman hanged for poisoning three little children for their insurance money.

There came the time when Holmes decided that he now needed better accommodation than his Montague Street rooms, and so he decided to look around and see if he could find a suitable flat to let. He was fortunate to come across one in Baker Street, No. 221B, in a house owned by a friendly landlady called Mrs Hudson. During his morning's work in the chemistry laboratory at Bart's Hospital, he spoke to a man called Stamford and told him that he had found some nice rooms, but that they

---

[9]Jack Prendergast in ACD, *The Gloria Scott*.

were too expensive for his purse. If only he could find a suitable companion to go halves. Stamford promised that if he heard of anyone he would let Holmes know. Holmes never realised then, how soon his wish would be granted.

Dr John H Watson

Dr Watson, faithfully following in Boswell's footsteps as a biographer for Sherlock Holmes, recorded little of himself for posterity. His school would appear to have been a private and expensive one, where his number was 31. During those early school years he was intimately associated with a brilliant scholar called Percy 'Tadpole' Phelps, who went on to Cambridge University.[10] Phelps was extremely well connected, for his uncle on the maternal side was Lord Holdhurst, the Conservative politician. Watson may have attended St Luke's College in one of our university towns. In 1895 he was with Holmes in this town, where his friend was carrying out research work. They received a visit in their furnished lodgings by an acquaintance, Mr Hilton Soames, a 'tall, spare man, of a nervous and excitable temperament', tutor and lecturer in Greek at St Luke's College. 'I had always known him to be restless in his manner,' wrote Watson.

Watson played rugby for Blackheath – perhaps his parental home – and on one occasion, at Old Deer Park, Richmond, Surrey, he was thrown over the ropes by an opponent, one Bob Ferguson. In later years they met again at Cheeseman's, Lamberley, near Horsham in Sussex, when Ferguson was a teabroker of Mincing Lane, London.

We do not know the date of Watson's birth; he had an elder brother and his father was H Watson.

Before 1878 Watson would appear to have been quite a traveller. At Pondicherry Lodge, Norwood, Watson noticed the great rubbish heaps which cumbered the grounds, looking like a gravel pit, the traces of the treasure seekers over six years, which reminded him of Ballarat in the colony of Victoria, Australia, where on a hillside he had seen the prospectors at work. Watson

---

[10]Dr Phelps McCarthy in ACD, *The Usher of Lea House School.*

had been in other countries.[11] 'I have coursed many creatures in many countries during my chequered career,' he recalled as they chased the *Aurora* in the police launch upon the Thames. He mentioned his travels when he first met Mary Morstan: 'In an experience of women which extends over many nations and three separate continents, I have never looked upon a face which gave a clearer promise of a refined and sensitive nature.' Watson was certainly a ladies' man. Later on, Holmes remarked that 'the fair sex was Watson's department'.

Watson does not record the date when he started his studies at Bart's Hospital, just that he took his degree of Doctor of Medicine of the University of London in 1878. He then went on to Netley on a course for army surgeons and was duly attached to the Fifth Northumberland Fusiliers, travelling to India as an assistant surgeon.

With the Second Afghan war (1878–1880) breaking out, he had to travel to Candahar to join the regiment. He was removed from his brigade and attached to the Berkshires, with whom he served at the Battle of Maiwand, where General Burrows was totally defeated with the loss of half of his brigade and chased back into Candahar. Here the garrison was liberated by General Roberts on 1 September 1880. At Maiwand, Watson was struck upon the shoulder by a Jezail bullet, which shattered the bone and grazed the subclavian artery (this caused him in later life to hold his left arm in a stiff and unnatural manner).[12] He also had a bullet through the leg, which damaged his Achilles tendon, causing him at times to nurse his wounded leg. It did not prevent him from walking, but it ached wearily at every change of the weather. (Later on, when Watson heard a true account of the family watch from Holmes, he sprang from his chair 'and limped impatiently about the room with considerable bitterness' – he wrongly thought that Holmes had pried into his brother's history. Watson managed to retain his nerve in this bloody battle, although his comrades fell, hacked to pieces by the natives. Certainly, Watson could say with truth, 'I have seen something of the rough side of life...' (In later years, Watson admitted that his hardened nerves

---

[11]John Turner was Black Jack of Ballarat. ACD, *The Boscombe Valley Mystery*.
[12]Jezail. Heavy Afghan gun.

shuddered when he saw Victor Hatherley's[13] hand, with a horrid red spongy surface where the thumb should have been, hacked off with a cleaver by Colonel Lysander Stark, at his home in Berkshire.[14]

Watson's orderly, Murray,[15] saved him from falling into the hands of the murderous Ghazis,[16] threw him upon a packhorse and brought him safely to the British Lines, from whence he was removed to the Peshawar base hospital. There he was struck down by enteric fever for some months, which nearly killed him. He became so weak and emaciated that the medical board sent him back to England on board the troopship *Orontes*, which brought him to Portsmouth jetty with his health in ruins, 'thin as a lath, brown as a nut', and haggard of face. The ship docked on the 30 November 1880.[17]

Having no relations, Watson decided to come to London, where he took accommodation at a private hotel in the Strand, living upon a government pension of just over £209 per annum, which gave him rather frugal living. This was why the faithful Murray never continued as the doctor's valet. Even so, Watson managed to keep a bull pup. As Watson recorded: 'There I stayed for some time… leading a comfortless, meaningless existence, and spending such money as I had, considerably more freely than I ought.' (He did have a flutter on the horses.) 'So alarming did the state of my finances become, that I soon realised that I must either leave the metropolis and rusticate somewhere in the country, or that I must make a complete alteration in my style of living. Choosing the latter alternative, I began by making up my mind to leave the hotel, and take up my quarters in some less pretentious and less expensive domicile.' He wished for a peaceful place, for arguments only upset his broken nerves. He was inclined to be

---

[13]Hatherley Farm. ACD, *The Boscombe Valley Mystery*.

[14]Name perhaps suggested by Dr Leander Starr Jameson, who led a raid into the Transvaal in 1896 with only 500 men.

[15]Dr Joseph Habakuk Jephson, 113 NY Regiment, wounded at Antietam in the American Civil War, would have died but for the help of a gentleman called Murray. See ACD, 'J Habakuk Jephson's Statement' *Cornhill Magazine*, 1883.

[16]A fanatical sect of death or glory boys.

[17]The data sent to me by Commander G S Stavert, MBE MA RN (Retd.), Hon. Secretary of the Sherlock Holmes Society of London.

lazy, pleasing himself what time he arose in the morning, and admitted to being rather Bohemian. Had Watson grown a moustache while on active service? He certainly had one in the July following his marriage to Mary Morstan, large enough to act as a disguise against recognition by his old school chum, Percy Phelps. He still carried his handkerchief in his coat sleeve – a lingering military sign.

On the same day that Watson's mind was made up (the year might well have been 1881 or 1882, for Watson had notes and records of the Sherlock Holmes' cases for 1882), he went out and into the Criterion Bar; here he met young Stamford, a former dresser of his at Bart's Hospital.[18] Each was so surprised to see the other, and although Stamford had never been a crony of his, Watson was pleased to find at least one person he knew in alien London. They lunched at the Holborn, where Watson gave him a short story of his adventures, and being asked 'What are you up to now?' replied, 'Looking for lodgings… Trying to solve the problem as to whether it is possible to get comfortable rooms at a reasonable price.'

'That's a strange thing… you are the second man to-day that has used that expression to me.'

Stamford said that the first man was, 'A fellow who is working at the chemical laboratory up at the hospital. He was bemoaning himself this morning because he could not get someone to go halves with him in some nice rooms which he had found, and which were too much for his purse.'

'By Jove! …if he really wants someone to share the rooms and the expense, I am the very man for him,' cried Watson, and was surprised at Stamford's lack of enthusiasm. 'You don't know Sherlock Holmes yet… perhaps you would not care for him as a constant companion.' He only knew Holmes from odd meetings in the laboratory, and so warned Watson not to blame him if they didn't get on together. Watson felt that there was something being withheld from him, but he was told that there was nothing against him, only that he was a little queer in his ideas – an enthusiast in some branches of science – otherwise a decent fellow but was not

---

[18]Stamford. Responsible for Watson meeting Holmes.

a medical student. 'I have no idea what he intends to go in for.' He knew that Holmes was well up in anatomy, a first-class chemist, desultory and eccentric, but a mine of out-of-the-way information, only communicative when the fancy seized him. 'It is not easy,' said Stamford, 'to express the inexpressible... Holmes is a little too scientific for my tastes – it approaches to cold-bloodedness. I could imagine his giving a friend a little pinch of the latest vegetable alkaloid, not out of malevolence, you under-stand, but simply out of a spirit of inquiry in order to have an accurate idea of the effects. To do him justice, I think that he would take it himself with the same readiness. He appears to have a passion for definite and exact knowledge.' He went on to tell Watson how he had seen Holmes in a most bizarre way, beat his subjects with a stick in order to verify how bruises could be performed after death.

'I should like to meet him, if I am to lodge with anyone, I should prefer a man of studious and quiet habits. I am not strong enough yet to stand much noise or excitement. I had enough of both in Afghanistan to last me for the remainder of my natural existence. How could I meet this friend of yours?'

'He is sure to be at the laboratory... He either avoids the place for weeks, or else he works there from morning till night. If you like we will drive round together after luncheon.'

So together they drove round to the hospital. Arriving, they turned down a narrow lane, and, passing through a small side door, passed into a hospital wing, ascended a bleak stone staircase – familiar to Watson – down a long corridor with white walls and brown doors, through a low-arched passage and into the chemical laboratory: a lofty chamber, lined and littered with countless bottles. Broad, low tables were scattered about, whereon lay retorts, test tubes and little Bunsen lamps, with their blue flickering flames.[19] Only one student was in the room, completely absorbed in his work.

'At the sound of our footsteps', wrote Watson, 'he glanced round and sprang to his feet with a cry of pleasure.'

'I've found it! I've found it,' shouted the stranger to Stamford,

---

[19]Invented by R W Bunsen, Victorian chemist.

running towards him with a test tube in his hand. 'I have found a re-agent which is precipitated by haemoglobin, and by nothing else.' It was as if a gold mine had been discovered. Stamford introduced the two men: 'Dr Watson, Mr Sherlock Holmes.'[20]

'How are you?' said Holmes cordially, shaking hands with a strength that surprised Watson. 'You have been in Afghanistan, I perceive,' which astonished Watson, the first of many astonishments to come in the years of their companionship. Holmes continued, 'The question now is about haemoglobin.'

Watson did not see the full significance of this. 'It is interesting, chemically, no doubt,' he said, 'but practically—'

'Why, man, it is the most practical medico-legal discovery for years. Don't you see that it gives us an infallible test for blood stains? Come over here now!'

And Holmes seized Watson by the coat sleeve in his eagerness, and drew him over to the table at which he had been working. 'Let us have some fresh blood,' Holmes dug a long bodkin into his finger, and drew off a drop of blood into a chemical pipette; he then added the blood to a litre of water, the proportion being one in a million. The water remained colourless until, with the addition of a few white crystals and some drops of a transparent fluid, the contents turned to a dull mahogany colour, and a brownish dust fell to the bottom of the container. Holmes clapped his hands with joy and cried, 'Beautiful! beautiful! The old guaiacum test was very clumsy and uncertain.[21] So is the microscopic examination for blood corpuscles. The latter is valueless if the stains are a few hours old. Now, this appears to act as well whether the blood is old or new.' Stains would no longer present a problem, for there was now the 'Sherlock Holmes test, and there will no longer be any difficulty.' Holmes then mentioned the names of people who might certainly have been hung, if his test had been in existence before – Von Bischoff of

---

[20]Holmes would have been twenty-seven or twenty-eight years old. 'What isn't generally realised is that Watson and Holmes were only twenty-nine when they first met.' Tim Piggott-Smith in an article by Francis Donnelly in *Radio Times,* 5–11 December 1987. Dr Watson does not appear to have recorded his age.

[21]A tropical American genus of trees of the bean-caper family. Greenish resin used in medicine.

Frankfurt, Mason of Bradford, Muller, Lefevre of Montpellier and Samson of New Orleans, to mention just a few. This provoked Stamford into calling Holmes 'a walking calendar of crime', and that he might start a paper called the *Police News of the Past*.

Sherlock Holmes and Dr Watson Agree on the Baker St Flat

Stamford mentioned to Holmes that the doctor had come upon business to discuss the idea of sharing rooms with him as he and the doctor sat down upon high three-legged stools. Holmes said that he had his eye upon a flat in Baker Street, 'which would suit us down to the ground.' Holmes listed some of his shortcomings: smoked strong tobacco (fortunately Watson was also a smoker), got in the dumps at times, didn't open his mouth for days on end, but if Watson just left him alone, he'd soon be all right; also played the violin. Watson mentioned that he kept a bull pup, objected to rows because of his shaken nerves, was extremely lazy and got up at all sorts of ungodly hours. With a merry laugh, Holmes said that they could consider the thing as settled, providing the rooms were agreeable. They agreed to meet at Bart's on the morrow at noon, and go together to see Mrs Hudson's spare flat.

As Watson and Stamford walked back, Watson suddenly stopped and turning upon his friend, asked, 'How the deuce did he know that I had come from Afghanistan?' With an enigmatical smile came the reply: 'That's just his little peculiarity... A good many people have wanted to know how he finds things out.' Watson rubbed his hands, 'Oh! a mystery is it? ...This is very piquant. I am much obliged to you for bringing us together. "The proper study of mankind is man," you know.'[22] 'You must study him, then,' replied Stamford. You'll find him a knotty problem, though. I'll wager he learns more about you than you about him.' With that Stamford bade Watson goodbye.

The next day, Holmes and Watson met as arranged, and to-

---

[22]'The true science and the true study of man is man' Pierre Charron, 1601. 'The proper study of mankind is man' Alexander Pope, 1688–1714.

gether they inspected the flat in Mrs Hudson's house at 221B Baker Street. As Watson recorded: 'So desirable in every way were the rooms, and so moderate did the terms seem when divided between us, that the bargain was concluded upon the spot, and we at once entered into possession.' Watson did not take his dog.

Watson never recorded how much they paid. That very evening, Watson moved his possessions from the Strand Hotel and Holmes the next morning brought several boxes and portmanteaux. For the next few days, their time was spent in unpacking and placing their property advantageously by mutual consent. They then settled down to enjoy their new surroundings. This was the beginning of a very happy partnership at Baker Street, which was to last for some years, Watson's stay there only being interrupted by his marriages.

Watson was still fascinated how, from a cursory glance, Holmes knew he had been in Afghanistan. He thought that someone had imparted knowledge of his movements to Holmes. 'Nothing of the sort. I *knew* you came from Afghanistan.' Holmes' train of reasoning ran thus: 'Here is a gentleman of a medical type but with the air of a military man. Clearly an army doctor, then. He has just come from the tropics, for his face is dark, and that is not the natural tint of his skin, for his wrists are fair. He has undergone hardship and sickness, as his haggard face says clearly. His left arm has been injured. He holds it in a stiff and unnatural manner. Where in the tropics could an English army doctor have seen much hardship and got his arm wounded? Clearly in Afghanistan.' Holmes knew that the war had finished in 1880; his whole train of thought had taken under one second. The deduction amazed Watson, for he only thought that people like Holmes existed in fiction, like Dupin and Lecoq.

Holmes gave Watson another early instance of his summing-up powers, just when there were no crimes to unravel or criminals to arrest, and Holmes would say querulously, 'What is the use of having brains in our profession? I know well that I have it in me to make my name famous. No man lives or has ever lived who has brought the same amount of study… to the detection of crime which I have done. And what is the result? There is no crime to detect, or, at most, some bungling villainy with a motive so transparent that even a Scotland Yard official can see through it.' What conceit, thought Watson, but had to readjust his views when he saw the master detective at work. When Holmes looked down upon the street beneath him, he diagnosed a stalwart, plainly dressed man as a 'retired sergeant of Marines', which startled Watson, but which was only a trifle to Holmes as he explained: 'Even across the street I could see a great blue anchor tattooed on the back of the fellow's hand. That smacked of the sea. He had a military carriage, however, and regulation side-whiskers. There we have the marine. He was a man with some amount of self-importance and a certain air of command. You must have observed the way in which he held his head and swung his cane. A steady, respectable, middle-aged man, too, on the face of him – all facts which led me to believe that he had been a sergeant.' Holmes' expression, 'commonplace', belied the real pleasure he derived from Watson's admiration.

Sherlock Holmes and Dr Watson – Early Days

Right from the beginning of their very close relationship, Sherlock Holmes and John Watson, always addressed each other by their surnames, never Sherlock and John.

Having no relations or friends to break the monotony of his daily existence, Watson eagerly hailed the mystery which surrounded Holmes, and attempted to unravel it. He found Holmes quite an easy man to live with, he being quiet in his ways and regular in his habits, for he was early to bed and early to rise during the time he worked at Bart's Hospital, where his day was divided between the chemical laboratory and the dissecting rooms. Sometimes he would stay there from morning till night.

Sometimes Holmes took long walks into the lowest places in London; other days he would while away the time upon the sitting room sofa, when the working fit was not upon him; there he would sit, neither speaking a word nor moving a muscle the whole day through. At these times, Watson noticed a dreamy vacant expression in his eyes and wondered if he was addicted to the use of some narcotic, but he dismissed the idea from his mind, for Holmes' temperance and cleanliness of his whole life forbade such thoughts. (Later on, Watson was to have his early thoughts shattered!) But whatever mood Holmes was in, his person and appearance struck the attention of the most casual observer as above reproach; even at a later date, when he lived for a while in a Neolithic hut upon Dartmoor, his dress, linen and clean-shaven face were exemplary.

Watson wondered what Holmes' definite goal was? Holmes had stated that he was not studying medicine, which puzzled Watson considerably; he did not seem to be reading for a science degree or something similar which might have been the open sesame to the learned world; his zeal for certain studies was remarkable, his knowledge ample and minute.

Watson wondered at his knowledge of some things and his lack of knowledge of others which he, Watson, considered necessary. Holmes could converse upon miracle plays, medieval pottery, violins, Ceylon Buddhism, warships of the future, George Meredith, and the Bible. He did admit to being a little rusty here, when he quoted the affair of Uriah and Bathsheba, not being sure whether it was in 'the first or second of Samuel'. Holmes could converse easily upon guns: seeing the word 'Pen...' upon a sawn-off shotgun, some two feet long, made for buckshot cartridges, and easily carried under the coat, Holmes immediately recounted that the gun was made by the well known American firm, the Pennsylvania Small Arms Company. This was told, a little later on, to the chief Sussex detective, White Mason, who gazed upon Holmes as the village GP might gaze with awe upon the Harley Street specialist.

Watson wondered at his ignorance of contemporary literature, philosophy, politics, the Copernican Theory of the famous fifteenth-century Polish astronomer, Copernicus.[23] Had the earth travelled round the moon, it would have meant no more to Holmes, for he had no interest in such studies, which astonished Watson. 'My mind', said Holmes, 'is like a crowded boxroom with packets of all sorts stowed away therein – so many that I may well have but a vague perception of what was there.'

Watson at first tried to pierce, what was to him, Holmes'

---

[23]Nicolaus Copernicus 1473–1543. The composition of the solar system in which the earth revolves about the sun.

seemingly dogmatic attitude, until he gradually realised the unique brain before him; for Holmes had a curious secretive streak in him, which sometimes left even Watson guessing what his exact plans might be. He liked to plot alone, to work out all the angles, and, when everything clicked into place to his satisfaction, then he might reveal all. He could be cold and inexorable in his manner, his face stern and Red Indian in its composure, when he wanted his own way.

Watson came to realise that Holmes was a first-class chemist, profound but eccentric, with a good knowledge of belladonna, opium and poisons generally. Chemistry was of course his first love, which gradually tended to predominate, as it became an invaluable source of income. His geology was practical, but limited, but he could tell at a glance one soil from another, and by colour and consistency of mud splashes could place their origin from any region, within fifty miles of London. His anatomy was accurate but unsystematic, his botany variable; his knowledge of sensational literature immense; his crime records unique, for he appeared to know every detail of every horror perpetuated in the nineteenth century. He was well up on British law. His approach to work, desultory, eccentric but scientific; he played the violin well, and was an expert single-stick player, boxer and swordsman. He surmised that bruises might be produced after death, and in order to verify this would beat with a stick subjects in the dissecting room. Holmes did say: 'My ramifications stretch out into many sections of society, but never, I am happy to say, into amateur sport, which is the best and soundest thing in England.' (Holmes had apparently forgotten that he was once an amateur boxer!) Watson was bewildered! 'If only I can find what the fellow is driving at by reconciling all these accomplishments, and discovering a calling which needs them all.'

As the first weeks of their companionship slipped by, Watson noted in his new journal, that there were no callers, and he thought that Holmes was a friendless man. But gradually, acquaintances in the most different classes of society called. These clients were interviewed alone in the sitting room, Watson absenting himself meanwhile, but Holmes always apologised to Watson for the inconvenience he caused him. Later on, as Watson became an integral part of the interview, Holmes would observe to a client, 'It is both or none. You may say before this gentleman anything which you say to me.' A client to Holmes was a mere unit, a factor in a problem, for he found that emotional qualities only upset his clear reasoning.

Among the early visitors from Scotland Yard were Inspectors, Lestrade, Tobias Gregson and Athelney Jones; a fashionably dressed young girl called and stayed for half an hour; a grey-headed, seedy visitor, much excited, looking like a Jew peddler; a slipshod elderly woman; an old white-haired gentleman; a railway porter in his velveteen uniform. When Holmes told Watson that he had to use their sitting room as a place of business, Watson wondered what kind of business. During the next seventeen years, Watson saw many more visitors pass through the portals of their sitting room.

Sherlock Holmes the only Unofficial Consulting Detective

Omnipotent as Holmes may well have thought himself, or certainly wished to be, he did admit that he was not the law, or even an official agent; but in the absence of the police he did declare himself the representative of the law; if his demeanour lacked anything to distil fear into the criminal, then his revolver filled the gap. As Holmes admitted to the Duke of Holdernesse, 'I am not in an official position, and there is no reason, so long as the ends of justice are served, why I should disclose all that I know.' Holmes preferred to work entirely unhindered, so that he became an independent investigator, which led him to become the only unofficial consulting detective. The greatest insult one could make to Holmes was to mistake him for a member of the police force. Certainly, it was his business, like any good citizen, to uphold the law; he said he represented justice, and at times he certainly acted as if he had special powers: how was he able, as an ordinary citizen, to obtain a police warrant just by the mere mention of his name? This perhaps shows the extraordinary respect in which the police held him. He said; 'I am the last and highest court of appeal in detection... I examine the data, as an expert, and pronounce a specialist's opinion. I claim no credit in such cases. My name figures in no newspaper. The work itself, the pleasure of finding a field for my peculiar powers, is my highest reward.' (Holmes was forgetting that he earned his living by this work, some of which was highly remunerative.) He followed his own methods and told as little or as much as he deemed fit. Sometimes he considered he could not be judge and jury, then he was inclined to leave some of the incriminating evidence behind for the police to discover, if they were able, and to act upon, if they were so inclined; for himself, his lips were sealed. If Holmes thought that a murderer was vindicated by his actions, and that no other man would be unlawfully apprehended by the police, then he would bow gracefully out, as he did with Dr Leon Sterndale, at Tredannick Wollas in Cornwall, John Turner of Boscombe Valley and Captain Crocker at the Abbey Grange, Marsham, Kent.

Holmes' razor-like brain was able to cut through that which was impenetrable to the police; he knew that he was superior to the inspectors of Scotland Yard, and also knew that they knew it, especially when he spoke to them in a high, quick voice. He knew that when he was out of the country Scotland Yard missed him, for they then lacked the ultimate help which Holmes might have given them.

When in a certain mood, Holmes might string along the police, an enigmatical smile spreading across his face; when he began to see daylight through a case, and generally not wishing to score at the expense of the police – for he preferred anonymity, not popular applause – his face would writhe with inward merriment, his eyes would shine like stars and he would rub his hands and chuckle with delight, his whole body wriggling with suppressed excitement, for he was not retained by the police to supply their deficiencies.

He would not disclose his own thoughts to the police while he had the case under consideration, for, as he said, he never guessed the final outcome, it being a shocking habit, destructive to the logical faculty; he never wasted words or repeated himself to the police. (Although he did once to Watson while at Thor Place in Hampshire. A revolver with one discharged chamber had been found on the floor of the wardrobe of Miss Dunbar, governess in Neil Gibson's house, which was very direct evidence. Holmes' eyes were fixed and he repeated in broken words: 'On–the–floor–of–her–wardrobe.')

After Holmes had reached his final conclusions, and not before, he would quite happily hand over the results to the police, although he never thought too highly of them. 'There may be an occasional want of imaginative intuition down there, but they lead the world for thoroughness, method, and great courage.'

He never liked to explain his deductions to the police, for they then appeared to his listeners to be so simple and he feared that his reputation would be shattered by being too candid. 'Results without causes are much more impressive,' said Holmes. The more bizarre, the less mysterious.

When no major case was on hand, which the police could not solve, then Holmes had to be content with minor ones, which led him to observe: 'As to my own little practice, it seems to be degenerating into an agency for receiving lost pencils and giving advice to young ladies from boarding schools.' This observation to Watson was triggered off by a letter from Violet Hunter of Montague Place, who wished to consult him as to whether she should accept a position as governess; she had no parents or relations to consult. Holmes thought that this really marked his zero point. Nevertheless, Holmes could never disappoint a damsel in distress. He not only interviewed her, but advised and helped her, bringing the matter to a successful conclusion.

Watson learnt over the years the wisdom of obedience, to do as Holmes desired, and, if no explanations were forthcoming, then he would hold back his question. Perhaps this tended towards Holmes taking Watson too much for granted. 'Watson, of course, comes with us,' Holmes said to Robert Ferguson of Lamberley. Of course, on the other hand, it could have epitomised Holmes' deep affection for his friend, so that he would on no account leave him out of things.

If Holmes did not intend to reveal information, he might well glide away to some other topic; he liked to feel he had a command over his friend; if moved, he could look formidable; a weary, heavy-lidded expression might veil his keen and eager nature.

How most trying Watson must have found his being, at times, kept in the dark, until the correct solution could be told to him, for Holmes' masterful dominating personality loved to surprise those about him. Later on, when Holmes told Watson about his several monographs, Watson observed: 'You have an extraordinary gift for minutiae,' for Holmes made deductions from signs so subtle that even when the reasoning was pointed out, other people found it hard to follow. Watson wondered why Holmes worked so hard to attain such precise information, unless there was a definite end in view, for no one saturated his mind with small matters unless there was a very definite reason behind it.

Holmes was familiar with the detectives of Poe and Gaboriau, Dupin and Lecoq, but they did not delve far enough for his liking. So there was nothing left for Holmes to do but to invent his own system. The study of criminology must be brought to an exact science, even to the nth capacity. So revolutionary were Holmes' methods that Dr Edmond Locard, head of the police laboratory at Lyons, applauded his ideas and methods. Holmes' methods were even way ahead of Hans Gross, who did not publish until 1891 his great textbook on 'criminal investigation', which laid down a base for all future police systems. In it, he applauded Holmes for having already used plaster, as the best way of preserving the impression of a footstep, and which he considered superseded the six popular ways of preservation then in current use.

Many times Watson was on the point of asking Holmes point-blank what actually was his profession, but delicacy prevented him from forcing Holmes to confide in him. Eventually, when the right moment arrived, Holmes told the Doctor all about his work.

It came about in this way. One morning in March, Watson came down to breakfast earlier than usual, and had to await the preparation of his breakfast. Holmes was busy eating so Watson picked up a magazine and, seeing that one of the articles called 'The Book of Life' had a pencil mark at the heading, he began to read it. He found that it attempted to show how much an observant man might learn by an accurate and systematic examination of all that came in his way. As Watson recorded:

It struck me as being a remarkable mixture of shrewdness and of absurdity. The reasoning was close and intense, but the deductions appeared to me to be far fetched and exaggerated. The writer claimed by a momentary expression, a twitch of a muscle or a glance of an eye, to fathom a man's inmost thoughts. Deceit, according to him, was an impossibility in the case of one trained to observation and analysis. His conclusions were as infallible as so many propositions of Euclid. So startling would his results appear to the uninitiated that until they learned the processes by which he had arrived at them they might well consider him as a necromancer.

The article continued:

From a drop of water, a logician could infer the possibility of an Atlantic or a Niagara without having seen or heard of one or the other. So all life is a great chain, the nature of which is known whenever we are shown a single link of it. Like all other arts, the Science of Observation, Deduction and Analysis,[24] is one which can only be acquired by long and patient study, nor is life long enough to allow any mortal to attain the highest possible perfection in it. Before turning to those moral and mental aspects of the matter which present the greatest difficulties, let the inquirer begin by mastering more elementary problems. Let him, on meeting a fellow-mortal, learn at a glance to distinguish the history of the man, and the trade or profession to which he belongs. Puerile as such an exercise may seem, it sharpens the faculties of observation and teaches one where to look and what to look for. By a man's finger-nails, by his coat-sleeve, by his boots, by his trouser-knees, by the callosities of his forefinger and thumb, by his expression, by his shirt-cuffs – by each of these things, a man's calling is plainly revealed. That all united should fail to enlighten the competent inquirer in any case is almost inconceivable.

---

[24]Monsieur C Auguste Dupin became friendly with a man he met in an obscure library in Rue Montmarte. They agreed to live together in a time-eaten, grotesque mansion in the Faubourg St German. One night they were strolling down a long dirty street, when Dupin surprised his friend by reading his thoughts, by observation, analysis and deduction, which was his friend's comprehension. Edgar Allan Poe, *Murders in the Rue Morgue*.

(At a later time, Holmes mentioned to Watson how a compositor could be known by his thumbnails, how a weaver might be known by his tooth, how important were the laces of a boot, how the first thing he looked at in a woman was the coat sleeve, how a poor Cabinet minister might be detected by the re-soling of his boots, and a coiner by the zinc and copper filings in the seam of his cuff. For Holmes was an omnivorous reader with a strangely retentive memory for such trifles; his unique mind regarded little things as important;[25] the gravest issues often depended upon small things, for he had trained himself to see as if through the eye of a camera, all being instantly recorded, but retaining only that which would assist him.)

Watson thought the article 'ineffable twaddle' and rubbish. He noticed that Holmes had read it, 'since you have marked it. I don't deny that it is smartly written. It irritates me though. It is evidently the theory of some armchair lounger, who evolves all these neat little paradoxes in the seclusion of his own study. It is not practical. I should like to see him clapped down in a third-class carriage on the Underground, and asked to give the trades of all his fellow-travellers. I would lay a thousand to one against him.'

Remarked Holmes calmly: 'You would lose your money... As for the article, I wrote it myself.' This astounded Watson. 'I have a turn both for observation and for deduction,' continued Holmes. 'The theories which I have expressed there, and which appear to you to be so chimerical, are really extremely practical – so practical that I depend upon them for my bread and cheese... Well, I have a trade of my own. I suppose I am the only one in the world. I'm a consulting detective, if you can understand what that is. Here in London we have lots of government detectives and lots of private ones. When these fellows are at fault, they come to me, and I manage to put them on the right scent. They lay all the evidence before me, and I am generally able, by the help of my knowledge of the history of crime, to set them straight. There is a strong family resemblance about misdeeds, and if you have all the

---

[25]Dupin recognised this before Holmes, as he said to the prefect of Paris police, 'Perhaps it is the very simplicity of the thing which puts you at fault.' Edgar Allan Poe, *The Purloined Letter*.

details of a thousand at your finger ends, it is odd if you cannot unravel the thousand and first.'

Holmes remarked that apart from members of the police, other people were sent to him by private inquiry agencies, people in a little trouble, who told their stories to an attentive Holmes, who made his appropriate comments and pocketed his fee. This astonished Watson, to think that without leaving his room, Holmes was able to unravel some knotty problem, impossible to other people. Holmes continued: 'I have a kind of intuition that way. Now and again a case turns up which is a little more complex. Then I have to bustle about and see things with my own eyes. You see I have a lot of special knowledge which I apply to the problem, and which facilitates matters wonderfully. Those rules of deduction laid down in that article which aroused your scorn are invaluable to me in practical work. Observation with me is second nature. The great advantage of being an unofficial detective,' said Holmes, 'was that as little or as much might be divulged as was considered necessary... They say that genius is an infinite capacity for taking pains,' said Holmes with a smile.[26] 'It's a very bad definition, but it does apply to detective work.' Watson thought that Holmes was bumptious and full of brag and bounce; but Watson did not there and then leave Holmes and Baker Street, good-hearted fellow that he was. Watson was to learn from long habit that a train of thoughts could run so quickly through Holmes' mind that he arrived at the conclusion without being conscious of the many intermediate steps.

Holmes never had any prejudices and followed docilely wherever fact led him; when a fact appeared to be opposed to a long train of deductions it invariably proved to be capable of bearing some other interpretation. Given all the facts of a case, Holmes could supply an explanation and reach a conclusion, but without data he was done, or, as he put it, without clay he could not make bricks. He could discover facts, but he could not change them; and he was always careful of an obvious fact, for it could be deceptive; his difficulty was to detach the framework of fact,

---

[26]Thomas Carlyle, 1795–1881. After dinner speech. Samuel Butler, 1835–1902. 'Genius... has been defined as a supreme capacity for taking trouble...', 'Genius... Jane Ellice Hopkins, 1836–1904. 'Genius is an infinite capacity for taking pains.'

absolute undeniable fact, from the embellishments of theorists. When two separate chains of thought were followed, he would find some point of intersection, which should approximate to the truth. If fresh facts fitted themselves into a scheme, the hypothesis might gradually become a solution; it sometimes happened that Holmes found it difficult to remember previous facts, for intense mental concentration had a curious way of blotting out what had passed.

As a rule, the more bizarre a thing was, the less mysterious it proved to be; it was the simple, commonplace, featureless crimes which were puzzling and difficult to unravel, as a commonplace face was the most difficult to identify. Perhaps the most difficult crime to track was the purposeless one, when Holmes might have to resort to imagination, for often it was found to be the 'mother of truth'. The more *outré*[27] and grotesque an incident was, the more carefully it deserved to be examined and the very point which appeared to compliment a case was, when duly considered and scientifically handled, the one which was most likely to elucidate it; from the grotesque to the horrible was only one step.

Holmes reduced the pursuit of a criminal to an exact science and could reconstruct the scene of a murder as if he had been there, but would only make his disclosures in his own time and in his own way. Holmes liked to sit in a room where a murder had been committed to see if the atmosphere brought him inspiration, for he was a believer in the genius loci, which made Watson smile. When Mortimer Tregennis found his two demented brothers and his dead sister, all with an expression of utmost horror upon their faces, in a Cornish cottage, he thought the cause was not of this world. But Holmes was of the opinion that all natural explanations must first be exhausted, for he had no belief in the supernatural. (The Duke of Holdernesse once said of Holmes, that he seemed to have powers that were hardly human.)[28]

Holmes' life was spent in one long effort to escape the commonplaces of existence, but he had the professional enthusiasm which kept him going through all tiredness, looking at a case as a mere abstract intellectual problem, for it was only boredom that

---

[27]*Outré*. Edgar Allan Poe, *Mystery of Marie Roget*.
[28]Lionel Dacre had a library of occult books. ACD, *The Leather Funnel*.

tired him, never work. If affairs were going slightly awry he would still approach the case with a 'half comic and wholly philosophic view'; he never liked to leave the odd trick with an opponent; when he had excluded the impossible, explained all contingencies, whatever remained, however improbable, must be the truth.[29]

Holmes' brain was so abnormally active that it was dangerous to leave it without any material to work upon; for then the fit might come upon him, and he could be the most incurably lazy devil that ever stood in shoe leather, which might lead him to the cocaine injection until something turned up: this was his only vice.

As an example of the lightning speed at which Holmes' brain worked, we may cite what happened at Reichenbach Falls. As Moriarty went over the cliff edge, and before he had time to hit the bottom, in such a short interval of time Holmes' rapidly acting brain had reached the conclusion that if the world was convinced that he was dead, then he would be able to get even with the remaining henchman of the professor, and so he instantly decided to stay away from London. (As he remarked to Miss Susan Cushing of Croydon, quickness at observing was his trade; mix imagination with reality, and there was the basis of his art.)

Watson once remarked that Holmes loathed every form of society, but this must have only been because he would not countenance any interruption in the workings of his immense faculties or his extraordinary powers of instinct, observation and intellectual deduction. His first rule in criminal investigation was to look for a possible alternative and provide against it; detection was, or ought to be, an exact science. This science of analysis and deduction was one which could only be acquired by a long and patient study if a person desired to attain the highest possible perfection in it, and would brook no interruption. Holmes kept his brain-attic stocked with the furniture that he was likely to use;

---

[29]ACD, *The Story of the Lost Special*. Of the missing train the Times amateur reasoner said: 'It is one of the elementary principles of practical reasoning, that when the impossible has been eliminated, the residuum, however improbable, must contain the truth.'

but he did allow a little room for the out-of-the-way knowledge, available should the need arise; unnecessary lumber had no place there, crowding out the useful knowledge, making it difficult to find the important information. His attic walls were not elastic, only having room for definite and exact knowledge. That was why Watson found Holmes deficient in what was to Watson necessary common knowledge.

It was necessary for Holmes to separate the essential from the accidental before an investigation got under way, and he had to be most careful of circumstantial evidence, occasionally very convincing, for this could be a very tricky thing. Holmes remembered Thoreau.[30] It was an error to argue in front of his data, for then he might find that he was insensibly twisting them round to fit his theories; he might form a provisional theory and then let time and a fuller knowledge agree or disagree with it, for he never guessed – such a habit was destructive to the logical faculty – and logic, Holmes knew, was rare; he always followed fact, bearing in mind to beware the obvious fact.

Watson's respect for Holmes' powers increased daily, and Holmes revelled in the doctor's continued surprise and admiration. As Watson saw more and more of Holmes at work, he summed him up as the most perfectly trained observing and reasoning machine that the world had ever seen, with a delicate and finely adjusted temperament, whose keen incisive reasoning, masterly grasp of a situation and quick subtle methods enabled him to disentangle the most inextricable mysteries. No doubt his fascination for the detection of crime stemmed from his boyhood days, for he was born some ten years after the death of Edgar Allan Poe, and so might well have been introduced to the French detective, Auguste Dupin, by his father, and imagined himself also a great detective who would solve world crime, and become the last and highest court of appeal.

Until Watson learned to the contrary, he thought that Holmes must be an orphan, for he was so reticent concerning his early life, that caused Watson to regard him as an isolated phenomenon, a brain without a heart, as deficient in human sympathy as he was

---

[30]'Some circumstantial evidence is very strong as when you find a trout in the milk.' H D Thoreau, 1854.

pre-eminent in intelligence; that beneath Holmes' quiet and didactic manner lay a terribly clever but vain and conceited person; he thus thought of him as a pure-blooded, well trained foxhound. Watson originally thought that Holmes was averse to women, and so formed no new friendship; he came to realise, that he was Holmes' only friend. Holmes mentioned this upon a wild and rainy September evening in 1887, as the bell rang at Baker Street and Watson surmised that it might be a friend of his. 'Except yourself, I have none, I do not encourage visitors.'

Holmes was impatient with less alert intelligences, and although not basically cruel, was sometimes callous from long over-stimulation, for in his time he had dealt with some fifty murders. He enjoyed practical joking, irrespective of his client's rank. Perhaps one of Holmes' best jokes (at least from his own point of view), was against Lord Cantlemere, when he slipped the Mazarin stone into his right-hand overcoat pocket and suggested that he should be arrested for possession of stolen property. As Cantlemere stood blinking and stammering as he looked at the yellow stone in his shaking palm, Holmes said, 'My old friend here will tell you that I have an impish habit of practical joking.' But Holmes never enjoyed the joke against himself. How fortunate for Holmes that Stamford brought Watson to his ken, who became his most understanding companion for so many years; no other man would have tolerated his vagaries.

Did not Holmes say that he loathed every form of society with his whole Bohemian soul, except Watson's. Perhaps not quite true, for he did not wish any outside influence to come between him and his work. He would readily devote his valuable time in helping a poor client, with no remuneration in sight, and treat an aristocrat in the same way, and if recompense there was, then so be it. 'I assure you, Watson, without affectation, that the status of my client is a matter of less moment to me than the interest of his case.' This was prompted by a letter from Lord Robert Walsingham de Vere St Simon, of Grosvenor Mansions, who carried a huge crest and monogram upon his envelope. Little wonder then, when Holmes received the King of Bohemia, and knew him through his disguise, that he spoke to him in a dry voice, saying he was well aware of what his visitor had told him, and settled himself in a languid, lounging way in his armchair, closed his eyes, and prepared himself to listen as if to any humble member of his realm.

Description of Sherlock Holmes

Sherlock Holmes was a tall man; at first, Watson thought that he was some six feet or more, but his height was put beyond all possible doubt one day by Holmes himself, who in his quiet factual way mentioned to Hilton Soames that he was six feet high, no more and no less; although it must be observed that when Holmes was tense and ready, his figure seemed to grow taller.[31]

He was an excessively lean, gaunt, loose-limbed, ascetic figure with a thin back, long thin legs, thin knees, and thin sinewy arms.

Because Holmes was blessed with superhuman powers of observation, he was inclined to belittle this lack of power in others, particularly the police and Watson, although Watson appreciated this intellectual gap between them; but, even so, Watson was very observant of his friend, as his writing testifies.

Perhaps it was Holmes' eyes that arrested Watson the most; did he not observe that early twinkle in his friend's eyes when Holmes guessed Watson's love for Mary Morstan? Holmes would sometimes look into Watson's eyes with the peculiarly mischievous gaze which was characteristic of his more imp-like moods, especially when his mind was absorbed by a problem and he had left his defence to his friend's revolver.

Holmes' eyes were grey, austere, beady, deep-set, sharp, piercing and inscrutable, with a steely glitter, like those of a bird, and as sharp as a rapier. With the game afoot, there was a subdued eagerness and a suggestion of tension in his brightened eyes and brisker manner, although to the casual observer he remained as impassive as ever. When a client was moved by his own story, and Holmes became excited and interested too, then the eyes had a hard glitter, and as Holmes became totally absorbed he would shut his eyes in order to obtain full concentration; a sudden

---

[31]*The Adventures of Sherlock Holmes*, second edition, London, George Newman Ltd, 1893 was dedicated to 'My old teacher Joseph Bell MD etc., of 2 Melville Crescent, Edinburgh.' He had contributed so much to Holmes' character.

opening and brightening of the eyes, together with a tightening of the lips, indicated that Holmes had at last seen a gleam of light in the darkness. As the eyes kindled and a slight flush sprang into his cheeks, Watson knew that Holmes was satisfied with the problem, more than words alone could imply, and that he would get his quarry; when Watson was astonished at Holmes reading his thoughts, a gleam of amusement would appear in his deep-set eyes, for he knew that in five minutes' time Watson would say that it was all so absurdly simple. Hilton Cubitt of Riding Thorpe Manor came to ask advice of Holmes over the mystery of the Dancing Men figures; Holmes tried to get him to stay, so that they could return together, but to no avail. He returned home and was murdered; when Holmes learnt this sad news, he knew that he had failed in his duty to his client, so that his face became haggard, out of which his inexorable eyes gleamed. Watson read in them Holmes' set purpose to devote his life to this quest, until his client had been avenged.

Holmes used his eyes to look at a criminal thoughtfully like a master chess player who meditated his crowning move; he could see to the very back of a person's mind as his eyes contracted and tightened until they were like two menacing points of steel. He could read in a man's eye when it was his own skin that he was frightened of saving. When Holmes listened to music (he was a composer and musician) his eyes became dreamy and languid, as they did also when, having observed and deduced, he would stare up at the ceiling. When the eyes shone with a faraway expression upon his slightly coloured, eager, aquiline face, then he would chatter away to himself under his breath, uttering exclamations, groans, whistles, even singing, and little cries suggestive of encouragement and hope, which were the battle signs when a crisis loomed.

Such a tense faraway expression Watson learned to associate with the supreme manifestations of his analytical genius. After a sleepless night pondering over a case, Holmes' bright eyes became the brighter for the dark shadows round them. With his gleaming eyes and straining muscles, Watson likened him to a foxhound as it ran upon a scent. Holmes in a period of intensive mental concentration, as shown by his eyes, told Watson that his friend needed solitude and seclusion, which prompted him to sally forth from the flat and go to his club. A mischievous twinkle would come into Holmes' eyes, as he said that although he understood his client's position, did the client understand his? And similarly when Homes watched Watson's intellectual entanglement over an obvious facet of a case.

Watson carefully noticed Holmes' bushy eyebrows, how they changed with the mood of the moment; how his drawn brows, like two hard black lines, and the deep furrows between them, showed that he needed no exhortation to concentrate all his attention upon a problem which, apart from the tremendous interests involved, must have appealed so directly to his love of the complex and the unusual. If the brow was ruffled, then the new evidence was not helping Holmes; a puzzled Holmes would sit for long spells with furrowed brow and vacant eye; the uncertainty whether he would be in time to stop a crime taking place would darken the brow with anxiety; a nonplussed Holmes for the moment, seeking a ray of light into a mystery, would smoke hard with his brows drawn down over his keen eyes, his lips compressed, and his head thrust forward in the eager way, characteristic of him. Holmes could become annoyed without having sufficient data to go upon, like trying to make bricks without clay, and he might sit for half an hour or so on end, with knitted brows and an abstracted air. When one police inspector tried to blame another inspector for allowing important footstep impressions to be churned up as if a herd of buffalo had passed along, he would glance at Watson and raise his eyebrows sardonically. A twitching of his bushy eyebrows, a gnawing of his lip, bespoke his disappointment, impatience and irritation, he would lean his chin upon his hands and stare into the log fire during a long silence.

Holmes' mouth was thin-lipped, his nose thin and hawk-like, which gave his whole expression an air of alertness and decision; his chin, prominent and square, which marked the man of determination. Watson often observed Holmes in the lamplight: 'The lamp beat upon his face, and so intent was it and so still, that it might have been that of a clear-cut classical statue, a personification of alertness and expectation.' At the house of Mr St Clair, near Lee, in Kent, Watson observed Holmes and noted: 'In the dim light of the lamp I saw him sitting there, an old briar pipe between his lips, his eyes fixed vacantly upon the corner of the ceiling the blue smoke curling up from him, silent, motionless, with the light shining upon his strong-set aquiline features.' Sometimes his face looked as if it was carved from old ivory; when in a perplexing position, he would be silently buried in thought, a pained expression upon his face; if there was a serious case in hand, then a stern gravity hardened his features. When conducting an experiment, the forehead might be wrinkled with speculation, and if the outcome appeared to be negative, an expression of the utmost chagrin and disappointment would appear upon his features; a sudden change to a positive conclusion might well cause him to wipe the perspiration from his forehead.

Holmes had, when he so willed it, the 'utter immobility of countenance of a Red Indian', thus not showing whether he was satisfied or not with the position of a case; or his face would assume a mask when his thoughts were elsewhere, that pale, clear-cut, sharp, austere and sallow-cheeked clean-shaven face.

His voice varied according to his mood – a high quick voice, a dogmatic tone, a languid voice, a strident or brisk business tone; and Watson knew the asperities of his temper. But Holmes could readily assume an easy air of geniality with a client, and, if a woman, he would talk most soothingly to her.

Was Holmes susceptible to sunburn? At least when he was driving on a sunny day, he would tilt his hat over his nose to keep the sun from his face.

He had an abnormally acute set of senses; he was able to smell the tarry odour of the gloves (impregnated with disinfectants), of Ralph, the elderly butler at Tuxbury Old Park, the house of Colonel Emsworth, and this gave him a clue towards discovering the true nature of the disease which affected Godfrey Emsworth. The colonel had thought it was leprosy; Holmes persuaded him to let him call in Sir James Saunders, the great dermatologist. He gave his opinion: 'It is not leprosy... A well-marked case of pseudo-leprosy or ichthyosis, a scale-like affection of the skin, unsightly, obstinate, but possibly curable, and certainly noninfective.'

We should never have known whether Holmes' skull was long or broad, had it not been for Dr James Mortimer, MRCS, (late of Charing Cross Hospital, winner of the Jackson Prize for Comparative Pathology, with an essay entitled 'Is Disease a Reversion?' A corresponding member of the Swedish Pathological Society, author of 'Some Freaks of Atavism', 'Do We Progress?' in the *Journal of Psychology*, and Medical Officer for the parishes of Grimpen, Thorsley and High Barrow, Dartmoor, Devon), who noted that Holmes had a dolichocephalic skull of 'such well-marked supra-orbital development. 'Would you have any objection to my running my finger along your parietal fissure? A cast of your skull sir, until the original is available, would be an ornament to any anthropological museum. It is not my intention to be fulsome, but I confess I covet your skull'[32]. (I wonder if Holmes ever left any bequest to a museum, in his will, regarding his skull?) Yet Professor Moriarty was somewhat disappointed with Holmes when he confronted him at Baker Street: 'You have less frontal development than I should have expected.'

Holmes' exceptionally nervous, strong, white thin hands were long fingered, the fingers often cold when upon the trail of a criminal. His hands were invariably blotted with ink and stained with chemicals; when he wished, those hands were capable of a hypnotic power of soothing and had a delicacy of touch as he manipulated, 'his fragile philosophical instruments'. Annoyed, and the hands were clenched; he would bite his nails when lost in thought, staring blankly out of the window; he would rub his hands together with delight, or with an appearance of avidity, which was a surprise to Watson who knew his frugal tastes. With his fingertips together, as if he were addressing a class, he would assume his most impassive and judicial expression with little dancing glances towards a curious visitor; sometimes he would be found with hands in his pockets, with a negligent air, which was not the norm but he had been known to indulge in this fancy, while at Briarbrae, Woking, Surrey, while walking round the grounds of the house keeping his hands in his pockets.

Oft-times Holmes would be found with his hands clasped

---

[32] ACD used the name Ward Mortimer in *The Story of the Jew's Breast-plate*.

behind him, his head sunk upon his chest, as he flung himself with characteristic eagerness into an investigation with a quick look of inward satisfaction, which indicated a congenial task before him as he paced eagerly and swiftly up and down the room. Sometimes the hands would be clenched in the air as he raved with annoyance if a client wasted his important time. He was inclined to tap with his fingers upon anything available, and his apparent air of nonchalance sometimes seemed to have an air of affectation, or he would lean his elbows upon the arm of a chair, like one who relishes conversation.

While in Camden House, the wait for the henchman of Moriarty, Colonel Moran (an elderly man with a gaunt swarthy face, scored with deep savage lines, a thin projecting nose, a high bald forehead and a huge grizzled moustache) was longer than Holmes expected; his impatience grew as he fidgeted with his feet, paced up and down in uncontrolled agitation, tapping rapidly with his fingers upon the wall. He was uneasy that his plans were not working out as he had hoped. In the utter silence of the dark room could be heard a thin, sibilant note which spoke of Holmes' intense suppressed excitement. A moment later he pulled Watson back into the blackest corner of the room and placed his warning hand upon his lips and clutched him with quivering fingers: Holmes' keener senses had already distinguished a low stealthy sound.

Watson noted that Holmes had a tendency to shrug his shoulders, sometimes at danger past, a typical example occurring on board the police launch as it chased the *Aurora* along the Thames. Holmes had not considered the possibility of Tonga retaining the last of his poisonous darts within his blowpipe and so the Andaman islander was given a chance to kill Holmes. Luckily the dart missed its intended victim and lodged in the wooden hatchway, but Holmes merely smiled and shrugged his shoulders in his easy fashion, realising that death had all but struck him down; Watson was sickened even at the thought of the horrible death which had been so narrowly avoided.

Another time, noted by Watson, occurred at Reigate, the Surrey house of Colonel Hayter, where Holmes was convalescing. Acton, a county magnate, had recently had his house burgled and a very odd assortment of articles stolen. This so intrigued Holmes that he forgot his recent illness and became instantly interested, which displeased Watson, who held up a warning finger. 'You are here for a rest, my dear fellow. For heaven's sake don't get started on a new problem when your nerves are all in shreds.' Holmes shrugged his shoulders with a glance of comic resignation towards the colonel, and the talk drifted on to less dangerous topics.

Holmes had a nimble and speculative mind, although he could at times be absent-minded. He had the power of throwing his brain out of action and switching all his thoughts on to lighter things, whenever he had convinced himself that he could no longer work to advantage. His usual habitual coolness was sometimes a cover for his deep agitation. He said of himself that he was an omnivorous reader with a strangely retentive memory for trifles. One drawback, he said, of an active mind, was that one could always conceive alternative explanations; seclusion and solitude were necessary to him in those hours of intense mental concentration during which he weighed every particle of evidence, constructed alternative theories, balanced one against the other, and made up his mind as to which points were essential and which immaterial. His mind became dejected and morose when things did not work out quickly enough for him. Once he told Watson that his reputation would not be improved by a certain mystery, for he had been sluggish in his mind and wanting in that mixture of imagination and reality which was the basis of his art, and he therefore blamed himself for not soon realising the clue which would have suggested to him the true solution.

His imagination could conceive no early solution to the mystery of the Lion's Mane, which brought him so completely to the limits of his powers, for he placed great value upon imagination, conceiving what might have happened, then acting upon the supposition, and, more often than not, he had found himself justified. He would put himself in the criminal's place, and, having first gauged his intelligence, would try to imagine how he would himself have proceeded under the same circumstances, an allowance being made for the 'personal equation, as the astronomers have dubbed it'.

When Watson saw Holmes absorbed in daydreaming thoughts, with a gleam in the eyes and a suppressed excitement in his manner, he was convinced that his friend had his hand upon a clue, even if Holmes himself was not capable of seeing it; he might be an introspective and pallid dreamer at Baker Street, but when upon the trail, he changed to a supple figure, alive with nervous energy, active and alert. No one would accuse him of being a nervous man generally, although he recognised that it was stupidity, rather than courage, that provoked the mind to refuse to recognise danger when it was close upon him; his strong masterful mind always dominated as if he really had the true authority of the law behind him. Perhaps Billy the pageboy summed up the magnitude of Holmes' mind. 'Mr Holmes always knows whatever there is to know', which was particularly so when he purposely starved himself in order to refine and heighten his mental faculties.

Holmes was a man of varying moods. When his affairs were going awry, then the mood might be melancholic, philosophic or partly comic, but with progress upon the scent, his face became flushed and darkened and the veins in his long sinewy neck stood out like whipcord. When in a taciturn or morose mood, he might run out and run in again, smoke incessantly, play snatches upon his violin, sink into a reverie, devour sandwiches at irregular hours, and ignore the casual questions put to him.

Holmes would run a new client over with one of his quick all-comprehensive glances, which at times could be stern, for he was impatient with a less active intelligence than his own. His attitude to those about him was habitually half humorous and half cynical: if he felt that the visitor was gaining the upper hand, his face went grey with anger and mortification, and he would question in a vibrant voice, telling of the fiery soul behind the cold face; if a visitor asked him not to break in upon his client's incognito, he would smile to himself and listen in a languid fashion, with closed eyes and fingertips together, but once he had ceased to be the centre of a problem, he would manifest no further interest in him. Holmes' quiet and systematic methods of work, coupled with his little digressions and his mocking smile, although proving to have a bearing upon the matter, would often irritate his clients, and should they be members of the police force, he might merely be amused. One moment Holmes could be elated and in a moving and chatty mood, and the next relapse into a silent, cold reverie if he was faced with aggression; a rigidity and alertness anticipated danger; a small vanity underlay his quiet and didactic manner, which might become severe when tragedy proved to lurk behind a curious train of events; his cold and proud nature was not always averse to public applause.

Holmes was seldom ill, but even his strong iron constitution had to succumb to exacting, long hours of work at times. On 14 April 1887 Watson received a telegram from Lyons, where Holmes was lying ill in the Hôtel Dulong. Within twenty-four hours, kind, friendly Watson was at his bedside, greatly relieved that Holmes' condition was not serious; it was a case of too much work, long hours and too little sleep. For two months Holmes had worked fifteen hours a day and five days at a time upon the track of the most accomplished European swindler, and had managed to succeed where the police of three continents had failed; Europe rang with his name.

Having taken Holmes back to Baker Street, Watson could see that he was not fully recovered and decided that Holmes needed to be taken right away from London crime, so that he could convalesce in peaceful surroundings. So the two went to stay with Watson's old friend of Afghanistan days, Colonel Hayter, who lived near Reigate. Holmes thought that he could find some peace and quiet here, away from it all with no crime to bother him; but he was proved to be wrong, which showed that even he still had something to learn. For as soon as murder was mentioned and an invitation from Inspector Forrester to investigate given, Holmes completely forgot his low state of health and became rejuvenated – better than all the doctor's advice. Suffice it to say, Holmes helped in the capture of the two Cunninghams, father and son, and his conscience was clear. Which was not so always: 'Once or twice in my career, I feel that I have done more real harm by my discovery of the criminal than ever he had done by his crime. I have learned caution now, and I had rather play tricks with the law of England, than with my own conscience.' Thus said Holmes to Watson at a later date.

When Holmes started upon his hobby, the detection of crime, he had no idea then how it would later dominate his life, but not to the total exclusion of his love of chemistry. Then there was no scientific system of criminology available, in print at least, which would enable a policeman to detect a criminal. Holmes was familiar with Lombroso and his work upon the criminal type, published in 1864; he knew of Monsieur Alphonse Bertillon of the Paris police, (as did Dr Mortimer), who photographed criminals and tried to identify them by a method he called anthropometric measurement. Holmes discussed with Watson the Bertillon system of measurements – for he was an enthusiastic admirer of the French savant – just after Watson's marriage, as they travelled down to Woking, to see Percy Phelps.[33]

Sherlock Holmes and Cocaine

In the early days, Watson became used to seeing Holmes lying upon the sofa, buried among his black-letter books, the whole day, for days on end, with little or no communication with him. He noticed the dreamy expression in his eyes that made him think that Holmes was taking some narcotic, although alien to his temperament and cleanliness of life. Gradually Watson realised the truth, that Holmes alternated between the soporific effect of cocaine and his own fierce energy to work. A drawn look upon his ascetic face and the brooding of his deep-set and inscrutable eyes told of the effect of idleness upon him. Watson was most worried how the cumulative effect of the drug would ultimately affect such a magnificent brain. He wanted to discuss this self-inflicted poisoning of his friend, but somehow every day never seemed to be the appropriate one.

Even by 1888 Holmes still had recourse to the drug habit; Watson watched him take his bottle from the corner of the mantelpiece, his hypodermic syringe from its neat morocco case and prepare his left sinewy forearm and wrist for the injection; his long, white, nervous fingers adjusted the delicate needle and rolled back his left shirt cuff. His eyes thoughtfully rested upon the innumerable puncture marks. 'Finally', wrote Watson, 'he

---

[33]Alphonse Bertillon, 1853–1914, Paris police officer.

thrust the sharp point home, pressed down the tiny piston, and sank back into the velvet-lined armchair with a long sigh of satisfaction.' Watson had watched Holmes take the drug daily, three times a day, until he no longer could control his pent-up exasperation. Perhaps the lunchtime Beaune wine gave him Dutch courage, for he could hold out no longer. 'Which is it today, morphine or cocaine?' Holmes raised his eyes languidly from the book he was reading. 'It is cocaine, a seven-per-cent solution.' Watson refused brusquely, for his constitution was not yet normal, to try the drug. Holmes agreed with Watson. 'I suppose that its influence is physically a bad one. I find it, however, so transcendently stimulating and clarifying to the mind that its secondary action is a matter of small moment.' Watson remonstrated with him, as a comrade and a medical man. Unoffended, Holmes with fingertips together tried to explain to Watson why he had recourse to drugs. He admitted that the effects of the drug were physically bad, but he could not be idle for long, his mind rebelled at stagnation; he needed problems, work, abstruse cryptograms, intricate analysis, mental exaltation – he could not tolerate the dull routine of existence. With a fully employed Holmes, Watson had no fear of the dominating drug, but he did keep his medical eye upon him for he knew the menace was never dead, only sleeping. A black depression could easily change into a mood of excellent spirits if work turned up. Holmes apparently never tried drenching his tobacco with laudanum like Thomas de Quincey in 1821.

Watson's First Case with Holmes

As Watson wrote the memoirs of his friend, he endeavoured to illustrate a few of his mental peculiarities, but found it difficult to pick out examples which in every way answered his purpose. Watson observed:

> For in these cases in which Holmes has performed some *tour-de-force* of analytical reasoning, and has demonstrated the value of his peculiar methods of investigation, the facts themselves have often been so slight or so commonplace that I could not feel justified in laying them before the public. On the other hand, it has fre-

quently happened that he has been concerned in some research where the facts have been of the most remarkable and dramatic character, but where the share which he has himself taken in determining their causes, has been less pronounced than I, as his biographer, could wish.

Many of the cases go undated: sometimes purposely, where discretion and reticence were entailed. Some involved the secrets of private families so that we find only some thirty dated cases. In recording his notes, Watson used foolscap paper.[34] He was also allowed to see the verbatim shorthand reports in Inspector Lestrade's notebook – presumably translated for Watson's benefit, there being no mention of his proficiency in that field of knowledge. Watson's notes took on a dramatic turn when he was able to record his first big case with Holmes, at the empty house, No. 3 Lauriston Gardens, Brixton, where Enoch J Drebber of Cleveland, Ohio, was found murdered. This might never have been recorded by Watson and called by him, *A Study in Scarlet*, had it not been for Watson's insistence that he should pay a visit; this followed after Holmes had received a police note, brought by the commissionaire which ran as follows:

My dear Mr Sherlock Holmes,
    There has been a bad business during the night at 3, Lauriston Gardens, off the Brixton Road. Our man on the beat saw a light there about two in the morning, and as the house was an empty one, suspected that something was amiss He found the door open, and in the front room, which is bare of furniture, discovered the body of a gentleman, well dressed, and having cards in his pocket bearing the name of 'Enoch J Drebber, Cleveland, Ohio, USA.' There had been no robbery, nor is there any evidence as to how the man met his death. There are marks of blood in the room, but there is no wound upon his person. We are at a loss as to how he came into the empty house; indeed the whole affair is a puzzler. If you can come round to the house any time before twelve, you will find me there. I have left everything in *status quo* until I hear from you. If you are unable to come, I shall give you fuller details, and would esteem it a great kindness if you would favour me with your opinions.

---

[34] Fool's cap and bells as watermark.

'Gregson is the smartest of the Scotland Yarders... he and Lestrade are the pick of a bad lot. They are both quick and energetic, but conventional – shockingly so. They have their knives into one another, too. They are as jealous as a pair of professional beauties. There will be some fun over this case if they are both put upon the scent,' observed Holmes.

Watson expected that this news would immediately turn Holmes into an alert person, but no, he remained calm, as if this were an everyday letter. 'Surely there is not a moment to be lost... shall I go and order you a cab?'

'I'm not sure about whether I shall go. I am the most incurably lazy devil that ever stood in shoe leather that is, when the fit is on me, for I can be spry enough at times.'

Watson knew that this was the moment that Holmes had awaited, when he could cease his cocaine injections and concentrate upon a new case; why then the lack of enthusiasm?

'My dear fellow, what does it matter to me? Supposing I unravel the whole matter, you may be sure that Gregson, Lestrade, and Co will pocket all the credit. That comes of being an unofficial personage.'

'But he begs you to help him,' said Watson.

'Yes. He knows that I am his superior, and acknowledges it to me; but he would cut his tongue out before he would own it to any third person. However, we may as well go and have a look. I shall work it out on my own hook. I may have a laugh at them, if I have nothing else. Come on!' An energetic fit had superseded the apathetic one, and away they both went in a hansom through the foggy cloudy morning to the scene of the crime.

As they drove along, Watson expected Holmes to chat upon the murder, but Holmes only said that it was a capital mistake to theorise without all the evidence; it would only bias his judgment.

The unoccupied house had a small front garden, with a narrow path of a clay and gravel mixture, sloppy from the overnight rain; a three-foot brick wall, topped by wooden rails, bounded the garden. Holmes was in no hurry to enter the house. Instead he nonchalantly lounged up and down the pavement, seemingly, to the onlooker, most unconcerned. But Holmes was taking note of the many marks of footsteps upon the path, confused except to his trained eye.

Holmes and Watson walked into the empty, large, square dining room. The walls blotched with mildew, uncertain light came through the dirty window; a thick layer of dust covered all.

As Watson recorded:

> At present my attention was centred upon the single, grim, motionless figure which lay stretched upon the boards, with vacant, sightless eyes staring up at the discoloured ceiling. It was that of a man about forty-three or forty-four years of age, middle-sized, broad-shouldered, with crisp curling black hair, and a short, stubbly beard. He was dressed in a heavy broadcloth frock coat and waistcoat, with light-coloured trousers, and immaculate collar and cuffs. A top-hat, well brushed and trim, was placed upon the floor beside him. His hands were clenched and his arms thrown abroad, while his lower limbs were interlocked, as though his death struggle had been a grievous one. On his rigid face there stood an expression of horror, and, as it seemed to me, of hatred, such as I have never seen upon human features. This malignant and terrible contortion, combined with the low forehead, blunt nose, and prognathous jaw, gave the dead man a singularly simious and ape-like appearance, which was increased by his writhing, unnatural posture. I have seen death in many forms, but never has it appeared to me in a more fearsome aspect than in that dark, grimy apartment, which looked out upon one of the main arteries of suburban London.

Both Gregson and Lestrade were nonplussed as they could find neither clue nor wound; some blood splashes were possibly those of the murderer.

Watson watched Holmes' nimble fingers, 'flying here, there, and everywhere, feeling, pressing, unbuttoning, examining, while his eyes wore the same faraway expression which I have already remarked upon. So swiftly was the examination made, that one would hardly have guessed the minuteness with which it was conducted. Finally, he sniffed the dead man's lips, and then glanced at the soles of his patent leather boots.'

As the body was lifted up to be taken to the mortuary, a woman's gold wedding ring was discovered beneath. To Holmes, this simplified matters. In the dead man's pockets were found the following as listed by Gregson: 'A gold watch, No. 97163, by Barraud, of London. Gold Albert chain, very heavy and solid. Gold ring, with masonic device. Gold pin bull-dog's head, with rubies as eyes. Russian leather card case, with cards of Enoch J Drebber of Cleveland, corresponding with the E J D upon the linen. No purse, but loose money to the extent of seven pounds thirteen. Pocket edition of Boccaccio's *Decameron*, with name of Joseph Stangerson upon the flyleaf. Two letters – one addressed to E J Drebber and one to Joseph Stangerson.' They were both from the Guion Steamship Company, referring to their New York return from Liverpool, and addressed to the Strand American Exchange.

Lestrade discovered a blood-red name on the wall – Rache, and thought it was for Rachel; Holmes thought otherwise. Holmes then proceeded to examine the room, while Watson watched his friend with great interest. Watson observed:

Holmes whipped a tape measure and a large round magnifying glass from his pocket. With these two implements he trotted noiselessly about the room, sometimes stopping, occasionally kneeling, and once lying flat upon his face. So engrossed was he with his occupation that he appeared to have forgotten our presence, for he chattered away to himself under his breath the whole time, keeping up a running fire of exclamations, groans, whistles, and little cries suggestive of encouragement and of hope. As I watched him I was irresistibly reminded of a pure-blooded, well-trained foxhound, as it dashes backward and forward through the covert, whining in its eagerness, until it comes across the lost scent. For twenty minutes or more he continued his researches, measuring with the most exact care the distance between marks which were entirely invisible to me, and occasionally applying his tape to the walls in an equally incomprehensible manner. In one place he gathered up very carefully a little pile of grey dust from the floor, and packed it away in an envelope. Finally he examined with his glass the word upon the wall, going over every letter of it with the most minute exactness. This done, he appeared to be satisfied, for he replaced his tape and his glass in his pocket.

To Holmes little things and trifles were infinitely the most important.

Holmes told the detectives that the murderer was a man, six feet tall, in the prime of life, with small feet, who wore coarse, square-toed boots and smoked a Trichinopoly cigar. He arrived with his victim in a four-wheeled cab, drawn by a horse with three old shoes and one new one on its off foreleg; he probably had a florid face and the fingernails of his right hand were remarkably long, and poison killed his victim. Holmes also informed Lestrade that *Rache* was the German for revenge. However, the detectives only evinced considerable curiosity and some contempt for the amateur at work.

Later on, Holmes explained to Watson how he arrived at his conclusions. While standing on the pavement, he had observed the cab marks near the kerb, as being there during the night and the hoof marks of different shoes. He determined the height of the murderer by his stride of four and a half feet, which also indicated good health; a man's bloody, long-nailed forefinger wrote on the wall, leaving the plaster scratched; the ash from the floor was dark in colour and flaky, which determined the particular cigar; *Rache* was printed in the Latin character, so not by a German. All these explanations put Watson's head in a whirl. But at this early stage of their partnership, Holmes did not intend to explain all the workings of his fast reasoning brain, otherwise Watson would think of him as a very ordinary person. But Watson had seen enough to know that he had witnessed the working of a superb, unique brain. 'I shall never do that,' he declared, 'you have brought detection as near an exact science as it ever will be brought in this world.'

The case involved three Americans from Salt Lake City – Enoch Drebber, murdered at Brixton, Joseph Stangerson, murdered at Halliday's Private Hotel, and Jefferson Hope, who called himself their judge, jury and executioner. Holmes summed up the case as a simple one: 'The proof of its intrinsic simplicity is, that without any help save a few very ordinary deductions I was able to lay my hand upon the criminal within three days... You see, the whole thing is a chain of logical sequences without a break or flaw.' 'It is wonderful!' responded Watson. 'Your merits should be publicly recognised. You should publish an account of the case. If you won't, I will for you... I have all the facts in my journal...' 'You may do what you like, Doctor,' replied Holmes, as he showed his friend the report in the *Echo* newspaper where the Scotland Yard officials, Lestrade and Gregson, gained all the credit for apprehending Hope, the killer. And so was born another 'Boswell'.[35] Holmes was eventually grateful to Watson. 'I must thank you for it all. I might not have gone but for you, and so have missed the finest study I ever came across.'

Dr Watson meets Mary Morstan

Watson's second case with Holmes was recounted in the story of *The Sign of Four*, in 1888, on 8 July which was a most memorable day in his life, as he met his future wife, Mary Morstan.

> She was a blonde young lady, small, dainty, well gloved, and dressed in the most perfect taste. There was, however, a plainness and simplicity about her costume which bore with it a suggestion of limited means. The dress was a sombre greyish beige, untrimmed and unbraided, and she wore a small turban of the same dull hue, relieved only by a suspicion of a white feather in the side. Her face had neither regularity of feature nor beauty of complexion, but her expression was sweet and amiable, and her large blue eyes were singularly spiritual and sympathetic.

Thus Watson recorded his first impressions. Her face promised a refined and sensitive nature. As she seated herself, her lip trembled and her hand quivered, signs of intense inward agitation. It would seem that there was an instant attraction between the two of them, for as Watson rose from his chair, intending to leave the room (for he felt rather embarrassed), she held up her gloved hand to detain him and said to Holmes, 'If your friend would be good enough to stop, he might be of inestimable service to me.' So Watson relapsed back into his chair.

Miss Morstan requested Holmes' help in her strange inexplicable case, knowing how he had helped her employer, Mrs Cecil Forrester, in the past. She told him how she had received annually

---

[35]James Boswell, 1740–1795. Biographer of Samuel Johnson, 1709–1784.

for the past six years a very large and lustrous pearl, and that very day an unsigned letter, asking her to come to the Lyceum Theatre at seven in the evening.

Holmes decided to go with her to the Lyceum Theatre, and as her correspondent had mentioned that she might bring two friends but no police with her, he suggested that Watson should go with them. 'But would he come?' she said, appealing with expression in her voice. 'I shall be proud and happy if I can be of any service,' said Watson fervently, which placed him in her eyes as a very kind person. Watson even watched from the window her brisk exit down Baker Street, and, turning to Holmes, exclaimed, 'What a very attractive woman!' Languidly replied Holmes, 'Is she? ...I did not observe.' (What a very odd remark to make by one who prided himself upon his unique observation!) Perhaps Holmes did not appreciate the signs of love for a woman in another man, as he would not permit himself the luxury of similar feelings. In those early days, a woman's heart and mind were insoluble puzzles to him. Watson really turned upon his friend. 'You really are an automaton – a calculating machine... There is something positively inhuman in you at times.' (Watson gradually came to realise, as the years slipped by, that Holmes did not deserve this reprimand.)

Holmes did not get angry or annoyed, he simply smiled. 'It is of the first importance not to allow your judgment to be biased by personal qualities. A client to me is a mere unit, a factor in a problem. The emotional qualities are antagonistic to clear reasoning. I assure you that the most winning woman I ever knew was hanged for poisoning three little children for their insurance-money, and the most repellent man of my acquaintance is a philanthropist who has spent nearly a quarter of a million upon the London poor.'

Holmes recommended that Watson should read Winwood Reade's *Martyrdom of Man*; Watson sat in the window with the book in his hand, but his thoughts were far from its daring speculations. He could only think of her sensitive smiling face, the deep rich tones of her voice and the mystery surrounding this sweet-faced woman of twenty-seven, whose youth had lost its self-consciousness and become a little sobered by experience. His mind ran on with such dangerous thoughts that he hurried to his desk to disperse the will-o'-the-wisp of his imagination. What was an ex-army surgeon with a weak leg and a weaker banking account thinking about! But the seeds of love had been sown.

But Holmes, even in his cold manner towards Miss Morstan, did appreciate her when he asked her if the handwriting of the letter and the address upon the pearl boxes were the same, and she immediately produced six pieces of paper as if by magic. 'You are certainly a model client. You have the correct intuition,' said Holmes. She showed a further example of her intuition by bringing and showing Holmes a curious paper found in her father's desk. 'I don't suppose it is of the slightest importance, but I thought you might care to see it, so I brought it with me.' The paper was of native manufacture, clean upon both sides, having been carefully preserved in a pocketbook. It showed a diagram of a large building with a red cross, and then four other crosses in a line, together with four signatures. 'Preserve it carefully, then, Miss Morstan, for it may prove to be of use to us. I begin to suspect that this matter may turn out to be much deeper and more subtle than I had at first supposed. I must reconsider my ideas.'

In the cab, as they travelled through the dense, drizzly fog, Watson and Miss Morstan chatted in an undertone about the pending journey and its possible outcome. Both were nervous and depressed, although her demeanour was resolute and collected. Watson tried to cheer and amuse her by recounting his Afghanistan adventures, but such were his feelings of love for Miss Morstan that his stories became somewhat tangled – for he fired a double-barrelled tiger cub, while a musket looked into his tent.

At the house in Cold Harbour Lane, Thaddeus Sholto upset her by a reference to her father's death and how he was secretly buried by the brothers – 'her face grew white to the lips'. As Thaddeus rambled on, she cut him short with, 'You will excuse me, Mr Sholto, but I am here at your request to learn something which you desire to tell me', but the answer necessitated a visit to his brother Bartholomew's house at Norwood. Watson had to revive her with water from a Venetian carafe, upon a side table.

The Sholto brothers, as trustees of the Agra treasure, decided that Mary Morstan, being an orphan, should have a fair share of the wealth as decreed by their dying father, Major John Sholto, late of the Indian Army. So they started to send her, at intervals, a single valuable pearl from a chaplet. 'It was a kindly thought... it was extremely good of you,' said an earnest Miss Morstan. Later they hoped that she would share in the wealth, estimated at not less than half a million pounds sterling.

Watson considered that if Miss Morstan could secure her rights, she would change from a needy governess to the richest heiress in England. He would have liked to have rejoiced and congratulated her, but he only saw her slipping away from his grasp and as he recorded he was 'ashamed to say that selfishness took me by the soul and that my heart turned as heavy as lead within me.' How was he going to aspire to the hand of so wealthy a woman?

Pondicherry Lodge, Norwood, the Sholto home, was a huge clump of a house, square and prosaic, plunged in shadow amid desolate grounds. No light shone amid the gloom, and the ominous silence 'struck a chill to the heart'. The shrill, broken whimpering of the housekeeper, Mrs Bernstone, could be heard from the interior of the black house, and Miss Morstan seized Watson's wrist for protection, their hearts thumping together. As they stood in the darkness outside together, Miss Morstan then placed her hand in Watson's. As he wrote afterwards: 'A wondrous subtle thing is love, for here were we two, who had never seen each other before that day, between whom no word or even look of affection had ever passed, and yet now in an hour of trouble our hands instinctively sought for each other. I have marvelled at it since, but at the time it seemed the most natural thing that I should go out to her so, and, as she has often told me, there was in her also the instinct to turn to me for comfort and protection. So we stood hand in hand like two children, and there was peace in our hearts for all the dark things that surrounded us.'

The housekeeper met them as they entered the house and appeared to be soothed by the presence of another woman. 'God bless your sweet, calm face!' she exclaimed. 'It does me good to see you.' Miss Morstan patted the thin worn hand and her few words of kindly womanly comfort brought the colour back into the bloodless cheeks.

After finding Bartholomew dead, Watson said, 'It is not right that Miss Morstan should remain in this stricken house.' Holmes agreeing, Watson took a further opportunity to be with her by taking her to Mrs Cecil Forrester's home in Lower Camberwell by cab. As Watson wrote:

> After the angelic fashion of women, she had borne trouble with a calm face as long as there was someone weaker than herself to support, and I had found her bright and placid by the side of the frightened housekeeper. In the cab, however, she first turned faint and then burst into a passion of weeping – so sorely had she been tried by the adventures of the night. She has told me since that she thought me cold and distant upon that journey. She little guessed the struggle within my breast, or the effort of self-restraint which held me back. My sympathies and my love went out to her even as my hand had in the garden. I felt that years of the conventionalities of life could not teach me to know her sweet, brave nature as had this one day of strange experiences. Yet there were two thoughts which sealed the words of affection upon my lips. She was weak and helpless, shaken in mind and nerve. It was to take her at a disadvantage to obtrude love upon her at such a time. Worse still, she was rich. If Holmes' researches were successful, she would be an heiress. Was it fair, was it honourable, that a half-pay surgeon should take such advantage of an intimacy which chance had brought about? Might she not look upon me as a mere vulgar fortune-seeker? I could not bear to risk that such a thought should cross her mind. This Agra treasure intervened like an impassable barrier between us.

Watson could see that he was not the only one fond of the young lady, for he saw how tenderly and motherly was Mrs Forester's welcome home to her very dear friend. Watson left with a picture of two graceful, clinging figures in the doorway, a glimpse of a tranquil English home amid the present dark business.

Watson knew that the Agra treasure in part or in whole belonged to Miss Morstan and knew that he must help all he could in its recovery, even if it meant that the finding of it might be his ultimate loss; at least he could dream, and dream of the sweet face of Mary looking down upon him.

Watson went out again to Camberwell to give the latest news, but actually to be near Mary again. Mrs Forrester called it 'A romance! …An injured lady, half a million in treasure, a black cannibal and a wooden-legged ruffian.' Mary glanced brightly at Watson – 'And two knights-errant to the rescue.' Watson was more than pleased to notice that by Mary's toss of her proud head she was not elated unduly; she thought only of the safety of Thaddeus Sholto.

After the iron treasure chest was secured, following the chase upon the Thames, Watson was landed at Vauxhall and, accompanied by a bluff, genial police inspector, took his treasure to Camberwell, so that Mary might be the first to see it, although he did so with a heavy heart. 'I have brought you something which is worth all the news in the world. I have brought you a fortune… Half of it is yours and half is Thaddeus Sholto's. You will have a couple of hundred thousand each. Think of that! An annuity of ten thousand pounds. There will be few richer young ladies in England. Is it not glorious?' Mary raised her eyebrows and, looking curiously at Watson, said, 'I owe it to you'. As Watson related how the poisoned dart had nearly killed him, she turned white and nearly fainted, thinking how she had nearly lost him. Small having thrown the key into the river, Watson had to forcibly prize open the hasp with the poker, and then with trembling fingers flung back the lid – to disclose an empty box!

'The treasure is lost,' said Mary, to which Watson in his suppressed joy ejaculated, 'Thank God!' 'Why do you say that?' 'Because you are within my reach again… Because I love you, Mary, as truly as ever a man loved a woman. Because this treasure, these riches, sealed my lips. Now that they are gone, I can tell you how I love you. That is why I said, "Thank God".' 'Then I say, "Thank God" too,' she whispered and Watson drew her to his side, knowing that he had gained the more worthy treasure. (Small had dumped the treasure overboard into the Thames.)

It just remained for Watson to impart his very good news to Holmes. After Athelney Jones had taken away his prisoner, Small, to be locked up, Watson said after they had sat for some time smoking in silence, 'I fear that it may be the last investigation in which I shall have the chance of studying your methods. Miss Morstan has done me the honour to accept me as a husband in prospective.'[36] 'I feared as much. I really cannot congratulate you,' Holmes replied with a groan. This really hurt Watson, coming from his nearest and dearest friend. 'Have you any reason to be dissatisfied with my choice?' 'Not at all. I think she is one of the most charming young ladies I ever met, and might have been most useful in such work as we have been doing. She had a decided genius that way; witness the way in which she preserved that Agra plan from all the other papers of her father. But love is an emotional thing, and whatever is emotional is opposed to that true cold reason which I place above all things. I should never marry myself, lest I bias my judgment.' Watson laughed. 'I trust that my judgment may survive the ordeal.'

Dr Watson's Marriages

Watson's marital affairs are not so easy to understand. In late September 1887 Watson recorded: 'My wife was a visitor to her mother's and for a few days, I was a dweller once more in my old quarters at Baker Street...' On 20 March 1888 'I was returning from a journey to a patient (for I had now returned to civil practice), when my way led me through Baker Street.' 'Wedlock suits you,' Holmes remarked, not effusively, for marriage had come between them, and interrupted a way of life to Holmes. 'I think, Watson, that you have put on seven and a half pounds since I saw you.' (Holmes just a little peeved?) Watson thought only seven. 'Indeed, I should have thought a little more. Just a trifle more, I fancy, Watson. And in practice again, I observe. You did not tell me that you intended to go into harness.' (Surprising that Watson was so remiss) Watson's general health had improved, he was now a more robust figure, with a stronger frame, a square jaw, thick neck and a 'modest' moustache, his handkerchief in the sleeve of his jacket. On 8 July 1888 Watson met Miss Morstan at Baker Street. Victor Hatherley visited Watson at his Paddington

---

[36]Watson remembered Charles Dickens' *London Recreations* '...husbands in prospective ordering bottles of ginger-beer for the objects of their affections.'

surgery in the summer of 1889, 'not long after my marriage'. This could have been before June 1889, when Kate Whitney (Isa, her husband, was one of Watson's patients) called late at night for Watson's help, at the house they had purchased from old Dr Farquhar, not far from Paddington Station. The practice had dwindled from twelve hundred to three hundred patients; for the former owner, old and suffering from St Vitus's dance, was no longer able to cure himself or his patients.

His neighbour, Dr Ansthruther, purchased a similar practice, as a newly built home; seemingly Watson purchased the better of the two, as indicated by the steps to his house, worn down three inches deeper than his neighbour's.[37]

The Watsons managed to afford a maid, Mary Jane, who being unsatisfactory did not stay long. Watson drove himself about in a hansom cab. Did he carry his medical instruments in a wicker basket like Dr Percy Trevelyan of Brook Street? A bulge on the right side of his top hat showed where he secreted his stethoscope.

Watson wrote little about his wife; she was a kindly person to folk in grief, who came to her like birds to a lighthouse, and she was a keen needlework woman. She does not appear to have had any children, for surely Holmes would have been their godfather, and Watson would have published the news. Now the very intimate relations which had existed between Holmes and Watson became to some extent modified. But Watson occasionally persuaded Holmes to forego his Bohemian habits and visit him and his wife.

The Watsons usually took an annual holiday, except when the bank account was depleted. Sometimes they would have a surprise visit from Holmes wishing Watson's assistance, when he would make himself at home in the rocking chair. Mary would put him up for the night, then in the morning they would be off in a four-wheeler to catch a train, even to faraway Birmingham, for distance was never an obstacle to these two intrepid travellers, the priority being just how interesting was the case. At these times one of his friendly medico neighbours, either Dr Ansthruther or

[37]At Edinburgh ACD may well have heard of the family name of Ansthruther and the fishing port of the same name.

Dr Jackson,[38] would step in and take Watson's surgery.

Mary Watson sometimes visited her friend, and at times like these Watson was able to spend a few days with Holmes, back in his familiar surroundings at the flat in Baker Street, just like the old days. There he would lean back in his old familiar chair, and after reading the newspaper would go off into a brown study, particularly if it was a cold day. With the room temperature up to ninety degrees, and with the blinds half drawn, the room was a veritable oven; even for Watson, used to such Indian temperatures, the close stuffiness of the room had a soporific effect upon him. Apart from these few contacts, Watson only learned of the activities of Holmes by the articles in the *Daily Press*; but come the festive season of the year, Watson would call round at Baker Street upon the second day after Christmas to wish Holmes the compliments of the season and to see if any case was afoot.

In 1890 Watson saw Holmes only three times. On 24 April 1891 Holmes paid an evening visit to Watson in his consulting room – Mrs Watson was away upon a visit. In the spring of 1894 Holmes visited Watson in his study at Kensington. 'In some manner he had learned of my own sad bereavement, and his sympathy was shown in his manner rather than in his words.' 'Work', said Holmes, 'is the best antidote to sorrow, my dear Watson.' A month or so later, Holmes persuaded Watson to sell his small Kensington practice to a young Dr Verner, who never quibbled over the price, much to Watson's surprise, and to move back to Baker Street. It was only some time later that Watson discovered that the buyer was a distant relative of Holmes – who incidentally had provided the money. Holmes must have missed Watson, very much!

In 1902 Watson was living in his own rooms, in Queen Anne Street, where his practice 'was not inconsiderable', in September Holmes asked him to come to Baker Street at all costs for he had a problem on his mind. 'Why does Professor Presbury's faithful wolfhound Roy, endeavour to bite him?' Watson's practice at this time was considerable, so that a trip with Holmes involved 'frantic

---

[38]Dr Habakuk Jephson, USA went on a voyage in the *Marie Celeste* and left his partner, Dr Jackson to look after the practice. ACD, 'J Habakuk Jephson's Statement', *Cornhill Magazine*, 1883.

planning and hurrying', but faithful Watson hurried round to Baker Street, where for half an hour Holmes totally ignored him, except to say, 'You will excuse a certain abstraction of mind, my dear Watson…' During the silence, Watson summed up the peculiar relations which existed between them:

> He was a man of habits, narrow and concentrated habits, and I had become one of them. As an institution, I was like the violin, the shag tobacco, the old black pipe, the index books, and others perhaps less excusable. When it was a case of active work and a comrade was needed upon whose nerve he could place some reliance, my rôle was obvious. But apart from this I had uses. I was a whetstone for his mind. I stimulated him. He liked to think aloud in my presence. His remarks could hardly be said to be made to me – many of them would have been as appropriately addressed to his bedstead – but none the less, having formed the habit, it had become in some way helpful that I should register and interject. If I irritated him by a certain methodical slowness in my mentality, that irritation served only to make his own flame-like intuitions and impressions flash up the more vividly and swiftly. Such was my humble rôle in our alliance.

These were early days in their relationship; as the years passed, Holmes came to appreciate Watson's many qualities.

In 1903 Watson married again; he never even revealed her name. Holmes now had to write his own accounts of his cases, so that Watson was not present to receive a further lecture upon his style of recording from Holmes, given 'with the air of a professor addressing his class'. Holmes had to now write his own account of 'The Blanched Soldier' and remembered his friend's retort: 'Try it yourself, Holmes!' So Holmes realised at last that the story had to interest the reader – like all Watson's accounts – and not be a canvas for self-adulation. Holmes found himself alone.

Dr Watson's Medical Knowledge

Watson, although not a practising surgeon, liked to keep abreast of modern surgical achievement and would read the latest treatise thereon. He also read the *British Medical Journal* and the latest report upon pathology. Even if he did not, with delicate precision, operate upon a human body, he nevertheless retained the delicacy of touch with his fingers, for did he not put this to good use when he made two burglars masks out of black silk, necessary for their nefarious expedition to Mr Milverton's house at Hampstead.

There were times when Watson's medical knowledge assisted Holmes, although with reticence he only recorded a few.

Holmes asked Watson to feel the arm and leg of the murdered man Bartholomew Sholto. He found that the muscles were as hard as a board, far exceeding the usual rigor mortis, and, coupled with the drawn muscles of the face, had no hesitation in diagnosing 'Death from some powerful vegetable alkaloid... some strychnine-like substance which would produce tetanus.'

Earlier in the evening, Watson had been introduced to Thaddeus Sholto, who cried in an excited voice, 'A doctor, eh? ...Have you your stethoscope? Might I ask you – would you have the kindness? I have grave doubts as to my mitral valve, if you would be so very good. The aortic I may rely upon, but I should value your opinion upon the mitral.' Watson listened to his heart, but could find nothing wrong, except that he was in an ecstasy of fear, for he shivered from head to foot. His comment that 'It appears to be normal. You have no cause for uneasiness', delighted the hearer.

Watson encountered another heart problem with Jefferson Hope, prisoner of Lestrade and Gregson at the police station. Asked if he had anything to say, Hope replied that he had. 'I may never be tried... You needn't look startled. It isn't suicide I am thinking of.' Turning his fierce dark eyes upon Watson, he asked him if he was a doctor, and, receiving an affirmative answer, he asked Watson to put his hand upon his chest. As Watson did so, he at once became aware of an extraordinary throbbing and commotion within. 'The walls of his chest seemed to thrill and quiver as a frail building would do inside when some powerful engine was at work.' Watson heard a dull humming and buzzing noise, which he declared was an aortic aneurism, and that there was immediate danger of death. In fact, on the very night after his capture, the aneurism burst, and Hope was summoned before a higher judge, where strict justice would be meted out to him.

Holmes appreciated the medical assistance that Watson gave to him; perhaps this was best highlighted after the visit to Baker Street of Culverton Smith, who had hoped to see a Holmes dying slowly from the poisoned box he had sent to him. Watson, out of necessity, had to believe in Holmes' illness and thus was kept in the dark. After Smith was taken away by the police, Holmes tried to placate his friend. 'It was very essential that I should impress Mrs Hudson with the reality of my condition, since she was to convey it to you, and you in turn to him. You won't be offended, Watson? You will realise that among your many talents dissimulation finds no place, and that if you had shared my secret you would never have been able to impress Smith with the urgent necessity of his presence, which was the vital point of the whole scheme.' Watson still could not understand Holmes keeping him away from the sickbed. 'Can you ask, my dear Watson? Do you imagine that I have no respect for your medical talents? Could I fancy that your astute judgment would pass a dying man who, however weak, had no rise of pulse or temperature?'

One November day, Robert Ferguson of Lamberley in Sussex, called in Holmes to investigate the supposed vampirism of his Peruvian wife and her attack upon their baby. He wrote Holmes a very long letter detailing the whole of the case, and adding that he had known Watson in his rugby-playing days. While Holmes and Watson were there, the son was asked to fetch from the sick bedroom Mrs Mason, the nurse, and the baby; Watson was able to cast his eye over this remarkable lad of fifteen, pale-faced, fair-haired and with excitable light blue eyes and a curious shambling gait. This told Watson that he was suffering from a weak spine. As Dolores, Mrs Ferguson's maid, said that her mistress needed to see a doctor, Watson consented to go upstairs and see her. She was clearly in a high fever, and only half conscious; Watson took her temperature and pulse; both were high. His impression was that her condition was rather that of mental and nervous excitement than of any actual seizure, but she was quite rational.

When Holmes and Watson were down in Devon, at King's Pyland, on Dartmoor, investigating a murder and the disappearance of the racehorse Silver Blaze, they were shown an 'ivory-handled knife with a very delicate inflexible blade marked Weiss & Co, London'; the tip was protected by a disc of cork, and the knife had been found upon John Straker, the murdered man. 'This is a very singular knife,' commented Holmes. 'I presume, as I see blood stains upon it, that it is the one which was found in the dead man's grasp. Watson, this knife is surely in your line?' Watson identified it as a cataract knife.

Watson, being a surgeon, was well up in osteology, which stood him in good stead and allowed him to shine in the presence of his master as he defined the name of a charred bone fragment from the furnace of Sir Robert Norberton of Shoscombe Old Place; he knew it to be the upper condyle of a human femur.

Watson was able to be of help after the murder of Joseph Stangerson (former Mormon Elder of Utah, USA, husband of Lucy Ferrier and murderer of her adopted father in 1860), at Halliday's Private Hotel in Little George Street. He had been stabbed through the heart. Inspector Lestrade found upon the bedroom window sill a small chipped ointment box containing two pills. 'It was the merest chance my taking these pills, for I am bound to say that I do not attach any importance to them,' commented the inspector. But Holmes was delighted and exultant. 'The last link… My case is complete.' He turned to Watson. 'Now, Doctor, he asked, 'are these ordinary pills?' Watson confidently replied that they were most unusual, being of a pearly grey colour, small, round and almost translucent; which latter quality told Watson that they were soluble in water, which they proved to be.

Watson helped to save the life of the chloroformed Lady Frances Carfax. Through all the darkness, Holmes had suddenly seen daylight when he reconsidered the depth of the coffin at Holy Peters house. With Watson, Holmes took a fast hansom to the Brixton Road, arriving there in forty minutes, just as Big Ben struck eight – the time of the funeral. The authoritative voice of Holmes stayed the exit of the hearse. By a united effort, the coffin lid was torn off and the body of Lady Carfax exposed. Holmes raised her to a sitting position. 'Is she gone, Watson? Is there a spark left? Surely we are not too late!' Watson worked away for half an hour, trying artificial respiration, injecting ether and every device that science could suggest, until at last he saw a flutter of life, a quiver of the eyelids and a dimming of a mirror, which showed the slow return to life.

Another time, Watson observed that Mr Blessington,[39] (or Sutton, the informer of the Worthingdon bank gang), of Brook Street, the resident patient with a weak heart of Dr Percy Trevelyan, had been dead three hours, 'judging by the rigidity of the muscles'.

Watson made an observation upon the dead man, Charles McCarthy, at Boscombe Pool, Ross ('a little reed-girt sheet of water some fifty yards across'). For having read the surgeon's report which stated that the posterior third of the left parietal bone and the left half of the occipital bone had been shattered by a heavy blow from a blunt weapon, he thought it worth while telling Holmes that the blow must have been struck from behind. Later on, when Watson met McCarthy's killer, Mr Turner (with ashen-white face and lips and corners of the nostrils tinged with blue), he knew that he was in the grip of some deadly and chronic disease, disclosed by Mr Turner as diabetes.

Mr Melas, a Greek interpreter, was abducted from his rooms in Pall Mall and taken to a large dark house 'standing back from the road in its own grounds' called The Myrtles, at Beckenham. Holmes' suspicions grew as he considered that the matter was taking a most serious turn. No answer came to knocker or bell; Holmes entered through the window. In an upstairs room full of poisonous fumes from a brazier, they discovered Melas, 'blue-lipped and insensible', with swollen, congested face and protruding eyes, his hand and feet securely strapped together. He was only just alive, but in less than an hour, with the aid of ammonia and brandy, Watson saw him open his eyes, and knew that he had managed to recall him to life.

Holmes and Watson, with Hall Pycroft, went to Birmingham (shortly after Watson's marriage,) to interview Arthur Harry Pinner in the temporary offices of the Franco–Midland Hardware Company, Limited, in Corporation Street. Here the managing director gave the three of them the slip by locking himself in an inner room, where he tried to hang himself with his own braces from a hook behind the door. Together they took Pinner down,

---

[39]The name Blessingtons mentioned in ACD, *The Tragedy of the Korosko*.

just in time to save him from the death he desired, for his clay-coloured face and purple lips showed how near he had been to death's door. Watson recorded:

> 'What do you think of him Watson?' asked Holmes.
>
> I stooped over him and examined him. His pulse was feeble and intermittent, but his breathing grew longer and there was a little shivering of the eyelids, which showed a thin white slit of ball beneath.
>
> 'It has been touch and go with him,' said I, 'but he'll live now. Just open that window, and hand me the water carafe.' I undid his collar, poured the cold water over his face, and raised and sank his arms until he drew a long natural breath. 'It's only a question of time now,' said I. [Watson used an alias here, Mr Price, a clerk; he never resorted to a disguise.]

In the spring of 1897 Watson was with Holmes in Cornwall and there met the revenge murderer of Mortimer Tregennis, Dr Leon Sterndale, lion hunter and explorer. He showed Watson, a paper packet whereon was written, *Radix pedis diaboli*, with a red poison label below, and asked him if he had ever heard of this reddish-brown, snuff-like powder. 'Devil's-foot rot! No, I have never heard of it.' Which was not surprising and no disparagement to Watson's medical knowledge, since the poison originated from the Ubangi country in West Africa, and was used as an ordeal poison by the medicine men; the only other specimen was at Buda.

Holmes asked Watson to visit Baron Adelbert Gruner at Kingston, in Surrey, with the alias of Dr Hill Barton of 369 Half Moon Street, London. He carried with him a priceless Ming, eggshell, deep-blue pottery saucer. With it, and his recently acquired knowledge of Chinese pottery, he hoped to beard the Austrian murderer in his den, at half past eight, which he was able to do. This was a ruse, which enabled wounded Holmes to gain undetected entry and steal the baron's brown-coloured love diary. Kitty Winter, a rejected former mistress of the baron, had her own plans for retribution. Hiding herself in the shrubbery, and as Holmes was chased by the baron, she threw vitriol in his face, and saw him roll and writhe in agony upon the carpet. In seconds, the vitriol had eaten into the face of the aristocrat of crime, leaving just a blurred, discoloured, inhuman mass of flesh. (Holmes later called it 'the wages of sin'.) Watson seized a carafe of water and rushed to his aid. He then bathed his face in oil, put cotton wadding on the raw surfaces and injected morphia, as the dead-fish eyes gazed up at him. A family surgeon later relieved Watson of his charge.

There were, no doubt, many more instances of Watson's medical help to Holmes, but, modest man that he was, he deigned not to recount them. He rather thought at first that Holmes regarded him only as a GP with mediocre qualifications and of limited experience, but when he heard Holmes refer to his astute medical talents and judgment, the inner man was pacified.

Watson tried to see Holmes as often as his medical practice permitted and would move heaven and earth to help, provided his patients did not suffer. Holmes rather expected Watson to down tools at the snap of his finger and obey his every whim, for he didn't like playing second fiddle to anyone and could be rather touchy. Once Holmes had said that there was important work for them to do. 'My practice—' began Watson. Said Holmes with some asperity, 'Oh, if you find your own cases more interesting than mine—' 'I was only going to say that my practice could get along very well for a day or two, since it is the slackest time in the year.' Holmes, somewhat mollified, having finally his own way, found his humour restored.

When pressure of work permitted, Watson would devote some time in looking over his notes of Holmes' cases and classifying the results. Two of these cases actually arose out of visitations of his clients to his surgery. One related to Colonel Warburton's madness (which Watson never published), and the other to Mr Hatherley's thumb, which was 'so strange in its inception and so dramatic in its details that it may be the more worthy of being placed upon record, even if it gave my friend fewer openings for those deductive methods of reasoning by which he achieved such remarkable results'. The latter case happened in the summer of 1889, not long after Watson's marriage, when he lived not far from Paddington Station; it was the station guard who brought in this new patient, and left before Watson could thank him. Round one of Mr Hatherley's hands was wrapped a bloodstained handkerchief, and when Watson saw what it had covered, even he shuddered. There were four protruding fingers and a horrid red spongy surface where the thumb should have been, hacked away by a cleaver. Watson 'sponged the wound, cleaned it, dressed it, and finally covered it over with cotton wadding and carbonised bandages'. Holmes took up the case, but even his ingenuity failed to capture the culprits, or discover the final whereabouts of the beautiful woman, the sinister German or the morose Englishman, Dr Becher, after their house was burnt down at Eyford, seven miles from Reading in Berkshire, and they were never seen again.

Dr Watson was a reader of non-medical publications, when time permitted. He liked to read a novel with his last pipe before going to bed, but he records little of the literature that he read; although he did mention skipping over the pages of Henri Murger's *Scenes de la Viè de Bohème* between nine o'clock and midnight, stolidly puffing at his pipe, while he awaited the homecoming of Holmes. I wonder if Watson ever found time to read the five books that the disguised Holmes brought him in 1894, among them writings by ancient Rome's poet, Gaius Valerius Catullus, John Bunyan's *Holy War*, *British Birds* and perhaps *The Origin of Tree Worship*, which Watson happened to knock out of Holmes' hands on his way home. This was the time when Watson fainted for the first and last time in his life. What happened to the little bookshop that Holmes had at the corner of Church Street, near Watson's house? Upon a winter's night Watson might have been discovered reading one of Clark Russell's fine sea stories, with the outside gale lending atmosphere. Holmes lent Watson his copy of Winwood Reade's, *Martyrdom of Man*, so that when Holmes mentioned, 'A strange enigma is man!' Watson was able to cap it with, 'someone calls him a soul concealed in an animal' – but Holmes needs must have the final say with a longer and final quotation.

'Are you well up in your Jean Paul?' 'Fairly so. I worked back to him through Carlyle.' 'That was like following the brook to the parent lake. He makes one curious but profound remark. It is that the chief proof of man's real greatness lies in his perception of his own smallness. It argues, you see, a power of comparison and of appreciation which is in itself a proof of nobility. There is much food for thought in Richter.'[40] (And yet strangely enough in the early days of their acquaintance, Watson had quoted Thomas Carlyle and Holmes had inquired in the naivest way who he might be and what he had done.)[41]

When Watson was staying at the Hereford Arms, in Ross, and awaiting the return of Holmes, in order to while away the time, he looked at a yellow-backed novel, but found the puny story of the plot so thin when compared with reality that he flung the book across the room, and concentrated instead upon the day's events. (How could a lover of books do such a thing?)

When it was required of him to do so, Watson could cast all matters aside and settle down to read and absorb sufficient knowledge of a particular subject, as was the case when Holmes asked him to study the intricate history of Chinese pottery so that he could appear sufficiently learned to be able to converse intelligibly upon the subject. Watson called upon his friend Lomax, the sub-librarian of the London Library in St James' Square, who gave Watson 'a goodly volume' upon the subject. He then proceeded to solidly read, for one evening, all through the night and the next morning, a glowing instance of Watson's powers of concentration which were not seemingly fully appreciated by Holmes.

Watson gradually came to live with, if not to wholly overcome, the two Afghanistan war wounds he sustained in the shoulder and leg, at the disastrous Battle of Maiwand in 1879–80, where his commander, General Burrows, was totally defeated. His general health as well had been undermined, so that it was not until he had left his London hotel (where his existence must have been somewhat frugal, on an army pension,), and went to live in the Baker Street flat that his health improved under the care of Mrs Hudson. His somewhat sedentary life forbade undue exercise, but time and his own determination improved his walking ability, although the shoulder never fully recovered. Was Watson mollified by Holmes' remark that 'weakness in one limb is often compensated for by exceptional strength in the others'?

---

[40]Johann Paul Friedrich Richter, 1763–1825.
[41]Thomas Carlyle, 1795–1881, historian and essayist.

The two of them often took a stroll along the London streets, Watson quite content to be walking with his friend wherever Holmes chose to go, knowing his knowledge of the metropolis to be infinite. One October evening, after the boisterous keen wind had died down and the stars were shining, Watson, muffled nose-high in his coat, accompanied Holmes for some three hours, from Baker Street, down the Strand, Fleet Street and so back home. Yes, his walking gradually improved from the limping of early days.

Watson walked to Camberwell to visit Mary Morstan; to Charlington Heath, from Farnham, by himself and with Holmes, where he even 'ran across the heath and peered through the trees'. He walked with Holmes and the dog, Toby, six miles from Pondicherry Lodge in Upper Norwood, to the Thames at the end of Broad Street; he walked with Holmes and Inspector Baynes to Wisteria Lodge, two cold and melancholy miles from Esher on a dark March evening, with a sharp wind blowing with a fine rain on their faces; with Sir Henry Baskerville on the track of the convict upon the Devon moor, who, being fleet of foot outdistanced his pursuers, although Watson described Sir Henry and himself as 'swift runners'. At Milverton's house, Appledore Towers, Hampstead, Watson and Holmes had to make a very quick exit, which entailed surmounting a six-foot wall, and then a run of two miles across the huge expanse of Hampstead Heath, where they stopped to listen for the sound of pursuit. Absolute silence. So they continued their leisurely way home. These few instances certainly show how well Watson managed with his bad leg, and tend to qualify Holmes' remark that Watson was born to be a man of action, his instinct always to do something energetic.

By the time of their trip to the Boscombe Valley, and the mystery surrounding the disappearance of Godfrey Staunton, the rugby player, both Watson and Holmes had become a couple of 'middle-aged London gentlemen', who found that the none too fast draghound Pompey was inclined to be too fast for them, so that he was put upon a leash in order to slow him down to their own speed.

Generally speaking, Watson was not credited by Holmes with very good powers of observation. But of course, Holmes was inclined to judge others by his very exceptional standards. His was a super intelligence, a super power of observation, a super power of deduction. His eyes looked, they saw and the image was stored in his photographic memory as if it were a card-index system, waiting to be tapped at the appropriate time. How could Watson, or anyone else for that matter, hope to compete with such a unique brain! Holmes instinctively knew at Bart's Hospital that Watson would make his ideal companion, but for all that, he withheld from Watson, initially, particular delicate matters, until he was more fully acquainted with his friend. The fact that Holmes permitted Moriarty (the mathematician, whom none could comprehend) to be considered as his intellectual equal showed Watson the gap that lay not only between the two of them, but all other mortals.

Watson certainly realised Holmes' intelligence, for as he said, 'I trust that I am not more dense than my neighbours, but I was always oppressed with a sense of my own stupidity in my dealings with Sherlock Holmes. Here I had heard what he had heard, I had seen what he had seen, and yet from his words it was evident that he saw clearly not only what had happened, but what was about to happen, while to me the whole business was still confused and grotesque.'

Nevertheless, Watson had his own attributes. He had, when necessary, the gift above all gifts: the grand gift of silence, when the situation warranted it. As a most sympathetic listener, he allowed Holmes to speak his thoughts aloud and so enable him to clear his brain and put his thoughts together in orderly fashion. Holmes knew that he could discuss all and sundry with Watson, and explain his observations, which, natural to him, were exceptional to others as well as Watson. Watson's mystification at the deductions might call forth a 'Pshaw, my dear boy', or 'it was simplicity itself' or 'I don't wish to be theatrical', which of course he actually did wish, as he was not able to 'tread the boards'. Holmes secretly revelled in revealing his powers to Watson. Watson averred that Holmes was not a difficult man to live with, which rather sums up the wonderful character of Watson.

Although not luminous, Watson was considered by his friend as a conductor of light. Some people, said Holmes, without genius, had a remarkable power of stimulating it, which placed Holmes very much in Watson's debt, for in noting Watson's fallacies, he was sometimes guided towards the truth. Not all Holmes' remarks were derogatory, or seemingly so, for he said Watson's appearance inspired confidence; did not Holmes say that if they both intended to barge in and interview without an appointment, then he thought that Watson had the necessary effrontery to put it through? He added that his intellect was Machiavellian and he was scintillating.[42] 'You will realise that among your many talents dissimulation finds no place…' He was Holmes' astute friend.

Watson often made a suggestion or a reflection which might have helped towards a solution, only to be rebuffed by Holmes' remark that it had already crossed his mind. Chatting upon the Blessington case, as they walked down Harley Street, Watson said, 'Is there not one alternative… grotesquely improbable, no doubt, but still just conceivable? Might the whole story of the cataleptic Russian and his son be a concoction of Dr Trevelyan's, who has, for his own purposes, been in Blessington's room?' This brought an amused smile to Holmes' face it being one of the first solutions which had occurred to him. Or Holmes might look at him thoughtfully and shake his head. 'I never get your limits, Watson. There are unexplained possibilities about you.' Watson had said of himself. 'If I have one quality upon earth it is common sense.' 'I suppose Watson, we must look upon you as a man of letters.' He even likened him to Scott Eccles, who gabbled his information. 'Come, come, sir… You are like my friend, Dr Watson, who has a bad habit of telling his stories wrong end foremost.' Could he not have given Watson just a little credit sometimes?

There were times when Holmes sent Watson upon a journey, ostensibly to observe for him. If, when Watson recounted his mission, he took the liberty of waxing lyrical, Holmes was not really amused; he could be lyrical upon nature, but frowned upon his biographer doing likewise. Watson was reporting upon the house of Josiah Amberley, The Haven at Lewisham:

'I think it would interest you, Holmes. It is like some penurious

---

[42] Niccolò Machiavelli of Florence, 1469–1527.

patrician who has sunk into the company of his inferiors. You know that particular quarter, the monotonous brick streets, the weary suburban highways. Right in the middle of them, a little island of ancient culture and comfort, lies this old home, surrounded by a high sun-baked wall mottled with lichens and topped with moss, the sort of wall—' 'Cut out the poetry, Watson,' said Holmes severely. 'I note that it was a high brick wall.'

Holmes had sent Watson on alone so that he could observe the place independently, disguised as a lounger, heavily moustached, and then he pulled good Watson to pieces, because he had not observed the wrinkled left and smooth right shoes of Josiah Amberley or his artificial limb. Surprisingly, Watson did not suggest to Holmes that next time he scouted by himself. But nevertheless, Watson in this instance had the last word and final laugh at Holmes expense; for he observed that the theatre ticket for Mr Amberley, to the Haymarket Theatre, which Amberley showed him as never having been used – his wife having a headache – bore the same number as he had used at school, thirty-one, and in B row. 'Excellent, Watson! His seat, then, was either thirty or thirty-two… That is most satisfactory.'

At Holmes' request, Watson travelled with Sir Henry Baskerville and Dr Mortimer down to Devon (so that Holmes could be there also, secretly and unobserved). While there, Perkins, from Baskerville Hall, drove Watson out to Coombe Tracey to interview Mrs Laura Lyons; strange that gentlemanly Watson opened the interview without even introducing himself. In the Neolithic hut (Holmes' temporary residence), Watson recounted the conversation that he had had; so interested was the detective that Watson 'had to repeat some of it twice before he was satisfied'. 'This is most important… It fills up a gap which I had been unable to bridge in this most complex affair.' Although Watson had been rather raw over Holmes' deception, the unusual praise which he received soon drove the anger from his mind.

Holmes, engaged upon the case of the missing Lady Frances Carfax, was desirous of knowing why she paid her last cheque for fifty pounds to her maid, Marie Devine. 'I have no doubt, however, that your researches will soon clear the matter up.' 'My researches!' said a mystified Watson. Hence Watson's health-giving expedition to Lausanne (where Lady Carfax was staying at the Hôtel National) at Holmes' behest. He travelled light, only a valise as his 'wants were few and simple'.[43] Holmes excused himself as he was as he said busy with the Abrahams case. Watson reported upon the lady's movements and sent back his report. Holmes replied by a 'telegram of half-humorous commendation'. Holmes next telegram asked for a description of Dr Shlessinger's left ear. Was this an ill-timed jest, another of Holmes' strange and sometimes offensive ideas of humour? Watson should have known that Holmes never dallied! Having left Baden, Watson was unable to help. It was a serious question, however, and answered by the manager of the Englischer Hof; the answer 'Jagged or torn', told Holmes that they were dealing with the Australian rascal, Holy Peters, bitten in the ear in a saloon fight in Adelaide in 1889.

Another journey Watson undertook for Holmes was to see Culverton Smith (the murderer of Victor Savage), and using all his powers of persuasion to convince him that Holmes was at death's door, and only he could save him. So well did Watson carry out Holmes' wishes that he was able to entice Smith to Baker Street. 'Admirable, Watson! Admirable! You are the best of messengers.' Watson certainly was invaluable as a companion.

It was some time in September 1887 that John Openshaw called and related the strange facts concerning some little dried orange pips which members of his family had received through the post and proved to be harbingers of death. 'Did you remark the postmarks of the letters?' asked Holmes. Watson recalled that 'The first was from Pondicherry, the second from Dundee and the third from London.' 'From East London,' corrected Holmes. 'What do you deduce from that?' 'They are all seaports. That the writer was on board of a ship.' 'Excellent' said Holmes.

As Watson once observed Holmes' particularly bright and joyous mood, with that somewhat sinister cheerfulness which was characteristic of his lighter moments, he probed Holmes' secret that he had a case. 'The faculty of deduction is certainly conta-

---

[43]Watson travelling alone, used only a travelling bag; together, when they intended to stay, they took suitcases.

gious, Watson,' Holmes replied. 'It has enabled you to probe my secret. Yes, I have a case.'

Holmes so often astonished Watson that it was a change for the boot to be upon the other foot. Holmes thought that Eduardo Lucas of Godolphin Street might well be one of three men capable of stealing a letter from a foreign potentate which had disappeared, from the locked despatch box of the Secretary for Foreign Affairs. Watson astonished Holmes as he looked up from reading the newspaper and said, 'You will not see him… He was murdered in his home last night.' This gave Watson a sense of exultation as he sensed Holmes' disbelief.

Concerning Mrs Douglas and Mr Barker at Birlstone Manor House, Watson observed, 'I am convinced myself that there is an understanding between those two people. She must be a heartless creature to sit laughing at some jest within a few hours of her husband's murder.' Holmes actually agreed!

When John Garrideb, an American gangster, placed a bogus advertisement in a Birmingham paper – 'Howard Garrideb. Constructor of Agricultural Machinery. Binders, reapers, steam and hand plows, drills, harrows, farmers' carts, buck-boards, and all other appliances. Estimates for Artesian Wells. Apply Grosvenor Buildings, Aston.' Holmes asked Watson if he saw anything curious about the advertisement. 'I saw that the word 'plough was misspelt.' 'Oh, you did notice that, did you? Come, Watson, you improve all the time. Yes, it was bad English but good American.' Holmes had to add, of course, that 'buckboards' and 'artesian wells' showed a typical American advertisement. Watson guessed that the American 'lawyer' put it in himself.

Perhaps Holmes did not appreciate Watson's exceptionally good eyesight. Evidence of this was certainly shown upon the Devon moor when he encountered the grey-whiskered, red-faced Mr Frankland (who was involved in legal actions in the Court of Queen's Bench, upon the behalf of the public) outside the gate of his garden; he was invited in to partake of a glass of wine. Frankland had seen a boy in the distance, every day, through his telescope upon the roof; he assumed that he was taking food to the convict, when actually it was to the unknown presence of Holmes. Watson suggested that the boy was likely taking food to his father, a moorland shepherd, which Frankland thought an absurd idea. 'You may be sure, sir, that I have very good grounds before I came to an opinion. I have seen the boy again and again with his bundle. Every day, and sometimes twice a day, I have been able – but wait a moment, Dr Watson. Do my eyes deceive me, or is there at the present moment something moving upon that hillside?' It was several miles off, but Watson distinctly saw a small dark dot against the dull green and grey. He was then able to verify this dot as a small urchin carrying a bundle with the aid of Frankland's formidable telescope.

Watson was particularly observant when he was with Holmes upon the track of the stolen racehorse, Silver Blaze, the five-year-old from the Isonomy stock, favourite for the Wessex Cup. They followed the tracks close to Mapleton; a man's track was visible beside the horse's, although alone before. The double track turned sharp off and took the direction of King's Pyland, which Holmes' eyes followed; Watson looked to the side of the tracks and noticed with surprise the same tracks coming back in the opposite direction. 'One for you, Watson… You have saved us a long walk, which would have brought us back on our own traces. Let us follow the return track.' This brought them to the Mapleton stables, and Silas Brown.

Watson showed great astuteness when he evaded Dr Mortimer's question as to why he was interested in Mrs Laura Lyons of Coombe Tracey, Devon (who had written a note to Sir Charles Baskerville), by asking him a question on craniology. As Watson related: 'I am certainly developing the wisdom of the serpent, for when Mortimer pressed his questions to an inconvenient extent I asked him casually to what type Frankland's skull belonged (he being Laura's father)… and so heard nothing but craniology for the rest of our drive. I have not lived for years with Sherlock Holmes for nothing.'

At times Watson could surprise Holmes with his non-medical knowledge. While in the chamber of the dead man, Bartholomew Sholto (who had been killed by a poisonous dart into the scalp at a point exposed to a hole in the ceiling), Holmes asked Watson to examine the long, sharp, black dart with some dried gummy substance near the point; he held it gingerly. 'Is that an English thorn?' asked Holmes. 'No, it certainly is not.'

Only occasionally, Watson managed to get a sly dig at his mentor. Mycroft sent a telegram to his brother concerning Cadogan West, which Watson read. 'Cadogan West? I have heard the name.' 'It recalls nothing to my mind,' said a peeved Holmes.

Did Watson not guess in Mrs Maberley's house that the recent urgent demands could only mean 'that the object, whatever it may be has only just come into the house'. 'Settled once again,' agreed Holmes.

Watson certainly scored a bullseye over Holmes when he was talking of Moriarty, to which Watson responded: 'The famous scientific criminal, as famous among crooks as—' Holmes thought, (somewhat pompously) that he was going to refer to himself and actually blushed! (Was this the only time?) 'I was about to say, as he is unknown to the public.' 'You are developing a certain unexpected vein of pawky humour,' said Holmes, not amused.

Watson showed his great tolerance when he said one day, 'I am inclined to think—' 'I should do so,' said Holmes, impatiently. Watson was annoyed at the sardonic interruption. 'Really, Holmes, you are a little trying at times.' He was more than trying, the time he chided Watson with 'Not one of your cases, Watson – mental, not physical. All right, come if you want to.' For Watson, in Holmes' estimation, was not quite upon the bottom rung of understanding. 'Watson, I have always done you an injustice. There are others.' He was referring to Mr Hilton Soames, tutor and lecturer at the College of St Luke's, who was unable to follow Holmes' line of reasoning.

But for all Watson's shortcomings in the eyes of Holmes, he did now and again receive praise. He was asked about Sir Robert Norberton, Holmes not knowing this man. He was told that he had been a Grand National jockey, with stables at Shoscombe Old Place, a boxer, athlete, turf plunger,[44] lover of fair ladies and a member of Queer Street,[45] a breeder of the most exclusive breed of spaniel and lived with his widowed sister, Lady Beatrice Falder. 'Capital, Watson! A thumb-nail sketch. I seem to know the man.'

---

[44]Reckless gambler.
[45]Queer Street, the feigned abode of persons in debt.

Again Watson was applauded in Camden House for spotting 'with unerring accuracy', the police in the street doorway, and he summed up the situation regarding Mr Melas the Greek interpreter and the attempt, by foul means, to secure Sophy Kratides' fortune. 'Excellent, Watson!' Holmes exclaimed. 'I really fancy that you are not far from the truth.'

Watson was certainly 'an ideal helpmate' for Holmes, being the very soul of discretion, and a person upon whom Holmes could thoroughly rely; he was called the 'stormy petrel of crime'. When the game was afoot, Holmes' habit was to say nothing and Watson's habit was to ask no questions. If Holmes' manner was cold, Watson read the sign and never argued; if ruffled and upset by Holmes' demeanour, he would not let it last too long, for there were numerous times when Holmes appeared to 'use' his friend and not trust him, and then understandably Watson would be bitter and his voice trembled as he spoke; but Holmes did at least explain his reasons and kindly Watson would be mollified. Watson once opened the door to Stanley Hopkins, late at night, when Holmes could just as easily have gone himself, but no, he had to command Watson: 'Run down, my dear fellow, and open the door, for all virtuous folk have been long in bed.' (I expect Watson would just as soon have kept his comfortable easy chair by the fire.)

Watson recorded that he co-operated with Holmes for seventeen years, and during that time he always had great faith in Holmes' judgments; he never expected Holmes to fail. If Holmes appeared to be behaving rather queerly to others he would say, 'I have usually found that there was method in his madness'; he would never stay ruffled for long; he would always respond to a Holmes' cry for help; he would become a humble 'ladder', as he did when Holmes wished to peep into the lighted window of the Fighting Cock Inn, near Mackleton, and the only way for Holmes to succeed was by putting his feet upon Watson's shoulders as he bent his back and supported himself against the wall. He kept copious notes of his own, was permitted at times to check some point of accuracy with Lestrade's notebook, had access to the yearbooks – for 1894 alone, there were three massive manuscript volumes – and documents in the dispatch cases, so that altogether there was a wealth of material to hand. Holmes' hard dry statements, caused by his mind being like a racing engine tearing itself apart because it was not connected up with the work for which it was built, often needed a little editing to soften them into the terms of real life, which Holmes only fully appreciated when he found that he had to write his own account, when the 'matter must be presented in such a way as may interest the reader'. So although Holmes admitted the necessity of Watson's embellishments, he was not above reminding Watson of his displeasure in the way they were written. In his introduction to *The Adventure of the Blanched Soldier* Holmes wrote:

> I have often had occasion to point out to him how superficial are his own accounts and to accuse him of pandering to popular taste instead of confining himself rigidly to facts and figures… If I burden myself with a companion in my various little inquiries it is not done out of sentiment or caprice, but it is that Watson has some remarkable characteristics of his own to which in his modesty he had given small attention amid his exaggerated estimates of my own performances. [Not quite sincere, Mr Holmes!] A confederate who foresees your conclusions and course of action is always dangerous, but one to whom each development comes as a perpetual surprise, and to whom the future is always a closed book, is indeed an ideal helpmate.

Holmes admitted that Watson had some power of selecting his stories which atoned for much which he deplored in his narratives. 'Your fatal habit of looking at everything from the point of view of a story instead of as a scientific exercise has ruined what might have been an instructive and even classical series of demonstrations. You slur over work of the utmost finesse and delicacy, in order to dwell upon sensational details which may excite, but cannot possible instruct, the reader.'

For Holmes preferred to give preference for publication to those cases which derived their interest from the ingenuity and dramatic quality of the solution, and Watson always tried to defer to his wishes, even when not fully understanding them, for he had the deepest respect for Holmes' extraordinary qualities. By long experience, Watson learned the wisdom of experience, asking for no explanation when none was forthcoming.

As Holmes' 'Boswell', Watson found it increasingly difficult to decide which to publish and which not to publish. He tried to choose the cases which illustrated the remarkable mental qualities of Holmes with the minimum of sensationalism, while still offering a fair field for his talents. He found it difficult to entirely separate the sensational from the criminal; he weighed up the pros and cons of a case and then chose those with the ingenuity and dramatic quality – for he called Holmes the dramatist in real life – of the solution, and wrote out his stories upon foolscap paper.

The choice of a memoir for Watson to publish with Holmes' permission was distinguished by the discretion and high sense of professional honour which Holmes maintained; writers of agonised letters, who wished that the family honour or the reputation of a famous ancestor be not disclosed, could rest assured that there would be no breach of confidence; he knew that he could rely upon Watson – did he not call him 'the very soul of discretion'? Most of the cases gave Holmes the opportunity of showing those curious gifts of instinct and observation that he had, but the most terrible human tragedies were often involved in those cases which brought him the fewest personal opportunities.

Watson rarely gave vent to his inner feelings, but sometimes he needed an outlet. Holmes had been displeased with Watson's sensational treatment of his cases, telling him that he had degraded what should have been a course of lectures, into a series of tales. 'You have erred, perhaps... in attempting to put colour and life into each of your statements, instead of confining yourself to the task of placing upon record that severe reasoning from cause to effect which is really the only notable feature about the thing.'

'It seems to me that I have done you full justice in the matter,' Watson remarked with some coldness, for he was repelled by the egotism which he had more than once observed to be a strong factor in Holmes' singular character.

'No, it is not selfishness or conceit... If I claim full justice for my art, it is because it is an impersonal thing – a thing beyond myself. Crime is common. Logic is rare. Therefore it is upon the logic rather than upon the crime that you should dwell.'

Watson thought that perhaps Holmes might be able to write the stories better himself. 'I will, my dear Watson, I will. At present I am, as you know, fairly busy, but I propose to devote my declining years to the composition of a textbook, which shall focus the whole art of deduction into one volume.' (I wonder if this book was ever written and, if so, have Scotland Yard the precious manuscript?) And yet, when Holmes had to be his own chronicler, after his retirement in July 1907, he missed his 'Boswell', for did he not say: 'Ah! had he but been with me, how much he might have made of so wonderful a happening...' (Holmes referred to his story of the Lion's Mane.) 'By cunning questions and ejaculations of wonder he could elevate my simple art, which is but systematised common sense, into a prodigy.'

Holmes oft-times used a most crushing remark to deflate the good Watson who was trying to be helpful. At King's Pyland, Dartmoor, Watson asked a very important question: 'Did the stable boy, when he ran out with the dog, leave the door unlocked behind him?' 'Excellent, Watson, excellent! …The importance of the point struck me so forcibly that I sent a special wire to Dartmoor yesterday to clear the matter up.' (Why did Holmes purposely keep Watson in the dark?) And the day that Watson, trying to help, misconstrued the meaning of the inscription upon Dr Mortimer's stick – 'To James Mortimer, MRCS from his friends of the CCH, 1884.' This the doctor construed as follows: 'I think… that Dr Mortimer is a successful, elderly medical man, well-esteemed, since those who know him give him this mark of their appreciation… I think also that the probability is in favour of his being a country practitioner who does a great deal of his visiting on foot… Because this stick, though originally a very handsome one, has been so knocked about that I can hardly imagine a town practitioner carrying it. The thick iron ferrule is worn down, so it is evident that he has done a great amount of walking with it.' Holmes voiced, 'Excellent!' and 'Perfectly sound.' 'And then again,' continued Watson, 'there is the "friends of the CCH". I should guess that to be the Something Hunt, the local hunt to whose members he has possibly given some surgical assistance, and which has made him a small presentation in return.' Holmes remarked that he was very much in Watson's debt. These words gave Watson keen pleasure, thinking that he had mastered Holmes observation and deduction. But he was soon to be deflated. 'I am afraid, my dear Watson, that most of your conclusions were erroneous. When I said that you stimulated me I meant, to be frank, that in noting your fallacies, I was occasionally guided towards the truth. Not that you are entirely wrong in this instance.' Holmes then suggested a more likely meaning for the initials – 'Charing Cross Hospital' – and surmised that Dr Mortimer was presented with the stick upon his leaving the hospital, intending to set up his own country practice.

Watson, no doubt, would have liked to voice an opinion more often but when he was sardonically interrupted time after time, he was inclined to forgo further comment, which of course he found most trying, and disapproved of the way Holmes looked into his eyes with a peculiar mischievous gaze. Holmes often chafed Watson, almost to the point of rudeness, or would say, 'My dear Watson, try a little analysis yourself.' With a touch of impatience: 'You know my methods. Apply them and it will be constructive to compare results.'

Certainly Watson did try to employ the methods. As he observed after Holmes had summed up Mr McFarlane: 'Familiar as I was with my friend's methods, it was not difficult for me to follow his deductions, and to observe the untidiness of attire, the sheaf of legal papers, the watch-charm, and the breathing which had prompted them.'

After the 'death' of Holmes in 1891, Watson continued to be interested in crime, following his very close intimacy with Holmes' methods. He never failed to read with care the various problems which came before the public, and he tried to employ Holmes' methods in their solution, though with indifferent success, for he was without the help of the master to guide him.

He became deeply interested in the wilful murder of the Honourable Ronald Adair, the second son of the Earl of Maynooth, living at 427 Park Lane. He tried to find that line of least resistance which Holmes had declared to be the starting point of every investigation, without success. His observations upon the house – low wall and railing, easy access to garden, the particular window concerned being entirely inaccessible – all puzzled Watson. But he was not allowed to publish the full story until 1904, when Holmes gave his formal permission. For so long as Holmes was in professional practice, the records of his successes were of some practical value to him, but not after he had left London, and Watson was then forbidden to publish without his sanction. But Holmes at times relented and gave his permission provided that the accounts were carefully guarded, so that these reports often went dateless for private and secret reasons.

Watson was not allowed to divulge the story of the second stain until after Holmes' retirement, when he consented to 'a carefully guarded account of the incident'; it was not until the year 1910 that permission was received by telegram to publish the case of the devil's foot:

WHY NOT TELL THEM OF THE CORNISH HORROR – STRANGEST CASE I HAVE HANDLED.

And it was not until as late as 1912 (presumably before Holmes became a government secret agent), that permission was given to Watson to publish the case which surrounded Baron Gruner and Violet de Merville, saying, 'It can't hurt now.'

It seemed only natural that Watson should highlight the successes rather than the failures in what Holmes chose to call his 'little fairy tales', for where Holmes failed, no one appeared to succeed. Watson noted just six cases where Holmes had gone wrong, which, considering that by the year 1891 Holmes had been concerned in over one thousand cases, was a very low percentage indeed. Some of these cases, Watson had found tragic, some comic, a large number merely strange, but none commonplace; for he knew that his friend worked rather for the love of his art than for wealth (although this was not totally ignored) and refused to associate himself with any investigation which did not tend towards the unusual and even fantastic.

Watson, like Holmes, was a smoker; a most important factor if they were going to live and work in harmony together; this was an early question put by Holmes at Bart's Hospital: 'You don't mind the smell of strong tobacco I hope?' 'I always smoke "ship's" myself,' answered Watson. 'That's good enough,' replied Holmes. For Holmes surely needed an understanding, kindred spirit to tolerate his strong shag tobacco. Once installed in the Baker Street flat, Watson found it more convenient to purchase his Bradley cigarettes and Arcadia pipe mixture at Bradley's of Oxford Street. He never mentioned that he purchased cigars there, so perhaps Holmes supplied both their wants: perhaps the army pension would not run to this expense. Certainly Watson supplied the wax vestas, for he was ever ready to supply a light whenever asked. Somewhat strange, was it not, that Holmes should once refer to Watson's smoking as indulging in filthy habits! 'What with your eternal tobacco, Watson, and your irregularity at meals, I expect that you will get notice to quit, and that I shall share your downfall...' Holmes even offered to share his tobacco with Watson, while at their small cottage in 1897, near Poldhu Bay, at the further extremity of the Cornish peninsula. After experimenting with a devil's poison, which nearly killed them both, Holmes sent Dr Sterndale a free man back to Africa. He observed to Watson, 'Some fumes which are not poisonous would be a welcome change', as he lit his pipe and handed his friend his tobacco pouch.

Watson still retained his old, short heavy army service revolver, an Eley's No. 2, which contained six cartridges. Watson carried his revolver upon many an expedition, in his hip pocket. It was used most effectively, in a peaceful way, by Holmes, in his experiment at Thor Bridge, Thor Place, Hampshire, to prove that Miss Dunbar, the family governess, had not committed murder, but that Maria Pinto, the Brazilian wife of Neil Gibson – a former American senator and the greatest gold-mining magnate in the world, hence his name of the Gold King – had shot herself. By a cunning device of sending her revolver over the bridge into the water, she made it appear that someone had shot her, and she hoped suspicion would fall upon the young Miss Dunbar.

Once, Watson forsook his Eley, and borrowed Holmes' spare revolver, when they both went to the house of Nathan Garrideb, in Little Ryder Street off the Edgware Road. Watson never copied Holmes in his indoor revolver practice – he felt strongly that neither the atmosphere nor the appearance of their room was improved by it. When Watson offered his services to the War Office in 1914, I wonder which type of army revolver he was given?

Watson was a billiards player; he played at his club with a man named Thurston. Holmes always knew when he had been there because of the chalk between his left finger and thumb, put there to steady the cue. Thurston had tried to get Watson to invest his money in some South African property, but sensible Watson declined.

Watson bought his footwear at Latimer's in Oxford Street. He had his particular method of doing up his boots, and when they were fastened with an unusually elaborate bow, Holmes knew that he had been to the Turkish bath, (for that bow was the hallmark of the boy who worked there). Did not Holmes once say, that much could be learned from the study of bootlaces! As well as shoes and boots, he also bought his patent leather slippers and his rubber-soled tennis shoes from there. Were they ribbed like those of Dr Leon Sterndale, the African explorer? They came in very handy during their illegal entry into the Hampstead home of Mr Milverton. Said Holmes: 'Have you a pair of silent shoes?' 'I have rubber-soled tennis shoes.' 'Excellent!' replied Holmes.

Among Watson's personal and prized possessions was a pocket watch, an expensive fifty-guinea watch some half a century old. Watson does not say whether the watch was of silver or of gold.[46] It came into his possession, a little before, or in early, 1888. The watch had originally belonged to his father, for there upon the back, were engraved his initials, H W. Upon his father's death the watch had passed into the possession of the elder son, who being of untidy habits and careless, and although left reasonably well off, did not make the most of his life and died from excess alcoholic drinking, in poverty: he had pawned the watch four times.

Watson kept a number of walking sticks, one more heavy than the rest, which he usually carried upon dangerous missions. Perhaps the head was loaded with lead, like the one of James

---

[46]'Whose gold watch was it that had been so mishandled?' Christopher Morley, writing in his introduction to *The Penguin Complete Sherlock Holmes*, 1981, p.7.

Armitage, and Mr Latimer, who carried one to intimidate Mr Melas. Sometimes Watson carried a cane; he also owned an umbrella, perhaps with an ivory crook, favoured by the Victorians. This umbrella came in most useful to Holmes at Birlstone Manor House, when at night-time he was enabled by the use of the crook to fish out from the moat a bundle of American clothes (made by Neal, Outfitter of Vermissa, USA, and belonging to Ted Baldwin), and the missing dumb-bell.

Watson also owned a most excellent field glass; he was particularly asked by Holmes to bring it with him, when they both journeyed down to King's Pyland, Dartmoor, by the Paddington train.

Dr Watson a Woman's Man

Watson was regarded by Holmes as a woman's man, the fair sex his department, and he spoke of him as follows: 'With your natural advantages, Watson, every lady is your helper and accomplice. What about the girl at the post office, or the wife of the greengrocer? I can picture you whispering soft nothings with the young lady at the Blue Anchor, and receiving hard somethings in exchange.' Certainly, Watson was attracted to the opposite sex, beginning (as far as we know), with Miss Morstan, who became a most understanding wife, letting Watson scamper off at a moment's notice at the snap of a Holmes' finger.

Then there was Miss Turner, daughter of John Turner, the man who murdered Charles McCarthy in Boscombe Valley, in the West Country. Watson spoke of her as 'one of the most lovely young women that I have ever seen in my life. Her violet eyes shining, her lips parted, a pink flush upon her cheeks, all thought of her natural reserve lost in her overpowering excitement and concern.'

Lady Hilda Trelawney Hope 'turned' Watson's head. The Baker Street flat was honoured 'by the entrance of the most lovely woman in London. I had often heard of the beauty of the youngest daughter of the Duke of Belminster, but no description of it, and no contemplation of colourless photographs, had prepared me for the subtle, delicate charm and the beautiful colouring of that exquisite head. And yet as we saw it that autumn morning it was not its beauty which would be the first thing to impress the observer. The cheek was lovely but it was paled with emotion, the eyes were bright, but it was the brightness of fever, the sensitive mouth was tight and drawn in an effort after self-command. Terror – not beauty – was what sprang first to the eye as our fair visitor stood framed for an instant in the open door.'

Miss Dunbar, the young governess of Neil Gibson's children at Thor Place, had a lasting effect upon Watson, for he had not expected to see such beauty. 'It was no wonder that even the masterful millionaire had found in her something more powerful than himself – something which could control and guide him. One felt too, as one looked at that strong, clear-cut, and yet sensitive face, that even should she be capable of some impetuous deed, none the less there was an innate mobility of character which would make her influence always for the good. She was a brunette, tall, with a noble figure and commanding presence, but her dark eyes had in them the appealing, helpless expression of the hunted creature who feels the nets around it, but can see no way out from the toils. Now, as she realised the presence and the help of my famous friend, there came a touch of colour in her wan cheeks and a light of hope began to glimmer in the glance which she turned upon us.'

Lady Brackenstall, wife of Sir Eustace Brackenstall of Abbey Grange, Marsham, in Kent, was described by Watson as no ordinary person.

> Seldom have I seen so graceful a figure, so womanly a presence and so beautiful a face. She was a blonde, golden-haired, blue-eyed, and would no doubt, have had the perfect complexion which goes with such colouring, had not her recent experience left her drained and haggard. Her sufferings were physical as well as mental, for above one eye rose a hideous, plum-coloured swelling, which her maid, a tall, austere woman, was bathing assiduously with vinegar and water. The lady lay back exhausted upon a couch, but her quick observant gaze as we entered the room, and the alert expression of her beautiful features, showed that neither her wits nor her courage had been shaken by her terrible experience. She was enveloped in a loose dressing-gown of blue and silver, but a black sequin-covered dinner-dress was hung

upon the couch beside her.

Letters from Dr Watson to Sherlock Holmes

Watson does not appear to have sent any letters or telegrams to Holmes from his private address. But he took a lot of trouble to send off telegrams and lengthy letters from Baskerville Hall in Devon to Holmes at Baker Street, keeping him well informed of the passage of events. Holmes, unbeknown to Watson, was also in Devon, spying, but not being seen. All correspondence was forwarded from Baker Street to Devon, and owing to the very excellent Victorian postal service, they were only delayed one day. When this was revealed to Watson, he was somewhat bitter, as he thought Holmes was busy upon a case of blackmail. 'Then you use me, and yet do not trust me …I think that I have deserved better at your hands Holmes.' Holmes had only kept Watson in the dark so that he himself might not be discovered, and so be able to work unhindered. After Holmes had explained to Watson how invaluable his letters had been, and how well thumbed they were, Watson was gradually pacified.

Watson did write a letter to Baron Gruner, but at Holmes' dictation, saying that he would be calling and why. It was an admirable document, short, courteous, and stimulating to the curiosity of the connoisseur. For the baron's interest had to be aroused in 'a delicate, little saucer of the most beautiful deep-blue colour… real egg-shell pottery of the Ming dynasty.'

Letters to Dr Watson

There was one letter written to Watson at his Paddington home, which triggered off a case for Holmes. It was from a former school chum called Percy Phelps of Woking:

> My dear Watson,
> I have no doubt that you can remember 'Tadpole' Phelps, who was in the fifth form when you were in the third. It is possible even that you may have heard that through my uncle's influence I obtained a good appointment at the Foreign Office, and that I was in a situation of trust and honour until a horrible

misfortune came suddenly to blast my career.

There is no use writing the details of that dreadful event. In the event of your acceding to my request it is probable that I shall have to narrate them to you. I have only just recovered from nine weeks of brain-fever and am still exceedingly weak. Do you think that you could bring your friend Mr Holmes down to see me? I should like to have his opinion of the case, though the authorities assure me that nothing more can be done. Do try to bring him down, and as soon as possible. Every minute seems an hour while I live in this state of horrible suspense. Assure him that if I have not asked his advice sooner it was not because I did not appreciate his talents, but because I have been off my head ever since the blow fell. Now I am clear again, though I dare not think of it too much for fear of a relapse. I am still so weak that I have to write as you see, by dictating. Do try to bring him.

Your old school-fellow,
Percy Phelps

Holmes saw to it that there was a happy outcome to the whole affair, recovering the grey roll of paper whereon was written the terms of a secret treaty between England and Italy.

Between the winter of 1890 and the spring of 1891, Watson received two notes from Holmes dated from Narbonne and Nîmes indicating a long stay in France upon important work for the French government.

Watson recorded only one major letter written to him by Holmes; this was at the Reichenbach Falls, just prior to his final contest with Professor Moriarty. The letter was written upon three pages torn from his notebook and addressed to his friend with precise directions, and in firm and clear writing as if he had written it at Baker Street:

My dear Watson,

I write these few lines through the courtesy of Mr Moriarty, who awaits my convenience for the final discussion of those questions which lie between us. He has been giving me a sketch of the methods by which he avoided the English police and kept himself informed of our movements. They certainly confirm the very high opinion which I had formed of his abilities. I am pleased to think that I shall be able to free society from any further effects of his presence, though I fear that it is at a cost which will give pain to my friends, and especially, my dear Watson, to you. I have already explained to you, however, that my career had in any case reached its crisis, and that no possible conclusion to it could be more congenial to me than this. Indeed, if I may make a full confession to you, I was quite convinced that the letter from Meiringen was a hoax, and I allowed you to depart on that errand under the persuasion that development of this sort would follow. Tell Inspector Patterson[47] that the papers which he needs to convict the gang are in pigeon-hole M done up in a blue envelope and inscribed, 'Moriarty'. I made every disposition of my property before leaving England and handed it to my brother Mycroft. Pray give my greetings to Mrs Watson, and believe me to be, my dear fellow,

Very sincerely yours,
Sherlock Holmes

The letter was weighed down by the silver cigarette case which Holmes used to carry, and his Alpine-stock was nearby. Watson was dazed with horror and could only conclude that the personal contest between the two men ended in their reeling over the precipice, locked in each other's arms. After Colonel Moriarty had written letters in defence of his brother, Watson felt that he must lay the true facts before the public exactly as they occurred, although he did so with a heavy heart.

There may well have been other letters that Watson did not publish. Certainly, there were some scribbled notes that Holmes wrote to his friend. In 1895, while Holmes was trying to trace the lost Bruce-Partington plans, he sent the following note by special messenger to Watson at Baker Street, shortly after nine o'clock in the evening:

Am dining at Goldini's Restaurant, Gloucester Road, Kensington. Please come at once and join me there. Bring with you a jemmy, a dark lantern, a chisel, and a revolver.
S H

Watson thought, 'It was a nice equipment for a respectable citizen to carry through the dim, fog-draped streets. I stowed them all

---

[47]There seems to be no published case in which this policeman is involved.

discreetly away in my overcoat and drove straight to the address given.'

While Holmes was considering the case of the junior partner of Brickfall and Amberley in 1899, he left a scribbled note for Watson upon the breakfast table among his toast crumbs and two empty eggshells:

> Dear Watson,
>
> There are one or two points of contact which I should wish to establish with Mr Josiah Amberley. When I have done so we can dismiss the case – or not. I would only ask you to be on hand about three o'clock, as I conceive it possible that I may want you.
> S H

One Sunday evening in early September 1902, Holmes sent Watson one of his laconic messages:

> Come at once if convenient – if inconvenient come all the same.

For Holmes was engaged upon the strange case of Professor Presbury and his unnatural creeping activities.

Over the years, Watson was called by Holmes various names, but he never used his first name, John: my dear Watson, Watson, friend Watson, – my friend Watson, Doctor, my dear Doctor, my dear fellow, my good fellow, my astute friend, my boy, and my intimate friend and associate. Watson was known to have called his friend, apart from Holmes, my dear chap. Both Watson and Holmes were called 'knights-errant' by Miss Mary Morstan, who after her marriage called her husband, James, not John. Could this have been the name of a previous lover, and she sometimes forgot?

By 1914, when Watson met Holmes at Harwich, with his little Ford car, he had become a 'thickset chauffeur,' but to Holmes he was still 'the same blithe boy as ever'. It would seem that he was about to offer his medical knowledge to the government, and return to the army, for before he and Holmes drove back to London with the captured German, Von Bork, Holmes said: 'As to you, Watson, you are joining us with your old service, as I understand, so London won't be out of your way.' (Presumably

Holmes continued with his war work.)

Dr John Watson will live in our memories, a man with a great gift of silence, a trusty comrade, a rare companion and a meticulous chronicler. Jack Douglas, who gave Watson the story called *The Valley of Fear* called Watson 'the historian of this bunch'.

Somewhere in the vaults of the bank of Cox & Co., of Charing Cross – I wonder if they also issued thousand-pound notes, as did the private bank in Threadneedle Street – there was, and possibly still is, a travel-worn and battered tin dispatch box, with the name painted on the lid of John H Watson, MD, late Indian Army. It was full of the records of cases, to illustrate the curious problems which Holmes had at various times examined. Some were complete failures; some unfinished tales; some of them private family secrets, never to be divulged to the public. Many were not edited. Some did not offer a field for those peculiar qualities which Holmes possessed to such a high degree. Some baffled his analytical skill, stories which began but had no ending; some were only partially solved upon conjecture and surmise, rather than upon that absolute logical proof, so dear to Holmes.

Perhaps, some day, a relative of Dr Watson may see fit to publish some of these cases and bring further enjoyment to the discerning reading public. Watson does not seem to have recorded what he considered might have been the total number of cases undertaken by Holmes while at Baker Street.

Did Dr Watson ever write a book about Sherlock Holmes, or himself, or both? White Mason, the Sussex provincial criminal officer, wondered also: 'Come along, Dr Watson and when the time comes, we'll all hope for a place in your book.'

After Holmes retired to Sussex, Watson still kept in touch with his friend, staying there for an occasional weekend, but no longer. They were still in touch in 1922, when Holmes gave Watson permission to publish the case of the 'Creeping' Professor Presbury, in 1902.

221B Baker Street Flat

Although Watson was so diligent in recording the many exploits of Sherlock Holmes, he unfortunately forgot to give a proper description of the first-floor flat which they shared together as tenants of Mrs Hudson. He simply referred to the flat as 'our modest apartment' and 'our lodgings'. Watson never even described Mrs Hudson, their landlady, or even mentioned her first name; Holmes just called her 'our worthy landlady', who came to stand in the deepest awe of him and never dared to interfere with him, however outrageous his proceedings might seem. She became fond of him over the years for he exhibited a remarkable gentleness and courtesy towards her. So it is only by the odd casual observation dropped by Watson at irregular intervals that any information can be gleaned as to the rooms themselves – the furnishings, possibly mid-Victorian.

We do not know the cost of the rental of the flat – Holmes and Watson had agreed to go halves – for Watson never mentioned the whole, or the half he paid. Could it have been similar to that paid by the Americans, Drebber and Stangerson, who each paid one pound a day at Charpentier's Boarding Establishment in Torquay Terrace, and in the slack season too?

The flat comprised the following rooms: a 'single large airy sitting room, cum dining room, cheerfully furnished, and illuminated by two broad windows', with raised blinds, which Mrs Hudson lowered in the evening, long before her stately footsteps could be heard going past the door at eleven o'clock, to bed, the maid's footsteps having pattered past an hour earlier. There was also a bow window in an alcove screened by a curtain. The room also served as Holmes' laboratory. The view from the windows looked down upon Baker Street below; sometimes awash with sunshine, sometimes muddy with shining wet pavements. Often the dense yellow winter fog could be seen as it rolled down between the lines of dun-coloured houses, and the opposite windows loomed like dark shapeless blurs through the heavy yellow wreaths, a greasy heavy brown swirl drifting past and condensing in oily drops upon the window panes. Come the snow, the traffic ploughed a 'brown crumbly band' down the centre of the street; at either side and on the heaped-up edges of the footpaths still as white as when it fell, except when cleaned and scraped, revealing the grey pavement. The street lit at night by the occasional gas lamp.

There was a table of humble lodging-house mahogany – Victorian furniture was mainly of Honduras mahogany – covered at mealtimes by a white cloth; no doubt a set of six mahogany chairs padded with horsehair, leather covered, with brass studs fixing the coloured gimp. Being a furnished flat, it is doubtful if Mrs Hudson needed to change the furniture and 'fittings' during Holmes' tenancy.[48] In one locked drawer of this table, Holmes kept Watson's cheque book, his own two revolvers, one his 'old favourite' and the other which Watson once borrowed, and a squat notebook, in which he recorded every action of the vile and dangerous life of Count Sylvius, who had possession of the stolen Mazarin stone. In another drawer were kept the spare clean white tablecloths.

On the wall above the fireplace was a mirror. The wooden mantelpiece was enhanced by Holmes' unanswered correspondence, 'transfixed by a jack-knife into the very centre'. Among those in the early days were to be found one from a fishmonger and one from a tidewaiter;[49] another from a most noble client. Holmes did observe that his letters had the charm of variety and that the more humble were often the more interesting. He was somewhat averse to replying by letter, preferring the use of telegrams in their yellow envelopes. (The speed of the Victorian letter service was not so much slower than the telegram, for a letter with a 10 p.m. postmark would reach its destination the next morning, and there was a second delivery in the day. No two-tier system then, all letters equal!)

Holmes oft-times would delight in putting his slippered feet upon the corner of the mantelpiece, his hands buried deeply in his trouser pockets, his chin sunk upon his chest, his head buried

---

[48]Mr Tulkinghorn's chambers in a once stately house in Lincoln's Inn Fields had 'Heavy broad-backed old-fashioned mahogany and horse-hair chairs not easily lifted…' Charles Dickens, *Bleak House*, 1853

[49]Tidewaiter. One who waited to see how things went before he acted.

in a cushion, listening with closed eyes.

Over the years the mantelpiece became the repository of other articles: pipes were placed there after smoking, tobacco pouches, syringes and, much later, the soft-nosed revolver bullet fired by Colonel Moran through the waxen head of Holmes, and retrieved by Mrs Hudson. At one time there rested thereon a little box, containing within a delicate, deep-blue saucer of Ming eggshell pottery wrapped in Eastern silk. In 1896 a small blue bottle bearing a red poison label, containing prussic acid took pride of place, a gift from Mrs Eugenia Ronder, the veiled lodger of Mrs Merrilow of South Brixton. The note with it read:

> I send you my temptation. I will follow your advice.

For Holmes had said to her, 'Your life is not your own. Keep your hands off it.'

The fire grate no doubt of the cast iron variety, needing to be cleaned with blacklead, and polished.[50] The fender was probably steel, as were the poker and tongs and doubtless there was a long-handled shovel to match, as generally they made a set of three. To one side was a coal scuttle, perhaps mahogany or brass, no longer for coal – being supplanted by logs – but containing pipes, cigars and tobacco.

They both enjoyed large fires, perhaps Holmes more than Watson, for the room temperature at times could be as high as ninety degrees Fahrenheit. This was no hardship to Watson, whose Indian service had trained him to withstand heat better than cold. Inside Watson liked some fresh air, Holmes the opposite. Holmes loved to stand in front of such a fire, warming the coat-tails of his frock coat, or his slippered feet, perhaps patent leather, like Watson's. Often Holmes stayed before the smouldering embers of the fire long after Watson had retired to bed.

In front of the fender was a bear-skin rug, on either side an easy chair, one a basket type and the other a low, well worn velvet armchair, with cushions, which Watson called Holmes' 'big armchair', where Holmes would curl himself, luxuriating in its comfort. To hand a pipe-rack, holding the favourite pipe of the

---

[50]Black lead. A black mineral, plumbago.

moment.

Near the couch (sofa) which was usually littered with papers, leaving just a favourite corner for Holmes, stood a wooden chair, a stool, a cane-backed chair and an armchair. A vacant chair was kept especially for visitors, where the lamplight could fall upon them. There was a chair with its back to the window, so that the occupant's expression could not be easily read; there was another pipe-rack to the right of the sofa; a cupboard where, among other things, Holmes kept his oranges; a sideboard, with whisky tumblers and a tantalus thereon.[51] When Holmes returned late one evening, having been out all day, without food since break-fast, 'he walked up to the sideboard and tearing a piece from the loaf, he devoured it voraciously, washing it down with a long draught of water'.

There was a small pedestal table in the window and a side table with a candlestick upon it: Holmes was able to judge the length of a client's stay by the length of the burnt candle. In one corner of the room stood a small strapped portmanteau and a spirit case, for both Holmes and Watson, and often their male visitors like Inspector Lestrade, liked a glass of spirits, and a gasogene, an apparatus for making aerated waters.

Both Holmes and Watson had a desk each, both kept locked. Among the things that Holmes kept there was a small casebook; among the things that Watson kept in his desk were a sheet of stamps, a thick bundle of postcards and sometimes his old service revolver, but generally that remained in his bedroom.

Holmes used a deal-topped side table and a bench – both well stained by acids – for his chemical experiments; he usually wore a dressing gown when experimenting, when he appeared to Watson like a strange lank bird, with dull grey plumage and a black topknot. When he was at his ease upon the sofa, he chose to wear his purple dressing gown; his large blue dressing gown he is known to have worn at Mr St Clair's house, in June 1889. Among his numerous early experiments was the one where he succeeded in dissolving hydrocarbon; another time he was experimenting upon salt, and found his answer in bisulphate of baryta. Once

---

[51]A case holding decanters which could be locked.

Watson found Holmes with a large curved retort 'boiling furiously in the bluish flame of a Bunsen burner, and the distilled drops were condensing into a two-litre measure'; he dipped into various bottles, drawing out a few drops of each with his glass pipette, and finally brought a test tube containing a solution over to the table. He then carried out his final test with a slip of litmus paper. 'If this paper remains blue, all is well. If it burns red, it means a man's life.' He dipped the paper into the test tube and it flushed immediately into a 'dull, dirty crimson'. Holmes cried: 'Hum! I thought as much!' Then there was Holmes' analysis of the acetones; frequently Holmes carried out all-night chemical researches: Watson would retire to bed, leaving him stooping over a retort and a test tube, and surprisingly enough would find him in the same position in the morning, when he came down to breakfast. It was at times like this that Holmes found his spirit lamp most useful, for he could make himself coffee at any ungodly hour that he wished, particularly so if an early-morning start was called for.

The floor had a carpet, possibly with a linoleum surround, this being rather the vogue at this time. Watson recorded, surprisingly, that Holmes dropped his cigarette ends around his chair upon the carpet. Poor Mrs Hudson! She did have to put up with a lot from her lodger, especially when Holmes was in one of his queer, humorous moods and decided upon some revolver practice in the sitting room, much to the anxiety of Mrs Hudson and the disapproval of Watson. There Holmes would sit in his velvet-lined armchair, armed with his hair-trigger revolver and a box of one hundred Boxer cartridges and proceed to decorate the wall with a V R of bullet marks, in honour of her Majesty.

The sitting room was originally lit by oil lamps; Watson recorded that Holmes, dressed as a rakish young workman, with a goatee beard, lit his clay pipe at the lamp, before going out. Candles were used in the bedrooms.

A candle to Holmes was not only a method of giving light in the darkness; there was another kind of 'light' visible to the eye accustomed to observe the most trivial and mundane of things, especially if the candle had been used. This in itself could reveal information to Holmes: witness his observation at Birlstone

Manor House, for here it was that Mr Douglas had entered the room with a lighted candle, which he must have placed upon the table sometime after eleven at night. Holmes was able to ascertain the time lapse between Douglas entering the room and his murder by noticing that the candle had burnt down not more than half an inch.

In March 1888 Watson recorded that the room was brilliantly lit. Did this mean that electric lighting had been installed? Certainly before or by 1899 the flat had electricity, for an electric bell was in use, which meant easy instant communication with downstairs, for when pressed, either Mrs Hudson or Mrs Turner would answer the summons. I wonder if Mrs Hudson installed the Swan and Edison electric lamps proposed by Sir Henry Baskerville to be put up outside the gloomy Baskerville Hall?[52]

Watson recorded in June 1902 that the telephone was in use. Holmes asked Watson, the telephone book being beside him, to ring Nathan Garrideb of 136 Little Ryder Street, to find out if he, like John Garrideb, was a fraud. Mr Nathan answered in a thin quavering voice, and asked to speak to Mr Holmes. There followed the only telephone conversation of Holmes that Watson bothered to record. Said Holmes, speaking of his previous visitor, John Garrideb: 'Yes, he has been here. I understand that you don't know him… How long? …Only two days! …Yes, yes, of course, it is a most captivating prospect. Will you be at home this evening? I suppose your namesake will not be there? …Very good, we will come then, for I would rather have a chat without him… Dr Watson will come with me… I understand from your note that you did not go out often… Well, we shall be round about six. You need not mention it to the American lawyer… Very good. Goodbye!'

Certainly Holmes made full use of the telephone, for he observed to Watson that thanks to the telephone and help from Scotland Yard, he could usually get his information without leaving the room. And yet he was prone to send Watson out upon an expedition to elicit information, when he, from the comfort of his room, could fill in the 'blanks' from over the 'air'. Watson

[52]Sir Thomas Baskerville sailed with Drake and Hawkins in 1595 with one thousand soldiers to seize Panama.

does not record that he had a telephone at his surgery, and whether Holmes communicated with him in that way. Certainly, Holmes visited Watson one June morning at his Paddington surgery interrupting Watson's after-breakfast reading of the *British Medical Journal*, and asked his friend to accompany him to Birmingham – in a first class carriage. Mrs Hudson had to visit Watson when she despaired of Holmes' life. So it seems that Watson had no telephone.

There were scientific charts and a newly framed picture of General Gordon[53] among the pictures of criminals which adorned the walls, and an unframed portrait of Henry Ward Beecher[54] upon the top of Watson's books. I wonder if Watson eventually framed it? The room was full of criminal relics, which had a way of wandering into the most unlikely places and positions, turning up even in the butter dish, or even less desirable places.[55]

Sherlock Holmes' Bedroom

Holmes' bedroom had two doors leading off from the sitting room and a third exit door, which Holmes referred to Watson just before the arrival of Count Negretto Sylvius. 'I think we, [Watson was going to warn Inspector Youghal], will go out through the bedroom. This second exit is exceedingly useful. I rather want to see my shark without his seeing me, and I have, as you will remember, my own way of doing it.' Later Holmes said, 'I shall try over the Hoffmann Barcarole upon my violin.[56] In five minutes I shall return for your final answer.' Holmes picked up his violin and withdrew into his bedroom. Count Sylvius then heard the haunting music upon the gramophone. The deception enabled Holmes to retrieve the Crown yellow diamond, worth one hundred thousand pounds.

Among the things Holmes kept in his bedroom was a large tin

---

[53]General Charles George Gordon, 1833–85. Killed at Khartoum.
[54]H W Beecher. American clergyman, brother of Harriet Beecher Stowe, authoress of *Uncle Tom's Cabin*. He undertook a mission on behalf of the North during the American Civil War.
[55]The waiter from the coffee house served dinner to Pip and Herbert Pocket, and put the melted butter in the armchair. Charles Dickens, *Great Expectations*, 1861.
[56]Jacques Offenbach, *The Tales of Hoffmann*.

strongbox, one 'third full of bundles of papers, tied up with red tape into separate packages', a collection of considerable trifling achievements, with little pecuniary gain. These were records of his early work, before Watson became his biographer, and he always handled these documents in a tender and caressing way. There were 'some pretty little problems among them', although they were not all successes. Over the years other documents came to reside there, particularly those relating to cases undertaken during Watson's absence from Baker Street during his marriages.

For safe keeping, certain valuables were kept in the strong box. The most famous jewel in the world, the black pearl of the Borgias, resided there for a short time only, for it rightfully belonged to the Prince of Colonna and was stolen from the Dacre Hotel; Holmes found the pearl in the sixth plaster cast copy of Devine's bust of Napoleon. The wholesale price had been six shillings and the retail price from twelve to fifteen shillings, and they had been manufactured by Gelder & Co., of Stepney. Holmes had purchased the plaster cast from Mr Sandeford, of Lower Grove, Reading, Berks., for ten pounds. So attractive was the price that Mr Sandeford made a special journey to Baker Street to deliver the cast. For a short time, the Countess of Morcar's blue carbuncle from South China resided there.

Just before Culverton Smith arrived at Baker Street, where he expected to find Holmes at death's door, and he could gloat over the 'dying' agonies, Watson looked at Holmes in bed, his face almost covered by clothes and apparently asleep. Watson, unable to settle down to reading, 'walked slowly round the room, examining the pictures of celebrated criminals with which the walls were adorned'. Finally he came to the mantelpiece, whereon was a 'litter of pipes, tobacco-pouches, syringes, penknives, revolver-cartridges, and other débris was scattered over it. In the midst of these was a small black and white ivory box with a sliding lid. It was a neat little thing…' Watson might have received the death prick, had he not been stopped by Holmes' dreadful yell.

Holmes was usually a late riser, except when he had been up all night, or wished a very early start – perhaps the earliest from Baker Street was about five in the morning, when he needed to catch the six o'clock train from Charing Cross to Chatham.

Perhaps his earliest start was at The Cedars, Lee, in Kent (for there Holmes never went to bed), when he awakened Watson at 4.25 a.m. when no one was stirring, in order to drive the horse and trap back to London, with a sponge in his Gladstone bag and a new theory in his head, concerning Neville St Clair. Many a time they made a start as the dawn was breaking over Baker Street; on the other hand, Holmes might not rise until the evening, or even spend several days in bed, from time to time.

Dr Watson's Bedroom

Watson's bedroom was upon the floor above, where the window with a pull-up and down blind was on the right-hand side; here Watson shaved when daylight permitted. The view from this window overlooked a yard behind the house, where grew a solitary plane tree. (Watson also shaved at his window in the early spring of 1897 while at Poldhu Cottage.) No gas, or electric, only candles were used; for Watson was awakened upon a frosty winter's morning in the same year, by Holmes' hand tugging at his shoulders: 'The candle in his hand shone upon his eager stooping face, and told me at a glance that something was amiss "Come, Watson, come," he cried. "The game is afoot.[57] Not a word! Into your clothes and come!"' Ten minutes later a cab was taking them to Charing Cross Station, as the first faint dawn was beginning to appear.

Holmes usually confided all the latest news to Watson at breakfast time, but during the early mystery surrounding the broken Napoleon plaster busts, he could not wait for Watson to come down, but went up to his bedroom, where Watson was still dressing and tapped at his door before entering. He held a telegram from Lestrade in his hand, which he read aloud: '"Come instantly, 131 Pitt Street, Kensington."' 'What is it?' asked Watson. 'Don't know – may be anything. But I suspect it is the sequel of the story of the statues. In that case our friend the image breaker has begun operations in another quarter of London. There's coffee on the table, Watson, and I have a cab at the door.'

---

[57]ACD used 'the game is afoot' in *The White Company*, 1891. 'The game's afoot', William Shakespeare, *Henry V*, III. i.

There was another instance of Holmes' intrusion into Watson's bedroom, although away from Baker Street, when Holmes had vital information to impart: this was in 1895, when Holmes was pursuing 'some laborious researches in early English charters' in one of the great university towns and, with Watson, resided in furnished lodgings close to the library. Here they were visited by an old acquaintance, Mr Hilton Soames of St Luke's College. He had found that proofs of the Greek examination papers upon his table had been tampered with and asked Holmes to help. One of a possible three students was thought to have been involved. Having solved the mystery, Holmes chose to call upon Watson in his bedroom just as he had finished his toilet, and asked him to forgo breakfast in order that Holmes could give Soames positive news early in the morning.

There was a spare bedroom, for here it was that Watson's old schoolfellow, Percy Phelps, slept in 1887. Holmes had considered the advisability of getting Phelps away from Woking, after he had experienced the attempted intrusion of a burglar through his bedroom window in the early hours of the morning; Watson, as a medical man, would be able to look after him, and they would be able to reminisce over their schooldays. For as Watson recorded: 'It was seven o'clock when I awoke, and I set off at once for Phelp's room to find him haggard and spent after a sleepless night.' Perhaps Holmes used this spare bedroom as a changing room for his many disguises, not wishing to clutter up his own bedroom, for Watson recorded at one time that Holmes, 'hastened upstairs' to his chamber, and was down again in a few minutes, having donned a disguise.

There were also lumber-rooms, which were used to store the old files of the daily newspapers, boxes, trunks and portmanteaux from Montague Street, and their fishing rods, reels and baskets. Holmes and Watson were recorded as using this angling gear when they stayed at the old-fashioned tavern called The Green Dragon at Shoscombe, in Berkshire, where they fished for trout in the millstream, and taken home a goodly supper. A staircase led up to these lumber-rooms.

Was there a separate bathroom? Perhaps because taking a bath was too mundane an affair (referred to by Holmes as the 'invigorating home-made article') Watson only once alluded to the bath. Whether this was taken in a common bathroom, a private one, or a yellow hipbath, the one to sit in with the high back, beside a fire in the privacy of his room, we are not told. 'A bath at Baker Street', said Watson, 'and a complete change freshened me up wonderfully. When I came down to our room I found the breakfast laid and Holmes pouring out the coffee.' Watson, it seems, was permitted to pour the tea. 'There is no great mystery in this matter,' said Holmes apropos of the disappearance of Captain Morstan, as he took the cup of tea which Watson had poured out for him.

There was always, of course, the other bath, the Turkish one. When Holmes and Watson both needed to relax and get away from the confines of their Baker Street flat, they would frequent the relaxing but expensive Turkish bath, on an upper floor in Northumberland Avenue. After luxuriating in their baths they would finally sit side by side upon couches, in the pleasant lassitude of the drawing room, in an isolated corner, enshrouded in sheets, contentedly smoking and chatting. Here of all places, Holmes, with a whimsical smile upon his face, was considered by Watson to have been less reticent and more human than anywhere else in London. Watson would sometimes come here by himself when he felt rheumatic and old, which he referred to as 'an alternative in medicine – a fresh starting point, a cleanser of the system.' Holmes always knew when Watson had been there by the unusual way his boots were fastened with an elaborate bow, the kind employed by the boy at the bath: did not Holmes say that much could be learned from the study of bootlaces? They were both known to have come here as late as the 3 September 1902.

There was a waiting room downstairs, where sometimes the clients would stay, waiting to be shown up to see Holmes; some clients sent up their visiting cards, brought in by Mrs Hudson on a brass salver, or were announced by Billy the young but wise and tactful pageboy in buttoned black clothes. Or the irate client might just burst in unannounced, such sometimes was their unbridled fury. There was a table in the hall.

The heavy front door had a semicircular fanlight of glass;

when the front doorbell was pulled, a clanging noise ensued, and the maid (who lived in) or Billy, giving a sharp click of the latch, would open the door; the visitor, after crossing the hall, climbed the seventeen stairs, (were they carpeted, with stair-rods of black cast iron or round or triangular brass ones, or just linoleum?) and made his way along a linoleum-covered passage to the sanctum of the famous detective. Holmes was given a front door latchkey by Mrs Hudson, perhaps as the premier tenant, for Watson never used one.

Mrs Hudson

It did not always mean a visitor for Holmes when the doorbell rang; when this happened upon a stormy evening in September 1887, Watson thought that it might have been a friend of Holmes, but the detective thought that it was 'more likely to be some crony of the landlady's.' So Mrs Hudson had visitors as well.[58]

Mrs Hudson seemingly occupied the rooms beneath the flat of Holmes and Watson, with apparently a bedroom upon the first floor; she once confided to Watson: 'After you was gone, he walked and he walked up and down and up and down, until I was weary of the sound of his footstep. Then I heard him talking to himself and muttering, and every time the bell rang out, he came on the stairhead, with, "What is that, Mrs Hudson?"'

Mrs Hudson was the owner of the house, 'our worthy land-lady' as Watson called her; Holmes was only the tenant, (even if he did pay her well), and yet at times he did tend to treat her as a servant; once when Inspectors Gregson and Baynes were about to leave, Holmes rang the bell: 'You will show these gentlemen out, Mrs Hudson', which too often, was an aspect of his somewhat dogmatic attitude towards other people.

But kindly Mrs Hudson trembled and wept when she thought that Holmes was going to die, and became so concerned about his state of health, that she actually visited Watson in his consulting room in the second year of his marriage to Mary Morstan, which must have preceded the installation of the telephone. 'He's dying,

---

[58]Mr Hudson, seaman of the *Gloria Scott*. Hudson Street in Aldershot where lodged Henry Wood. ACD, *The Adventure of the Crooked Man*.

Dr Watson… For three days he has been sinking, and I doubt if he will last the day. He would not let me get a doctor. This morning when I saw his bones sticking out of his face and his great bright eyes looking at me I could stand no more of it. "With your leave or without it, Mr Holmes, I am going for a doctor this very hour," "Let it be Watson, then," said he. I wouldn't waste an hour in coming to him, sir, or you may not see him alive.' (Unfortunately for the criminal world, the illness was faked.)

While Holmes was abroad for three years, after the death of Professor Moriarty, Mrs Hudson gave her attention and 'immediate care' to the rooms of the flat; when Holmes returned to Baker Street, Mrs Hudson was thrown into violent hysterics by the arrival of one whom she thought had perished at the Reichenbach Falls. Yes, she certainly had a great affection for her tenant.

Mrs Hudson kept a terrier dog, old and nearing its lifespan; its muzzle was snow-white, its breathing laboured, its eyes glazed. Mrs Hudson had asked Watson to be kind enough to put the dog out of its misery, which somehow kindly Watson had failed to do. Holmes remembered this and asked Watson if he would mind going down and fetching the poor little devil of a terrier which had been bad so long and which Mrs Hudson wanted to be put out of his pain.

Watson went downstairs and carried the dog upstairs in his arms, and placed it upon a cushion on the rug. Holmes thought that he could please his landlady, while carrying out an experiment of his own which would test a theory of his regarding the small white box of pearly grey, small, round pills, which Lestrade had found in Joseph Stangerson's room, at Halliday's Private Hotel; the inspector had attached no importance to them.

With his penknife, Holmes cut one of the pills in two, and placed one half in a teaspoon of water in a wine glass and, adding a little milk, found it dissolved easily. Lestrade thought Holmes was laughing at him, but he was assured that the experiment concerned the death of Stangerson, if he would just have a little patience. Holmes poured the contents of the wine glass into a saucer, and the dog speedily licked it dry; minutes ticked by and no startling effect happened, causing the inspector to smile, and

Holmes to gnaw his lip and drum his finger upon the table with acute impatience, for he had not expected the pill to be inert and himself a failure in the presence of the police. Then his deducing powers came to his aid – the other pill of course! This he cut in half and, following the previous procedure, gave the drink to the dog. 'The unfortunate creature's tongue,' wrote Watson, 'seemed hardly to have been moistened in it, before it gave a convulsive shiver in every limb, and lay as rigid and lifeless as if it had been struck by lightning.' Thus was Mrs Hudson's plea attended to, and the murderer of Enoch Drebber and Joseph Stangerson – another American, Jefferson Hope – apprehended.

Sherlock Holmes' Waxen Busts

Holmes had two waxen coloured busts made of himself; the first was made by Monsieur Oscar Meunier of Grenoble, who spent some days in the making of it. He used this bust in the sitting room window as a decoy to force the hand of Moriarty's bosom friend, the second most dangerous man in England, Colonel Sebastian Moran, of Conduit Street, late of Her Majesty's Indian Army and a very fine game shot. He was an elderly man with a gaunt, swarthy, virile yet sinister face, scored with deep, savage lines and two cruel blue eyes with drooping cynical lids, a thin, projecting, fierce aggressive nose, a high, bald, philosopher's deep-lined forehead, a grizzled, long moustache, with the jaw of a sensualist; Moriarty had paid him a yearly salary of six thousand pounds. Holmes observed, 'That's paying for brains, you see, the American business principle. It's more than the Prime Minister gets.' He it was who had tried unsuccessfully to kill Holmes by dropping rocks over the cliff at the Reichenbach Falls.

Moran knew that Holmes was alive, and so kept a constant watch upon the Baker Street flat (using as his sentinel a man called Parker, a garrotter by trade), awaiting the homecoming of the detective.

Holmes, wishing to delude his attackers (knowing that a watch was kept upon his movements) into believing that he was at Baker Street, when in reality he was elsewhere, set up the Meunier bust in the window, and draped it in his old mouse-coloured dressing gown, thus showing, with the blind down, a brilliant yellow screen with a black figure outlined upon its centre. In order to create a sense of reality, Mrs Hudson had been instructed to change the position of the bust once every quarter of an hour, going carefully down on her knees and working from the front, so that her shadow would not be seen.

So in order that the watchers could be watched, and the trackers tracked, with the bust as bait and Holmes and Watson as the hunters, Holmes took Watson by cab from his Kensington consulting room to the corner of Cavendish Square. From here they travelled upon foot, and with Holmes' extraordinary knowledge of London's byways, 'passed rapidly and with an assured step, through a network of mews and stables, the very existence of which I had never known. We emerged at last into a small road, lined with old, gloomy houses, which led us into Manchester Street, and so to Blandford Street. Here he turned swiftly down a narrow passage, passed through a wooden gate into a deserted yard, and then opened with a key the back door of a house.' This was Camden House, opposite the Baker Street flat. Holmes led Watson by the wrist, with his cold thin fingers, down a long hall, into a large, square, empty room, dimly lit by the street lights.

Holmes stared into the street, into the bleak and boisterous night, while the wind whistled shrilly down the long street; he expected an attack from without, keeping his eyes intently fixed upon the stream of passers-by, wondering from whence the shot would come.

Watson looked up at the window opposite and saw the shadow of the perfect reproduction of Holmes, and being utterly surprised gave a gasp of amazement as he said, 'Good heavens! It is marvellous.' He put out his hand to make sure that his friend was actually beside him. Holmes enjoyed this, and quivered with silent laughter as he said, remembering Shakespeare, and twisting it to his own advantage: 'I trust that age doth not wither nor custom stale my infinite variety...[59] It really is rather like me, is it not?' Watson looked at the window again: 'The shadow has

---

[59]Enobarbus, friend of Antony, 'Age cannot wither her nor custom stale Her infinite variety.' William Shakespeare, *Antony and Cleopatra,* II. ii.

moved!' which surprised him even more. 'Of course it has moved' said Holmes with some asperity. 'Am I such a farcical bungler, Watson, that I should erect an obvious dummy, and expect that some of the sharpest men in Europe would be deceived by it?'

As midnight approached and Baker Street had cleared of pedestrians, Holmes keen senses distinguished a low stealthy sound from the back of the house; a door opened and shut; steps crept down the passage, reverberating harshly in the empty house; a man's outline, blacker than the blackness of the open doorway, crept forward, crouching, menacing, into the room, unaware of the other occupants, and they, not expecting an intruder. He raised the window six inches, the street light showing him to be dressed in evening clothes; he carried a sort of stick, and took a bulky object from his overcoat pocket. There was a loud sharp click, as of a spring or bolt falling into place, a long, whirling, grinding noise from a lever depressed, and then a powerful click. Watson saw that it was a kind of gun with a curiously misshapen butt; he put something into the breech, cuddled the butt into his shoulder and pulled the trigger. Then followed a 'strange, loud whiz and a long, silvery tinkle of broken glass'. The soft-nosed expanding revolver bullet hit the bust plumb in the middle of the head, and smack through where the brain might have been, and flattened itself on the opposite wall, and was retrieved by Mrs Hudson.

Holmes attacked, springing like a tiger onto the marksman's back, and hurled him flat upon his face. But he was quickly up, and with tremendous strength seized Holmes by the throat, and it might well have gone badly with him had not Watson hit the stranger on the head with the butt of his revolver, dropping him to the floor, where he sat upon him, giving Holmes the chance to summon Lestrade by his whistle. The inspector arrested his man, not at first appreciating that he had caught Colonel Moran, the murderer of Ronald Adair (shot with a similar bullet through the open window of the front room on the second floor of No. 427 Park Lane).

Holmes made Lestrade a present of the airgun, for the Scotland Yard museum. 'An admirable and unique weapon…

noiseless and of tremendous power: I knew Von Herder, the blind German mechanic, who constructed it to the order of the late Professor Moriarty. For years I have been aware of its existence, though I have never before had the opportunity of handling it.'

The colonel gave Holmes his last look of hatred and amazement, muttering, 'You fiend! You clever, clever fiend,' which brought Holmes' rejoinder: 'Ah, Colonel…! Journey's end in lover's meetings,' as he arranged his crumpled collar.[60] (Holmes must have been rather fond of this Shakespearean quotation, for he used it again when he met Inspector Gregson of Scotland Yard at the doorway to the Howe Street flats.)

At a later date, post-1892, when Holmes lived a solitary bachelor's life, he had another waxen bust made of himself by Tavernier, the French modeller; he placed it in the alcove of the bow window, complete with one of his dressing gowns, the 'body' seemingly sunk deep in an armchair. It was Billy's job, when the blind was down, to place the detachable head at different angles, to give the appearance of Holmes' reading an invisible book; the window was being watched from a window across the road. Holmes expected an attack from Count Negretto Sylvius of 136 Moorside Gardens, possibly from the window opposite, where he judged there was a man with an airgun, made by old Straubenzee in his Minories workshop, for the count; for Holmes had followed the count there, disguised first as a sporting man and then as an elderly woman with a parasol. Holmes anticipated that at any moment the assassin's bullet might spoil the beautiful head.

But the count had other ideas, to beard Holmes in his den and ask why his 'agents' had been following him, and to settle accounts; his visiting card preceded him into the sitting room. Holmes confronted him with an account of his vile life: of the death of Mrs Harold, the history of Mrs Minnie Warrender, the Riviera train robbery, the Crédit Lyonnais forged cheque and evidence, through Ikey Sanders, that he was involved in stealing the Crown jewel, the great yellow Mazarin stone, which it was Holmes' first aim to retrieve. He gave the count and Merton, his

---

[60]An adaptation by Holmes of a quotation from William Shakespeare, *Twelfth Night*, II. iii.

prizefighter henchman, five minutes to consider the proposition of whether he would give up the stone, valued at one hundred thousand pounds, or be jailed for his crimes; then Holmes passed into his bedroom to play Hoffmann's 'Barcarole', which instead was played upon a gramophone record, a modern remarkable invention.

This gave Holmes the opportunity to pass through his second bedroom door, and substitute himself for his dummy, thus misleading the count to think that he still saw the waxen bust. As Sylvius showed the jewel to Sam Merton, in the light of the window, Holmes snatched the diamond from the outstretched hand, and clapped his revolver to the count's head. Holmes pressed the electric bell to summon Watson and Inspector Youghal of the CID Scotland Yard, who soon clicked his handcuffs upon the prisoners. Fortunately, this time no airgun bullet defaced the waxen 'Holmes'. I wonder if the two busts found their way into the Scotland Yard Museum?

Sherlock Holmes' use of Telegrams

Before the telephone was installed in the sitting room at Baker Street, Holmes sent and received telegrams in their yellow envelopes, for urgent information; the continental telegrams were more expensive, being tuppence a word. When Holmes received a reply-paid telegram, he knew the sender was a man, because no woman would ever have dreamed of sending such a telegram, for she would have called herself. Watson recorded some of the telegrams.

After the murder of Charles McCarthy at the pool in Boscombe Valley, near the little country town of Ross, Inspector Lestrade asked Holmes to help him; Holmes, wishing the company of his friend, sent a telegram to Watson, which came to him one morning while he breakfasted with his wife. It ran:

> HAVE YOU A COUPLE OF DAYS TO SPARE? HAVE JUST BEEN WIRED FOR FROM THE WEST OF ENGLAND IN CONNECTION WITH BOSCOMBE VALLEY TRAGEDY. SHALL BE GLAD IF YOU WILL COME WITH ME. AIR AND SCENERY PERFECT. LEAVE PADDINGTON BY THE 11.15.

His wife urged him to go, knowing that Dr Ansthruther would look after his practice while he was absent.

While Holmes was investigating the movements of the suspicious Josiah Amberley, he sent one of his agents to Little Purlington, Essex, and got him to send a telegram to Amberley, as if coming from the local vicar, the Reverend J C Elman, MA who held the living of Mossmoor cum Little Purlington, the name Holmes had taken from his *Crockford's Clerical Directory*; Holmes desired to get Amberley as far away from The Haven, Lewisham, as possible. The telegram simply said:

COME AT ONCE WITHOUT FAIL. CAN GIVE YOU INFORMATION AS
TO YOUR RECENT LOSS.
ELMAN.
THE VICARAGE.

With the suspect upon a wild goose chase, Holmes was able to examine Amberley's house at his leisure.

While Holmes was masquerading as Captain Basil, he asked Watson to write out on a telegram form the following:

SUMNER, SHIPPING AGENT, RATCLIFF HIGHWAY. SEND THREE
MEN ON, TO ARRIVE TEN TO-MORROW MORNING. BASIL.

This was to lure, and secure, Patrick Cairns, harpooner and murderer of Peter Carey. In order that the police should be on hand to make an arrest, Watson wrote out for Holmes a telegram to Inspector Stanley Hopkins, 46 Lord Street, Brixton:

COME BREAKFAST TO-MORROW AT NINE-THIRTY. IMPORTANT.
WIRE IF UNABLE TO COME. SHERLOCK HOLMES.

Holmes employed another ruse, in order to cover his presence upon the Devon moor: he sent his helper, the small boy, Cartwright, back to London by train, telling him to send from there a telegram to Sir Henry Baskerville, in Holmes' name, to say that if he found a pocketbook that he had dropped, to send it by registered post to Baker Street.

During the time that Holmes was investigating the loss of the naval treaty by Percy Phelps of the Foreign Office, he sent telegrams from Woking Station to every London evening newspaper; he hoped thereby to elicit information concerning the thief, who must have come from outside the building, there being no hiding place within. Although the night was wet there was no trace of damp upon the linoleum, so Holmes deduced that he must have come in a cab. The advertisement read as follows:

> £10 reward. The number of the cab which dropped a fare at or about the door of the Foreign Office in Charles Street at a quarter to ten in the evening of May 23rd. Apply 221B, Baker Street.

Holmes had hoped that this might bring forth information, but no cabby came forward to claim the reward.

While Watson was travelling abroad upon the trail of the Lady Frances Carfax, before he left Baden, he sent a letter to Holmes giving an account of his progress. In reply, Holmes sent a telegram to Watson, asking for a description of Dr Shlessinger's left ear. Watson did not realise, unfortunately, the true significance of this request, simply thinking that it was another of Holmes' ideas of humour, strange and sometimes offensive, so he took no notice of the apparently ill-timed jest.

Towards the end of March 1892 Holmes received a telegram at lunchtime which ran:

> HAVE JUST HAD MOST INCREDIBLE AND GROTESQUE EXPERIENCE.
> MAY I CONSULT YOU?
> SCOTT ECCLES
> POST-OFFICE, CHARING CROSS.

The use of the word 'grotesque' immediately intrigued Holmes, so much so that he scribbled an answer on the reply-paid telegram. Holmes was told by this client of his most singular and unpleasant experience, for never in his life had he been placed in such an improper and outrageous situation. This led to Holmes and Watson going down to Wisteria Lodge, near Esher, in Surrey, the home of Aloysius Garcia, who had been murdered on Oxshott Common.

Wishing to obtain information concerning people living in the

Oxshott area, which might help him in not only finding the murderer, but in exonerating Scott Eccles, Holmes sent a telegram to the local house agent, with a pre-paid reply. Back came the answer:

LORD HARRINGBY, THE DINGLE; SIR GEORGE FFOLLIOTT, OXSHOTT TOWERS; MR HYNES HYNES, JP, PURDEY PLACE; MR JAMES BAKER WILLIAMS, FORTON OLD HALL; MR HENDERSON, HIGH GABLE; REVEREND JOSHUA STONE, NETHER WALSLING.

Holmes knew that the other end of his 'tangled skein' must lie among these houses, thus limiting his field of operations. Holmes was going to keep the news to himself, and was going to place the telegram in his notebook, without showing it to Watson, when he was pulled up in time by Watson's expectant face; (there was now no need for Holmes' secrecy). It is true that in the early days, not knowing Watson very well, he had had to be careful and discreet over high matters of state. Evading the English law, Mr Henderson, (otherwise known as Don Murillo, the yellow and sapless, but tough as whipcord, Central American dictator) missed the Guildford Assizes and escaped to Madrid, where he was murdered in the Hotel Escorial.

Holmes was fairly accustomed to receiving weird telegrams at Baker Street, but there was one in particular which gave him a puzzled quarter of an hour; it ran as follows:

PLEASE AWAIT ME. TERRIBLE MISFORTUNE. RIGHT WING THREE-QUARTER MISSING, INDISPENSABLE TO-MORROW.
OVERTON.

It bore a Strand postmark sent at 10.36 a.m. This led Holmes, on behalf of Cyril Overton of Trinity College, to travel to Cambridge from King's Cross Station, on the trail of Godfrey Staunton, who was eventually found in a lonely cottage, sitting at the foot of a bed, whereon lay his wife, dead from consumption.[61]

Seldom did Holmes call upon the superior brain of his brother

---

[61]Joseph Overton, solicitor and Mayor of Great Winglebury. Charles Dickens, *The Great Winglebury Duel.*

Mycroft, but after Sherlock was consulted over Cadogan West and the Bruce-Partington plans, he needed to know more about the men who might have been involved. So at London Bridge he sent a telegram to his brother:

> SEE SOME LIGHT IN THE DARKNESS, BUT IT MAY POSSIBLY FLICKER OUT. MEANWHILE, PLEASE SEND BY MESSENGER, TO AWAIT RETURN AT BAKER STREET, A COMPLETE LIST OF ALL FOREIGN SPIES OR INTERNATIONAL AGENTS KNOWN TO BE IN ENGLAND, WITH FULL ADDRESS.
> SHERLOCK.

The reply came in the form of a note, brought post-haste by a government messenger, so important did Mycroft consider the case:

> There are numerous small fry, but few who would handle so big an affair. The only men worth considering are Adolph Meyer, of 13 Great George Street, Westminster; Louis La Rothière, of Campden Mansions, Notting Hill; and Hugo Oberstein, 13 Caulfield Gardens, Kensington. The latter was known to be in town on Monday and is now reported as having left. Glad to hear you have seen some light. The Cabinet awaits your final report with the utmost anxiety. Urgent representations have arrived from the very highest quarter. The whole force of the State is at your back if you should need it. Mycroft.

Colonel Walter, who stole the submarine plans (hoping to repay a Stock Exchange debt), and Oberstein, who received them and tried to sell them in all the naval centres in Europe, were subsequently caught and jailed.

During Holmes' investigation into the case known as The Sign of Four he sent a telegram to Inspector Jones from Poplar, at midday:

> GO TO BAKER STREET AT ONCE. IF I HAVE NOT RETURNED, WAIT FOR ME. I AM CLOSE ON THE TRAIL OF THE SHOLTO GANG.[62] YOU CAN COME WITH US TO-NIGHT IF YOU WANT TO BE IN AT THE

---

[62]Oscar Wilde brought an unsuccessful action for criminal libel against Sir John Sholto Douglas, 8th Marquis of Queensbury, 1844–1900.

This brought Jones to Baker Street, and subsequently upon the trail and capture of Jonathan Small.

On 14 April 1887 Watson received a telegram from Holmes in Lyons, where he was lying ill, after his arduous task in apprehending the most accomplished swindler in Europe. In consequence thereof, Holmes was inundated by telegrams from Europe to such an extent that his room was literally ankle-deep with congratulatory telegrams. Kindly Watson was in the sickroom within twenty-four hours.

Holmes received a lot of information concerning the underworld of crime from a man called Mercer; he was Holmes' general utility man, who kept his eyes upon routine business. In September 1902 Holmes sent him a telegram asking for information concerning a man call A Dorak, who was the English agent for H Lowenstein of Prague, who had produced a wondrous strength-giving serum from the black-faced crawling and climbing monkey, the langur. This was the biggest and most human monkey from the Himalayan mountains. Lowenstein was searching for the secret of rejuvenescence and the elixir of life, and supplied Professor Presbury with bottles of this serum. Back came a telegram from Mercer:

HAVE VISITED THE COMMERCIAL ROAD AND SEEN DORAK. SUAVE PERSON, BOHEMIAN, ELDERLY. KEEPS LARGE GENERAL STORE.

This gave Holmes information connected with the source of supply and the man himself, and helped him to form his final analysis.

In order to assist the British government against the German spy-network, Holmes was persuaded to come out of his Sussex retirement in 1912. In August 1914, just before the outbreak of the First World War, Holmes sent off two telegrams: the first to Von Bork, the German secret agent (his employer of the moment), under his Irish-American alias, from Portsmouth – he was then lodging with a landlady at Fratton:

WILL COME WITHOUT FAIL TO-NIGHT AND BRING NEW SPARKING

PLUGS.
ALTAMONT.

This referred to phoney naval signals Holmes was selling to the Germans, and was one of the code words used relating to a motor car. The second telegram was to Watson, asking him to come to Harwich with his car, which he did, and after the capture of Von Bork, drove Holmes and the tied-up German to London, for intelligence interrogation.

It is most interesting to note, that such had been Holmes' high standing with the Post Office, over the years, that he was able to arrange that any telegram sent to him, would reach him wherever he happened to be.

If great urgency was needed in ensuring that a letter was promptly delivered, then Holmes would ask Watson to ring for an express messenger. Watson recorded two particular instances, although there were no doubt others.

When Holmes wished to advise Baron Adelbert Gruner of Vernon Lodge, near Kingston, that 'Dr Hill Barton' would be coming to see him with a very rare Ming eggshell saucer, he dictated the letter to Watson, no reply being needed. 'It was an admirable document, short, courteous, and stimulating to the curiosity of the connoisseur', for the baron owned and was an authority upon priceless Chinese porcelain. A messenger was duly dispatched with it, preceding Watson's visit. The mission carried with it possible danger to Watson if his identity were penetrated: had Holmes fully considered this? But Watson's interview did afford extra valuable time for Holmes to find the baron's 'love diary', with which he hoped to break off the marriage of the baron to Violet de Merville, for was he not the detested Austrian murderer? This book, combined with the vitriol attack by Kitty Winter – a discarded lover – did the trick, much to the gratification of General de Merville, of Khyber fame.

While Holmes was trying to locate the various 'homes' of the six Napoleon plaster casts, he learned from Harding Brothers of Kensington that one had been sold to Josiah Brown of Laburnum Lodge, Laburnum Vale, Chiswick; so Holmes sent a letter to him by express messenger, thus ensuring that Brown would be prepared for an anticipated entry of a burglar that night into his house. Holmes asked him to lock every door on the inside and await developments, so that they were able to capture Beppo the Italian with the plaster bust as Holmes had planned.

It is known that Holmes sometimes dictated letters for the ordinary post. Holmes made Colonel Valentine Walter write a letter at his dictation to Hugo Oberstein, at the Hôtel du Louvre, Paris, (who had murdered Cadogan West with a blow upon the head, with a short life-preserver, and stolen the invaluable naval submarine plans). The letter ran:

> Dear Sir,
>
>   With regard to our transaction, you will no doubt have ob-
> served by now that one essential detail is missing. I have a tracing
> which will make it complete. This has involved me in extra trou-
> ble, however, and I must ask you for a further advance of five
> hundred pounds. I will not trust it to the post, nor will I take
> anything but gold or notes. I would come to you abroad, but it
> would excite remark if I left the country at present. Therefore I
> shall expect to meet you in the smoking-room of the Charing
> Cross Hotel at noon on Saturday. Remember that only English
> notes, or gold, will be taken.

Oberstein, eager to complete the coup of his lifetime, came to the hotel, was arrested and imprisoned for fifteen years.

Another time, Holmes dictated a letter to Inspector MacDonald, to be taken by hand (presumably by a policeman) to Mr Cecil Barker at Birlstone Manor House, as follows :

> Dear Sir,
>
>   It has struck me that it is our duty to drain the moat, in the
> hope that we may find something which may bear upon our in-
> vestigation. I have made arrangements, and the workmen will be
> at work early to-morrow morning diverting the stream; so I
> thought it best to explain matters beforehand.

It was then signed by the inspector and sent off at four o'clock. This prompted Cecil Barker to work quickly in hauling a bundle from the moat, containing the clothes of the American, Ted Baldwin, who had been blasted in the face by his own twin-barrelled gun; this gave Jack Douglas the chance to take refuge in a secret hiding place used by King Charles, leaving the police to assume that his was the dead body. But this did not fool Holmes!

Sometimes Holmes' communication would just take the form of a note; after the death of Willoughby Smith (the young university man employed as a secretary by Professor Coram, an elderly man, living at his country home, Yoxley Old Place), the detective Stanley Hopkins called to see Holmes at Baker Street, as he could make neither head nor tail of it. After hearing all the facts of the case, Holmes wrote the following note upon a sheet of paper, and tossed it across to the detective. It ran:

> Wanted a woman of good address, attired like a lady. She has a remarkably thick nose, with eyes which are set close upon either side of it. She has a puckered forehead, a peering expression, and probably rounded shoulders. There are indications that she has had recourse to an optician at least twice during the last few months. As her glasses are of remarkable strength, and as opticians are not very numerous, there should be no difficulty in tracing her.

Hopkins was duly astonished, as having all that evidence in his hand, he never realised it. He did however meet the Russian girl Anna, the professor's wife, the unintentional murderess, but was too late to arrest her, she dying from self-administered poison.

Letters to Sherlock Holmes

Watson does not seem to have published many of the letters which Holmes received; among them we have the following:

Claridge's Hotel
October 3rd.

Dear Mr Sherlock Holmes,

I can't see the best woman God ever made, go to her death without doing all that is possible to save her. I can't explain things – I can't even try to explain them, but I know beyond all doubt that Miss Dunbar is innocent. You know the facts – who doesn't? It has been the gossip of the country. And never a voice raised for her! It's the damned injustice of it all that makes me crazy. That woman has a heart that wouldn't let her kill a fly. Well, I'll come at eleven to-morrow and see if you can get some ray of light in the dark. Maybe I have a clue and don't know it. Anyhow, all I know and all I have and all I am are for your use if only you can save her. If ever in your life you showed your powers, put them now into this case.

Yours faithfully

J Neil Gibson

This was the American called the Gold King, who, having married a Brazilian woman, settled down in their Hampshire home at Thor Place, with Miss Dunbar as a governess for their two children.[63] The wife was shot in the brain and Miss Dunbar was accused of her murder. Eventually Holmes proved that it was suicide, intended to look like murder. As Holmes said to Watson: 'Whether Miss Dunbar was her rival in a physical or in a merely mental sense seems to have been equally unforgivable in her eyes. No doubt she blamed this innocent lady for all those harsh dealings and unkind words with which her husband tried to repel her too demonstrative affection. Her first resolution was to end her own life. Her second was to do it in such a way as to involve her victim in a fate which was worse than any sudden death could be.'

While Holmes was with Watson at Cambridge, he received the following letter after breakfast:

Sir,

I can assure you that you are wasting your time in dogging my movements. I have, as you discovered last night, a window at the back of my brougham, and if you desire a twenty-mile ride which will lead you to the spot from which you started, you have only to follow me. Meanwhile, I can inform you that no spying upon me can in any way help Mr Godfrey Staunton, and I am convinced that the best service you can do to that gentleman is to return at once to London and to report to your employer that you are un-able to trace him. Your time in Cambridge will certainly be wasted.

Yours faithfully,

---

[63]Mr Everard King married a Brazilian woman in ACD, 'The Story of the Brazilian Cat', *Strand Magazine*, 1898.

But the letter only excited Holmes' curiosity. Cyril Overton of Trinity College, had implored the detective's help in finding his rugby player, Godfrey Staunton and Holmes meant to find him. With the help of Jeremy Dixon's dog, Pompey, who followed the aniseed scent, Holmes and Watson were eventually taken to the hideout of the missing three-quarter.

It was on 3 September 1902, while in the Turkish bath in Northumberland Avenue, that Holmes showed the following letter, written the day before, to Watson. It was addressed from the Carlton Club:

> Sir James Damery presents his compliments to Mr Sherlock Holmes and will call upon him at 4.30 to-morrow. Sir James begs to say that the matter upon which he desires to consult Mr Holmes is very delicate, and also very important. He trusts, therefore, that Mr Holmes will make every effort to grant him this interview, and that he will confirm it over the telephone to the Carlton Club.

The 'matter' concerned the marriage of General de Merville's daughter, Violet, to a known murderer, one Baron Gruner; the father disapproved and feared that his headstrong daughter would have her own way. Luckily Holmes secured the 'love or lust book' of the baron and with Kitty Winter's vitriol attack, the marriage did not take place.

Vampires in Transylvania, with stakes driven through the heart of the corpse, perhaps, but not surely in everyday England! But nevertheless, such was the bombshell received by Holmes. It was dated 19 November, from 46 Old Jewry. 'Re Vampires' it said:

> Sir,
>
> Our client, Mr Robert Ferguson, of Ferguson and Muirhead, tea-brokers, of Mincing Lane, has made some inquiry from us in a communication of even date concerning vampires. As our firm specialises entirely upon the assessment of machinery the matter hardly comes within our purview, and we have therefore recommended Mr Ferguson to call upon you and lay the matter before

you. We have not forgotten your successful action in the case of Matilda Briggs.

We are, sir,

faithfully yours,

Morrison, Morrison and Dodd per E JC

The letter from Robert Ferguson came in the same post. He gave as his only personal introduction that he knew Watson as a former rugby player; it was a very long letter. After Ferguson had called at Baker Street, Holmes decided to investigate the mystery at Cheeseman's, Lamberley, in Sussex. The Peruvian wife had been found leaning over her baby, apparently biting his neck and sucking his blood, an act alien to her sweet and gentle disposition. Holmes was able to show that it was actually the mother's affection for her child that caused her to suck out the poison from a South American arrow, a wound caused by her jealous stepson Jack.

Holmes then replied by letter to the solicitor's letter on 21 November:

Sir,

Referring to your letter of the 19th, I beg to state that I have looked into the inquiry of your client, Mr Robert Ferguson, of Ferguson and Muirhead, tea brokers, of Mincing Lane, and that the matter has been brought to a satisfactory conclusion. With thanks for your recommendation, I am, sir, faithfully yours,

Sherlock Holmes

(I wonder why Holmes did not send a telegram, which he preferred to writing a letter!)

Sherlock Holmes' Newspaper Advertisements.

When Holmes wanted an advertisement to appear in every London evening newspaper, he would usually send it by telegram, which would be attended to by Watson or Billy the pageboy. As Holmes observed: 'The Press, Watson, is a most valuable institution, if you only know how to use it.' The newspapers included the *Globe*, *Star*, *Pall Mall Gazette*, *St James*, *Evening News*, *Echo* and apparently there were others.

With reference to the Norwood tragedy, he placed the following in the *Standard*:

LOST – WHEREAS MORDECAI SMITH, BOATMAN, AND HIS SON JIM, LEFT SMITH'S WHARF AT OR ABOUT THREE O'CLOCK LAST TUESDAY MORNING IN THE STEAM LAUNCH *AURORA*,[64] BLACK WITH TWO RED STRIPES, FUNNEL BLACK WITH A WHITE BAND, THE SUM OF FIVE POUNDS WILL BE PAID TO ANYONE WHO CAN GIVE INFORMATION TO MRS SMITH, AT SMITH'S WHARF, OR AT 221B, BAKER STREET, AS TO THE WHEREABOUTS OF THE SAID MORDECAI SMITH AND THE LAUNCH *AURORA*.

There was no reply to Baker Street, so that Holmes was left to his own methods of capturing the launch and Jonathan Small.

After Peterson the commissionaire had found the Countess of Morcar's blue carbuncle in his Christmas goose, Holmes placed the following advertisement in all the evening papers:

FOUND AT THE CORNER OF GOODGE STREET, A GOOSE AND A BLACK FELT HAT. MR HENRY BAKER CAN HAVE THE SAME BY APPLYING AT 6.30 THIS EVENING AT 221B, BAKER STREET.

This time, Holmes got Peterson to run down to the advertising agency to see to the insertion. Mr Baker subsequently arrived at Baker Street, but was quite certain that he knew nothing concerning the carbuncle. He did give Holmes useful information concerning his goose – he purchased it through a goose club run by Mr Windigate of the Alpha Inn, near the British Museum, which led Holmes upon the right scent, and to the capture of the thief, James Ryder, head attendant at the Hotel Cosmopolitan.

After Tobias Gregson informed Holmes of the murder of Enoch Drebber at Brixton, and of a woman's gold wedding ring being found under his body, Holmes inserted the following advertisement in the 'Found' column of every evening newspaper:

IN THE BRIXTON ROAD, THIS MORNING, A PLAIN GOLD WEDDING

---

[64]Anson Stone, first Lieutenant on the *Aurora* frigate, engaged in cutting off supplies from Genoa. ACD, *Rodney Stone*.

RING, FOUND IN THE ROADWAY BETWEEN THE WHITE HART TAVERN AND HOLLAND GROVE. APPLY DR WATSON, 221B, BAKER STREET, BETWEEN EIGHT AND NINE THIS EVENING.

By this, Holmes had hoped to catch the suspected man in the brown coat, who wore coarse, square-toed boots: he did not expect to be outwitted by the visitor who called in reply to the advertisement.

When Holmes advertised in the London daily newspapers he chose *The Daily Telegraph*. There was the time when he wished to pose as 'Pierrot', the man who inserted four successive advertisements in the agony column of the *Daily Telegraph* appearing on the right-hand top corner of a page. So Holmes and Watson drove round to the offices of the *Daily Telegraph* and put in the following advertisement:

TO-NIGHT. SAME HOUR. SAME PLACE. TWO TAPS. MOST VITALLY IMPORTANT. YOUR OWN SAFETY AT STAKE.

Holmes had cunningly used the code conned from the previous advertisements. Holmes had his reply in the shape of Colonel Valentine Walter, with the soft, handsome, delicate features, and the long light beard, at the house in Caulfield Gardens; he it was who had stolen ten of the thirty Bruce-Partington submarine plans, but it was Oberstein who killed Cadogan West with his short life preserver.

Meals at Baker Street and Other Places

So many of the humdrum everyday events go unrecorded, and insufficiently so, like the meals that were eaten at Baker Street.

Holmes appreciated the value of exercise before breakfast to provide an excellent appetite, which was the ideal situation, but one which it was not always possible to execute. So often his breakfast went untasted because of the nature of a telegram or letter which he had just received. If an early start to the day was called for, before the usual breakfast time, then Holmes and Watson would breakfast later on, upon their journey.

Such an occasion, (one of many) took place after the death of

Willoughby Smith at Yoxley Old Place, seven miles from Chatham in Kent.[65] Following a request from Inspector Hopkins, the three of them were away early, after Holmes had provided coffee made on his spirit lamp. After a long and weary journey, they alighted at a small station some miles from Chatham. While a horse was being put into a trap at the local inn, they snatched a hurried breakfast.

Holmes was known to say, 'We shall order breakfast.' Did he mean that he would press the bell to let Mrs Hudson know that they were ready, or were they allowed to choose what to have?

Watson did mention breakfast tea, or coffee in a well polished silver-plated coffee pot (the first poured by Watson, the latter by Holmes). There might be curried chicken, or ham and eggs and toast; or eggs might be boiled, scrambled, or fried with bacon. Holmes was certainly fond of eggs, for he was known to have devoured four of them for breakfast while staying with Watson in a double-bedded room at the Westville Arms, Birlstone. Did Watson drink cocoa at Baker Street? He certainly did while at Mackleton and seemingly Holmes was also not averse to this beverage. Holmes would conclude his breakfast with a cigarette, during which time Watson made a special point of never arguing with him, knowing how this unsettled him.[66]

Holmes and Watson did not always breakfast alone, for they often had company, which extra work does not appear to have inconvenienced Mrs Hudson.

There was one rather special breakfast partaken with Percy Phelps after Holmes had retrieved the naval treaty. Mrs Hudson brought in the tea and coffee and the breakfast under three separate covers. Holmes uncovered a dish of curried chicken:

'Mrs Hudson has risen to the occasion. Her cuisine is a little limited… but she has as good an idea of breakfast as a Scotch woman.'

Watson uncovered ham and eggs. 'What are you going to take, Mr Phelps – curried fowl or eggs, or will you help yourself?'

---

[65]Smith. ACD used the name again: Culverton, Violet, Mordecai, Smith's Wharf, and Abercrombie Smith in *Lot 249*.
[66]In the film of *The Creeping Man*, ITV, 28 March 1991, Holmes stubbed out his cigarette, but not in the ashtray.

asked Holmes. 'Thank you. I can eat nothing,' replied Phelps. 'Oh come! Try the dish before you.' 'Thank you I would really rather not.' 'Well, then, said Holmes with a mischievous twinkle, 'I suppose that you have no objection to helping me?'

As he raised the cover, he uttered a terrible scream, for there in the dish, lay the little cylinder of blue-grey paper. As Watson recorded: 'He caught it up, devoured it with his eyes, and then danced madly about the room, pressing it to his bosom and shrieking out in his delight. Then he fell back into an armchair, so limp and exhausted with his own emotions that we had to pour brandy down his throat to keep him from fainting.'

This may have appealed to Holmes' sense of the dramatic, but the shock to Phelps could well have been fatal; luckily it was not. Both the honour of Phelps and Holmes was saved, for he never liked to fail: it was his business to know things. (I wonder if Holmes, as the lodger, asked Mrs Hudson's permission to invite an extra guest to breakfast and how much he was charged – no comment from Watson!)

Luncheon must often have been an erratic meal, according to Holmes' movements. It might have been at a railway buffet, or a hasty meal in a restaurant, with the cruet stand used as a prop for Holmes' newspaper. If the meat was beef, then Holmes liked a glass of beer. Sometimes a bottle of Beaune for luncheon; sometimes a bottle of Montrachet with a cold partridge. One blazing hot day in August, after Holmes and Watson had visited Miss Sarah Cushing at New Street, Wallington, they partook of a pleasant little meal of an hour's duration in that Surrey village, washed down by a bottle of claret. (Holmes was very fond of this wine at home, particularly with a biscuit, and it was a biscuit mixed with milk that at one time revived Dr Thorneycroft, of the Priory School, Mackleton, after his fatiguing journey.)

In October 1890 Watson recorded that they had a luncheon of a sandwich and a cup of coffee, before they went to hear the afternoon recital of the violin virtuoso, Signor Pablo Sarasate, at the St James' Hall. 'I observe', said Holmes, 'that there is a good deal of German music on the programme, which is rather more to my taste than Italian or French. It is introspective, and I want to introspect. Come along!' All the afternoon, Holmes sat with

Watson in the stalls perfectly happy, gently waving his long nervous, thin-fingered hands in time to the music, while his gently smiling face and his languid, dreamy eyes were 'as unlike Holmes, the sleuth hound, Holmes the relentless, keen-witted, ready-handed criminal agent as it was possible to conceive.'

Holmes was also fond of going to hear Norman Neruda of whom he said; 'Her attack and her bowing are splendid. What's that little thing of Chopin's she plays so magnificently: Tra-la-la-lira-lay.' Holmes was certainly in a good position himself to appreciate such artistry. Before he went to Hallé's afternoon concert, he would snatch a quick lunch somewhere. Holmes would return to Baker Street in sparkling mood and greet Watson with another facet of his wide knowledge. 'Do you remember what Darwin said about music? He claims that the power of producing and appreciating it existed among the human race long before the power of speech was arrived at.'

When possible, they dined at home at seven in the evening, unless urgent business took them away from Baker Street, so that their meal had to be taken later. Mrs Hudson's food was good, but somewhat unenterprising, so that it would seem Holmes was apt to embellish the standard cooking with ideas of his own. A favourite dish, when in season was woodcock.

Now and again, Holmes would play housekeeper, an unusual asset to his other merits, and one which he thought Watson did not fully appreciate. Such a time happened when Holmes entertained Athelney Jones of Scotland Yard with oysters, a brace of grouse, a choice white wine followed by a glass of port to drink success to their proposed expedition upon the Thames, in a police boat.

Another occasion arose when Holmes ordered and paid for, from a confectioner's man, food for an evening meal for five people, including Lord Robert Walsingham de Vere St Simon, and the Americans Mr and Mrs Francis Hay Moulton, from McQuire's Camp in the Rockies. The food arrived in a very large flat box, 'a quite epicurean little cold supper,' consisting of a couple of brace of cold woodcock, a pheasant, a pâté de foie gras pie, with a 'group of ancient and cobwebby bottles.' His Lordship was somewhat taken aback at the assembled company, and showed his offended dignity, for he was bitterly hurt. Holmes had hoped that he would have stayed, and partaken of a friendly supper, but this was too much for his Lordship, to be expected to sit down with the girl found to be already married and therefore not his lawful wife, so making a wide sweeping bow, he stalked out of the room.

But if something special arose, like a concert, a Wagner night at Covent Garden, or Carina singing at the Albert Hall, then Holmes and Watson would don their dress clothes, sally forth and dine at Marcini's or Simpson's in the Strand, sitting at a small front window table watching the rushing stream of life go by outside.

After some weeks away at Baskerville Hall, and returning to London, they felt that they both needed to relax, and so they went to hear the De Reszkes in *Les Huguenots*, (Holmes having a box), and dined at Marcini's on the way.

They were known also to have dined at Goldini's garish Italian restaurant in Gloucester Road, Kensington, where the meal might finish with a coffee and a curaçao, perhaps with one of the proprietor's cigars, which were less poisonous than one would have expected. They were still patronising these London restaurants as late as 1902.

Watson recorded a visit to him from Holmes when he refused the kind offer of food, saying that he had partaken of supper at Waterloo Station.

Later on at Baker Street, a new cook was employed – Holmes was not impressed by the cooking of his eggs. When Watson came down to breakfast, Holmes said that he would discuss a letter from J Neil Gibson, the Gold King, after Watson had 'consumed the two hard-boiled eggs with which our new cook has favoured us. Their condition may not be unconnected with the copy of the *Family Herald*, which I observed yesterday upon the hall-table. Even so trivial a matter as cooking an egg demands an attention which is conscious of the passage of time and incompatible with the love romance in that excellent periodical.'

Holmes would appear to have started his Index of Crime and Criminals early in his life, for his records certainly went back as far as the case of Jansen in Utrecht in 1834, some twenty years before his birth; he mentioned also the Worthingdon bank robbers of 1875 and the Andover case of 1877. Yet it was only once in every year or so that he would master sufficient energy to docket and arrange his material and, as neatly tied bundles, place them into his chest in his bedroom, and so his index increased accordingly.

Thus his papers were allowed to accumulate, until every corner of the room was stacked with bundles of manuscripts, which were on no account to be touched, let alone burnt; but they did make the room untidy and uninhabitable, so much so that Watson came to refer to their little sitting room, as being an untidy one.

No wonder that the musty smell of papers and continual heavy smoking ate up the oxygen in the room, which caused Watson, when he was permitted, to open the windows for some fresh air. Holmes never approved of open windows: 'It is a singular thing, but I find that a concentrated atmosphere helps a concentration of thought. I have not pushed it to the length of getting into a box to think, but that is the logical outcome of my conviction.'

As the years passed by, the shelves became full of books of reference, scrapbooks, ponderous commonplace books into which Holmes pasted the agony columns from the daily newspapers – an index concerning men and things which furnished him with information at a moment's notice. He kept a separate index list of his own cases.

There was a bulky world geographical dictionary newly published, to which were added succeeding volumes as they were published; a Continental Gazetteer, an American encyclopaedia – a heavy brown volume – a red covered volume of the English nobility, a *Bradshaw*[67] for train times (Watson's department), his own Index of Biographies, a yellow-covered volume of *Whitaker's Almanac*, some 'black-letter editions' and Watson's Medical Directory. I wonder if Watson added to his collection the three books that Holmes gave him, namely, *British Birds*, *The Holy War*[68]

---

[67]George Bradshaw, 1801–1853. Engraver and Printer, originator of the *Railway Timetables*, 1839, which developed into *Bradshaw's Monthly Railway Guide* of 1841–1961.

[68]John Bunyan, *The Holy War*.

and poems by Catullus.[69]

For 1894 alone there were three massive manuscript volumes. The dispatch cases, filled with documents, would have been a perfect hunting ground for the student, not only of crime, but of the social and official scandals of the late Victorian era. Some cases were so delicate in their content that several attempts by burglars were made, in order to secure and destroy these papers, luckily without success. In 1891 they even resorted to fire, but little damage was done. Watson, in his choice of publication, never abused Holmes' confidence in him, and so the delicate cases remained unpublished.

Oft-times Holmes, searching for information from many sources, would sit upon the floor with all his material around him and could become so excited in his work that he would not rise, but sat like some strange Buddha with crossed legs, one book upon his knees, checking with his long thin forefinger the points of interest upon the palm of his left hand.

Mycroft Holmes

Holmes had a great respect for his elder brother Mycroft. He remarked to Watson: 'When I say, therefore, that Mycroft, [Holmes called his brother either Mycroft or my dear Mycroft], has better powers of observation than I, you may take it that I am speaking the exact and literal truth.' Watson wondered how it was that Mycroft was not publicly known, he having such singular powers. Holmes laughed at the thought that it was his modesty which made him acknowledge Mycroft as his superior. 'My dear Watson,' he said, 'I cannot agree which those who rank modesty among the virtues. To the logician, all things should be seen exactly as they are, and to underestimate one's self is as much a departure from truth as to exaggerate one's own powers.' This, said Holmes was not conceit, for logic was rare, and guessing a shocking habit.

Holmes explained to Watson, Mycroft's unique position:

He has made it for himself. There has never been anything like it

---

[69] Gaius Valerius Catullus, the bisexual lyrical poet of ancient Rome.

before, nor will be again. He has the tidiest and most orderly brain, with the greatest capacity for storing facts, of any man living. The same great powers which I have turned to the detection of crime he has used for this particular business. The conclusions of every department are passed to him, and he is the central exchange, the clearing-house, which makes out the balance. All other men are specialists, but his specialism is omniscience. We will suppose that a minister needs information as to a point which involves the Navy, India, Canada and the bimetallic question; he could get his separate advices from various departments upon each, but only Mycroft can focus them all, and say offhand how each factor would affect the other. They began by using him as a short-cut, a convenience; now he has made himself an essential. In that great brain of his everything is pigeon-holed and can be handed out in an instant. Again and again his word has decided the national policy. He lives in it. He thinks of nothing else save when, as an intellectual exercise, he unbends if I call upon him and ask him to advise me on one of my little problems.

Whereas Mycroft's problems were international, he referred to Sherlock's detective work as 'petty puzzles of the police-court'.

Mycroft Holmes was a tall, portly, heavily built and massive man with a suggestion of uncouth physical inertia in him; a gross body with a dominant mind. He had a masterful browed head, firm lips, alert, deep-set, light watery grey eyes, with that faraway introspective look of the thinker. His hands were broad and flat, like the flippers of a seal; his face retained something of the sharpness of expression, which was so remarkable in Sherlock's. He was addicted to snuff, which he took from a tortoise-shell box, and brushed away any surplus grains upon his coat with a large red silk handkerchief.

He could have been the world's greatest criminologist, but he lacked ambition and energy; his explanations were always proved to be right, yet he was absolutely incapable of working out the practical points which needed to be considered before a court case. Observation and deduction were only a hobby to him. As Mycroft observed to his brother: 'Give me your details, and from an armchair I will return you an excellent expert opinion. But to run here and run there, to cross-question railway guards, and lie on my face with a lens to my eye – it is not my métier.' He left the solving of a case to Sherlock; he would tell Sherlock to act! To use his powers, go to the scene of the crime, see the people concerned, and to leave no stone unturned.

The only exercise that Mycroft took was to walk from his Pall Mall lodgings, round the corner into Whitehall and back again. For Mycroft to deviate from his usual daily route and call at Baker Street was 'as if you met a tram-car coming down a country lane', said Sherlock. 'Mycroft has his rails and he runs on them... A planet might as well leave its orbit.'

Mycroft had no ambition, remaining always a subordinate, receiving neither honour nor title. In consequence, his salary was a paltry four hundred and fifty pounds per annum; he had an extraordinary faculty for figures, and audited the books in some of the government departments; yet he remained the most indispensable man in the country; in fact he really was the British Government.

He was a founder member of the Diogenes Club, which was opposite his rooms, some little distance from the Carlton, where he went at a quarter to five and stayed until seven forty; he was one of the queerest members of this queer club, which contained the 'most unsociable and unclubable men' in London, no member taking any notice of the others. Only in the Stranger's Room was talking allowed. Here it was that Sherlock found the atmosphere 'very soothing'.

As far as is known, Mycroft only visited Sherlock three times at Baker Street (by hansom cab) upon matters of the utmost importance to the State; the matter had to be of paramount importance to make Mycroft deviate from his routine life – as he said, 'You don't expect such energy from me, do you, Sherlock?' These were some of Sherlock's most interesting cases. The first time, Mycroft wished to confer over the case of the Greek interpreter; the other times in 1895, when he wished to discuss the death of Arthur Cadogan West, an unmarried clerk at Woolwich Arsenal, concerned with the theft of the Bruce-Partington submarine plans. But he did warn Holmes, by telegram, that he was coming to see him.

Once, Mycroft, not being able to leave his office, and wishing to divulge some information quickly, sent a government messenger post-haste to Baker Street with a note upon the aforementioned submarine plans; in it he gave valuable information concerning three of the most likely suspects.

How many times did Sherlock visit Mycroft? He certainly visited in April 1891, travelling by cab, after he had been attacked by Moriarty's minions in Welbeck Street and Vere Street; there he spent the day in safety.

Mycroft and Sherlock (they always used first names when addressing each other) had a very close understanding between them; Mycroft said that his brother had all the energy of the family. When Sherlock went abroad to escape the attacks of Moriarty, he made Mycroft his sole confidant – he was the only person who knew that his brother was alive; he provided Sherlock with money, and preserved his rooms and papers at Baker Street in apple-pie order. (Unhappy, good-hearted Watson had to presume that Sherlock died at the Reichenbach Falls for security reasons.)

Mycroft was particularly well informed upon calligraphy. Having inserted the following advertisement in the *Daily News* – 'Anybody supplying any information as to the whereabouts of a Greek gentleman named Paul Kratides, from Athens, who is unable to speak English, will be rewarded. A similar reward paid to anyone giving information about a Greek lady, whose first name is Sophy. X 2473' – he received a reply from J Davenport of Lower Brixton:

> In answer to your advertisement of to-day's date, I beg to inform you that I know the young lady in question very well. If you should care to call upon me, I could give you some particulars as to her painful history. She is living at present at The Myrtles, Beckenham.

It was, observed Mycroft: 'Written with a J pen on royal cream paper by a middle-aged man with a weak constitution.'

Only once in his life was Mycroft known to have resorted to disguise, and that was as a coachman, dressed in a heavy black cloak, tipped at the collar with red, when he drove Watson (he did not recognising his cabby) in a brougham to Victoria Station in order to try and elude Moriarty, Sherlock arriving by a different route.[70]

Sherlock Holmes' Private Police Force

Holmes referred to himself and Watson as the 'Irregulars', as opposed to the regular police force. A fond quotation of Holmes was 'Thrice is he armed who hath his quarrel just', which might well have been his own personal motto.[71]

Clever as Holmes was at disguise, there were times when even he could not journey into certain areas, where he might be known by an undesirable of the criminal world. So Holmes banded together a troop of urchins, whom he called his Baker Street Irregulars, his own private 'police force'. They comprised between six and twelve of the dirtiest, barefooted and most ragged street Arabs that it was possible to find in London; they were able to infiltrate into some of the most unsavoury places, and, fitting into the background of squalor, could wander around unobserved, whereas Holmes' presence would have stuck out like a sore thumb. Watson first met these boys while he was discussing with Holmes the murder of the American, Enoch Drebber. There was the 'pattering of many steps in the hall and on the stairs, accompanied by audible expressions of disgust upon the part of our landlady', and six of these urchins rushed into the room, to be called to attention by Holmes in a sharp voice, as they formed a line of 'disreputable statuettes'. Such was the unruly entry of the boys that Holmes told Wiggins, his dirty little lieutenant, to report alone, and leave his cronies in the street. 'There's more work to be got out of one of those little beggars than out of a dozen of the force,' remarked Holmes. 'The mere sight of an official-looking person seals men's lips... They are as sharp as needles, too; all they want is organisation.' Their pay was one shilling each, even if their report was negative. Once they were reimbursed three shillings and sixpence. Sometimes Holmes communicated with Wiggins by telegram – hopefully he was able to read! Later one of

---

[70]A one horse closed carriage named after Lord Brougham, 1778–1868.
[71]William Shakespeare, *Henry VI Part II*, III. ii. Henry Wheeler Shaw (American essayist, 1818–1885) added in *Josh Billings*, 'But four times he who gets his blow in fust.'

the boys earned an extra guinea by waving his handkerchief as a sign of having located the *Aurora*; surely the boy must have stolen this handkerchief from some kindly old gentleman, as if he were a Fagin employee. The next time these boys came to Baker Street there were twelve of them, and they still ignored the guv'nor's warning for only one to report.

If any one of these street urchins could be of particular help to Holmes, then apparently distance was no object, for in early 1888 Holmes employed 'Irregular' Simpson to act as a scout in Aldershot. (Watson never recorded how much Holmes paid the boy for this lengthy trip.) There Holmes was investigating the presumed murder of Colonel Barclay, of the Royal Munsters, and wished to interview Henry Wood, (late corporal in the 117th Foot, in India), living in Hudson Street – 'a short thoroughfare lined with plain two-storied brick houses'. In order to ensure that Wood was in his house, Holmes posted Simpson to mount guard and to follow the man wherever he went, for the boy would stick to a man like a burr. 'He's in all right, Mr Holmes,' he said, and Holmes patted him on the head with a congratulatory hand. Holmes sent in his card, saying he had come upon important business, and was admitted to see Wood.

Use of Dogs in Detection

It was while Holmes was involved in the case of the murder of Bartholomew Sholto that he confided to Watson his preference for using a dog, instead of members of the police force, in tracking down his quarry.

He asked Watson to go to No. 3 Pinchin Lane, down near the water's edge at Lambeth. It was the third house on the right-hand side, the home of Sherman, the bird stuffer, whose sign of business was indicated in the window by a weasel holding a young rabbit. Watson was told to knock the owner up (a 'lanky, lean old man, with stooping shoulders, a stringy neck, and blue-tinted glasses'), give him Holmes' compliments (for a friend of Mr Sherlock was always welcome), ask for Toby and bring him back in the cab to Pondicherry Lodge. Said Watson: 'A dog, I suppose.' 'Yes, a queer mongrel with a most amazing power of scent. I would rather have Toby's help than that of the whole detective force of London.'

Inside the house, by the uncertain, shadowy candlelight, Watson found Toby, No. 7 on the left-hand side, among the most queer animal family which he had ever seen. Toby was an 'ugly, long-haired, lop-eared creature, half-spaniel and half lurcher,[72] brown and white in colour, with a very clumsy gait.' Watson sealed the dog's friendship with a lump of sugar and took him back to Holmes at Norwood,[73] just as the palace clock struck three in the morning.

As the east gradually whitened, in the cold, grey morning light, Holmes and Watson set off on their journey with Toby, having made him smell the creosote handkerchief as he stood with his 'fluffy legs separated, and with a most comical cock to its head, like a connoisseur sniffing the bouquet of a famous vintage. Holmes then threw the handkerchief to a distance, fastened a stout cord to the mongrel's collar, and led him to the foot of the water-barrel. The creature instantly broke into a succession of high, tremulous yelps and, with his nose to the ground and his tail in the air, pattered off upon the trail at a pace which strained his leash and kept us at the top of our speed.'

Toby followed the creosote trail, and led Holmes and Watson upon a six-mile trudge to the Thames near Broad Street, close upon the heels of Jonathan Small.

Holmes introduced Watson to another dog – 'a detective who is a very eminent specialist in the work that lies before us'. This was Pompey, a 'squat, lop-eared, white-and-tan dog, something between a beagle and a foxhound', one trained to follow the hunt, 'the pride of the local draghounds – no very great flier... but a staunch hound on a scent', and fast enough no doubt for a 'couple of middle-aged London gentlemen'. This took place at Cambridge, in February, where Holmes and Watson had journeyed in order to help Cyril Overton find his friend Godfrey Staunton. In order to do this, Holmes needed to follow the brougham of Dr Leslie Armstrong (pulled by a pair of grey

---

[72]Dog with a distinct cross of greyhound.
[73]Professor Andreas lived in a small villa in Upper Norwood. ACD, *Story of the Jew's Breast-plate.*

horses), hoping to be led to the object of his search. Having failed in his mission previously, Holmes chose the ultimate in detection; he filled his tiny hypodermic syringe with aniseed[74] – Watson at first was horrified, thinking it the instrument of evil – but Holmes reassured him, saying that he hoped that it would be the key to unlock the mystery and, although only a threadbare and venerable device, useful upon occasion. He shot the aniseed over the hind wheel of Armstrong's carriage. 'A draghound', said Holmes, 'will follow aniseed from here to John o' Groats', providing that the trail did not lead through water. A leather leash was fastened to the dog's collar, who then 'sniffed round for an instant, and then with a shrill whine of excitement started off down the street, tugging at his leash in his efforts to go faster. In half an hour, we were clear of the town and hastening down a country road.' The dog followed the aniseed trail, which eventually led to a cottage in a field where Godfrey Staunton's wife of only a year lay dead from a most virulent form of consumption, bewailed by her distraught husband.

Members of the Police Force

When Holmes thought it necessary to communicate with the police (before the installation of the telephone), he would do so by the very efficient telegram service. While Holmes and Watson were away on the Continent keeping Moriarty at bay, Holmes telegraphed from Strasbourg in the morning to the London police, and received a reply in the evening to say that they had secured Moriarty's gang but not the leader.

Holmes knew very well that his powers went far above those of the London and county police. 'After all, it is a question of money with these fellows, and I have the British Treasury behind me. If it's on the market I'll buy it – if it means another penny on the income tax.' In a letter to Holmes, Mycroft, (with reference to the Bruce-Partington plans), wrote:

> The Cabinet awaits your final report with the utmost anxiety. Urgent representations have arrived from the very highest quar-

---

[74]The seed of anise, an umbelliferous plant used in making cordials.

ter. The whole force of the State is at your back if you should need it.

When Holmes was working upon the country's most secret affairs, he would get almost hourly reports from the government. (Surely Holmes could not have reached a higher pinnacle of fame!)

During Holmes' early years at Baker Street, before he gained world renown, he was apt to be only tolerated by the police inspectors, until they gradually came to realise his unique position among detectives. Although he at times took the law into his own hands as a private citizen, he was never a member of the police force and certainly never wished to be; for as he said, 'I am not in an official position, and there is no reason, so long as the ends of justice are served, why I should disclose all that I know.' It was his business to know what other people didn't know.

Holmes generally desired no accolade, no mention in the newspapers, he just listened to the general chorus of misplaced approbation; he only wished his name to be associated with crimes which presented some difficulty in their solution: he played the game for the game's sake. 'It is art for art's sake,' said Holmes to Watson.[75]

How puerile could the police become, thought Holmes, when they took no action after John Openshaw had received a death threat from the Ku Klux Klan, accompanied by five little dried orange pips. They assumed it to be a practical joke, and, apart from placing a policeman in the house, took no further interest. Holmes raved and clenched his hands in the air as he cried out, 'Incredible imbecility!'

Holmes never bothered to explain to his police friends the enigmatic clue, their intelligence was not really up to it. The case of the stolen racehorse, Silver Blaze, is a good example. John Straker, retired jockey and trainer of the horse for Colonel Ross, hoped to nobble the favourite, by a slight nick upon the tendons of the horse's ham, and to do it subcutaneously, so as to leave no trace. Luckily Holmes had grasped the significance of the silence of the dog, which gave him the clue that he wanted; the dog did

---

[75]'Art for Arts sake...' Benjamin Constant, 1804.

not bark in the night – which he would have done had the nocturnal visitor been a stranger. As Holmes observed: '...a dog was kept in the stables, and yet, though someone had been in and had fetched out a horse, he had not barked enough to arouse the two lads in the loft. Obviously the midnight visitor was someone the dog knew well.'

Holmes came to know most of the heads of the police force, and, as he said, he cleared up the mysteries which they had abandoned as hopeless, thus recognising him as the 'final court of appeal' in doubtful cases. Perhaps this helped to mitigate his crime of being a common burglar – for he had all the necessary tools – and should have found himself in the dock, but for the intervention of an illustrious client stepping in between him and the law. Power in the right quarter could cock a snook at the law.

He called himself 'an irregular pioneer who goes in front of the regular forces of the country', and one who could 'hush up that which others will be bound to publish'. Holmes was always willing to give the police the benefit of his deductions. 'My results are always very much at your service if you care to apply to me for them.'

Inspector Lestrade Holmes came to know very well, so that in time he dropped the 'inspector', and he in turn was called, first, 'Master Holmes' and then 'Holmes'. Watson called Lestrade 'the little professional'; presumably he had a first name, but it goes unrecorded, but began with a G. Holmes declared that Lestrade and Inspector Gregson, were the pick of a bad lot; quick and energetic, but conventional; they had their knives into each other and were as jealous as a pair of professional beauties'.

Perhaps it was Lestrade who gave Holmes his police whistle; the only other known receiver of such a whistle was Horace Harker, journalist of the Central Press Syndicate, of 131 Pitt Street, Kensington, a quiet little backwater; he had purchased cheaply a bust of Napoleon from Harding Brothers to place in his sitting room, and had it stolen and smashed into fragments in the front garden of an empty house in Campden House Road.

Lestrade was a thin, wiry, dapper, sallow, austere, little rat-faced or ferret-like man, with dark beady eyes. He was obtuse but resolute, lacked imagination, was usually out of his depth, was devoid of reason, but was tenacious as a bulldog; his left foot had an inward twist. His sense of smell was suspect – for he was unable to detect the smell of coffee in the brown paper wrapping round the yellow cardboard box sent to Miss Cushing of Croydon.

Lestrade wrote his notes in pencil shorthand and probably employed the new form of shorthand writing by Sir Isaac Pitman.[76] When he walked abroad upon a country case, he was known to wear a light brown dust coat and leather leggings; at other times, a pea-jacket[77] and cravat which gave him a nautical appearance; sometimes he carried a black canvas bag.

At first Lestrade, with many years' experience behind him, was apt to just tolerate the amateur detective, until, with closer association, he realised the vast chasm which existed between them in the profession of the detection of crime, and eventually acknowledged Holmes as his superior. For as Watson recorded: 'Lestrade had learned by more experiences than he would care to acknowledge, that that razor-like brain could cut through that which was impenetrable to him.'

The methods employed by Holmes and Lestrade were poles apart; as the former said to the inspector: 'You work your own method, and I shall work mine.' The case of the murder of Charles McCarthy by John Turner and how Holmes gradually built up all the evidence, which showed him the kind of person he was looking for, is a good example: following Lestrade's question as to who was the murderer, Holmes replied: 'He is a tall man, left-handed, limps with the right leg, wears thick-soled shooting boots and a grey cloak, smokes Indian cigars, uses a cigar-holder, and carries a blunt pen-knife in his pocket.' This provoked Lestrade's laughter: 'I am afraid that I am still a sceptic. Theories are all very well, but we have to deal with a hard-headed British jury... Who was the criminal, then?' Holmes told him that it was the gentleman he described, who would not be difficult to find being in a rather unpopulated neighbourhood. Lestrade

---

[76]Sir Isaac Pitman, 1813–1897. Learned shorthand system of Samuel Taylor. He published *Stenographic Sound Hand*, 1837, substituting phonographic for the mainly orthographic methods adopted by former shorthand authors.

[77]Ernest Lana wore a pea-jacket. ACD, *The Story of the Black Doctor*.

could see himself as being the laughing stock of Scotland Yard if he roamed about looking for a left-handed gentleman with a game leg, and refused to take advantage of Holmes' superior talents. Said Lestrade, 'I find it hard enough to tackle facts, Holmes, without flying after theories and fancies.' 'You are right,' replied Holmes demurely, 'You do find it very hard to tackle facts.' It is little wonder, therefore, that Holmes sometimes called the inspector, 'imbecile'.

If Lestrade could puzzle the famous expert, he would chuckle with delight, for such an opportunity was rare. The inspector had his chance at the residence of Eduardo Lucas, 16 Godolphin Street, Westminster. A great deal of blood had stained the carpet right through, but on taking hold of the corner of the carpet and turning it over there was no corresponding stain on the white woodwork. Holmes was astounded that no mark was left; then Lestrade gloated as he turned over another portion of the carpet, to show a great crimson spill upon the square white facing of the old-fashioned floor. Holmes said that the explanation was simple enough. 'The two stains did correspond, but the carpet has been turned round. As it was square and unfastened, it was easily done.' This piqued the inspector: 'The official police don't need you, Mr Holmes, to tell them that the carpet must have been turned round. That's clear enough, for the stains lie above each other – if you lay it over this way.'

Nothing pleased Lestrade so much as if he were able to find an opportunity to score (he hoped) over Holmes. He even bothered to send a telegram from Norwood, so smug was he that he had his 'murderer':

IMPORTANT FRESH EVIDENCE TO HAND. MCFARLANE'S GUILT DEFINITELY ESTABLISHED. ADVISE YOU TO ABANDON CASE.

But Holmes never accepted this kind of police advice – he would either confirm or destroy a Lestrade theory, by means which Lestrade was quite incapable of employing or even of understanding. Lucky for Lestrade that Holmes' deductions led him to a far different conclusion, and that an innocent man did not hang – otherwise his police reputation would have been ruined. Holmes suggested a few changes in the police report, thus enhancing Lestrade's reputation, for no one threw dust in the eyes of Inspector Lestrade with impunity; his overbearing manner gave way to that of a child before his teacher as Holmes explained the facts of the case but desired no publicity. For he only chose to be associated with those crimes which presented some difficulty in their solution, so only rarely did his name appear in connection with crime.

The maddening insolent days of yesteryear receded when Lestrade would say: 'Yes, some of us are a little too much inclined to be cock-sure, Mr Holmes', which Holmes countered in a scathing and dictatorial way: 'What, you see nothing remarkable? Well, well, let it pass. Perhaps when a man has special knowledge and special powers like my own, it rather encourages him to seek a complex explanation, when a simple one is at hand.' And then Holmes would tap his forehead three times and shake his head solemnly.

Another instance of Holmes' dictatorial attitude towards Lestrade happened at 16 Godolphin Street, the eighteenth century residence of the murdered man, Eduardo Lucas:

'Look here, Lestrade,' said he, 'has that constable in the passage been in charge of the place all the time?'

'Yes, he has.'

'Well, take my advice. Examine him carefully. Don't do it before us. We'll wait here. You take him into the back room. You'll be more likely to get a confession out of him alone. Ask him how he dared to admit people and leave them alone in this room. Don't ask him if he has done it. Take it for granted. Tell him you know someone has been here. Press him. Tell him that a full confession is his only chance of forgiveness. Do exactly what I tell you!'

Once Lestrade suggested that Alexander Holder of the banking firm of Holder & Stevenson, of Threadneedle Street, should consult Sherlock Holmes over the loss of a gold corner, with three beryls, of the Beryl Coronet, belonging to one of the highest, noblest, most exalted names in England; the mystery was beyond the understanding of the police mind, so he had bowed to the superior brain of Holmes.

Over the Lord Simon affair, Lestrade had mentioned that he had no objection to Mr Holmes' co-operation, since he himself could see no light in the darkness that surrounded the sudden disappearance of the newly married Lady Simon.

Lestrade certainly bowed to Holmes, when it came to burglary: 'We can't do these things in the Force, Mr Holmes. No wonder you get results that are beyond us.'

Among the notes sent to Holmes from Lestrade was the following, concerning the two human ears sent to Miss Cushing:

> I think that this case is very much in your line. We have every hope of clearing the matter up, but we find a little difficulty in getting anything to work upon. We have of course, wired to the Belfast post-office, but a large number of parcels were handed in upon that day, and they have no means of identifying this particular one, or of remembering the sender. The box is a half-pound box of honeydew tobacco and does not help us in anyway. The medical student theory still appears to me to be the most feasible, but if you should have a few hours to spare, I should be very happy to see you out here. I shall be either at the house or in the police-station all day.

Later, Lestrade arrested Jim Browner, who had murdered his wife, Mary Cushing, and her lover, Alec Fairbairn, (a 'dashing, swaggering chap, smart and curled', whose manner was 'more of the poop than the forecastle'), with a heavy oak stick, tied the bodies into their rowing boat, stove in a plank, and sank them in the sea at New Brighton. He then wrote the following letter – rather a long one for the inspector – to Holmes:

> My dear Mr Holmes,
>
> In accordance with the scheme which we had formed in order to test our theories... [Holmes was rather tickled by the use of the word 'we'] I went down to the Albert Dock yesterday at 6 p.m. and boarded the SS *May Day*, belonging to the Liverpool, Dublin, and London Steam Packet Company. On inquiry, I found that there was a steward on board of the name of James Browner and he had acted during the voyage in such an extraordinary manner that the captain had been compelled to relieve him

of his duties. On descending to his berth, I found him seated upon a chest with his head sunk upon his hands, rocking himself to and fro. He is a big, powerful chap, clean-shaven, and very swarthy – something like Aldridge, who helped us in the bogus laundry affair. He jumped up when he heard my business, and I had my whistle to my lips to call a couple of river police, who were round the corner, but he seemed to have no heart in him, and he held out his hands quietly enough for the darbies.[78] We brought him along to the cells, and his box as well, for we thought there might be something incriminating; but bar a big knife, such as most sailors have, we got nothing for our trouble. However, we find that we shall want no more evidence, for on being brought before the inspector at the station he asked leave to make a statement, which was, of course, taken down just as he made it, by our shorthand man. We had three copies typewritten, one of which I enclose. The affair proves, as I always thought it would, to be an extremely simple one, but I am obliged to you for assisting me in my investigation. With kind regards,

Yours very truly,

G Lestrade

(The inspector was still trying to belittle Holmes' help, although he knew it to be unjustified.)

Gradually, over the years, Lestrade mellowed in his approach to Holmes and showed himself more magnanimous. 'We're not jealous of you at Scotland Yard. No, sir, we are very proud of you, and if you come down to-morrow, there's not a man from the oldest inspector to the youngest constable, who wouldn't be glad to shake you by the hand.' Lestrade appreciated the master brain and would gaze at Holmes with reverence, for did not Holmes say that he was the last and highest court of appeal?

We are inclined to think that policemen, subjected as they are to all forms of violent crime in all its aspects, become, with time, hardened to any happening. But not Lestrade. Even after twenty years of police experience, hardened to the viciousness of criminals, he could still feel sick when he saw at Halliday's Private Hotel a little ribbon of blood, curling from under the door, 'which had meandered across the passage and formed a little pool

---

[78]Slang for hand-cuffs – personal name of Darby.

along the skirting at the other side'.

Inspector Tobias Gregson, Holmes also came to know very well, and he thought him the smartest of them all: quick and energetic, shockingly conventional, but unfortunately he lacked imagination. Tall, white-faced, with bulldog eyes, flaxen hair and fat hands, he was pompous, gallant and, within his limitations, a capable officer, always ready with a notebook in his hand. He was athletic – he ascended Holmes' staircase three steps at a time. He also used shorthand for his notes and smoked cigars. When Gregson was offered whisky and water he replied: 'I don't mind if I do… The tremendous exertions which I have gone through during the last day or two have worn me out. Not so much bodily exertion you understand, as the strain upon the mind. You will appreciate that, Mr Sherlock Holmes, for we are both brain-workers.' Holmes did not like being allied in any way with a member of the 'Yard', and if he was ever mistaken for a London detective, he was exceedingly annoyed. He replied gravely to the inspector: 'You do me too much honour.'

Gregson knew in the early days that Holmes was his superior and acknowledged this to Holmes, 'but he would cut his tongue out before he would own it to any other person.' 'I'll do you this justice, Mr Holmes, that I was never in a case yet that I didn't feel stronger for having you on my side.' He even called Holmes 'a smart man'. He admired the professional way in which Holmes opened a window catch in order to gain illegal entry into a house. 'It is a mercy that you are on the side of the Force, and not against it, Mr Holmes.'

The inspector might blunder in the matter of intelligence, but never in that of courage; while he was on the trail of the American murderer, Black Gorgiano of the Red Circle, with Mr Leverton of Pinkerton's American Agency, he climbed the stair of the Howe Street flat, in order to arrest him with the same absolutely quiet and businesslike bearing with which he would have ascended the official staircase of Scotland Yard; Leverton tried to precede him, but Gregson elbowed him back, for London dangers were the privilege of the London police, and not for a visiting American detective.

Both Gregson and Lestrade did not appreciate that Holmes'

smallest actions were all directed towards some definite and practical end, and when they both asked his opinion of the word 'Rache' in blood-red letters upon the wall of No. 3 Lauriston Gardens, he replied with a world of sarcasm: 'It would be robbing you of the credit of the case if I were to presume to help you... You are doing so well now that it would be a pity for anyone to interfere.' Holmes knew that the inspectors together would not get very far, for there was great rivalry between them. With great sarcasm in his voice, Holmes asked, 'If you will let me know how your investigations go, I shall be happy to give you any help I can.' His tongue must have been a little in his cheek, for he knew that Gregson referred to 'that fool Lestrade' and the feeling was no doubt mutual.

Inspector Gregory, although he lacked imagination, was rapidly making his name in the English detective service. Watson described him as a 'tall, fair man with lion-like hair and beard and curiously penetrating light blue eyes'; he sent a telegram to Holmes, inviting his co-operation in unravelling a murder and the mystery of the missing racehorse, Silver Blaze, at King's Pyland, Dartmoor: conversation through the whole of England had been dominated by this event. As Colonel Ross, the owner, said to Holmes, 'The inspector here has done all that could possibly be suggested, but I wish to leave no stone unturned...' Hence the call to Baker Street for help. When the inspector met Holmes at Tavistock Station, he apologised for his lack of progress in the case, for all his evidence was circumstantial. Here his comfortable open landau was waiting to take the four of them through the Devon countryside to a 'neat little red-brick villa with overhanging eaves which stood by the road', with the low curve of the moor behind.

The inspector showed Holmes a bag containing a boot of Straker, the retired jockey-trainer, and a shoe of Fitzroy Simpson the stable boy, and a cast horseshoe of Silver Blaze. 'My dear Inspector, you surpass yourself!' said Holmes. In a hollow on the moor, Holmes found a vital clue, a half-burned wax vesta, coated with mud, but only because he expected to find one. Gregory was annoyed with himself. 'I cannot think how I came to overlook it.' He also missed the significance of the three lame sheep, a 'singular epidemic'. Colonel Ross, having been somewhat cavalier to Holmes, had the tables turned upon him when Holmes disclosed the horse as the murderer of Straker.

Then there was Inspector MacDonald of Scotland Yard; a tall, bony figure, with a great cranium, deep-set lustrous eyes, and bushy eyebrows, who was exceptionally strong; a silent and precise man with a hard Aberdonian accent, and of a very dour nature. Although of a very good Scots upbringing, he had found that a book upon eclipses, lent to him by Professor Moriarty (whom he regarded as 'a very respectable, learned, and talented sort of man', whose hand upon the inspector's shoulder at parting, was 'like a father's blessing before you go out into the cold, cruel world'), had been a wee bit above his head. When Holmes told him that the delightful person of Moriarty – as surmised by the inspector – was really the master brain behind London's criminal world, the inspector really thought that he was joking. He smiled and his eyelid quivered as he glanced at Watson and said: 'I won't conceal from you, Mr Holmes, that we think in the CID that you have a wee bit of a bee in your bonnet over this professor.' MacDonald could recognise Moriarty's talent, but not his evilness.

In the early days, at the end of the 1880s, Holmes had helped MacDonald to attain success, accepting as his sole reward, the intellectual joy of the problems. So there arose within him affection for Holmes and he consulted him over all his difficulties; thus talent recognised genius – Holmes not being prone to friendship did not allow the association to go beyond his tolerance.

MacDonald was a practical man, not a theorist, and when Holmes congratulated him with all his heart upon his approach to detection work, he was very satisfied, although he did not take quite so happily to a suggestion from Holmes while at Birlstone Manor House that he should read a penny book which Holmes had purchased from the local tobacconist, which gave a short clear and interesting account of the old building, including the concealment of Charles I which became the vital clue to Holmes. MacDonald showed a little unusual temper as he considered Holmes to be making a fool of him. Replied Holmes, 'The interplay of ideas and the oblique uses of knowledge are often of extraordinary interest. You will excuse these remarks from one who, though a mere connoisseur of crime, is still rather older and perhaps more experienced than yourself.' This the inspector admitted heartily. 'You get to your point, I admit; but you have such a deuced round-the-corner way of doing it.' He also admitted that when it came to questioning a suspect, he preferred that the interrogation be carried out by Holmes, being 'in better hands'.

MacDonald, knowing his inferiority to Holmes, would seize any opportunity to score a point against him, as an example at the Birlstone Manor House showed. While being shown the open window which had been left open purposely for police examination, as it was found the previous night, Holmes observed that it was rather narrow for a man to pass. Here was the inspector's chance: 'Well, it wasn't a fat man anyhow. We don't need your deductions, Mr Holmes, to tell us that. But you or I could squeeze through all right.'

Perhaps this was the type of incident which brought out the dictator in Holmes, particularly towards a police inspector whom he considered to be on a lower intellectual level than himself and to whom he dictated a note:

'I want you to write a note to Mr Barker.'

'Well?'

'I'll dictate it, if you like. Ready? Dear Sir: It has struck me that it is our duty to drain the moat, in the hope that we may find sooner—'

'It's impossible,' said the inspector. 'I've made inquiry.'

'Tut, Tut! My dear sir, please do what I ask you.'

'Well, go on.'

'—in the hope that we may find something which may bear upon our investigation. I have made arrangements, and the workmen will be at work early to-morrow morning diverting the stream—'

'Impossible!'

'—diverting the stream; so I thought it best to explain matters beforehand.

'Now sign that, and send it by hand about four o'clock. At that hour we shall meet again in this room. Until then we may each do what we like; for I can assure you that this inquiry has come to a definite pause.'

Inspector Mortan of Scotland Yard was an old acquaintance of Holmes and yet Watson never published any case which involved this policeman. Watson did however record how he met Mortan outside the Baker Street house, as he waited for a cab in the dense London fog to take him to see Mr Culverton Smith of Lower Burke Street, a 'line of fine houses lying in the vague borderland between Notting Hill and Kensington'. He had to impress upon Smith the necessity of speed, in coming to Holmes before he died. Mortan, dressed in unofficial tweeds, suddenly materialised through the fog; he had heard rumours of Holmes' illness. 'How is Mr Holmes, sir?' he asked Watson and was told, 'He is very ill.' This, in all sincerity, for Watson really believed his friend to be near death's door, not appreciating that it was just another of Holmes' specialist acting parts to ensure that Smith believed the illness to be real. As Watson recorded: 'He looked at me in a most singular fashion. Had it not been too fiendish, I could have imagined that the gleam of the fanlight showed exultation in his face.' 'I heard some rumour of it,' said he. Watson was only too pleased to escape in the cab, thinking that perhaps some acute jealously still simmered over the years between the two men, and a chance encounter had brought it to a head.

Other inspectors known to Holmes were Merryvale and Lanner of Scotland Yard. The latter Holmes met at 403 Brook Street, where Dr Percy Trevelyan had been set up in practice by a Mr Blessington, who had been murdered by hanging – a cord tied to a hook from which the lamp usually hung. The smart-looking police inspector was just making notes in his pocketbook as Holmes and Watson arrived. His greeting was hearty: 'Ah, Mr Holmes, I am delighted to see you.' 'Good-morning Lanner, you won't think me an intruder, I am sure,' although he was called in by Dr Trevelyan. Asked if he had formed an opinion, the inspector told Holmes: 'As far as I can see, the man has been driven out of his senses by fright. The bed has been well slept in, you see. There's his impression, deep enough. It's about five in the morning, you know, that suicides are most common. That would be about his time for hanging himself. It seems to have been a very deliberate affair.' Holmes explained to Lanner, after collecting the evidence, that it was no suicide, but a deeply planned and cold-blooded murder; this he had deduced from signs so subtle and minute that, even when he had pointed them out, Lanner could scarcely follow his reasoning; he had overlooked the vital information which could be deduced from the four cigar ends.

Holmes solved the St Pancras case for Inspector Merryvale through the use of his microscope, detecting glue in the cap of the accused man.

Inspector Bradstreet of Bow Street, B division was well known to Holmes; he was a tall, stout official in a frogged jacket and a peaked cap who had been twenty-seven years in the Force.[79] When Holmes took out a very large bath-sponge from his Gladstone bag[80] at the Bow Street cells, it caused a chuckle from the inspector: 'He! he! You are a funny one.' Holmes asked Bradstreet to open the cell door where lay the sleeping prisoner, Hugh Boone. Then Holmes demonstrated his little bit of magic; first he dipped his sponge into the water jug and then vigorously rubbed twice across and down the prisoner's face. Like the bark from a tree, the face peeled off, the coarse brown tint disappeared; the scar disappeared and likewise the twisted lip. Beneath the tangled red hair was black hair and a smooth skinned face. It was none other than the missing man, Neville St Clair. All the astonished inspector could say was: 'Great Heavens! It is, indeed, the missing man. I know him from the photograph' But he really did not know what charge to prefer. But seemingly no crime had been committed, and the inspector, being of a magnanimous nature, decided that no further steps would be taken against him. Holmes admonished St Clair, saying that he should have trusted his wife, not leaving her to think that the worst had happened. The inspector had the last word – no more of Hugh Boone. Whether Holmes knew Inspector Barton, who was previously in charge of the case, is not clear.

---

[79]Ornamental stripes or workings of braid or lace on the breast of a coat.
[80]Travelling thick leather bag, named in honour of William Ewart Gladstone, 1809–1898, four times prime minister.

Inspector Stanley Hopkins was an exceedingly alert man, of eager youthful face, thirty years of age, who usually dressed in a quiet tweed suit, but still retained the erect bearing of one who was accustomed to the police uniform. Holmes rated him highly and knew that he was destined to make his mark in the criminal world; Hopkins gave Holmes his professional admiration and respect for his scientific methods, as a pupil to his master. Hopkins was known to have consulted Holmes at least seven times, and all the summons were found to be entirely justified; although Watson recorded the information given, he did not publish all the results.

In 1895 Holmes told the inspector that he was going to Norway, which journey, unfortunately, Watson never published. In the same year Holmes and Watson journeyed to Forest Row, Woodman's Lee, at the request of Hopkins, to investigate the murder of Captain Peter Carey who had been a most daring and successful seal and whale fisher with his steam sealer, the *Sea Unicorn* of Dundee.[81] Hopkins had given a cry of joy to know that Holmes was giving up his valuable time to investigate. 'Thank you, sir. That will, indeed, be a weight off my mind.' Holmes then used his authoritative tone to the inspector: 'If you will call a four-wheeler, Hopkins, we shall be ready to start for Forest Row in a quarter of an hour.' Down there they met John Hopley Neligan, a nocturnal visitor to the hut in the garden at the unlikely hour of two thirty in the morning, which placed him under suspicion. He endeavoured to explain himself by asking Hopkins if he had heard of Dawson and Neligan, the latter being his father. But the inspector's face showed a blank, for he had not that fund of useful knowledge like Holmes, who, tapping his attic of general information, knew them to be West Country bankers in Cornwall. Some of Holmes' ironical comments made the inspector wince.

But Hopkins was determined to have the last word, and arrested Neligan upon the evidence of a notebook with the initials J H N. He was cock-a-hoop and, turning to Holmes, said, 'Well, Mr Holmes, I am very much obliged to you and to your friend for

---

[81]ACD was surgeon for seven months in 1880 on a whaling ship the *Hope,* and later wrote 'Life on a Greenland Whaler', *Strand Magazine*.

coming down to help me. As it turns out your presence was unnecessary, and I would have brought the case to this successful issue without you; but none the less, I am very grateful.' This example of imperfect police methods did not meet with Holmes' approbation, for he had expected better deduction and was disappointed that Hopkins had not looked for a possible alternative and provided against it. It is the first rule of criminal investigation.

Holmes explained to Hopkins how he had reached the conclusion that a seaman harpooner called Patrick Cairns was the murderer. As he listened, the policeman's face grew longer and longer as his hopes and ambitions crumbled about him, and he could only stare in amazement. He had imagined that he had a complete case, and had not realised that his case was intrinsically impossible. 'I don't know what to say, Mr Holmes... It seems to me that I have been making a fool of myself from the beginning.' 'Well, well... We all learn by experience,' said Holmes good-humouredly.

In the winter of 1897 Hopkins sent Holmes a plea for help. The note was written upon crackling paper with the monogram E B and a coat of arms and the writing showed considerable agitation, although Hopkins was generally not an emotional man. It referred to the death of Sir Eustace Brackenstall, whose head was knocked in with his own poker, and it ran as follows:

> Abbey Grange, Marsham, Kent,
> 3.30 a.m.

My Dear Mr Holmes,

    I should be very glad of your immediate assistance in what promises to be a most remarkable case. It is something quite in your line. Except for releasing the lady, I will see that everything is kept exactly as I have found it, but I beg you not to lose an instant as it is difficult to leave Sir Eustace there.

    Yours faithfully,
    Stanley Hopkins.

Hopkins had blundered two years before, but still hoped that Holmes would be forgiving and answer his cry for help! Which of course he did. Hopkins got on the wrong trail, thinking that because three wine glasses had apparently been used, the murder was committed by the Randall gang. He didn't appreciate the clue which Holmes gave him, that the missing silver found in the pond was merely a 'blind'. He didn't read the clues of the bees wing in the third glass (sediment from the other glasses), the cut bell rope, and the blood mark upon the oaken chair whereon Lady Brackenstall had been bound, and her story being an absolute fabrication. The inspector thought that Holmes had powers that were not human: certainly Holmes discovered the true murderer, but took no action against him; Hopkins continued his own line of thought with no result. Constable Wilson, presumably, was no help either.

Holmes met Inspector Forrester in April 1887, at Reigate, at the house of Colonel Hayter (he had come under Watson's professional care in Afghanistan). He was a smart, keen-faced official, who hearing that the famous Mr Holmes of Baker Street was staying at the colonel's, wondered if Holmes would care to step across to the house of the Cunninghams, where William Kirwan the coachman had been shot. Watson disapproved, but convalescing Holmes accepted the invitation with alacrity. He was able to help the inspector in arresting the murderers, the father and son Cunningham. Holmes observed to his friend, 'Watson, I think our quiet rest in the country has been a distinct success, and I shall certainly return much invigorated to Baker Street to-morrow.' Watson recorded one of the few times that Holmes became demonstrative towards the police in as much as he actually clapped Forrester upon the back and said that it had been a pleasure working with him. Said the colonel, 'I consider it the greatest privilege to have been permitted to study your methods of working. I confess that they quite surpass my expectations, and that I am utterly unable to account for your result.'

Inspector Martin of the Norfolk Constabulary, Holmes met at the home of Hilton Cubitt of Riding Thorpe Manor, Norfolk, when he was investigating the mystery of the Dancing Men, the death of the owner, and the apprehension of the killer Abe Slaney, the American, who although he was condemned to death at the winter assizes at Norwich, was given penal servitude in consid-eration of mitigating circumstances, for Cubitt had fired the first shot. When Holmes met the inspector he was greeted with: 'Why, Mr Holmes, the crime was only committed at three this morning. How could you hear of it in London and get to the spot as soon as I?' (Holmes and Watson had taken the first morning train.) 'I anticipated it. I came in the hope of preventing it.' 'Then you must have important evidence, of which we are ignorant...' 'I have only the evidence of the Dancing Men... Will you associate me in your investigation, or will you prefer that I should act independently?' 'I should be proud to feel that we were acting together, Mr Holmes.'

The inspector contented himself with watching Holmes at work and carefully noting the results; he observed the way that Holmes carried out his interrogation of Mrs King, the cook, and Saunders, the housemaid, sitting in a great old-fashioned chair in the oak-panelled and high-windowed hall – the court of investigation.

Holmes pointed out some of the salient points to Martin. There was a third bullet, fired from inside the room, which had drilled right through the lower window sash, seen only because, expecting it, he had looked for it; he highlighted the importance of the servants smelling gunpowder and the fact that the door and window were only open a short time, as witnessed by the non-guttered candle. Much as the inspector would have liked to have asserted his authority, being overcome with admiration for Holmes' deductions he was just content to listen – just so long as he eventually captured his man. As the inspector seemed not to sense danger, Holmes had to ask him to telegraph for an escort, for he just couldn't comprehend that the murderer would arrive at Holmes' invitation.

As the case closed, the inspector was magnanimous in his praise for Holmes. 'It is a privilege to be associated with you in the handling of a case'; he hoped that he would have Holmes beside him in any future case.

It was while Holmes was at Lewisham, investigating the movements of Josiah Amberley that he met Inspector MacKinnon, a smart young policeman. Amberley was found to have murdered both his wife and her lover, Dr Ray Ernest, which would never have been discovered through the inspector's methods – a compulsory warning to Amberley, that whatever he said might be used against him, which would never have bluffed the murderer into saying what was virtually a confession. But the inspector was sure that, without Holmes to help, he would eventually have reached the correct solution, having formed his own views upon the matter. But he was a little afraid of losing the credit (perhaps even face!) and was somewhat relieved when Holmes told him that having solved the problem he would step aside. 'That is very handsome of you, Mr Holmes. Praise or blame can matter little to you, but it is very different to us when the newspapers begin to ask questions.' He thanked Holmes in the name of the police force; but he did rather wonder why Holmes had been consulted at all by Amberley. 'Pure swank!' said Holmes. 'He felt so clever and so sure of himself that he imagined no one could touch him. He could say to any suspicious neighbour, 'Look at the steps I have taken. I have consulted not only the police but even Sherlock Holmes.' The inspector laughed and forgave Holmes his 'even'.

Inspector Algar of the Liverpool Police Force was a friend of Holmes; how they originally met is not recorded, but he did consult him over the movements of Mrs Mary (Cushing) Browner, and her husband Jim Browner. Holmes sent Algar a telegram, wishing to know if the wife was still at home and if the husband had departed on the SS *May Day*, belonging to the Liverpool, Dublin and London Steam Packet Company; he was asked to send his reply to the police station. Back came the information that Mrs Browner's house had been closed for more than three days and she was thought to have travelled south to see relatives. Jim Browner (as a steward), had left aboard the *May Day* and would berth in the Albert Dock in the Thames. Sarah Cushing, Mary's sister, fell in love with her brother-in-law; this love, being spurned, turned to poisonous hate, when she knew that her sister Mary's footmark in the mud meant more to her husband than her whole body and soul. Mary turned her love upon another seaman, Alec Fairbairn, which eventually caused their murders by her husband, and the sending of an ear of each, packed in salt, to Miss Susan Cushing of Croydon; this triggered off Holmes' involvement in the case, being invited by Inspector

Lestrade, as he found that he had 'a little difficulty in getting anything to work upon'.

Holmes knew an inspector of the Harrow police and met him subsequently at the house of Mrs Maberley, The Three Gables, Harrow Weald. She called Holmes in as she had recently experienced a succession of strange incidents in connection with her house, for she remembered that her late husband Mortimer had been a former client of the great detective. Holmes remembered her husband and their debonair son, Douglas, who had recently died of pneumonia while attaché at Rome; his personal effects in several trunks and cases, had been sent home. Then followed a burglary, with Mrs Maberley being chloroformed. Thus it was that Holmes met the local bustling, rubicund inspector (whose name goes unrecorded), who greeted Holmes as an old friend, and treated the affair as an ordinary one. 'Well, Mr Holmes, no chance for you in this case, I'm afraid. Just a common, ordinary burglary, and well within the capacity of the poor old police. No experts need apply.' He tapped his bulky notebook. 'It is all here,' he said, which included a folded sheet of foolscap, the page numbered 245. 'I never pass anything, however trifling… That is my advice to you, Mr Holmes. In twenty-five years' experience I have learned my lesson. There is always the chance of finger-marks or something.' The inspector failed to realise that the fragment of paper held the key to the mystery – not so Holmes. His perseverance winkled out the real reason for the burglary – Douglas's infatuation with the celebrated beauty, Isadora Klein, his revealing manuscript in his trunk, ready for the publishers which could have cast a scandal upon Isadora's intended marriage to the young Duke of Lomond. The inspector had simply thought the writing 'mighty poor stuff'. The inspector still had much to learn and could only smile, as much as to say: 'These clever fellows have always a touch of madness.'

It was not until Holmes had retired to Sussex that he met, in July 1907, Inspector Bardle of the Sussex Constabulary, who had been summoned from Lewes by Anderson the village constable (a 'big, ginger-moustached man of the slow, solid Sussex breed', which covered 'much good sense under a heavy silent exterior'). Bardle was born and bred in Sussex, and had certainly never before encountered the fearful stinger, *Cyanea capillata*. He was a steady, burly, phlegmatic, bovine man, with thoughtful ox-like eyes. He wondered whether he should arrest Ian Murdock for the murder of Fitzroy McPherson, and asked Holmes' candid opinion, for he was surely troubled in his own mind and, being uncertain of himself, needed the master's assurance as to what he should or should not do, lest he let the murderer slip away with all the evidence against him. But Holmes assured him that his case was too weak for an arrest. The inspector, having only seen the weals upon the dead body, gave them no intensive study, unlike Holmes. He had enlarged his photograph of them and studied them through his strong lens, and thus had seen that the weal was unequal in its intensity, with a dot of extravasated blood here and another there. The inspector suggested that the marks could have been made if a red-hot net of wires had been laid across the back, which certainly was ingenious thinking; Holmes thought that perhaps a stiff cat-o'-nine-tails with small hard knots upon it might be a nearer description. When Holmes disclosed the name of the murderer, the inspector was absolutely staggered. 'Well, you've done it! …I had read of you but I never believed it. It's wonderful.' Whereupon Holmes shook his head, for to accept such praise was to lower his own standards.

There was also Youghal of CID, Montgomery of Shadwell Police Station and Baynes of the Surrey Constabulary (with a fat red face wreathed in smiles, with small glittering eyes), of whom Holmes said that he would rise high in his profession, as he had instinct and intuition. He congratulated him, which caused a deep flush upon the inspector's face. Baynes was concerned with the death of Aloysius Garcia, of Wisteria Lodge, Esher; Holmes gave him a word of friendly warning, thinking he was not on the right lines and did not wish him to be committed too far unless he was sure of his facts. They both agreed to work upon their own lines, for as Baynes said: 'But we all have our own systems, Mr Holmes. You have yours, and maybe I have mine.' And Baynes added that Holmes was always welcome to any information that he might have. Baynes never caught the culprits, but he did visit Baker Street and showed Holmes and Watson a printed description of the murderers, who were themselves murdered. Constable

Walters assisted Baynes by detecting and pursuing the hideous mulatto, which helped with the arrest, but not before Constable Downing was badly bitten by the savage.

White Mason, the chief Sussex detective, was called out to Birlstone Manor House, (where murder had been committed) by Sergeant Wilson from the small local police station; a slow, bucolic, common-sense man with big fingers, who had been unnerved and troubled by the tremendous responsibility which had suddenly come upon him. Scratching his puzzled head in his perplexity, he thought that the case was a deal too thick for the likes of him, a bit rummy.

Mason arrived from headquarters in a light dog cart behind a breathless trotter, at noon, in the cold winter sunshine. He was a very live and smart man, a quiet and comfortable-looking person in a loose tweed suit, clean-shaven, with ruddy face and fat hands, a stoutish and powerful body and bandy, gaitered legs, who looked very unlike the accepted provincial criminal officer: he could easily have passed for a farmer or a retired gamekeeper.

The detective scribbled an account and sent it to his personal London friend, Inspector MacDonald, by the 5.40 a.m. milk train, which notified him far more promptly than was usual at Scotland Yard when provincials needed their assistance, as usually the scent was already cold when the notification was received. The note ran as follows:

> Dear Inspector MacDonald,
> Official requisition for your services is in separate envelope. This is for your private eye. Wire me what train in the morning you can get for Birlstone, and I will meet it – or have it met if I am too occupied. This case is a snorter. Don't waste a moment in getting started. If you can bring Mr Holmes, please do so, for he will find something after his own heart. You would think the whole thing had been fixed up for theatrical effect, if there wasn't a dead man in the middle of it. My word, it *is* a snorter!

White Mason was honoured by Holmes' presence and wondered if he would co-operate fully and place his observations at the disposal of the police. MacDonald reassured him:

'I have worked with Mr Holmes before. He plays the game.'

'My own idea of the game at any rate,' said Holmes with a smile. 'I go into a case to help the ends of justice and the work of the police. If ever I have separated myself from the official police, it is because they have first separated themselves from me. I have no wish ever to score at their expense. At the same time Mr White Mason, I claim the right to work in my own way and give my results at my own time – complete, rather than in stages.'

Mr Mason put forward his case, with his 'cool, clear, common-sense brain' and his solid grip upon fact, which impressed Watson. Holmes, usually impatient with members of the police force, certainly recognised Mason's quality for he 'listened to him intently, with no sign of that impatience which the official exponent too often produced.' (Holmes expected to be informed by others, but seldom made any acknowledgement to the giver of information.) But being so unusually very impressed caused him to say: 'You put it very clearly. I am inclined to agree with you.' Certainly one up for Mr Mason!

Holmes also became known to lesser mortals in the police hierarchy, such as the detective Forbes of Scotland Yard, whom he met during his investigation of the case of the missing naval treaty from the Foreign Office, on 23 May. The treaty 'defined the position of Great Britain towards the Triple Alliance and fore-shadowed the policy which this country would pursue in the event of the French fleet gaining a complete ascendancy over that of Italy in the Mediterranean'.

Forbes was a 'small, foxy man with a sharp but by no means amiable expression'; he was decidedly frigid in his manner at first, especially when he learned the nature of Holmes' errand.

'I've heard of your methods before now, Mr Holmes,' said he tartly. 'You are ready enough to use all the information that the police can lay at your disposal, and then you try to finish the case yourself and bring discredit on them.'

'On the contrary,' said Holmes, 'out of my last fifty-three cases my name has only appeared in four, and the police have had all the credit in forty-nine. I don't blame you for not knowing this, for you are young and inexperienced, but if you wish to get on in your new duties, you will work with me and not against me.'

'I'd be very glad of a hint or two,' said the detective, changing his manner. 'I've certainly had no credit from the case so far.'

But he gave Holmes all the information that he collected. Tangey the commissionaire had been shadowed, his wife also, by one of his women and although a bad lot and a drinker, there was nothing against her; the brokers in her house had been paid off with her husband's pension; she had answered the bell as her husband was very tired; she had made a hasty departure from the building simply because she was late. The reason for her getting home later than Mr Phelps, was that her bus was slower than the hansom; she had seen no one in Charles Street except the constable. After he had shadowed the clerk Gorot for nine weeks, the result was nil. Holmes thanked him for the information and hoped that he would be able to apprehend the culprit and pass him to the police.

Holmes, after a fight with Joseph Harrison, managed to secure the stolen naval treaty papers, and then let the man go, wiring information to Forbes. If the detective caught his man, well and good, if not, better for the government who really did not wish the matter to be bandied about in the police court.

Another detective was Athelney Jones, whom Holmes met at Pondicherry Lodge, Upper Norwood, in 1888, the former home of a retired Indian Army officer, Major John Sholto, and his twin sons, Thaddeus and Bartholomew. They had met previously in the Bishopgate jewel case, when Holmes lectured them all on causes, inferences and effects, and set Jones upon the right track by a piece of very simple reasoning. Jones had suggested that it was more by good luck. Here Bartholomew Sholto was found murdered; his brother Thaddeus reported this at the police station, which brought Jones to the house. He commented:

'Bad business! Bad business! Stern facts here – no room for theories. [He was having a dig at Holmes.] How lucky that I happened to be out at Norwood over another case! I was at the station when the message arrived. What d'you think the man died of?'

'Oh, this is hardly a case for me to theorise over,' said Holmes dryly…

'Ha! I have a theory. These flashes come upon me at times… What do you think of this, Holmes? Sholto was, on his own confession, with his brother last night. The brother died in a fit, on which Sholto walked off with the treasure? How's that?'

'On which the dead man very considerately got up and locked the door on the inside.'

'Hum! There's a flaw there. Let us apply common sense to the matter. [Hardly the make-up of a policeman!] This Thaddeus Sholto *was* with his brother; there *was* a quarrel: so much we know. The brother is dead and the jewels are gone. So much also we know. No one saw the brother from the time Thaddeus left him. His bed has not been slept in. Thaddeus is evidently in a most disturbed state of mind. His appearance is – well, not attractive. You see that I am weaving my net round Thaddeus. The net begins to close upon him.'

'You are not quite in possession of the facts yet,' said Holmes.

He could see that Jones was going to make a fool of himself, which he did, as he arrested Thaddeus in the Queen's name as being concerned in the death of his brother. The prisoner looked at Holmes and Watson – he knew how the mind of the police worked. Holmes tried to pacify him, for that he thought that he would be able to clear him of the charge. But the inspector was sure that he had the right man. 'Don't promise too much, Mr Theorist…! You may find it a harder matter than you think,' snapped Jones. Holmes gave him a picture of the right men to seek, which only called forth a sneer from the detective. But Jones eventually had the sense to admit that he was on the wrong track and admitted it in the *Standard* newspaper; which was rather a pointer to Holmes' real opinion of Athelney Jones: an absolute imbecile in his profession but one whom he would not wish to hurt professionally.

In reply to Holmes' telegram, Jones came to Baker Street. His police brusqueness and masterful presence had given way to a meek downcast man and even apologetic as he accepted a cigar and a whisky and soda, and mopped his face with his red bandanna handkerchief. He could see no light in the darkness, his professional credit was at stake and he was willing to accept any possible assistance. His opinion of Holmes had increased, as he spoke in a husky and confidential voice to Watson. 'Your friend, Mr Sherlock Holmes, is a wonderful man, sir… He's a man who is not to be beat. I have known that young man go into a good many cases, but I never saw the case yet that he could not throw a light upon. He is irregular in his methods and a little quick perhaps in jumping at theories, but, on the whole, I think he would have made a most promising officer, and I don't care who knows it.' But when Watson suggested that Holmes had picked up the scent again, Jones detected a chink in the master's armour, and was most satisfied. 'Ah, then he has been at fault too… Even the best of us are thrown off sometimes. Of course this may prove to be a false alarm but it is my duty as an officer of the law to allow no chance to slip.' Jones no longer referred to Sherlock Holmes as the theorist, and grudgingly, perhaps, admitted that Holmes 'hit the nail on the head sometimes'. He even admitted that Scotland Yard would esteem it a great kindness if Holmes would favour them with an opinion upon any mysterious case that came to hand.

Jones, with Holmes' help, apprehended John Clay the murderer, thief, smasher and forger, although he didn't wholly hold with Holmes' theoretical methods.

Inspector Sam Brown was on the police launch with Holmes, Watson and Jones, chasing the *Aurora* on the Thames, and went with Watson to Mrs Cecil Forrester's house with the empty treasure chest.

J Neil Gibson, the greatest American gold-mining magnate in the world, of Thor Place in Hampshire, implored Holmes (by letter sent from Claridge's Hotel in London) to employ all his powers in proving the innocence of Miss Dunbar, the attractive family governess after the shooting of Mrs Gibson at the bridge over Thor Mere.

So down to Hampshire went Holmes and Watson, and called upon Sergeant Coventry in the little front room of his humble cottage which served as the local police station.

> He was a tall, thin, cadaverous man, with a secretive and mysterious manner which conveyed the idea that he knew or suspected a very great deal more than he dared say. He had a trick, too, of suddenly sinking his voice to a whisper as if he had come upon

something of vital importance, though the information was usually commonplace enough. Behind these tricks of manner he soon showed himself to be a decent, honest fellow who was not too proud to admit that he was out of his depth and would welcome any help.

'Anyhow, I'd rather have you than Scotland Yard, Mr Holmes,' said he. 'If the Yard gets called into a case, then the local loses all credit for success and may be blamed for failure. Now, you play straight, so I've heard.'

'I need not appear in the matter at all... If I can clear it up I don't ask to have my name mentioned.'

'Well, it's very handsome of you, I am sure. And your friend, Dr Watson, can be trusted, I know.'

The sergeant provided Holmes with ten yards of stout twine from the village shop, and with many critical and incredulous glances which showed he had doubts about Holmes' sanity, lurched along beside Holmes to the bridge. The astonished sergeant was treated to an interesting show by Holmes showing how, with the help of Watson's revolver, Mrs Gibson had shot herself, attempting to fasten the crime upon her governess. Then Holmes gave his orders to Sergeant Coventry: 'You will of course, get a grappling-hook and you will easily restore my friend's revolver. You will also find beside it, the revolver, string and weight...' (The murder weapon.)

Holmes also knew another private detective, his friend Mr Barker, a stern-looking, dark impassive man, who usually wore grey-tinted glasses, and sported a large Masonic pin in his tie. Where their two paths came together, and the work was mutual, they would work together as they did over the case of Mr Amberley of The Haven,[82] Lewisham. It was at his house that Holmes was slipping through the pantry window, prior to a bit of lawless burglary, when Mr Barker's hand took a grip of Holmes' collar, as he said: 'Now you rascal, what are you doing in there?' They both smiled at each other as recognition took place.

Later on, when Amberley was asked by Holmes what he had done with the bodies of his wife and Dr Ray Ernest, he found the

---

[82]Perhaps suggested by John Russell, Viscount Amberley, 1842–1876. (*Dictionary of National Biography*).

retired colourman suddenly a different person – 'a misshapen demon with a soul as distorted as his body' – as he tried to commit suicide by swallowing a white pellet; but he was forestalled as Holmes sprang at his throat like a tiger. Barker, anticipating trouble, had a cab waiting at the door, whither Amberley was dragged, wriggling and twisting, by Holmes and Barker, who took him to the police station a few hundred yards away; there Barker stayed to attend to the formalities, while Holmes returned to Watson.

Holmes knew both Monsieur Dubugue of the Paris police and Fritz von Waldbaum, the well known specialist of Dantzig; Watson retained an almost verbatim report of the interview given by Holmes to these two gentlemen, in which he demonstrated the true facts of the most important international case caused by the loss of a letter from a foreign potentate, and how its publication abroad could have caused a diplomatic breach perhaps involving Britain in a war; they had wasted their time and energy upon side issues, and totally missed the true significance of the value of the second bloodstain upon the beautiful, old-fashioned, square-blocked wood flooring.

Holmes was introduced to Mr Leverton, an American detective from Pinkerton's American Agency[83], in Howe Street by Inspector Gregson; a quiet, businesslike young man, with a clean-shaven, hatchet face, who posed as a London cabby, complete with whip and four-wheeler. 'The hero of the Long Island cave mystery? Sir, I am pleased to meet you,' said Holmes, which commendation caused a flush upon the American's face, for this was their first meeting. 'I am on the trail of my life now… If I can get Gorgiano—' 'What! Gorgiano of the Red Circle?' For Holmes knew all about Giuseppe Gorgiano.

This surprised the American. 'Oh, he has European fame, has he? Well, we've learned all about him in America. We *know* he is

---

[83]Mr Leverton of Pinkerton's American Agency, said of Gennaro Lucca who murdered Giuseppe Gorgiano of the American Red Circle secret society, that in the USA he would receive 'a pretty general vote of thanks'. After Holmes killed Moriarty, he was accorded similar treatment, for there were no legal proceedings against him.

at the bottom of fifty murders, and yet we have nothing positive we can take him on. I tracked him over from New York, and I've been close to him for a week in London, waiting some excuse to get my hand on his collar. Mr Gregson and I ran him to ground in that big tenement house, and there's only the one door, so he can't slip us. There's three folk come out since he went in, but I'll swear he wasn't one of them.' Holmes suggested that they all went into the house to investigate, although they had no warrant. Gregson agreed. 'He is in unoccupied premises under suspicious circumstances… That is good enough for the moment. When we have him by the heels we can see if New York can't help us to keep him. I'll take the responsibility of arresting him now.' So Holmes, Watson, Gregson and Leverton went upstairs, to the left-hand flat upon the third floor. Here they found the Italian, dead upon the deal boards of the carpetless floor. He was an enormous man, his clean-shaven, swarthy face grotesquely horrible in its contortion, with a knife blade driven deeply into his broad, brown, upturned throat. This was the end of the leader of a secret Neapolitan society, the Red Circle, whose oaths and secrets were frightful, and escape from membership impossible. Leverton was not sure how the British law would view this murder, but in America, he said, the killer would receive a 'pretty general vote of thanks'.

Although Holmes never met William Hargreave of the New York Police Bureau, he was upon very friendly terms with him. Holmes would impart information to him by cable, of his knowledge of crime and American criminals in London, and Hargreave would reciprocate with information concerning American criminals in England. He told Holmes that Abe Slaney was the most dangerous crook in Chicago.

There is a most interesting sidelight upon the impact which Holmes had upon the professional police detective. James Bradshawe, a professional police detective, speaking to his friend Wilfred Underhill, an amateur detective, said that the professional was always supposed to be wrong, having the disadvantage of going by a rule. His friend said that Sherlock Holmes went by a logical rule. They were talking presumably in the year 1929, with Holmes very much in their mind, and if he was living still in

Sussex, after his First World War experiences, he would have been some seventy-five years old.

Sherlock Holmes' Informers

Apart from the Baker Street Irregulars, Holmes employed other people to gather information for him. One of these was a lad of fourteen, called Cartwright, with a bright keen face, who gazed with great reverence upon the famous detective, for he knew from his manager of the district messenger office, Mr Wilson, how Holmes had saved not only his good name but his life.

Holmes was anxious to gather information concerning an anonymous letter sent to Sir Henry Baskerville at the Northumberland Hotel; it was post marked 'Charing Cross' and consisted of a half-sheet of foolscap paper folded into four. Thereon was only one sentence, across the middle, composed of printed words which ran thus:

> As you value your life or your reason keep away from the moor.

Only the last word was printed in ink. Holmes traced the message as having been extracted from the previous day's *Times* newspaper – Dr Mortimer was amazed by this example of Holmes' powers of deduction. Holmes deduced that the sender was an educated man, who had addressed the envelope in a hotel. Cartwright was commissioned by Holmes to check twenty-three hotels taken from the Hotel Directory, all in the neighbourhood of Charing Cross, to see if he could find the centre page of *The Times*, with holes cut from the leading article by short-bladed scissors. He was to inspect the waste-paper baskets, with the excuse that he was looking for a miscarried telegram. Although Cartwright was given fifty-six shillings towards 'tips' for the outside and hall porters, (with ten shillings extra for emergencies), he was unable to trace the cut newspaper sheet; even Holmes admitted: 'The odds are enormously against your finding it.' Later, Cartwright became invaluable to Holmes, when he took him down to the Devon moor near Baskerville Hall, where he secretly supplied all Holmes' daily wants, and reported upon Watson's movements.

'Porky' Shinwell Johnson was an informer who supplied

Holmes with information from the early 1900s. He was a 'huge, coarse, red-faced, scorbutic man' with vivid black eyes, quick observation and a cunning mind, initially a very dangerous villain, serving two terms at Parkhurst Prison. After repenting he became Holmes' agent in the vast criminal underworld of London, and often supplied him with vitally important information. He refused to be a copper's 'nark', only dealing with non-court cases, and so screened himself from his companions. As an ex-jailbird, he had entry into nightclubs, dosshouses, and gambling dens in London, and so could pick up any garbage in the darker recesses of the underworld.

Johnson and Holmes corresponded by telegram, never by letter. When Johnson burgled a house, he only stole saleable articles or that which would melt down. One of his old mates was Miss Kitty Winter; together they helped Holmes to break off the intended marriage of Miss Violet de Merville to Baron Gruner.

Mercer was another agent of Holmes; he was employed in the later years, particularly in 1903, during the time that Watson was away from Baker Street. Holmes spoke of him as 'my general utility man who looks up routine business'. He was very helpful over the Professor Presbury case; Holmes had learnt that the professor, having been to Prague, was corresponding with a gentleman named A Dorak, whose letters, marked with a cross under the stamp, were never to be opened by Mr Bennett, his private secretary. Holmes needed to know something of this Dorak with whom the professor was secretly corresponding. Holmes despatched a telegram during the day, and had a reply from Mercer in the evening:

HAVE VISITED THE COMMERCIAL ROAD AND SEEN DORAK. SUAVE PERSON, BOHEMIAN, ELDERLY. KEEPS LARGE GENERAL STORE.

Said Holmes: 'His nationality connects up with the Prague visit.' So Holmes then formed a provisional theory 'that every nine days the professor takes some strong drug which has a passing but highly poisonous effect', and that he was being supplied by a Bohemian intermediary in London, the agent for a Mr Lowenstein of Prague, an obscure scientist who was trying to find the secret of rejuvenescence and the elixir of life.

Another of Holmes' informers was Landale Pike, whom Holmes referred to as, 'his human book of reference upon all matters of social scandal.' Watson has left us the following picture of him:

> This strange languid creature, spent his waking hours in the bow window of a St James' Street Club, and was the receiving station as well as the transmitter for all the gossip of the metropolis. He made, it was said, a four-figure income by the paragraphs which he contributed every week, to the garbage papers which catered to an inquisitive public. If ever, far down in the turbid depths of London life, there was some strange swirl or eddy, it was marked with automatic exactness by this human dial upon the surface. Holmes discreetly helped Landale to knowledge, and on occasion was helped in turn.

Fred Porlock (one of Moriarty's minions of the underworld) was another cog in Holmes' machine of information. His fear of being found out that he was divulging information to Holmes was always uppermost in his mind; this was shown in an ensuing letter which he wrote after first sending a coded note:

> Dear Mr Holmes,
>
> I will go no further in this matter. It is too dangerous – he suspects me. I can see that he suspects me. He came to me quite unexpectedly after I had actually addressed this envelope with the intention of sending you the key to the cipher. I was able to cover it up. If he had seen it, it would have gone hard with me. But I read suspicion in his eyes. Please burn the cipher message, which can now be of no use to you.
> Fred Porlock

(Moriarty was always referred to as 'he', for safety's sake.)

Porlock sent his information by letter in cipher, and his writing was known to Holmes by the Greek *e* with the peculiar top distinctive flourish. Holmes explained the man to Watson:

'Porlock, Watson, is a nom de plume, a mere identification mark; but behind it lies a shifty and evasive personality. In a former letter he frankly informed me that the name was not his own, and defied me ever to trace him among the teeming millions of this great city. Porlock is important, not for himself, but for the great man [Moriarty] with whom he is in touch. Picture to yourself the pilot fish with the shark, the jackal with the lion – anything that is insignificant in companionship with what is formidable; not only formidable, Watson, but sinister – in the highest degree sinister. That is where he comes within my purview.'

Holmes sent him money, the occasional ten-pound note, to be called for at Camberwell post office usually, although other devious methods were employed for his invaluable information, for Holmes had promised when he first wrote, that he would not try to trace him, and Holmes' word was his bond and he never broke faith. (The fact that Holmes could keep faith with such a person certainly surprised Inspector MacDonald.)

In March 1892 Holmes employed John Warner as an informer. He was the late gardener of Mr Henderson – a rich, strong active man of fifty, with iron-grey hair, great bunched black eyebrows, a parchment face, with the step of a deer and the air of an emperor, and as tough as whipcord. (It was later on that it transpired that the real name of Henderson was Don Murillo, the Tiger of San Pedro, wanted by the Spanish police since 1886.) He was not averse to using a dog whip. The servants feared and disliked him. He lived in a double-winged Jacobean grange, High Gable, near Oxshott in Surrey, not far from Wisteria Lodge.

Warner was told to keep an eye upon the gates and report any happenings to Holmes. He was able to report that the family had departed from the house, by the late train. They had tried to take Miss Burnett, their English governess (whose real name was Signora Victor Durando, wife of the San Pedro minister in London – who was shot by Murillo – who was keeping track of the murderer), heavily drugged by opium, with them. But she had struggled, and Warner went to her assistance, and managed to tear her away, and get her into a cab. He brought her in a half-collapsed, nervous condition to Holmes at The Bull public house. 'Excellent, Warner!' cried Holmes as he sprang to his feet, ready to help in carrying Miss Burnett upstairs, laying her upon a sofa and administering strong coffee to clear her brain from the effects of the drug.

Sherlock Holmes Nearly Dies

The fact that Holmes was often responsible for the apprehension of a criminal, either with the police, his own 'Irregulars', or his own informers, certainly made him a likely target for an attack. For there were a few times when Holmes' life was in jeopardy, and he might well not have lived to enjoy his Sussex retirement.

How fortunate that the life of the world's most famous detective was not untimely stopped by a poisoned dart from the blowpipe of Tonga, the Andaman islander; luckily it missed its intended target and buried itself into the wooden hatchway of the police launch while they were chasing the *Aurora*.

Holmes nearly lost his life upon the Devon moor, although the incident was of his own making, when he ventured into the Grimpen Mire, trying to retrieve Sir Henry Baskerville's missing black boot. He sank in up to his waist and would never have seen dry land again had not Watson and Lestrade been there to drag him out.

It was while Holmes and Watson were staying at Poldhu Cottage in Cornwall that an experiment was carried out by Holmes, with the poisonous devil's foot root powder, the fumes from which reacted quickly upon the two of them. Developments were not long in coming. Watson had hardly settled in his chair before he was:

> conscious of a thick, musky odour, subtle and nauseous. At the very first whiff of it my brain and my imagination were beyond all control. A thick, black cloud swirled before my eyes, and my mind told me that in this cloud, unseen as yet, but about to spring out upon my appalled senses, lurked all that was vaguely horrible, all that was monstrous and inconceivably wicked in the universe. Vague shapes swirled and swam amid the dark cloud-bank, each a menace and a warning of something coming, the advent of some unspeakable dweller upon the threshold, whose very shadow would blast my soul. A freezing horror took possession of me. I felt that my hair was rising, that my eyes were protruding, that my mouth was opened, and my tongue like leather. The turmoil

within my brain was such that something must surely snap. I tried to scream and was vaguely aware of some hoarse croak which was my own voice, but distant and detached from myself. At the same moment, in some effort of escape, I broke through that cloud of despair and had a glimpse of Holmes' face, white, rigid, and drawn with horror – the very look which I had seen upon the features of the dead. It was that vision which gave me an instant of sanity and strength. I dashed from my chair, threw my arms round Holmes, and together we lurched through the door, and an instant afterwards had thrown ourselves down upon the grass plot and were lying side by side, conscious only of the glorious sunshine which was bursting its way through the hellish cloud of terror which had girt us in. Slowly it rose from our souls like the mists from a landscape until peace and reason had returned, and we were sitting upon the grass wiping our clammy foreheads, and looking with apprehension at each other to mark the last traces of that terrific experience which we had undergone.

Sherlock Holmes Attacked in Regent Street

In 1902 Holmes was attacked in London. 'Murderous Attack Upon Sherlock Holmes', said the black upon yellow news-sheet, displayed by a one-legged newsvendor between the Grand Hotel and Charing Cross Station. This stunned Watson so much that in his confused state of mind he snatched away a newspaper, failed to pay the man and then stood in the doorway of a chemist's shop, reading the fateful paragraph which ran thus:

> We learn with regret that Mr Sherlock Holmes, the well-known private detective, was the victim this morning of a murderous assault which has left him in a precarious position. There are no exact details to hand, but the event seems to have occurred about twelve o'clock in Regent Street, outside the Café Royal. The attack was made by two men armed with sticks, and Mr Holmes was beaten about the head and body, receiving injuries which the doctors describe as most serious. He was carried to Charing Cross Hospital and afterwards insisted upon being taken to his rooms in Baker Street. The miscreants who attacked him appear to have been respectably dressed men, who escaped from the bystanders by passing through the Café Royal and out into

Glasshouse Street behind it. No doubt they belonged to that criminal fraternity which has so often had occasion to bewail the activity and ingenuity of the injured man.

Holmes suffered two lacerated scalp wounds which needed some stitches, and some considerable bruises, but Sir Leslie Oakshott reported no immediate danger. Lucky for Holmes, being a single-stic`k expert, he took most of the blows on his guard. All this happened because Holmes had 'crossed swords' with Baron Adelbert Gruner, the Austrian murderer ('cool as ice, silky voiced... poisonous as a cobra', a fiend incarnate), who had previously warned Holmes that if he did not desist from inter-fering in his life, he might well be crippled like Le Brun, the French agent, who had been beaten up by Apaches in Montmarte.

Professor James Moriarty

Over the years, Holmes had felt that there was some deep organising power, some master brain behind London's criminal underworld, but it was some time before he discovered the secret which eventually led him to the central power: none other than a man called Professor Moriarty. Through his contacts in the underworld of crime, with men like Porlock, Holmes was able to build up a useful dossier upon him.

Holmes learned that the professor was a man of good birth and education endowed by nature with a phenomenal mathemati-cal faculty.[84] He had two brothers, one a stationmaster in the west of England, and younger than himself, and Colonel Moriarty. Watson called him also James – possibly some confusion in his notes. The colonel later tried to defend his brother, following his death at the Reichenbach Falls, near Meiringen, in Switzerland.

At the age of twenty-one, he wrote a treatise upon the binomial theorem which had a European vogue, and the dynamics of an asteroid, a book which ascended to the heights of pure mathematics.[85] Upon the strength of the first book, he won

---

[84]The French Minister, a mathematician who wrote learnedly on the differential calculus. Edgar Allan Poe, *The Purloined Letter*.

[85]Sir Isaac Newton discovered the binomial theorem while absent from Cambridge during the London plague of 1665–1666.

the mathematical chair at one of our smaller universities, and had to all appearances, a most brilliant career before him. But the man had hereditary tendencies of the most diabolical kind. A criminal strain ran in his blood, which, instead of being modified, was increased and rendered infinitely more dangerous by his extraordinary mental powers. Dark rumours gathered round him in the university town, and eventually he was compelled to resign his chair and come to London, where he set up as an army coach.

At the end of the 1880s Holmes said to Watson:

'You have heard me speak of Moriarty?'

'The famous scientific criminal, as famous among crooks as...'

'My blushes, Watson!' Holmes murmured in a deprecating voice.

'I was about to say, as he is unknown to the public.'

'A touch! A distinct touch!' cried Holmes. You are developing a certain unexpected vein of pawky humour, Watson...'

(Seldom was Watson allowed to score a point off his friend!)

On the evening of 24 April 1891 a paler and thinner Holmes visited Watson at his consulting room, after a unique morning visit from Professor Moriarty. Holmes put his fingertips together and, resting his elbows on his knees, asked Watson, 'You have probably never heard of Professor Moriarty?' 'Never'. 'Aye, there's the genius and the wonder of the thing,' cried Holmes. The man pervades London and no one has heard of him. That's what puts him on a pinnacle in the records of crime.' (Watson's memory slightly at fault?) Holmes told Watson that the professor was the Napoleon of crime:

'He is the organiser of half that is evil and of nearly all that is undetected in this great city. He is a genius, a philosopher, an abstract thinker. He has a brain of the first order. He sits motionless, like a spider in the centre of its web, but that web has a thousand radiations, and he knows well every quiver of each of them. He does little himself. He only plans. But his agents are numerous and splendidly organised. Is there a crime to be done, a paper to be extracted we will say, a house to be rifled, a man to be removed – the word is passed to the professor, the matter is organised and carried out. The agent may be caught. In that case money will be found for his bail or his defence. But the central power which uses the agent is never caught – never so much as suspected. This was the organisation which I deduced, Watson…'

By calling Moriarty a criminal, Watson was certainly uttering a libel in the eyes of the law, for evidence would be lacking to convict him; he was the greatest schemer of all time, the organiser of every deviltry, the controlling brain of the underworld, a brain which might have made or marred the destiny of nations, but it was impossible to ascribe any crime to him. Moriarty was the only man Holmes recognised as his equal, note, mark you, not the reverse.

One of the far-reaching radiations from the spider's London web had enmeshed Jack Douglas and murdered him at sea in a storm off St Helena. Holmes explained to Cecil Barker, Jack's friend, how it had been very well stage-managed.

'There is a master hand here. It is no case of sawed-off shotguns and clumsy six-shooters. You can tell an old master by the sweep of his brush. I can tell a Moriarty when I see one. This crime is from London, not from America.' Barker beat his head with his clenched fist in his impotent rage. 'Do not tell me that we have to sit down under this?'

'No, I don't say that,' said Holmes, and his eyes seemed to be looking far into the future. ' I don't say that he can't be beat. But you must give me time – you must give me time!'

On the morning of 24 April 1891 Professor Moriarty, unannounced either by Billy or Mrs Hudson, visited Holmes in his room: a most unexpected visitor. This was the first time that the two of them had come face to face, although Holmes had visited Moriarty's rooms three times, but found nothing compromising except a most valuable Greuze painting on the wall above where the professor usually sat at his writing desk. This had posed an interesting question as to how Moriarty could afford to buy such a painting on a nominal salary of seven hundred pounds per annum? Holmes thought that perhaps he had some twenty different bank accounts, the bulk of his fortune in crime, abroad in the Deutsche Bank or the Crédit Lyonnais, as likely as not.

Holmes was certainly startled by the very man himself standing before him. He was an extremely tall and thin man, his forehead domed out in a white curve, his puckered eyes deeply sunken in his head. He was clean-shaven, pale and ascetic-looking, his thin face protruded forward, and was 'forever slowly oscillating from side to side in a curiously reptilian fashion'. Moriarty was disappointed at the lack of Holmes' frontal development. Holmes had instantly recognised his extreme danger, and slipped his revolver from the drawer into the pocket of his dressing gown; this called forth a rebuke from Moriarty: 'It is a dangerous… habit to finger loaded firearms…' So Holmes laid the cocked weapon upon the table, and told the professor that he could spare him five minutes. Moriarty took out his memorandum book, and ticked off dates: Holmes had crossed his path on 4 January, had incommoded him on 23 January, seriously inconvenienced him by the middle of February, had hampered his plans by the end of March, and now, at the close of April, through continual persecution, he was in danger of losing his liberty. The position was an impossible one, and Holmes was told to desist. 'It has been an intellectual treat to see the way in which you have grappled with this affair, and I say, unaffectedly, that it would be a grief to me to be forced to take any extreme measure. You smile, sir, but I assure you that it really would.' If Holmes did not steer clear of a mighty organisation, he would be trodden underfoot; this did not deter Holmes, for danger was his trade, but it would mean inevitable destruction for Holmes if he persisted in crossing Moriarty. Said Moriarty, 'It seems a pity, but I have done what I could. I know every move of your game. You can do nothing before Monday. It has been a duel between you and me, Mr Holmes. You hope to place me in the dock. I tell you that you will never beat me. If you are clever enough to bring destruction upon me, rest assured that I shall do as much to you.' Holmes replied that if he knew that he would overcome his arch-enemy, he would willingly die for it. Moriarty snarled and went peering and blinking out of the room, but nevertheless Holmes was convinced of his sincerity by his soft, precise fashion of speech.

Moriarty soon swept into battle through his minions. They attacked Holmes at midday, for as he passed from Bentinck Street on to the Welbeck Street crossing, he was nearly knocked down by a two-horse van, furiously driven, with the intent to kill; but Holmes luckily gained the footpath. In Vere Street, a brick fell from a roof and nearly killed him. Holmes sought the safety of a cab, and spent the day with his brother Mycroft. On his way to visit Watson in the evening, he was attacked by a ruffian with a bludgeon; Holmes knocked him down with a blow on his teeth, barking his knuckles. Watson was surprised at such a visit of a pale and thin Holmes, and sensed that he was frightened. When Holmes closed his shutters and said he was afraid of airguns, and wanted Watson to go with him for a week to the Continent – seemingly on a purposeless visit – which was so unlike his friend that Watson was certainly worried. Holmes put his fingertips together and, with his elbows on his knees, told Watson of Moriarty's visit and the attacks upon his person in the streets; a day of horror.

Holmes realised that Moriarty certainly meant business and that London was no longer a safe haven. Watson happily agreed to the holiday, his wife being away at the time, and there was no problem with his practice as a neighbour would stand in for him.

They were to meet at Victoria for the Continental express (each arriving separately by devious ways), where the second first-class carriage had been reserved – not just two seats – Holmes never did things by halves. Holmes disguised himself as an Italian priest, in order to arrive incognito; not that it fooled Moriarty, who, full of murderous intent, was hot upon their trail. Watson did wonder why a priest was in their reserved carriage, until a voice said, 'My dear Watson, you have not even condescended to say good morning.'

Holmes knew that Moriarty would do what he would do, given similar circumstances, and that was to engage a special steam engine and carriage to speed the chase; expense was no worry to the arch-fiend.[86]

---

[86]M Louis Caratal hired a special train with two carriages and a guard's van, from the superintendent of the Central and West Coast Station in Liverpool, to London, costing fifty pounds and five shillings. ACD, *The Story of the Lost Special*, 1894. Sir Omicron Pie was to arrive by the 9.15 p.m. train at Barchester, to see the sick Dean. 'I wonder why they didn't have a special.' Dr Proudie to Mr Slope. Anthony Trollope, *Barchester Towers*, 1857.

They travelled to Canterbury, where they alighted, leaving their luggage on the train, which would eventually arrive in Paris; this would keep the watchful eye of Moriarty busy for two wasted days. They then purchased a 'couple of carpet-bags', intending to buy their requirements as necessary.

They made a cross-country journey to Newhaven, and then on to Brussels and Strasbourg, making their leisurely way to Switzerland, via Luxembourg and Basle. Holmes kept in touch with the London police by telegram, who informed him that the whole of the gang had been secured, which only left Moriarty and Colonel Moran at large. Commented Holmes: 'Of course, when I had left the country, there was no one to cope with him. But I did think that I had put the game in their hands.' Holmes now wished Watson to return to England for there was danger ahead and he did not wish to embroil Watson; but after consulting for half an hour, they continued their journey together.

They travelled up the valley of the Rhône and over the Gemmi Pass deep in snow and along the border of the melancholy Daubensee, where Moriarty first showed his hand. A huge rock was cast down upon them, but they escaped. Holmes was ever watchful and alert, but never depressed. 'The air of London is the sweeter for my presence. In over one thousand cases I am not aware that I have ever used my powers upon the wrong side. Your memoirs will draw to an end, Watson, upon the day that I crown my career by the capture or extinction of the most dangerous criminal in Europe.'

They reached the village of Meiringen on 3 May 1891 (by way of Interlaken), where they put up at the Englischer Hof. They set off together on 4 May intending to spend the night at Rosenlavi, and they were told not to miss seeing the Reichenbach Falls; here the path was cut halfway round the falls, so that the traveller had to retrace his steps. At the falls on 4 May Watson received a bogus letter asking for medical help, which called him instantly away. Holmes sensed that the hand of Moriarty was in this but said nothing to Watson. Shortly afterwards, Moriarty confronted Holmes upon the three foot wide path, with a sheer wall on one side and a sheer drop on the other. With Moriarty's permission, Holmes left a note for Watson, written on three pages of his notebook, under his silver cigarette case near his Alpine-stock.[87] As Watson later related: 'It was characteristic of the man that the direction was as precise, and the writing as firm and clear, as though it had been written in his study.'

Watson was asked to contact Inspector Patterson, and tell him that the papers which he needed to convict the gang were at Baker Street, in pigeonhole M, done up in a blue envelope and inscribed, 'Moriarty'.

Moriarty drew no weapon, but rushed upon Holmes and threw his long arms around him, hoping to throw him over the precipice. This was when Holmes' knowledge of Japanese wrestling stood him in good stead, as he slipped through Moriarty's grip and toppled him over the edge of the precipice, striking a rock below and splashing into the water. Holmes had at last come to grips with and defeated his greatest enemy.

It only remained now to defeat, later on, the second enemy, Colonel Sebastian Moran, of Conduit Street, London. (Holmes had a record of him, and knew that he had served in Her Majesty's Indian Army and was a fine heavy-game shot; an elderly man with a philosopher's brow and a sensualist's jaw, a fierce aggressive nose, high bald forehead and a huge grizzled bristling moustache; a gaunt, swarthy, virile, sinister face, scored with deep savage lines and cruel blue eyes with drooping cynical lids; he lived by his ill-gotten card gains and a salary of six thousand pounds a year from Moriarty. His lookout man was Parker, a garrotter by trade and a performer on the Jew's harp.)

Holmes then tried to scale the cliff, but was attacked from above by Colonel Moran, who pushed a heavy boulder down upon him. He then scrambled down again to the narrow path, with an almost sheer wall on one side, having a few small footholds and a ledge, and the other side a sheer drop into the water below.

Holmes now made a hurried exit, travelled ten miles over the mountains in darkness, until a week later he arrived in Florence. Watson returning to the Falls, and finding only the letter, presumed that his friend was dead; this was what Holmes hoped

---

[87]Holmes told Watson that he left his cigarette box. Watson writing from memory, perhaps confused these two things.

would happen, that the world would believe him dead. Holmes must have pondered upon this rather churlish attitude towards his friend, but decided that secrecy was absolutely vital.

Holmes' only confidant now was his brother Mycroft, who kept in touch, sent him money and looked after the Baker Street flat. He thought it wise that any London criminal should think him dead, and so elected to stay abroad.

There were three accounts of the death of Sherlock Holmes in the public press in 1891 in the *Journal de Genève* on 6 May; Reuters' dispatch in the English papers on 7 May and letters by Colonel James Moriarty defending the memory of his brother. Now that Professor Moriarty was dead and his gang of criminals in police hands, the greatest criminal trial of the century was expected, with some forty mysteries to be cleared up, and hanging for them all.

Holmes travelled for three years abroad. As he related to Watson:

> I travelled for two years in Tibet, and amused myself by visiting Lhassa, and spending some days with the head Llama. You may have read of the remarkable explorations of a Norwegian named Sigerson, but I am sure that it never occurred to you that you were receiving news of your friend. I then passed through Persia, looked in at Mecca, and paid a short but interesting visit to the Khalifa at Khartoum, the results of which I have communicated to the Foreign Office. Returning to France, I spent some months in a research into the coal-tar derivatives, which I conducted in a laboratory at Montpelier, in the south of France.[88]

Holmes return to England was hastened by hearing of the unusual murder of the Honourable Ronald Adair in the spring of 1894 in London. And so back to Mrs Hudson and Baker Street.

After Moriarty's death, Holmes felt that there was a void in London from the point of view of the criminal expert. Watson disagreed. Holmes merely smiled.

---

[88]Black fluid, obtained by the distillation of tar, used for medicines, dyes and waterproofing. Tuxbury Old Hall butler had 'tarry' odour on his gloves. Watson remarked upon the 'tar-like odour' of the Pondicherry Lodge garret.

'Well, well, I must not be selfish… The community is certainly the gainer, and no one the loser, save the poor out-of-work specialist, whose occupation has gone. With that man in the field, one's morning paper presented infinite possibilities. Often it was only the smallest trace, Watson, the faintest indication, and yet it was enough to tell me that the great malignant brain was there, as the gentlest tremors of the edges of the web remind one of the foul spider which lurks in the centre. Petty thefts, wanton assaults, purposeless outrage – to the man who held the clue all could be worked into one connected whole. To the scientific student of the higher criminal world, no capital in Europe offered the advantages which London then possessed. But now—' Holmes shrugged his shoulders in humorous deprecation of the state of things which he had himself done so much to produce.

Sherlock Holmes Refuses a Knighthood

Was Holmes offered a knighthood in 1894 or 1895, after he had rid the London criminal world of its arch-villain? He certainly deserved one. In the latter end of June 1902, shortly after the conclusion of the South African War, he was offered a knighthood for services rendered. Holmes carried out his detective work, like any other true artist, for art's sake, and to satisfy first himself. How therefore would he increase his greatness by accepting a knighthood? He had no wish to offend the monarch, but he just couldn't bring himself to accept this accolade. He disappointed Watson, who declared: 'You have brought detection as near an exact science as it ever will be brought in this world. Your merits should be publicly recognised.' Perhaps Holmes considered that he received the highest accolade from Stapleton,[89] when as John Clayton's disguised passenger in his London cab, he called himself 'Sherlock Holmes'. This prompted Holmes to observe, after a hearty laugh: 'a touch, Watson – an undeniable touch. I feel a foil as quick and supple as my own. He got home upon me very prettily that time.' Watson in his role of partner and confidant never enlarged upon the knighthood affair, simply hoping that at a later date he might be given permission from Holmes to enlarge

---

[89]Jack Stapleton, former almoner of Sir Charles Baskerville – a Baskerville throwback, entomologist at Merripit House.

and place it upon a permanent record.

Sherlock Holmes' Laughter

Holmes seldom laughed, although he was always ready to have a sly dig at the inadequate police inspectors. Usually it was inclined to be a dry chuckle, or something of a smile, which might break into laughter, light or hearty. Holmes and Watson unexpectedly met together in one of the prehistoric hut dwellings upon Dartmoor. As they chatted, the sun gradually set, and night settled upon the moor, and the stars faintly shone in a violet sky. The silence of the night was suddenly rent by a terrible scream and a prolonged yell of horror, which turned Watson's blood to ice in his veins and even Holmes, the usual man of iron, was deeply shaken as he said it was the hound. They both ran blindly through the gloom, hindered by boulders and gorse bushes; they panted up hills and rushed down the slopes, making their way towards the point from whence came the sounds. They eventually came to the figure of a prostrate man, face down upon the ground. By the light of a match they recognised the ruddy tweed suit of Sir Henry Baskerville. As Watson recorded: 'the head doubled under him at a horrible angle, the shoulders rounded and the body hunched together as if in the act of throwing a somersault. So grotesque was the attitude that I could not for the instant realise that that moan had been the passing of his soul.' They both blamed themselves for not keeping a constant vigilance upon their host. Then, as Holmes peered closer at the body, he uttered a cry, a cry from the usual stern and self-contained Holmes, and there he was dancing, laughing and wringing Watson's hand, for he had seen that the man was bearded and was none other than the convict, Selden.

While at Baskerville Hall, Holmes and Watson examined the 1647 portrait of the old Cavalier roysterer, Hugo Baskerville, hanging in the banqueting hall; he was depicted in black velvet and lace, in a broad plumed hat, white lace collar, with curling lovelocks round the straight severe face. Watson thought that there was something of Sir Henry about the jaw; standing upon a chair, Holmes curved his right arm over the hat and round the hair, and in the candlelight Watson was amazed to see the face of Stapleton spring out of the canvas, as if it were his own portrait. 'Yes, it is an interesting instance of a throwback which appears to be both physical and spiritual…' said Holmes. 'The fellow is a Baskerville – that is evident… We have him, Watson, we have him, and I dare swear that before to-morrow night he will be fluttering in our net as helpless as one of his own butterflies. A pin, a cork, and a card, and we add him to the Baker Street collection!' with that, Holmes 'burst into one of his rare fits of laughter as he turned away from the picture. I have not heard him laugh often,' recorded Watson, 'and it has always boded ill to somebody.'

At Deep Dene House, Lower Norwood, Mr Oldacre's house, Holmes made 'desperate efforts to restrain a convulsive attack of laughter', over Lestrade's finding of McFarlane's bloody thumb mark upon the whitewashed wall, which he knew had not been there the day before. He could not conceal his amusement as he said, 'It is final.' His face was 'writhing with inward merriment. His two eyes were shining like stars.' He made desperate efforts to restrain a sudden attack of laughter. Holmes was outwardly calm, but his whole body gave a wriggle of suppressed excitement as he spoke in a hilarious manner; on the top corridor of the house, Holmes was seized with a spasm of merriment.

The finale at Deep Dene House saw Mr Cornelius being taken into custody by Lestrade upon a charge of conspiracy, perhaps even of attempted murder, and the likelihood of his banking account being impounded by his creditors. The malignant eyes of the little man turned upon Holmes. 'I have to thank you for a good deal. Perhaps I'll pay my debt some day.' 'I fancy that, for some years, you will find your time very fully occupied,' said Holmes, and although he might have wished to have laughed in the face of the local builder, he merely smiled indulgently.

Holmes had cause to have a sovereign bet with Mr Breckinridge, who had a large game stall in Covent Garden Market, over geese and whether they were town or country bred – actually he was seeking the address of the supplier, and by this ruse gained the necessary information, that it was Mrs Oakshott of the Brixton Road. Holmes pretended to be disgusted with his lost bet, left the stall, and under a nearby lamp post 'laughed in the hearty, noiseless fashion which was peculiar to him'.

Cyril Overton, following upon the heels of his telegram to Baker Street, asked Holmes to find Godfrey Staunton, the rugby player of Trinity College Cambridge, for he was vitally needed to play against Oxford.[90] So Holmes and Watson travelled from King's Cross down to Cambridge to see Dr Leslie Armstrong (a thinker of European reputation in more than one branch of science), who had receipted a bill for thirteen guineas to Godfrey Staunton, and yet he had never known his patient to be ill. Asked whether he had heard from Staunton in London, the doctor replied, 'Certainly not.' An urgent telegram which had been sent from Staunton to the doctor, had not been received in Cambridge and Holmes said that he would go to the post office and register a complaint. This made the doctor furious, as he rang for John, his pompous butler, who ushered the visitors severely to the door and into the street, where Holmes burst out laughing. 'Dr Leslie Armstrong is certainly a man of energy and character, perhaps even another Moriarty, should his talents turn to crime.'

Jabez Wilson came to see Holmes in June 1890 and related the most extraordinary story of a Red-Headed League, founded by an American, Ezekiah Hopkins. There was now a vacancy for a new member to earn the princely sum of four pounds a week for purely nominal services. So unusual was the story, that Holmes could not resist chuckling and wriggling in his chair, as was his habit when in high spirits.

Mr Eduardo Lucas was murdered in his eighteenth-century house at 16 Godolphin Street, lying between the Thames and Westminster Abbey. As Holmes and Watson left this house, having discovered the secret hiding place in the floor of the murder room, Holmes showed something to the duty constable, who stared in amazement. 'Good Lord, sir!' Holmes placed his finger upon his lips, replaced his hand in his breast pocket, and burst out laughing as they turned down the street.

Holmes laughed when Lord St Simon placed him on a par with the aristocracy as he said: 'I am afraid that it will take wiser

[90]Perhaps suggested by Howard Staunton, chess player, awarded prize medal for design of chessmen, 1862.

heads than yours or mine', as he bowed himself out in a stately old-fashioned manner. Holmes laughed so much that it needed a whisky and soda and a cigar to restore him after all the cross-questioning. A few minutes later, Holmes again laughed heartily as Lestrade came into their sitting room and announced that he had dragged the Serpentine for the body of Lady St Simon; he laughed again as Lestrade showed him a note in a card case, from a pocket of the wet, watered silk wedding dress of the aforesaid lady, which tended to compromise Miss Flora Millar (a woman from the Allegro, who had been on very friendly terms with Lord St Simon), for she had apparently written:

You will see me when all is ready. Come at once. F H M.

which Lestrade thought was a decoy note. Holmes was more interested in the reverse side of the note, which was a fragment of a hotel bill, which placed Holmes upon the true scent and the discovery of the mystery.

At times, Holmes needed to go out alone, and when he returned he would recount his adventures to Watson, and if they tickled his sense of humour, then he would laugh heartily as he recounted them.

Holmes, dressed as a drunken-looking groom, returned to Baker Street on 21 March 1888, having had some adventures at Briony Lodge, the bijou villa of Irene Adler, and while attending her marriage ceremony. His day had been quite entertaining, and as he recounted his exploits to Watson, they appealed so much to his sense of fun, that he cried: 'Well, really!' and then he choked, and laughed again until he was obliged to lie back, limp and helpless in the chair.

Holmes once read to Watson an excerpt from one of Edgar Allan Poe's stories, wherein a close reasoner followed the unspoken thoughts of his companion; when Holmes said that he was able to do likewise, Watson expressed incredulity. When Holmes actually gave Watson an example of his art, Watson sat up in his chair and stared at Holmes in blank amazement, at which Holmes actually laughed heartily at his friend's perplexity.

One winter's night as Holmes and Watson sat on either side of the fire, Holmes explained to his friend the extraordinary case of the *Gloria Scott* and how the Justice of the Peace, Trevor, was struck dead with horror at receiving an enigmatical message to do with fly-papers and hen pheasants. Watson glanced up at Holmes in a bewildering fashion. 'I cannot see how such a message as this could inspire horror. It seems to me to be rather grotesque than otherwise.' Holmes merely chuckled at the expression on his friend's face.

While Holmes and Watson were on the moors at Mackleton, in the north of England, endeavouring to solve the mystery of the abduction of the son of the Duke of Holdernesse, they were surprised to see James Wilder, the duke's secretary, ride hurriedly past on his cycle and dismount at the Fighting Cock Inn and go inside. This was mystery enough, and Holmes and Watson, needing to investigate further, cautiously approached the inn; there Holmes struck a match and inspected the rear wheel of the cycle, and chuckled to himself as he saw that the tyre was a Dunlop one: this was the needed clue.

Following the visit of Mr Grant Munro to Baker Street, Holmes took up his case concerning the unusual movements of his wife down at Norbury, in an adjacent cottage to his own house. There in a cosy, well furnished, upstairs room, with two candles burning upon the table and two upon the mantelpiece, was discovered a little girl, stooping over a desk in a corner of the room; her face was of the strangest livid tint and the features devoid of any expression. Holmes with a laugh peeled off a mask from her face, revealing a coal-black Negress with flashing white teeth, who was amused at her visitors' amazed faces. She was Lucy Hebron, an American from Atlanta, where her father (of African descent) had died, and afterwards she was brought to England by her white mother. The rather comic situation also affected Watson, who burst out laughing as well, which for him was unusual.[91]

Inspector Forrester visited Colonel Hayter's house because he had heard that Mr Holmes of Baker Street was there. 'We thought that perhaps you would care to step across, Mr Holmes.' 'The

---

[91]The name Munro was also used by ACD in *The Adventures of the Copper Beeches* – Colonel Spence Munro.

fates are against you, Watson,' said Holmes laughing, for he was being dragged into a case of murder, and Watson realised that his protection of Holmes from work was impossible.

Holmes was discussing his brother Mycroft with his friend and Watson suggested that it was Holmes' modesty which made him acknowledge his brother as his superior; this suggestion brought laughter from Holmes, for he did not rank modesty among the virtues, but simply recognised Mycroft's superior powers of observation.

The living members of the Worthingdon bank raid of 1875 (when they stole seven thousand pounds) called upon their police informer, Sutton, in his sombre flat-faced house in Brook Street, London, expecting to wreak their vengeance upon him, only the first time their prey was out upon his customary walk. Holmes guessed that these unknown intruders were actually known to Sutton, having read fright in his eyes. Watson suggested another line of thought: 'Is there not one alternative... grotesquely improbable, no doubt, but still just conceivable? Might the whole story of the cataleptic Russian and his son be a concoction of Dr Trevelyan's, who has, for his own purposes, been in Blessington's rooms?' In the gaslight, Watson saw that Holmes forbore to laugh – he just gave an amused smile at his friend's brilliant departure from his usual observations.

Holmes and Watson travelled by train down to Ross, in the west of England, for the detective had received a telegram which called for help in the unravelling of the Boscombe Valley mystery. Watson read the account in the Hereford newspaper. 'I see... that the coroner in his concluding remarks was rather severe upon young McCarthy. He calls attention, and with reason, to the discrepancy about his father having signalled to him before seeing him, also to his refusal to give details of his conversation with his father, and his singular account of his father's dying words. They are all, as he remarks, very much against the son.' Thereupon Holmes laughed softly to himself and stretched himself out upon the cushioned seat, for he saw the remarks as being favourable to the son.

Kate Whitney called late one night in June 1889 upon the Watsons, seeking their help. She knew that her husband Isa, when the fit was upon him, made use of an opium den at the Bar of Gold in Upper Swandam Lane, where he usually had a one-day orgy, and then returned home; but he now had overstayed his usual time to two days and Kate was worried; Watson promised to bring him home in his hansom. There he most surprisingly found Holmes posing as a drug addict. Once they were together in the street, Holmes burst into a hearty fit of laughter. 'I suppose, Watson,' he said, 'that you imagine that I have added opium-smoking to cocaine injections, and all the other little weaknesses on which you have favoured me with your medical views.'

Mr Hatherley, a hydraulic engineer, having lost his thumb through Colonel Stark's vicious attack upon him, accompanied Holmes and Watson back to the scene of the crime, where they found the house burnt and the criminals flown.[92] Upon their return to London, the engineer commented ruefully: 'Well... it has been a pretty business for me! I have lost a thumb and I have lost a fifty-guinea fee, and what have I gained?' 'Experience,' replied Holmes. 'Indirectly it may be of value, you know; you have only to put it into words to gain the reputation of being excellent company for the remainder of your existence.' And Holmes actually laughed! (Had it been Holmes who had lost a thumb, I doubt if he would have found it a laughing matter!)

At Victoria Station in 1891, Watson, as arranged, met Holmes in a carriage of the Continental express – once Holmes had discarded his disguise as a venerable Italian priest, which had startled Watson, and shown himself in his true form. As their train moved out, Moriarty was seen waving, trying to stop the train. 'With all our precautions, you see that we have cut it rather fine,' said Holmes laughing, as he threw off his black cassock and hat.

It was in 1894 that Holmes took Watson to Camden House, in Baker Street, which stood opposite Mrs Hudson's flat. Here he enjoyed Watson's gasp and cry of amazement as he saw the side view of Holmes' black silhouette upon the luminous screen of the

---

[92]Mr Septimus Goring of New Orleans, passenger on the *Marie Celeste,* had his fingers of the right hand lopped off leaving a great sponge-like hand with the thumb protruding from it. ACD, 'J Habakuk Jephson's Statement' in *Cornhill Magazine,* 1883.

window – a Meunier masterpiece. Holmes enjoyed the startling effect that he had caused, as he quivered with laughter, saying: 'It really is rather like me, is it not?' (What conceit!)

When Holmes and Watson were upon the trail of the murderer of Bartholomew Sholto, they hoped that the dog Toby would follow the smell of the creosote, and so lead them to their quarry; instead of which, a side trail was followed, finishing up in a timber yard, where the creosote was used for wood seasoning. As Watson recorded: 'Sherlock Holmes and I looked blankly at each other, and then burst simultaneously into an uncontrollable fit of laughter.' A little later on when they were on the very fast police launch which was chasing the *Aurora* on the Thames, the launch shot past long lines of loaded barges as though they were stationary. As they overhauled a river steamer and left her far behind, Holmes smiled with satisfaction, so often a prelude to a laugh. (So even the simple things tickled his sense of humour.)

At Aldershot, in Hudson Street (a short thoroughfare lined with plain two-storeyed brick houses), Major Murphy of the Irish regiment, the Royal Mallows, related to Holmes that Colonel Barclay died of apoplexy. 'You see it was quite a simple case after all.' 'Oh, remarkably superficial,' agreed Holmes, smiling, when he might have laughed at the major, knowing that the truth lay with Corporal Henry Wood, whose unexpected appearance at the colonel's window had brought premature death.

In April 1887 Watson took Holmes down to Reigate, to the home of his old friend Colonel Hayter, where he hoped Holmes could convalesce after his trying time abroad. There had been a recent burglary in the neighbourhood with no apparent clues. 'But the affair is a petty one, one of our little country crimes which must seem too small for your attention Mr Holmes, after this great international affair.' (Concerning the Netherlands–Sumatra Company and the 'colossal schemes' of Baron Maupertuis.) A smile from Holmes showed his pleasure at international recognition, although normally he would have laughed away the compliment.

Sherlock Holmes' Conceit

Watson at first thought Holmes clever, but conceited, bumptious, dogmatic and egotistical, with a small vanity underlying his quiet and didactic manner, which was not far from the truth. But for all these things, as Watson witnessed more and more of Holmes and his methods, he learnt to appreciate him as the greatest living detective.

Yet conceit there was. 'What is the use of having brains in our profession? I know well that I have it in me to make my name famous. No man lives or has ever lived who has brought the same amount of study and of natural talent to the detection of crime which I have done.' And later: 'There, Watson! What do you think of pure reason and its fruit? If the greengrocer had such a thing as a laurel wreath, I should send Billy round for it.' This was after Holmes had deciphered the Birlstone code sent by Fred Porlock. (Holmes was certainly not backward in self-adulation!)

Holmes, speaking of Moriarty's genius to Watson, said, 'But if I am spared by lesser men, our day will surely come.' Of the most brilliant bit of thrust-and-parry work in the history of detection with the professor, Holmes observed: 'Never have I risen to such a height, and never have I been so hard pressed by an opponent. He cut deep, and yet I just undercut him... this man may be taken as being quite on the same intellectual plane as myself.' (Not the other way round, you will notice!) As Moriarty sped after Holmes for the final conflict in 1891, Holmes explained to Watson that under similar circumstances, he would have whistled up an engine and carriage as if he were whistling for a cab, expense no problem. At Canterbury Station, Holmes commented upon Moriarty's train as it passed through with a rattle and a roar, beating a blast of hot air into their faces. 'There he goes... There are limits, you see, to our friend's intelligence. It would have been a coup-de-mâitre had he deduced what I would deduce and acted accordingly.' (Holmes just a little superior?)

When Holmes first met Watson at Bart's Hospital, Holmes explained his new infallible test for bloodstains, far better than the old uncertain guaiacum test. Had his test been invented before, many men now alive would have paid the extreme penalty, with the reliable Sherlock Holmes' test. 'His eyes faintly glittered as he spoke, and he put his hand over his heart and bowed as if to some applauding crowd conjured up by his imagination.'

Holmes had not one but two waxen busts made of himself, by Meunier and Tavernier; he admitted to carrying a portable Newgate Calendar in his memory. He spoke to Mrs Hudson at times as if he, and not she, was the landlord; just because he paid her princely sums of money to mollify her for his shortcomings, it certainly gave him no reason to forget that he was only the lodger; he irritated Watson when he said that all his writing 'should be devoted to his own special doings', with an emphasis upon his analytical reasoning. What conceit thought Watson.

Holmes loved to be recognised by people holding important positions in society: 'Your name is very familiar to me, Mr Holmes,' said Lord Holdhurst, Cabinet minister and future prime minister. Did he not have an audience with a certain lady at Windsor? When Holmes felt that he had reached the top of the pinnacle in his profession, then no reward no recognition could increase his stature, not even a knighthood; he even refused to shake the hand of the King of Bohemia, simply bowing and turning away. (This was not just conceit, but purely bad manners.)

In 1903 Holmes wished to arrest Professor Presbury, the famous sixty-one-year-old physiologist of the university town of Camford, but as he said to Watson, 'We cannot arrest the professor because he has done no crime, nor can we place him under constraint, for he cannot be proved to be mad.' Certainly, Holmes must have found the situation somewhat galling, for he would dearly have loved to have exercised his assumed mantle of power.

After Holmes had related to Watson the story of the Musgrave Ritual, and that the ancient crown of the kings of England resided at Hurlstone Manor House in western Sussex, he could not prevent a little of his conceit surfacing as he said to Watson: 'I am sure that if you mentioned my name they would be happy to show it to you.'

As to Gaboriau's Lecoq, Holmes gave him the credit for his energy, but called him a 'miserable bungler'; whereas he took six months to solve a crime Holmes did it in a day. No wonder that such conceit made Holmes regard Lestrade and Gregson as his minions. Note how he spoke to those inspectors after he had finished swiftly examining the dead body of Enoch Drebber, the American, in a house in Brixton. 'You can take him to the mortuary now. There is nothing more to be learned.' So Gregson and his four men obeyed the civilian command, placed the body upon a stretcher and took Drebber away; this was the kind of situation which made Holmes raise his eyebrows sardonically.

Further conceit showed when Holmes was trying to gather information concerning the disappearance of Lady Frances Carfax; he tried to locate the Australian rogue, Holy Peters, alias the Reverend Dr Shlessinger. At last a clue arrived with the pawning of a 'silver-and-brilliant pendant of old Spanish design' at Bovington's in the Westminster Road; Holmes expected that Holy Peters would call again at the jeweller's, and this would provide an opportunity for the Honourable Philip Green (son of a Crimean War admiral), to see the customer. Said Holmes, 'I will give you a note to them, and they will let you wait in the shop. If the fellow comes you will follow him home.' Green was also told to be discreet and to offer no violence. Holmes also spoke to Green concerning his possible entry into No. 36 Poultney Square, Brixton, the home of Peters, into which a deeper than usual coffin had been taken. 'We can do nothing legal without a warrant.' So Holmes sent Green down to the authorities to obtain one from Inspector Lestrade. As Holmes thought that the murder of Lady Frances was imminent and the arrival of the warrant might be too late, he took the law into his own hands and forced his way into the house, saying that his revolver would serve as his warrant for the time being. Peters called Holmes a common burglar, which indeed he was, but this did not deter Holmes from pouring fuel upon the flames by calling Watson a dangerous ruffian. Eventually Holmes was shown the coffin containing the body of a poor old woman, one Rose Spender, from the Brixton Workhouse Infirmary. Holmes remained impassive, but clenched his hands in acute annoyance (for he never liked to be thwarted) and said: 'I am going through your house.' By this time, Peters had summoned the police, a sergeant and a constable, and told them of

Holmes' forced entry. The police, knowing Holmes' identity, told him: 'But you can't stay here without a warrant… Sorry, Mr Holmes but that's the law.' 'Of course not. I quite understand that.' And Holmes and Watson left defeated, with their tails between their legs, but only for the moment.

Holmes became involved over the death of Maria Pinto, Brazilian wife of Neil Gibson, the American gold magnate, of Thor Place when the children's governess, Miss Grace Dunbar, was accused of murder and taken to Winchester, where she was lodged in Sergeant Coventry's humble cottage, which served as the local police station. Holmes told Neil Gibson at Baker Street: 'I have no doubt we can get the necessary permits [to see Miss Dunbar] this morning and reach Winchester by the evening train.' The pass was obtained but only after some delay. Holmes' reputation had certainly soared to dizzy heights when he could quite easily obtain an official pass or warrant; no need to present himself in person – a scribbled note to the inspector, and a warrant would be forthcoming to the bearer! If all else failed, there was his revolver!

When Holmes found upon the northern moor the dead body of Herr Heidegger (the German master at the Priory School) with his skull partially crushed in, he said to Watson that the police must be informed; but he could not dispense with Watson. 'But I need your company and assistance,' said Holmes, as Watson suggested that he should take a note back. Holmes was in a fix. 'Wait a bit! There is a fellow cutting peat up yonder. Bring him over here, and he will guide the police.' Watson fetched the man, and Holmes dispatched him with a note to Dr Huxtable. Perhaps the man was too frightened to tell Holmes to deliver his own note.

Watson called Holmes the benefactor of the race; he compared him to the early nineteenth century, first private detective, created by Edgar Allan Poe. (Holmes disliked being compared to anyone!) Holmes was not even born when Dupin disappeared from the Paris of 1849, so that he had plenty of time to absorb, utilise and develop the Frenchman's methods.

Both men were intellectuals and both men solved crimes by means of almost superhuman analytical genius, but Dupin was not a phenomenon, and far inferior to himself! What absolute conceit! Holmes at least might have accorded credit where it was due, and pointed this out to Watson. They both saw things unnoticed by others: Dupin said that the large excessively obvious things escaped observation; Holmes observed that: 'It has long been an axiom of mine that the little things are infinitely the most important.' They both solved the crimes which baffled the French and English police; they both read the inner thoughts of people by observing the small surface indications. Yes, there is no doubt that Dupin exercised a great influence over Holmes.

As it was, Holmes merely explained his logical train of reasoning to Watson, as if he had initiated it; Watson had expressed incredulity in such powers and so Holmes explained how he could from Watson's features, especially the eyes, read his train of thought, like his predecessor, Dupin.

It was a rainy day in October, with the blinds half drawn. Finding nothing to interest him in the newspaper, Watson leaned back in his chair and fell into a brown study. Although Holmes was reading and rereading a letter he had received that morning, he still had time to observe Watson. 'You are right, Watson,' he said. It does seem a very preposterous way of settling a dispute.' 'Most preposterous!' exclaimed Watson, unwittingly admitting Holmes' insight into his inner most thoughts. 'What is this, Holmes! This is beyond anything which I could have imagined.' Holmes actually laughed heartily at Watson's perplexity and his incredulity.

Holmes then went on to explain to Watson how he had been able to enter his train of thought. 'In the example which you read to me the reasoner drew his conclusions from the actions of the man whom he observed,' said Watson. 'If I remember right, he stumbled over a heap of stones, looked up at the stars, and so on. But I have been seated quietly in my chair, and what clues can I have given you?'

Holmes replied: 'The features are given to man as the means by which he shall express his emotions, and yours are faithful servants.' This astounded Watson. 'Your features, and especially your eyes.'

Holmes then told Watson how his reverie commenced with

the throwing down of the newspaper, followed by a short vacant expression.

'Then your eyes fixed themselves upon your newly framed picture of General Gordon, and I saw by the alteration in your face that a new train of thought had been started. But it did not lead very far. Your eyes turned across to the unframed portrait of Henry Ward Beecher... You then glanced up at the wall, and of course your meaning was obvious. You were thinking that if the portrait were framed it would just cover that bare space and correspond with Gordon's picture over there...

So far I could hardly have gone astray. But now your thoughts went back to Beecher, and you looked hard across as if you were studying the character in his features. Then your eyes ceased to pucker, but you continued to look across, and your face was thoughtful. You were recalling the incidents of Beecher's career. I was well aware that you could not do this without thinking of the mission which he undertook on behalf of the North at the time of the Civil War, for I remember you expressing your passionate indignation at the way in which he was received by the more turbulent of our people. You felt so strongly about it that I knew you could not think of Beecher without thinking of that also. When a moment later I saw your eyes wander away from the picture, I suspected that your mind had now turned to the Civil War, and when I observed that your lips set, your eyes sparkled, and your hands clinched, I was positive that you were indeed thinking of the gallantry which was shown by both sides in that desperate struggle. But then, again, your face grew sadder; you shook your head. You were dwelling upon the sadness and horror and useless waste of life. Your hand stole towards your old wound and a smile quivered on your lips, which showed me that the ridiculous side of this method of settling international questions had forced itself upon your mind. At this point I agreed with you that it was preposterous and was glad to find that all my deductions had been correct.'

Even after the explanation, Watson was still amazed.

Perhaps Holmes reached his pinnacle of conceit when he accosted James Ryder in Covent Garden Market. Having speedily overtaken the little man, Holmes touched him upon the shoulder; the gaslight showed a colourless face.

'Who are you,? What do you want?'

Holmes, having overheard Ryder's questions to the salesman, thought that he could help him.

'You? Who are you? How could you know anything of the matter?'

'My name is Sherlock Holmes. It is my business to know what other people don't know.'

'But you can know nothing of this?' He was referring to his goose being sold.

'Excuse me, I know everything of it.'

Holmes was not the man to be easily ruffled, but when his ego suffered a severe stab from Dr Mortimer, it was a different story, for he had placed himself upon a pinnacle, and there was no one to supplant him.

'Recognising, as I do, [said Dr Mortimer], that you are the second highest expert in Europe—'

'Indeed, sir! May I inquire who has the honour to be first?' asked Holmes with some asperity.

'To the man of precisely scientific mind the work of Monsieur Bertillon must always appeal strongly.'[93]

'Then had you not better consult him?'

'I said, sir, to the precisely scientific mind. But as a practical man of affairs it is acknowledged that you stand alone. I trust sir, that I have not inadvertently—'

'Just a little,' said Holmes [somewhat peeved].

Did this remark still rankle a little later on, after Dr Mortimer had read the contents of the eighteenth century manuscript relating to the Baskerville legend, for Holmes yawned, and tossed the end of his cigarette into the fire?

Sherlock Holmes' Visiting Card

Holmes believed in the power of his visiting card always com-

---

[93]Alphonse Bertillon, Paris police officer (1853–1914) who developed his system for identification of criminals involving measurements of the body, photos and descriptions.

manding respect and generally acting as an 'open sesame', to people and places where others might well have failed: another aspect of his strong masterful personality. (Watson also left his visiting card when he called at Lower Burke Street, to see Culverton Smith.)

When Holmes went to the Woolwich Arsenal office, concerning the Bruce-Partington submarine plans, he was met by Sidney Johnson, the senior clerk, a silent and morose, thin, gruff and bespectacled man of middle age, with haggard cheeks and hands that twitched from recent nervous strain. Upon Holmes presenting his visiting card, he was received with that respect which his card always commanded, and divulged all the information that Holmes required.

During the winter of 1897, Holmes and Watson paid a visit to the shipping office of the Adelaide–Southampton line, which stands at the end of Pall Mall. He sent his card to the manager and was assured of instant attention, and it was not long before he acquired all the information he needed which would help him towards solving the death of Sir Eustace Brackenstall of the Abbey Grange, Marsham, Kent, and also give a new lease of life to Captain Crocker.

Before Holmes returned to Baker Street from Charlington Hall (six miles from Farnham in Surrey) in 1895, he said to Bob Carruthers of Chilton Grange that he thought that he had done what he could to make amends for his share in an evil plot. 'There is my card, sir, and if my evidence can be of help to you in your trial [for he had wounded Roaring Jack Woodley with his revolver, hoping that Miss Violet Smith would be his widow and not his wife], it shall be at your disposal.' It would appear that Holmes was never called upon to give evidence.

Holmes found it necessary to call upon Lord Holdhurst, the foreign minister, in Downing Street on behalf of his nephew, Percy Phelps, who was his client. Holmes' name was well known in ministerial circles, and after his visiting card was sent in, he and Watson were instantly shown up. Certainly Holmes commanded respect from all ranks of society.

Sherlock Holmes' Love of Nature

While Holmes resided at Baker Street, London crime was as life itself to him; away from the metropolis, Watson saw him 'as an uncomfortable man', without his scrapbooks, chemicals and his homely untidiness, and in consequence his temper was apt, sometimes, to become a little frayed. Watson, at first, tended to misconstrue Holmes' apparent preference of some four or five million Londoners around him to nature; he even said that his 'appreciation of Nature, found no place among his many gifts'. How wrong Watson was, and over the succeeding years he had to alter his misconception.

Holmes' love of nature was there, nevertheless, an inborn thing, but the nature of his work required his full concentration, so that he was seldom permitted this luxury.

As Holmes observed to Watson upon their first case together: 'One's ideas must be as broad as Nature, if they are to interpret Nature.' If a case took him away from London, Holmes regarded this as a bonus; as he said: 'I should be none the worse for a quiet, peaceful day in the country... I get so little active exercise that it is always a treat.' He was quite ready to make time available to run down to the countryside in order to test one or two theories which he had in mind.

Holmes not only saw nature, but felt its presence: 'How small we feel,' he observed, 'with our petty ambitions and strivings in the presence of the great elemental forces of Nature.' Watson realised when he was at Briarbrae, Woking, Surrey, how he had mistakenly prejudged his friend, never before having seen Holmes take an interest in nature. 'It was a new phase of his character to me, for I had never before seen him show any keen interest in natural objects.' Here it was in the July following Watson's first marriage, at the home of his old schoolfellow, Percy Phelps, that Watson noticed particularly his friend's interest in nature, when Holmes walked to the open window and held up the drooping stalk of a moss-rose, looking down at the dainty blend of crimson and green. 'What a lovely thing a rose is!' he said. 'Our highest assurance of the goodness of Providence seems to me to rest in the flowers. All other things, our powers, our desires, our food, are all really necessary for our existence in the first instance. But this rose is an extra.' Later, after Holmes had seen Watson and Phelps off to London, he went for a walk by himself. 'After leaving you at the station I went for a charming walk through some admirable Surrey scenery, to a pretty little village called Ripley, where I had my tea at an inn and took the precaution of filling my flask and of putting a paper of sandwiches in my pocket. There I remained until evening, when I set off for Woking again and found myself in the highroad outside Briarbrae just before sunset.'

Holmes could also become lyrical over an early morning sky: 'How sweet the morning air is! See how that one little cloud floats like a pink feather from some gigantic flamingo. Now the red rim of the sun pushes itself over the London cloud-bank.'

It was during his early married life with Mary Morstan that Watson received a telegram asking him to go with Holmes down to Ross, to investigate the Boscombe Pool tragedy. Holmes added: 'Air and scenery perfect.' They put up at the Hereford Arms, arranged by Inspector Lestrade, who had also ordered a carriage to take him to the scene of the crime. 'It was very nice and complimentary of you,' said Holmes. 'It is entirely a question of barometric pressure.' 'I do not quite follow you,' said a startled Lestrade. 'How is the glass? Twenty-nine, I see. No wind, and not a cloud in the sky,' observed Holmes, thinking that he might be better employed having a quiet smoke, sitting upon a rather superior hotel sofa, than going forth in the night.

In 1891, while in Switzerland, Holmes said to Watson, 'Of late I have been tempted to look into the problems furnished by Nature…'

In 1892 Holmes and Watson travelled down to Wisteria Lodge near the pretty Surrey village of Esher, where Aloysius Garcia had been murdered. Mr Scott Eccles, being under suspicion by the police, asked Holmes that he might retain his services, and so the two friends found themselves in the country. Here Holmes was very busy, but still had some time for Mother Nature. 'I'm sure, Watson, a week in the country will be invaluable to you. It is very pleasant to see the first green shoots upon the hedges and the catkins on the hazels once again. With a spud, [a small narrow digging tool], a tin box, and an elementary book on botany, there are instructive days to be spent.' Holmes prowled about with this equipment, but he was not too successful in finding plant specimens, before the evening brought him back to the Bull Inn.

In July 1895 Holmes and Watson journeyed down to Woodman's Lee in Sussex to investigate the death of Captain Peter Carey, a most daring and successful seal and whale hunter. Having satisfied himself that there was no more to be gained by staying in the outhouse, Holmes said: 'Let us walk in these beautiful woods, Watson, and give a few hours to the birds and the flowers.' There was time later, to discuss the case with Hopkins.

The same year, the two friends went down to Charlington Heath, near Farnham, in Surrey, to assist Miss Violet Smith, who had taken a post as music teacher to the only daughter of Mr Carruthers at Chilton Grange, at the unusual salary of one hundred pounds per annum. Miss Smith cycled to and from Farnham Station every weekend and while she cycled along the road by Charlington Heath, she noticed a man following her on a bicycle, keeping about two hundred yards behind her; she found this repeated incident so perplexing that she sought the advice of the great detective. So Holmes and Watson found themselves walking from Farnham Station towards their destination. As Watson related: 'A rainy night had been followed by a glorious morning, and the heath-covered countryside, with the glowing clumps of flowering gorse, seemed all the more beautiful to eyes which were weary of the duns and drabs and slate greys of London. Holmes and I walked along the broad, sandy road inhaling the fresh morning air and rejoicing in the music of the birds and the fresh breath of the spring.' Certainly they both had ample time to appreciate nature.

Nature again called out to Holmes in the spring of 1897; he was nearing a nervous breakdown from overwork which was taking its toll of his iron constitution. He needed to be rejuve-nated. He was advised by his medico, Dr Moore Agar of Harley Street, to take a holiday, which resulted in Holmes and Watson staying in a small, whitewashed cottage near Poldhu Bay, on the Cornish peninsula. There they walked together or Holmes would go for long solitary walks up on the moor, and meditate upon the simple life, the peaceful and healthy routine. Holmes was not yet in possession of sufficient material to reach a conclusion upon the Tregennis case, and so thought that here, nature would help him. 'Let us walk along the cliffs together and search for flint arrows. [He really meant arrowheads.] We are more likely to find them than clues to this problem. To let the brain work without sufficient material is like racing an engine. It racks itself to pieces. The sea air, sunshine, and patience, Watson – all else will come.' They discussed the difficulties of the case before them as they walked. 'And yet, with a little more material, we may prove that they are not insurmountable... Meanwhile, we shall put the case aside until more accurate data are available, and devote the rest of our morning to the pursuit of Neolithic man.' The holiday must have done Holmes a power of good, for he observed, 'I think, Watson, that I shall resume that course of tobacco poisoning which you have so often and so justly condemned.'

It was while Holmes was investigating the mystery of the missing racehorse, Silver Blaze, and slowly walking back across the moor with his friend that Watson, with no problem upon his mind, absorbed the delights of nature, which Holmes appeared not to appreciate under his pensive mood, or so thought Watson wrongly; he thought that all the glories of the landscape went unnoticed by Holmes, that he saw not that 'The sun was begin- ning to sink behind the stable of Mapleton, and the long, sloping plain in front of us was tinged with gold, deepening into rich, ruddy browns where the faded ferns and brambles caught the evening light.' Holmes saw, but was not allowed the complete fulfilment, for, as he had observed before, it was one of the curses of a mind with a turn like his that he must look at everything with reference to his own special subject. He was not at the moment free entirely to indulge in the delights of nature.

Having finished reading the newspapers while on his journey with Watson to Winchester, Hampshire, Holmes looked out of the window and began to admire the scenery – the spring day, a light blue sky, fleecy white clouds and bright sunshine, with an exhilarating nip in the air. Watson admired the little red and grey roofs of the farmsteads, which peeped out from amid the light green of the new foliage. 'Are they not fresh and beautiful?' he cried with enthusiasm, having left the fog of London behind him. 'It is my belief, Watson, founded upon my experience, that the lowest and vilest alleys in London do not present a more dreadful record of sin than does the smiling and beautiful countryside.' For Holmes was thinking of their isolation and how crime might so easily be committed there, in spite of the surrounding natural beauty.

In order that Holmes could get Josiah Amberley, the retired colourman of The Haven, Lewisham, out of his house, he sent him, with Watson, upon a false trail to see Mr Elman, the vicar at Little Purlington, in Essex, not far from Frinton. Watson telephoned Holmes from the Railway Arms in the wilds of the countryside, explaining the abortive journey and the anger of the vicar. Replied Holmes: 'I have unwittingly condemned you to the horrors of a country inn. However, there is always Nature, Watson – Nature and Josiah Amberley – you can be in close commune with both.' And his dry chuckle ended the conversation.

Holmes was very much alive to the country air while he was with Watson at Shoscombe, where Josiah Barnes (mine host of The Green Dragon) asked them if they were 'on the turf themselves'. 'No, indeed,' said Holmes. 'Just two weary Londoners who badly need some good Berkshire air.'

Holmes seldom took exercise for exercise's sake. But there were times when he needed to relax, away from the close air of their sitting room. Early spring often found them taking a walk in the park, 'where the first faint shoots of green were breaking out upon the elms, and sticky spear-heads of the chestnuts just beginning to burst into their five fold leaves'. They would ramble about together, for an hour or so, finding solace in the observation of nature, talking if necessary, but happy to stroll in silence, as befitted men who knew each other intimately.

Holmes must often have had visions of a country retirement, for even as late as 1903 he made this known to Watson. 'It's surely time that I disappeared into that little farm of my dreams.'

But before Holmes retired, he did have an insight into some rough living in the country; for he secretly followed Watson down to Baskerville Hall and, unbeknown to him, lived in one of the Neolithic huts upon the Devon moor, which still retained sufficient roof to act as a screen against the weather. It was only Holmes' strong and immutable purpose, which kept him in such an inhospitable abode. The boy Cartwright kept Holmes supplied with necessities – blankets, waterproofs, cooking utensils, a bucket of water, bread, tinned tongue, peaches, a pannikin and a half-full bottle of spirits. Holmes was able to make a fire in an improvised grate – possibly the only time that Holmes kindled a fire! From the cosseted life of Baker Street, Holmes ably coped with such spartan living, knowing that thus he would be able, incognito, to keep his eye upon the happenings in the locality.

As Holmes did eventually retire to the Sussex countryside, nature must have eventually called him home, once the onus of detection work was lifted off his shoulders and he could deservedly revel in peace. There he gave himself up 'entirely to that soothing life of Nature for which I had so often yearned during the long years spent amid the gloom of London.'

It was during his retirement in Sussex in July 1907, that he observed: 'On the morning of which I speak the wind had abated, and all Nature was newly washed and fresh. It was impossible to work upon so delightful a day, and I strolled before breakfast to enjoy the exquisite air.'

It was the same year in Sussex, that Holmes became involved in the mystery of the Lion's Mane. As he walked to the village of Fulworth to see Miss Maud Bellamy, he had time to pause as he particularly became aware of 'the thyme-scented downs'. So great was Holmes' love and feeling for nature that he was prompted to say: 'When one tries to rise above Nature, one is liable to fall below it.'

So many people had threatened his life in London, and yet he had survived through thick and thin to eventually reap the benefit of a busy life, to add to his knowledge of living through his great interest in bees and photography, and to enjoy his country retirement to the full.

Sherlock Holmes' and Dr Watson's Revolvers

Both Holmes and Watson owned revolvers, sometimes referred to as pistols. Holmes possessed two; Watson only his old army service revolver from his Afghanistan days, an Eley's No. 2. Did they hold a gun licence? Did Lestrade supply the necessary authority? Watson does not clarify this. Did Holmes think that just because he had promoted himself to the position of the only unofficial consulting detective in the world, the last court of appeal, that he was above the law of the country and that he had the legal right to shoot to kill? He did admit sometimes that he was not the law, but was still perfectly happy to represent it in the absence of the police.[94]

When Holmes was still under the shadow of Colonel Moran, and liable to be killed by him, he had some doubts as to using his revolver. He observed to Watson, 'I could not shoot him at sight, or I should myself be in the dock.'

But Holmes had no qualms over the Andaman islander. When Holmes and Watson were following the trail of Jonathan Small and Tonga, Holmes made sure that Watson carried his revolver, and he himself loaded two chambers of his own, then began the chase on the Thames, the police boat chasing the launch *Aurora*. 'Fire if he raises his hand,' said Holmes quietly as the gap narrowed between the two boats. Holmes had promised that if the islander turned nasty, he would shoot him dead. Tonga raised his blowpipe to his lips and, as he did so, both revolvers fired together, and the native whirled round, threw up his arms, and fell sideways into the river. This was the end of the savage, bestial and cruel Tonga. Should Holmes and Watson have been apprehended for murder? They were not! Was it carried out in the name of self-defence? Supposing Tonga had been a white man? Did the Victorians call this racial prejudice?

After all, Holmes was only a member of the community, not even a policeman; sometimes he seemed to have no misgivings as to his assumed authority.

Holmes told Watson to be prepared to shoot John Clay (thief,

---

[94]Abercrombie Smith bought a heavy revolver, with a box of central-fire cartridges at Clifford's, High Street, Oxford. ACD, *Lot 249*.

murderer, forger and smasher, and with royal blood flowing in his veins), with whom he had had one or two little turns.[95] This took place in the cellar of one of the principal London banks, the Coburg branch of the City and Suburban. 'If they fire, Watson, have no compunction about shooting them down.' Watson placed his revolver, cocked, upon the top of a wooden case, behind which he waited expectantly, with the intent to use it, but there was no necessity. Holmes in this instance used his hunting crop to smash down upon John Clay's wrist, and a revolver clinked upon the stone floor.

Watson used his revolver when he was in the empty Camden House, across the road from their flat. There, Colonel Moran fired his gun at Holmes' effigy in the window opposite, across the street. Holmes then sprang like a tiger onto the marksman's back, and hurled him flat upon his face. But Moran was soon up again, and with convulsive strength, seized Holmes by the throat. Watson then struck him upon the head with the butt of his revolver, and Moran dropped to the floor, and Watson fell upon him and held him until he became Lestrade's prisoner.

While in the house of Mr Nathan Garrideb, in Little Ryder Street, off the Edgware Road, Holmes carried his 'old favourite' revolver, and Watson was given Holmes' other revolver. As the head of Killer Evans, (the American from Chicago) emerged from the small cellar, through a square opening in the floorboards, two revolvers pointed at it. He coolly scrambled to the surface. 'I guess you have been one too many for me, Mr Holmes. Saw through my game, I suppose, and played me for a sucker from the first. Well, sir, I hand it to you; you have me beat—' This was to put Holmes off his guard, for he suddenly whisked out a revolver from his breast pocket, and fired two shots. Watson was hit superficially in the thigh as Holmes crashed his revolver down on the man's head, which sprawled him upon the floor and gave him a bloody face; Holmes then frisked him for further weapons.

In 1895, prior to travelling with Watson down to Chiltern Grange, six miles from Farnham, Holmes slipped his revolver into his pocket; he was hoping to help Miss Violet Smith (who

---

[95]Smasher. One who passed bad money.

taught music – hence the 'spatulate finger-ends') to the ten-year-old daughter of her employer, Mr Carruthers. Miss Smith, on her cycle, had been followed by a bearded cyclist and was very frightened – thus she sought help from the great detective. Holmes and Watson arrived at Chilton Grange, only to find Miss Smith 'married' to Mr Woodley, by an unfrocked clergyman, Mr Williamson, and with a dubious marriage licence. Undeterred, Carruthers sought to change the wife into a widow, and shot Woodley, just wounding him. The 'clergyman', mouthing foul oaths, pulled out his revolver, but before he could raise it, Holmes threatened him with his own revolver:

> 'Enough of this… Drop that pistol! Watson, pick it up! Hold it to his head! Thank you. You, Carruthers, give me that revolver. We'll have no more violence. Come, hand it over!'
>
> 'Who are you, then?'
>
> 'My name is Sherlock Holmes.'
>
> 'Good Lord!'
>
> 'You have heard of me, I see. I represent the official police until their arrival. Here, you!' he shouted to a frightened groom, who had appeared at the edge of the glade. 'Come here. Take this note as hard as you can ride to Farnham… Give it to the super-intendent at the police-station. Until he comes, I must detain you all under my personal custody.'

Such was the power of a revolver, and as Watson recorded: 'The strong, masterful personality of Holmes dominated the tragic scene, and all were equally puppets in his hands.'[96]

Holmes did not always carry his revolver with him, but he knew that he could rely upon thoughtful Watson. 'Watson,' he said, 'I have some recollection that you go armed upon these excursions of ours.' (Watson carried his heavy, short, handy, but serviceable weapon, containing six cartridges, in his hip-pocket.) 'It was as well for him that I did so,' reported Watson, 'for he took little care for his own safety, when his mind was once absorbed by a problem, so that more than once, my revolver had been a good friend in need.' When Holmes was reminded of this he said, 'Yes, yes, I am a little absent-minded in such matters.' But this time, at

---

[96]Homes and Watson took Archie Stamford, forger, Farnham 1887.

Thor Bridge, Watson's revolver was only used by Holmes in his experiment at the bridge.

Watson was of the opinion that revolver practice should distinctly be an open-air pastime. Holmes disagreed, for he preferred to do this in the comfort of the Baker Street flat, where he would sit in an armchair with his hair-trigger revolver and one hundred Boxer cartridges; he would then proceed to adorn the opposite wall with a patriotic V R. Poor Mrs Hudson, to have such a lodger, even if he paid over and above the odds for the rent!

Sherlock Holmes and Art

In the early days at Baker Street, Watson thought that Holmes was so immersed in chemical experiments and the detection of crime that he was lacking in knowledge and appreciation of art; Watson even used the words 'abysmal' and 'crude', for their viewpoints differed. After all, had not Holmes some Vernet blood in his veins? Over the years, Watson gradually came to change his views upon this other aspect of Holmes' knowledge, and to realise that he had in a very remarkable degree, the power of detaching his mind at will.

For instance, Holmes could be immersed in the affairs of Sir Henry Baskerville, one minute, while the next he could switch off from crime and on to an appreciation of art. Having endeavoured unsuccessfully to hail a cab in order to follow the bearded stranger who was dogging the footsteps of Sir Henry, Holmes then took Watson into one of the Bond Street picture galleries; here he became entirely absorbed in the pictures of the modern Belgian masters and talked of nothing but art for a whole two hours. Even so, Watson still thought that his friend only had the crudest ideas about the subject.

Holmes also had a fund of knowledge concerning the French artists. He asked Inspector MacDonald (after he had visited Professor Moriarty), if he had noticed a picture over the professor's head. 'I don't miss much, Mr Holmes. Maybe I learned that from you. Yes, I saw the picture – a young woman with her head on her hands, peeping at you sideways.' 'That painting was by Jean Baptiste Greuze… a French artist who flourished between the years 1750 and 1800. I allude, of course, to his working career. Modern criticism has more than endorsed the high opinion formed of him by his contemporaries.' Holmes continued, trying to show the inspector how all knowledge could be useful in the art of detection. 'Even the trivial fact that in the year 1865, a picture by Greuze entitled *La Jeune Fille à l'Agneau*, fetched one million two hundred thousand francs – more than forty thousand pounds – at the Portalis sale may start a train of reflection in your mind.' The inspector was honestly interested. 'I may remind you,' returned Holmes, that the professor's salary can be ascertained in several trustworthy books of reference. It is seven hundred a year.' 'Then how could he buy—' Holmes used the example of the expensive picture being in the possession of a lowly paid man so that the true financial position of the king of the underworld could be understood and brought within the limited range of the inspector's observation and understanding.

Holmes gave a further example of his knowledge of art while at Baskerville Hall, when he became impressed by the line of family portraits upon the wall in the banqueting hall. His fixation surprised both Watson and Sir Henry. 'Excuse the admiration of a connoisseur… Watson won't allow that I know anything of art, but that is mere jealousy because our views upon the subject differ. Now, these are a really fine series of portraits.' Sir Henry wondered how it was that a detective of Holmes' calibre found time to absorb the niceties of painting. 'I know what is good when I see it, and I see it now. That's a Kneller. I'll swear, that lady in the blue silk over yonder, and the stout gentleman with the wig ought to be a Reynolds. They are all family portraits, I presume?' Holmes was particularly interested in the portrait of the wicked Hugo Baskerville in a broad plumed hat, curling lovelocks, white lace collar and black velvet coat, with a straight severe face, not brutal, but prim hard and stern, with a firm set, thin-lipped mouth and a coldly intolerant eye, and dated 1647 upon the back of the canvas. 'Dear me,' commented Holmes, 'he seems a quiet, meek-mannered man enough, but I dare say that there was a lurking devil in his eyes. I had pictured him as a more robust and ruffianly person.' Holmes showed Watson that by taking away the trimmings there was revealed the face of Stapleton, an interesting instance of a throwback, with designs upon the succession, and proving the first quality of a criminal investigator, that he should see through a disguise. (Did Holmes remember Irene Adler?)

Sherlock Holmes' Exercise and Agility

Holmes was a man who never took exercise without good reason nor an aimless holiday while he lived in London; few men were capable of greater muscular effort. Aimless bodily exercise was to him a waste of energy, and he seldom bestirred himself, only when his profession called upon him to do so. He was then absolutely untiring and indefatigable. A usually spare diet and simple habits helped to keep him in training; cocaine was his only vice when there was no game afoot.

Holmes did observe that, 'There can be no question, my dear Watson, of the value of exercise before breakfast.' The two of them would occasionally take a walk in the park, perhaps just to escape from the smoke-laden atmosphere of their sitting room. Sometimes they would embark on an evening ramble of some two hours when they would go further afield, returning about five or six o'clock. At times, should there be a pleasant evening breeze, then they would go on a London ramble of some three hours, when they would stroll about together, passing along the Strand and Fleet Street, watching the ebb and flow of life.

When it was really necessary, for Holmes was always in training, he was able to draw upon his inexhaustible store of nervous energy, which gave him his springy step. Usually Watson was not far behind, even if his leg did trouble him at times; his sedentary life and gradually increasing weight, were not always in his favour.

Certainly, Holmes was more agile than Watson; once they made a forced entry into Appledore Towers, the Hampstead home of Mr Milverton, in their black silk masks. Their object was to find the pocketbook of this notorious blackmailer, and any incriminating papers and letters which might affect the marriage of Lady Eva Blackwell to the Earl of Dovercourt. But one of Milverton's previous victims stepped in with her own method of revenge, by shooting Milverton with her little gleaming revolver. After her departure, Holmes emptied the safe of all incriminating letters upon the fire. The revolver shots having roused the household, Holmes and Watson made a quick exit. 'This way, Watson, we can scale the garden wall in this direction.' Holmes seemed to know the grounds well as they made their way through a plantation of small trees. A six-foot wall barred their way, but Holmes sprang easily to the top and over. As Watson did the same, he felt the hand of the man behind him grab at his ankle, but he kicked himself free and scrambled over a grass-strewn coping, and fell upon his face among some bushes. Holmes helped him to his feet in an instant and together they dashed away across the huge expanse of Hampstead Heath. After they had run two miles, they halted and listened intently: absolute silence. They had shaken off their pursuers and were safe. Inspector Lestrade – unknowingly – described the escaping Watson as 'a middle-sized, strongly built man – square jaw, thick neck, moustache, a mask over his eyes'. Watson was still fleet of foot, seemingly.

The next day at lunch, Holmes suddenly sprang to his feet. 'By Jove, Watson, I've got it! Take your hat! Come with me!' And Holmes hurried at his top speed down Baker Street and along Oxford Street, until they had almost reached Regent Circus. There, in a photographer's window, they saw photographs of many celebrities and beauties and among them a stately lady in court dress with a high diamond tiara upon her noble head. Holmes and Watson looked knowingly at each other.

Another instance of their agility happened at 13 Caulfield Gardens, the home of Hugo Oberstein. Realising that they could not gain entry through the massive front door, they helped each other over the railings and into the back area, where they could hear the policeman's footsteps in the fog above.

Wishing to get into the grounds at Briarbrae, Woking, Holmes clambered over the perimeter fence, which surprised Percy Phelps who wondered why he did not enter through the gate, which surely must have been open. 'Yes,' said Holmes, 'but I have a peculiar taste in these matters. I chose the place where the three fir-trees stand, and behind their screen I got over without the least chance of anyone in the house being able to see me.'

In 1891, upon the evening of 24 April, Holmes surprised

Watson by appearing in his consulting-room. He hurriedly explained the position regarding Moriarty and how he must get away to the Continent; Watson agreed to go too. Then they went into the garden and Holmes climbed over the back garden wall and into Mortimer Street, thus eluding the vigilant eye of any of Moriarty's henchmen.

While at Sholto's house at Norwood, Holmes likened himself to Blondin, the tightrope walker, for he climbed out of the garret, in his bare feet, and onto the roof. There he crawled along the roof-ridge, looking as Watson said, like an enormous glow-worm. Then Holmes climbed down the water pipe onto a barrel and from there to the ground. There he put his stockings and boots on again. Ahead of them lay a six-mile trudge down to the Thames, which Watson managed in spite of his leg.

Holmes and Watson went down to Abbey Grange, Marsham, Kent, upon the invitation of Stanley Hopkins. Lady Brackenstall had been secured to an oaken dining room chair by the cut bell rope. In order to test his theory about his rope, Holmes, to Watson's astonishment, climbed up onto the massive mantelpiece. Far above his head hung the few inches of red cord which were still attached to the wire. Holmes looked for some time up at it, and then, in an attempt to get nearer to it, he rested his knee upon a wooden bracket on the wall. This brought his hand within a few inches of the broken end of the rope, which he observed was not frayed, but had been cut with a knife – for fear of giving the alarm by ringing the bell. The impression of a knee in the dust on the bracket gave Holmes the clue he sought. Finally Holmes sprang down with an ejaculation of satisfaction.

Another instance of Holmes' speed of foot happened at Baker Street. After taking neither food nor drink for three days, Holmes feigned death in order to catch a murderer, Culverton Smith. When Watson suggested fetching Dr Ainstree, the 'greatest living authority upon tropical disease', and turned to the door to go out, Holmes in an instant, with a tiger spring, intercepted him. Watson heard the sharp snap of a twisted key, and Holmes had staggered back to his bed, exhausted and panting after his tremendous burst of energy, the key safe with him.

Holmes and Watson had occasion to go down to the Copper

Beeches near Winchester, the home of Jephro Rucastle, in order to be of assistance to Miss Hunter and to get to the bottom of the missing daughter, Alice Rucastle. When Holmes found the upstairs room with its little pallet bed empty and the prisoner gone, he guessed the exit was by way of the skylight. So he also swung himself up through the skylight and onto the roof, where he discovered the long light escape ladder, used by Mr Fowler to take his intended bride away.

Holmes and Watson, with Inspector MacDonald of Scotland Yard, travelled down to Birlstone Manor House at Birlstone, in Sussex, following upon the murder of the owner, Mr Douglas. Holmes, wishing to put a theory of his to the test, persuaded the other two men to accompany him, in the dark, to a screen of laurel bushes, which lay nearly opposite to the main door and the drawbridge. Their vigil was a long one and bitterly cold, a damp reek from the moat chilling them to the bone and setting their teeth chattering. At last the window was thrown open, with a whining of hinges, and a man peered forth furtively, not wishing to be observed. He leaned forward and hauled in from the moat a large round object into the room. (This was precipitated by the inspector pretending that he was to have the moat drained.) 'Now!' cried Holmes, and with 'one of those outflames of nervous energy which could make him on occasion both the most active and the strongest man that I have ever known, ran swiftly across the bridge and rang violently at the bell.' As Ames opened the door, Holmes brushed him aside and rushed into the room lit by a solitary oil lamp, where he confronted Cecil Barker with the sodden bundle of clothes belonging to the American, Ted Baldwin.

While down in Cornwall in the spring of 1897, Holmes and Watson were taken to the vicarage of Tredannick Wollas by Mr Roundhay in his dog cart, where his lodger, Mortimer Tregennis, had died during the night under unusual circumstances. So urgent Holmes felt the matter to be, that he and Watson postponed their breakfast. Watson described another aspect of Holmes' agility as he entered the death room:

> In an instant he was tense and alert, his eyes shining, his face set,

his limbs quivering with eager activity. He was out on the lawn, in through the window, round the room, and up into the bed-room, for all the world like a dashing foxhound drawing a cover. In the bedroom he made a rapid cast around and ended by throwing open the window, which appeared to give him some fresh cause for excitement, for he leaned out of it with loud ejaculations of interest and delight. Then he rushed down the stairs, out through the open window, threw himself upon his face on the lawn, sprang up and into the room once more, all with the energy of the hunter who is at the very heels of his quarry.

Perhaps Holmes' most impressive display of speed and agility took place on Dartmoor, when he chased the gaunt, savage, coal-black bloodhound-cum-mastiff, as large as a small lioness, which Stapleton had purchased from Ross and Mangles in the Fulham Road, London. Stapleton brought it down by the North Devon line, and walked a long way over the moor in order to evade suspicion. He then kept it kennelled in a safe hiding place in the dangerous Grimpen Mire. Once before, Holmes had heard the terrible scream of Selden the convict, and a prolonged yell of horror and anguish as the hound attacked him, which shook Holmes' nerves. 'Where is it? …Where is it waiting?' he had whispered, and Watson knew by the thrill of his voice that the usual man of iron was shaken to his very soul. Came the time when the hound chased Sir Henry Baskerville in the moonlight, and as it leaped down the track, past the watchers, Holmes and Watson both fired their revolvers at the creature, through the dense, white fog, and gave instant chase. Watson related:

> Never have I seen a man run as Holmes ran that night. I am reckoned fleet of foot, but he outpaced me as much as I outpaced the little professional [Lestrade]. In front of us as we flew up the track we heard scream after scream from Sir Henry and the deep roar of the hound. I was in time to see the beast spring upon its victim, hurl him to the ground, and worry at his throat. But the next instant Holmes had emptied five barrels of his revolver into the creature's flank.

There was no need for Watson to do likewise – the hound was dead. (But Watson did blow out the brains of another dog, Carlo, the huge black mastiff of Jephro Rucastle.)

Sherlock Holmes as a Burglar

Although Holmes' art was directed towards apprehending the criminal, he was not above undertaking a little burglary some-times (for he rather fancied himself as a master burglar), when he considered that it was the only way to secure some vital informa-tion. He kept a good assortment of shining housebreaking tools in a leather case in a drawer. As Holmes observed: 'This is a first-class up-to-date burgling kit, with nickle-plated jemmy, diamond-tipped glass-cutter, adaptable keys, and every modern improvement which the march of civilisation demands.' Add also a dark lantern, a pair of silent shoes and a black silk mask, to turn him into one of the most truculent figures in London. Opening safes was one of his hobbies; how grateful were the police to find Holmes upon the side of the law and not against them.

One of Holmes' burglaries took place at the Hampstead home of Mr Milverton. Both he and Watson, attired in evening dress clothes and wearing masks of black silk, arrived at the house at midnight. Holmes chose to enter the drawing room by way of the greenhouse, it being less noisy. 'The place was locked,' wrote Watson, 'but Holmes removed a circle of glass and turned the key from the inside. An instant afterwards he had closed the door behind us, and we had become felons in the eyes of the law.'

The next morning, just after breakfast was finished and Holmes and Watson were smoking their morning pipe, a very solemn and impressive Lestrade was ushered into the sitting room. The inspector asked for Holmes' assistance in a most remarkable and dramatic murder, that of Milverton, at Hampstead, by criminals of good position, wishing to prevent social exposure. 'Criminals? Plural?' said Holmes. 'Yes, there were two of them. They were nearly as possible captured red-handed. We have their footmarks, we have their description, it's ten to one that we trace them. The first fellow was a bit too active, but the second was caught by the under-gardener, and only got away after a struggle. He was a middle-sized, strongly built man – square jaw, thick neck, moustache, a mask over his eyes.' (Considering that the time was around midnight, windy and bitterly cold, the gardener's eyes were extremely good.) 'That's rather vague. Why, it might be a description of Watson!' said Holmes. 'It's true… It might be a description of Watson,' said Lestrade with amusement. Holmes declined to help. 'The fact is that I knew this fellow Milverton, that I considered him one of the most dangerous men in London, and that I think there are certain crimes which the law cannot touch, and which therefore to some extent, justify private revenge. No, it's no use arguing, I have made up my mind. My sympathies are with the criminals rather than with the victim, and I will not handle this case.'

Holmes and Watson also broke into the house of Hugo Oberstein, in order to see how the body of Arthur Cadogan West, the twenty-seven-year-old Woolwich Arsenal clerk, came to be found outside Aldgate Station, in the London Underground. The house was one of a line of 'flat-faced pillared, and porticoed houses' of the middle Victorian period in the West End of London. The fog screened them with its friendly shade. By the light of his lantern, Holmes could see that the massive door was locked and bolted and presented a problem. 'We would do better in the area,' said Holmes. After the policeman's steps had died away, they helped each other over the railings. Holmes set to work upon the lower door, stooped and strained, until with a sharp crash it flew open. They sprang through into a dark passage, closing the door behind them; Holmes led the way, by the aid of his little fan of yellow light, up the curving uncarpeted stairs, until a window was reached. Holmes threw it open and the lamp light disclosed the window sill to be thickly coated with soot from passing engines, the black surface being blurred and rubbed in places. Holmes now had the clue he needed. The next night they took Mycroft and Lestrade with them.

In 1899 Josiah Amberley of Brickfall and Amberley, manufacturers of artistic materials, came to Baker Street and told Holmes his tale of woe; how his wife and a friend, Dr Ray Ernest, had eloped together to an unknown destination, taking with them his deed-box containing a good part of his life's savings. In Holmes' imagination, he had some doubts as to the story ringing true. He first sent Watson down to the house at Lewisham to report upon any possible useful evidence. Then Holmes sent Amberley and Watson on a false trail down to Essex in order that the coast would be clear for his own inspection of the house. For Watson had given Holmes a useful clue when he mentioned the use of new green paint in the house. As Holmes told Inspector MacKinnon: 'There being no fear of interruption, I proceeded to burgle the house. Burglary has always been an alternative profession had I cared to adopt it, and I have little doubt that I should have come to the front.' (A common burglar, without a warrant who received praise instead of chastisement from the Law!) Holmes continued:

'Well, then came an incident which was rather unexpected to myself. I was slipping through the pantry window in the early dawn, when I felt a hand inside my collar, and a voice said: 'Now, you rascal, what are you doing in there?' When I could twist my head round I looked into the tinted spectacles of my friend and rival, Mr Barker. It was a curious foregathering and set us both smiling. It seems that he had been engaged by Dr Ray Ernest's family to make some investigations and had come to the same conclusion as to foul play. He had watched the house for some days and had spotted Dr Watson as one of the obviously suspicious characters who had called there. He could hardly arrest Watson, but when he saw a man actually climbing out of the pantry window there came a limit to his restraint. Of course, I told him how matters stood and we continued the case together.'

This must have been an unusual experience for Holmes, working with another private detective, although he did have occasion to meet up with Mr Leverton, of Pinkerton's American Agency.

John Mason, head trainer of the horses of Sir Robert Norberton of Shoscombe Old Place, wanted Holmes' opinion; he thought that his employer was going mad with the strain of the necessity to win The Derby with his colt, Shoscombe Prince, to avoid bankruptcy. He wasn't sleeping, his eyes were wild and his conduct to his sister, Lady Beatrice Falder, had ended in a bitter, savage, spiteful quarrel; and why had the master gone at midnight in the rain to the haunted crypt under the old ruined chapel in the park? Why should he want to dig up a dead body? So it was that Holmes was persuaded to go down and investigate. In the crypt:

Holmes set to work making a very careful examination of the graves, ranging from a very ancient one, which appeared to be Saxon, in the centre, through a long line of Normans, Hugos and Odos, until we reached the Sir William and Sir Denis Falder of the eighteenth century. It was an hour or more before Holmes came to a leaden coffin standing on end before the entrance to the vault. I heard his little cry of satisfaction and was aware from his hurried but purposeful movements that he had reached a goal. With his lens he was eagerly examining the edges of the heavy lid. Then he drew from his pocket a short jemmy, a box-opener, which he thrust into a chink, levering back the whole front, which seemed to be secured by only a couple of clamps. There was a rending, tearing sound as it gave way, but it had hardly hinged back and partly revealed the contents before we had an unforeseen interruption.

Inside was a body swathed in a sheet, 'with dreadful, witch-like features all nose and chin, projecting at one end, the dim, glazed eyes staring from a discoloured and crumbling face. It was the dead body of Lady Beatrice, who had died naturally of the dropsy. Sir Robert explained to Holmes the whole situation, which seemed a little irregular although perhaps still within the law. Said Holmes the burglar: 'this matter must, of course, be referred to the police. It was my duty to bring the facts to light, and there I must leave it.'

In order to watch the shooting of his effigy in the window of the flat in Baker Street, probably by an assassin in the street (who could then be apprehended by Lestrade and his officer), Holmes took Watson to the empty Camden House opposite. Here they passed through a wooden gate into a deserted yard, where Holmes opened the back door with a key and made his illegal entry into the pitch-dark dwelling. Watson never mentioned how Holmes obtained the key, or was it one of his own adaptable keys?

When Holmes broke into the house called Vernon Lodge, near Kingston, Surrey, the home of Baron Gruner, he was able to steal the baron's love or lust diary, owing to Watson keeping him occupied by a discourse upon Chinese pottery. Holmes hoped to use this diary as a weapon to prevent Miss Violet de Merville's marriage, which it did eventually. As Watson wrote: 'Sherlock Holmes was threatened with a prosecution for burglary, but when an object is good and a client is sufficiently illustrious, even the rigid British law becomes human and elastic. My friend has not yet stood in the dock.'

Holmes certainly would have made the master criminal. As he said to Watson after John Turner had killed Charles McCarthy at Boscombe Pool, near Ross, in Herefordshire – thinking of Baxter's words: 'There, but for the Grace of God, goes Sherlock Holmes.'

Sherlock Holmes the Actor

'The best way of successfully acting a part, is to be it,' said Holmes.

Holmes was the consummate actor; he did not merely change his costume, but his expression, his manner, his make-up, his very soul, seemed to vary with every fresh part that he assumed. Even when he first met Watson, and explained his infallible test for bloodstains – the Sherlock Holmes' test – he could not subdue his theatrical streak, despite the smallness of his audience. Watson recorded that: 'His eyes fairly glittered as he spoke, and he put his hand over his heart and bowed as if to some applauding crowd conjured up by his imagination.'

After Count Sylvius, the murderer, had complimented Holmes upon his acting abilities, which had deceived him into thinking that Holmes had placed an old sporting man and an elderly woman upon his trail, Holmes observed, 'Really, sir, you compliment me. Old Baron Dowson said the night before he was hanged that in my case what the law had gained the stage had lost.[97] And now you give my little impersonations your kindly praise?' With menacing eyes, the count called Holmes a 'play-acting, busybody self'.

As the years went by, and Holmes became a noted figure to the police and to the criminal underworld, he found it necessary at times to adopt a variety of disguises. Sometimes he would change in the upstairs room at Baker Street; at other times in one of the many refuges that he had in London, where he could come

---

[97] Perhaps suggested by John Dowson (1820–1881), Orientalist. *Dictionary of National Biography*, 1903.

and go in secret, unknown even to Watson. His friend insisted that he was the dramatist in real life. Holmes thrived upon such adulation. 'Some touch of the artist wells up within me, and calls insistently for a well-staged performance.'

While Holmes was on the trail of Jonathan Small – he with the wooden leg – he resorted to the disguise of a seaman, and returned to Baker Street, to see if he might deceive even Watson and Athelney Jones; as soon as he was through the front door, his impersonation began. Watson described the scene so well:

> A heavy step was heard ascending the stair, with a great wheezing and rattling as from a man who was sorely put to it for breath. Once or twice he stopped, as though the climb were too much for him, but at last he made his way to our door and entered. His appearance corresponded to the sounds which we had heard. He was an aged man, clad in seafaring garb, with an old pea-jacket buttoned up to his throat. His back was bowed, his knees were shaky, and his breathing was painfully asthmatic. As he leaned upon a thick oaken cudgel his shoulders heaved in the effort to draw the air into his lungs. He had a coloured scarf round his chin, and I could see little of his face save a pair of keen dark eyes, overhung by bushy white brows and long grey side-whiskers. Altogether he gave me the impression of a respectable master mariner who had fallen into years and poverty.

Although Watson had seen Holmes depart in the early dawn, in seaman's dress, he still didn't penetrate the disguise. Holmes continued his fun with both of them, saying that he knew where Smith's boat was, the wanted men and the treasure, but he would only tell Mr Holmes and he could not afford to wait. 'No, no; I ain't going to lose a whole day to please no one. If Mr Holmes ain't here, then Mr Holmes must find it all out for himself. I don't care about the look of either of you, and I won't tell a word.' He shuffled towards the door, but Jones blocked his path. 'Pretty sort o' treatment this,' he said '...I come here to see a gentleman, and you two, who I never saw in my life, seize me and treat me in this fashion!' And he stamped his stick to add emphasis to his words. Watson assured him that he would be recompensed for his loss of time, and invited him to rest on the sofa. Then he suddenly surprised the two of them, having shed his false make-up, by asking for a cigar, for the others were already smoking. Jones was highly delighted. 'Ah, you rogue! …You would have made an actor and a rare one. You had the proper workhouse cough, and those weak legs of yours are worth ten pound a week. I thought I knew the glint of your eye, though. You didn't get away from us so easily, you see.'

Holmes was called in by the King of Bohemia to endeavour to retrieve some compromising letters written to Irene Adler, the American actress and singer, together with a photograph of the two of them together, before his impending marriage took place to Clotilde Lothman von Saxe-Meningen of Scandinavia.

So he resorted to two disguises. First he took the part of an out-of-work, drunken-looking groom (ill-kempt and side-whiskered with an inflamed face and disreputable clothes), for Holmes relied upon the sympathy and freemasonry which existed among horsy men, to divulge information about this particular lady, which they did as Holmes lent a hand to some ostlers in rubbing down their horses in a nearby mews. In the same disguise he attended the wedding of Miss Adler to Godfrey Norton, as the sole witness of the marriage ceremony.

Later, in order to obtain admittance to Irene Adler's residence, he adopted the disguise of an amiable and simple-minded Nonconformist clergyman, with a broad black hat, baggy trousers, white tie, and a sympathetic smile, peering through spectacles with benevolent curiosity. (Watson does not mention Holmes normally wearing them.) With the aid of accomplices engaged for the evening to stage a fight as Mrs Norton descended from her smart little landau, Holmes dashed into the crowd to protect the lady and got 'knocked down', and, feigning injuries with the aid of red paint, was carried into the house and into the sitting room.

Holmes had previously given Watson instructions that when the window was opened (ostensibly to give him fresh air), and he saw Holmes hand signal, he was to throw in the long cigar-shaped roll – an ordinary plumber's smoke rocket, with a cap at either end to make it self-lighting – and call out 'Fire!' and the paid crowd of onlookers would join in.[98]

Mrs Norton saw through the disguise and prevented Holmes from achieving his objective; she later on fooled Holmes himself – and Holmes was a past master at penetrating a disguise – by disguising herself as a slim young youth in an ulster. She followed him home, and called out: 'Goodnight, Mister Sherlock Holmes', as he searched for his door key. 'I've heard that voice before. Now, I wonder who the deuce that could have been,' said Holmes, staring down the dimly lit Baker Street.

Mrs Neville St Clair of Lee, in Kent, had business to attend to at the offices of the Aberdeen Shipping Company in Fresno Street, which branched out of Upper Swandam Lane. As she walked down the lane at 4.35 p.m., on her way home, she happened to look up at the second floor open window of an opium den, and was struck cold by seeing the agitated face of her husband, who waved frantically and then disappeared. She called the police, who inspected the upstairs room, but found no St Clair, only Hugh Boone, a professional beggar of Threadneedle Street, a crippled wretch of hideous aspect. Also there strangely enough, were St Clair's clothes and a box of bricks which he had promised to bring home for their little boy. The police were mystified and arrested Boone and took him to the police station.

In order to help Mrs St Clair find her husband, Holmes visited the opium den, the vile, stupefying fumes of the drug wafting over the double row of sleepers, and played the rôle of another customer; he hoped to glean some helpful information. He sat himself down beside a brazier, a very thin, very wrinkled, old man bent with age, an opium pipe dangling down from between his knees, as though it had dropped in sheer lassitude from his fingers, a picture of doddering, loose-lipped senility.

Holmes needed to ponder over the question of the missing man, which he did at the home of the St Clairs, staying up all night, smoking heavily and reaching a conclusion by morning that Neville was masquerading as Boone. Later, Holmes' wet sponge upon the face with the twisted lip proved him right, as with

---

[98]Dupin, wishing to replace the stolen letter by his own facsimile to gain time, employed a man to fire a musket, so causing a disturbance. Edgar Allan Poe, *The Purloined Letter*.

Inspector Bradstreet's permission he visited the prisoner in his cell. His hands had been washed but his face was as black as a tinker's, this did not conceal its repulsive ugliness: a broad weal from a former scar ran right across it from eye to chin, and by its contraction had turned up one side of the upper lip, while he had a shock of very bright red hair. Holmes moistened his sponge from the water jug and rubbed the prisoner's face vigorously to reveal St Clair's features, much to the inspector's astonishment.

When Holmes travelled down to Aldershot to assist the police in finding the murderer of Colonel Barclay, he posed as a registration agent, and in that capacity had a most interesting gossip with the landlady of Henry Wood of Hudson Street. Wood had accidentally met Nancy Barclay in the street, his love of some thirty years ago; Holmes interviewed Wood and although he usually concealed his emotions, he was in a state of suppressed excitement as he did so. Wood had followed Nancy home, and through the window had witnessed an altercation between husband and wife, whereupon he stormed in on them. The shock of seeing Nancy's former lover from India caused the colonel to collapse, hitting his head on the fender. The inquest concluded that death was naturally due to apoplexy.

While Holmes was investigating the disappearance of the son of the Duke of Holdernesse of Mackleton, he resorted to the pretence of having a sprained ankle and, clutching Watson by the shoulder, he limped up to the door of the Fighting Cock Inn, telling Reuben Hayes, the landlord, that he was unable to walk, and asked him to hire a carriage, as he could not put his foot to the ground. However, there was no carriage available, and if Holmes could not walk, he was advised to hop. Holmes tried other tactics and offered a sovereign for a bicycle, but the demand still fell upon stony ground.

In the case of the Beryl Coronet, Holmes resorted to the dress of a common loafer. 'Yes,' said Holmes, in reply to Watson's 'Strange how terms of what in another man I should call laziness alternate with your fits of splendid energy and vigour.' 'There are in me the makings of a very fine loafer, and also of a pretty spry sort of a fellow.' With turned-up collar, a shiny, seedy coat, red cravat and worn elastic-sided boots, he looked, as Watson noted, 'a perfect sample of the class'. Before he departed from Baker Street, he cut a slice of beef from the joint upon the sideboard, sandwiched it between two rounds of bread, put it in his pocket, and made his way to Streatham. Going to the house of Sir George Burnwell, he made acquaintance with his valet and for six shillings obtained a pair of the master's cast-off shoes; these he found fitted the tracks at Streatham and so those of the thief, who had sold the three beryls from the coronet.

While Holmes was staying as a guest of Colonel Hayter, at Reigate, he became involved, against Watson's advice, in the hunt for the murderer of William Kirwan, coachman to the Cunninghams. In order to prevent Inspector Forrester telling the Cunninghams of the existence of the torn piece of paper from the note sent to Kirwan, Holmes quickly resorted to the art of throwing a sudden and severe fit, his face assuming the most dreadful expression. As Watson recorded: 'His eyes rolled upward, his features writhed in agony, and with a suppressed groan he dropped on his face upon the ground.' Holmes was carried into the kitchen, 'where he lay back in a large chair and breathed heavily for some minutes'. Explaining that he had only just recovered from a severe illness, he said that he was liable to these sudden nervous attacks. Later, when he explained the truth to the colonel, he laughed: 'Good heavens! ...do you mean to say all our sympathy was wasted and your fit an imposture?' Watson too, had been amazed at the admirable and professional piece of acting, to which Holmes only said, 'It is an art which is often useful.'

In order to escape the vigilance of Moriarty, Holmes, as he boarded the Continental express at Victoria, travelled in the garb of a venerable decrepit Italian priest, who in broken English told a porter that his luggage was booked through to Paris; he was aged, wrinkled, dull of eye, with a mumbling mouth with a protruding lower lip and he wore a black cassock and hat. As the first-class carriage had been reserved, Watson was surprised to find a stranger seated there and a chill of fear came over him as he thought that some accident had overtaken his friend; the doors were all shut and the whistle blown and still no Holmes to greet the worried Watson. Then the 'priest' spoke: 'My dear Watson...

you have not even condescended to say good-morning.' Cried out the startled and astonished Watson, 'Good heavens! How you startled me.' Whispered Holmes: 'Every precaution is still necessary. I have reason to think they are hot upon our trail.'

In the case of the king of the blackmailers, Charles Augustus Milverton, Holmes, was to help Lady Eva Blackwell (due to be married to the Earl of Dovercourt), retrieve some important letters, which he later burnt. In order to gain entry to the house and spy out the land, Holmes posed as Mr Escott, a plumber, a rakish young workman with a goatee beard, a swagger and smoking a clay pipe. He became engaged to Agatha the maid, although he had no intention of marrying, and walked out with her for several evenings. Thus he was able to learn the plan of the house, and that the letters he wanted were in a safe in the study; this was necessary groundwork before he and Watson committed a burglary.

Holmes pretended that he had been pricked by the poisonous needle, sent in a little box by Culverton Smith, who was perfectly familiar with Holmes' whereabouts. He told Watson that he had caught a rare Asiatic disease from Sumatra. For three days Holmes tasted neither food nor drink, so that his bones stuck out of his face, his eyes were unnaturally bright and he looked at death's door. He spoke of odd things to Watson, in order to accentuate his rôle of a raving maniac. He added vaseline on his forehead, belladonna in the eyes, rouge over the cheekbones and crusts of beeswax round the lips. His thin hands twitched upon the bedcover: a sight to please Holmes' would-be murderer.

When Lady Frances Carfax, the sole survivor of the direct family of the late Earl of Rufton, ceased to correspond from abroad with her old governess, Miss Dobney, the anxious family (being exceedingly wealthy, and who would spare no expense if the matter could be cleared up) called in Holmes to take up the case. So Watson was sent off, alone, to Lausanne to elicit information. While there, he accosted a huge, swarthy man with a bristling black beard, hoping he might gather useful information. As Watson recounted:

The fellow gave a bellow of anger and sprang upon me like a tiger. I have held my own in many a struggle, but the man had a grip of iron and the fury of a fiend. His hand was on my throat and my senses were nearly gone before an unshaven French *ouvrier* in a blue blouse darted out from a cabaret opposite, with a cudgel in his hand, and struck my assailant a sharp crack over the forearm, which made him leave go his hold. He stood for an instant fuming with rage and uncertain whether he should not renew his attack. Then, with a snarl of anger, he left me and entered the cottage from which I had just come. I turned to thank my preserver, who stood beside me in the roadway.

This turned out to be none other than Holmes, who, finding that he could get away from London, had followed close upon Watson's heels. Having saved his friend from a serious attack, all Holmes could say was: 'Well, Watson, a very pretty hash you have made of it! I rather think you had better come back with me to London by the night express.'

In the spring of 1894 Holmes returned to London from his foreign travels. Wishing for the time to remain incognito and hidden from such people as Colonel Moran, he set up as a bookseller at the corner of Church Street, not far from Watson's Kensington abode. No one recognised Holmes – not even Watson – in this elderly deformed man, his curved back inside a seedy frock coat, his sharp wizened face with white side-whiskers, and white hair; he looked thinner and keener than of old, with a dead-white tinge in his aquiline face, an indication of recent bad health. He spoke in a strange croaking voice, with a gruff snarling manner.

In July 1895 several rough-looking men called at Baker Street to see 'Captain Basil', the disguise of Holmes while he was on the trail of Black Peter. He had spent some days in the East End of London, devising an Arctic expedition and asked for harpooners to sign on with him.[99]

In June, after Watson's marriage, Holmes posed as Mr Harris of Bermondsey when he applied for a job as an accountant at

---

[99]In 1880 ACD aged twenty, went as surgeon on the steam whaling ship *Hope* from Peterhead to the Arctic Seas for seven months. Pay two pounds, ten shillings a month plus three shillings a ton oil money. ACD, 'Life on a Greenland Whaler', *Strand Magazine*.

126B Corporation Street, Birmingham; he went with Watson who posed as Mr Price. Neither was a serious contender for employment, but went simply to assist Mr Hall Pycroft in solving the mystery of Arthur Pinner's 'brother'.

Dr Trevelyan of Brook Street, London, an authority upon cataleptic attacks, was visited by a bogus Russian nobleman with a presumed similar complaint. Holmes explained to Watson that the catalepsy was a fraudulent imitation. 'It is a very easy complaint to imitate. I have done it myself.'

When Holmes went down to the Devon moors, in order to unravel the mystery surrounding the murder of Sir Charles Baskerville, he went unbeknown to Watson, for he wished to observe without his presence being known. He wore a tweed suit and cloth cap, and with his thin, worn, alert face, bronzed by the sun, and roughened by the wind, he looked like any other moorland tourist.

Watson was asked if he would mind going in his place to interview Josiah Amberley at The Haven, Lewisham, as he was rather busy: mere subterfuge, for he merely wished to study at first hand things for himself, without being recognised. Holmes went as a lounger – a tall, dark, heavily moustached, military-looking smoking man; Watson failed to penetrate the disguise, but he noted that he was given a curiously questioning glance, which he recalled later on as he explained his visit to Holmes.

During Holmes' three years travelling abroad, after Moriarty's death, he posed as Sigerson, a Norwegian explorer.

Holmes once observed to Watson, 'My eyes have been trained to examine faces and not their trimmings. It is the first quality of a criminal investigator that he should see through a disguise.' Strange, that both 'Mrs Sawyer' and Irene Adler, both fooled Holmes.

There must have been so many other disguises that Holmes used, but alas, they go unrecorded by Watson, and still await the researcher among the vast amount of unpublished material.

Sherlock Holmes the Smoker

Holmes was a great smoker and generally smoked a black shag

tobacco; when he visited Watson he would smoke a pipe of his Arcadian mixture.

His first pipe was smoked before breakfast, composed of all the dottles left over from his smokes of the previous day, all carefully dried and collected upon the corner of the mantelpiece; after breakfast, a cigarette. During the day, the smoke might be one of a variety of pipes, a cigarette or a cigar from his cigar case, with which he would often enjoy a whisky and soda. He kept his strong black shag tobacco in the toe-end of a Persian slipper, which he spoke of to Watson as his 'lamentable tobacco'.[100]

Holmes kept more than one rack of pipes – briars (one favourite with an amber mouthpiece), clays and cherrywoods. Did he have a meerschaum pipe? In neither text nor illustration is there any evidence of one being smoked.[101] Holmes might have smoked such a pipe in 1914, after he took Von Bork to London in Watson's car.[102] I wonder if Holmes owned an ADP briar-root pipe, like that smoked by John Straker, and would he have cared for his long-cut Cavendish tobacco.[103]

Holmes kept certain pipes for certain moods; when in a disputatious mood, then a long cherrywood pipe, perhaps lit by a glowing chip from the wood fire, held in the steel claws of the tongs, or by a wax vesta, or perhaps a thin spill of paper or wood; for the meditative mood, the old black oily clay pipe thrusting out like the bill of some strange bird. Maybe, this was the pipe referred to by Watson as Holmes' 'oldest and foulest of pipes'. When in a judicial mood he would place his fingertips together, but which particular pipe he then smoked goes unrecorded.

---

[100]Everard King of Greylands Court, near Clipton-on-the-Marsh, Suffolk wore a pair of red Turkish slippers. ACD, 'The Story of the Brazilian Cat', *Strand Magazine*, 1898.

[101]William Gillette, American actor, smoked a meerschaum pipe. Claire Hills, copywriter to the Folio society, gave me the following information. 'When Gillette was rehearsing the title part in his play, *Sherlock Holmes*, his jaw ached to such an extent through speaking with a pipe clenched between his teeth, that a solution had to be found to relieve this painful problem. Thus was born the myth of the meerschaum, the large bowl of which, thanks to the shape of the pipe's stem, Gillette could support in his collarbone.'

[102]Frank Wiles's colour portrait of Holmes first appeared in the *Strand Magazine* in September 1914; he smoked a straight-stem pipe.

[103]Tobacco moistened and pressed into quadrangular cakes Mr Cavendish?

While he was deliberating upon the Baskerville legend and pouring over a very large-scale Ordnance Survey map of the Devon moorland (acquired from Stamford's of Long Acre), he consumed 'two large pots of coffee and an incredible amount of tobacco, in his black clay pipe'. Watson, entering the room full of the acrid fumes of strong coarse tobacco, thought that a fire had broken out, as he began coughing. 'Caught cold, Watson?' said Holmes, coiled up in an armchair in his dressing gown. 'No, it's this poisonous atmosphere.' 'I suppose it is pretty thick, now that you mention it.' 'Thick! It is intolerable.' 'Open the window, then!' Which was a most unusual remark for Holmes to make, as he preferred his windows shut! Sometimes it was the reeking amber mouthpiece of his pipe, which he used as a pointer to show Watson certain positions upon a map.

If the disguise called for it, then Holmes was not averse to smoking two fills of an ostler's shag tobacco, with a glass of half and half, and earning tuppence as he assisted in rubbing down the horses.[104] I wonder if he kept these coins as a further memento of Irene Adler?

When Holmes was listening to the facts of a case, his wreaths of acrid smoke from his pipe seemed to curl up more thickly, as if to emphasise each curious episode; sometimes as he leaned back in his velvet-covered chair, he would blow little warning rings of smoke up to the ceiling. With a cigarette, he would draw in the smoke, 'as if the soothing influence was grateful to him'.

Holmes usually needed more than one pipe when working upon a case; often he needed several pipes when trying to separate crucial facts from incidental ones. Some problems, like the one concerning John Clay, the City and Suburban bank robber, were a three pipe one lasting some fifty minutes, during which time Holmes begged Watson not to speak to him.

Perhaps Holmes' longest smoking period was an all-night sitting at The Cedars, when he contemplated the problem of the missing person, Neville St Clair. As Watson recorded:

---

[104] Mr Smallweed, Mr Guppy and Mr Joblin go to a dining house known as a Slap-Bang, where they order: 'Three pint pots of half and half.' Charles Dickens, *Bleak House*, 1853.

He took off his coat and waistcoat, put on a large blue dressing-gown and then wandered about the room, [a large and comfortable double bedded room], collecting pillows from his bed and cushions from the sofa and armchairs. With these he constructed a sort of Eastern divan, upon which he perched himself cross-legged, with an ounce of shag tobacco and a box of matches laid out in front of him. In the dim light of the lamp I saw him sitting there, an old briar pipe between his lips, his eyes fixed vacantly upon the corner of the ceiling, the blue smoke curling up from him, silent, motionless, with the light shining upon his strong-set aquiline features. So he sat as I dropped off to sleep, and so he sat when a sudden ejaculation caused me to wake up, and I found the summer sun shining into the apartment. The pipe was still between his lips, the smoke still curled upward, and the room was full of a dense tobacco haze, but nothing remained of the heap of shag which I had seen upon the previous night.

Holmes was most interested in the pipe left behind at Baker Street by Mr Grant Munro. 'A nice old briar,' observed Holmes, 'with a good long stem of what the tobacconists call amber. I wonder how many real amber mouthpieces there are in London? Some people think that a fly in it is a sign. Well, he must have been disturbed in his mind to leave a pipe behind him which he evidently values highly' 'How do you know that he values it highly?' asked Watson. 'Well, I should put the original cost of the pipe at seven and sixpence. Now it has, you see, been twice mended, once in the wooden stem and once in the amber. Each of these mends, done, as you observe, with silver bands, must have cost more than the pipe did originally. The man must value the pipe highly when he prefers to patch it up rather than buy a new one with the same money.' Holmes continued: 'Pipes are occasionally of extraordinary interest. Nothing has more individuality, save perhaps watches and bootlaces. The indications here, however, are neither very marked nor very important. The owner is obviously a muscular man, left-handed, with an excellent set of teeth, careless in his habits, and with no need to practise economy.'

Rather strange that Holmes never published a monograph upon pipes; he surely must have made numerous notes with the full intention of publication: the reader is the loser.

His stock of cigars Holmes kept in the coal scuttle (for they had wood fires), from whence he could fill his case for a journey.[105] Watson does not mention where Holmes kept his cigarette stock from where he could fill his silver cigarette case. Did he order them by the thousand, like Professor Coram? For he was not averse to smoking the professor's Egyptian cigarettes at Yoxley Old Place in Kent, made especially for him by Ionides of Alexandria. There, Holmes smoked cigarette after cigarette with extraordinary rapidity, even faster than the professor, while he paced up and down near a high bookcase in the corner of the room. Watson thought that he did this because he enjoyed the unusual flavour. But it was purely a ruse, covered up by a smiling Holmes with 'I am a connoisseur.' It was simply done in order to cover the carpet with ash, for he wished to verify his suspicions that someone was hiding behind the bookcase; the foot impressions turned out to be those of Anna Coram, the professor's wife.

Holmes' knowledge of tobacco and their ash was vast, for he knew of at least one hundred and forty varieties; just by looking at the ash left in a pipe-bowl he could say, 'This is Grosvenor mixture at eight pence an ounce.'

Tobacco Ash and Revelations

Holmes could read a book out of even a very short burnt cigarette stub. Mrs Warren, a neighbouring landlady, visited Holmes at Baker Street, imploring his help over her mysterious lodger. Holmes was prepared to wave her away, but she held her ground firmly with the 'pertinacity and also the cunning of her sex'. (Holmes had arranged, the previous year, an affair for Mr Fairdale Hobbs, a lodger of hers.) Flattery won her the day and Holmes put down his gum-brush and gave her his undivided attention.

Mrs Warren then shook out from an envelope, two burnt matches and a cigarette end upon the table, for she had heard that Holmes was able to read great things out of small ones. 'There is nothing here,' said Holmes. 'The matches have of course, been used to light cigarettes. That is obvious from the shortness of the

---

[105]The dish of potatoes was mislaid in the coal-scuttle, during dinner at Mrs Jellyby's house. Charles Dickens, *Bleak House*, 1853.

burnt end. Half the match is consumed in lighting a pipe or cigar. But, dear me! This cigarette stub is certainly remarkable. The gentleman was bearded and moustached, you say? …I don't understand that. I should say that only a clean-shaven man could have smoked this. Why, Watson, even your modest moustache would have been singed.' Watson suggested a holder. 'No, no the end is matted… It may, of course, be trivial – individual eccentricity; or it may be very much deeper than appears on the surface. The first thing that strikes me is the obvious possibility that the person now in the rooms may be entirely different from the one who engaged them.'

Sherlock Holmes' Other Attributes

Among Holmes' many attributes was that of great strength: this was put to the test when he was confronted by Dr Grimesby Roylott in his siting room at Baker Street in April 1883. He flung open the door without any ceremony or warning, wanting to know what Holmes had said to his stepdaughter, Helen Stoner. To all the questions Holmes kept a calm exterior and parried them with inconsequential statements, which rattled the doctor so much that he told Holmes that he was a dangerous man to fall foul of. He then exhibited his strength by seizing the steel poker and bending it into a curve, and throwing it dramatically into the fireplace. He then strode from the room. Holmes picked up the bent poker, and with a sudden effort straightened it again, demonstrating that he had even greater strength.[106]

But even this exceptional strength failed Holmes once; he was demonstrating to Mr Holder that no ordinary man could have broken the piece from the Beryl Coronet. Holmes, with a grip of iron, exerted his strength upon the heirloom, but without result. 'I feel it give a little, he commented; but, though I am exceptionally strong in the fingers, it would take me all my time to break it.'

---

[106]Michael Henchard went into the Three Mariners Inn to partake of his first drink after twenty-five years abstinence. Before he left he spoke of Donald Farfrae. 'I could double him up like that and yet I don't.' Saying which, he laid the poker across his knees, bent it as if it were a twig, flung it down and departed. Thomas Hardy, *The Mayor of Casterbridge*, 1886.

Holmes then explained how it had taken the strength of two men, that of Sir George Burnwell, the thief, and that of Arthur Holder, who was only trying to retrieve the coronet, having chased the thief in his bare feet.

In Holmes' college days, he had been both a fencer and a boxer.[107] Watson called Holmes 'undoubtedly one of the finest boxers of his weight that I have ever seen. Few men were capable of greater muscular effort.' But did Watson ever see Holmes box? He certainly heard how Holmes could use his fists!

There was an early case of Holmes being in a brawl, which was recorded in his Index of Biographies, which must have happened before he knew Watson. A certain man called Mathews knocked out Holmes' left canine in the waiting room at Charing Cross. Holmes must have been just a little bit slow with his defence.[108]

As an amateur, Holmes fought the prize fighter McMurdo over three rounds at Alison's rooms on his benefit night, and gave McMurdo something to remember him by – a cross-hit under the jaw. As McMurdo said to Holmes four years later, when they met at Pondicherry Lodge, 'Ah, you're one that has wasted your gifts, you have! You might have aimed high, if you had joined the fancy.' 'You see, Watson,' said Holmes, laughing, 'if all else fails me, I have still one of the scientific professions open to me.'

Certainly, Holmes, although not in practice, could still give a good account of himself; on one of his trips to see Watson he was attacked by a rough with a bludgeon – one of Moriarty's henchmen – but he knocked him down, barking his knuckles upon the man's front teeth.

Again, he found his amateur skill most handy when he came up against Cyril Woodley in April 1895, a rather odious, coarse, puffy-faced, red-moustached young man, who was hoping to marry Miss Violet Smith against her will. He was a guest of Mr Williamson, tenant of Charlington Hall, Charlington Heath,

---

[107]ACD was a boxer. On the Greenland Whaler, *Hope*, he blackened the eye of Jack Lamb, the steward. He wrote two boxing stories, *Rodney Stone* and *The Croxley Master*. Also a prize fighting play, *The House of Temperley*.

[108]David Copperfield knocked out the tooth of the Canterbury butcher. Charles Dickens, *David Copperfield*, 1850.

Surrey. Holmes was talking to the landlord of the local inn when Woodley came in from the taproom, and in an argumentative way, with the colourful use of adjectives, asked what Holmes meant by asking questions – for he had overheard the conversation. He ended a string of abuse by a vicious backhander which totally surprised Holmes, and gave him a cut lip and a discoloured lump upon his forehead. But as Holmes related to Watson: 'The next few minutes were delicious. It was a straight left against a slogging ruffian. I emerged as you see me. Mr Woodley went home in a cart.'

Another case of Holmes the pugilist occurred at Woking. He had been asked by Watson's nervous and sensitive old school chum, Percy Phelps, to hurry urgently down to Briarbrae to assist him over the recovery of a naval treaty. Having sent Watson and Phelps back to London, Holmes waited patiently, squatting down in a clump of rhododendrons just opposite Phelps's bedroom window, until the church clock struck two in the morning. Then Holmes saw Joseph Harrison, the suspected thief, bareheaded with a black cloak thrown over his shoulder. He entered the house by the window, the catch of which he pushed back with a long-bladed knife, and, pushing the knife through a crack in the shutters he prised the bar up and swung them open. As Holmes later related:

> From where I lay I had a perfect view of the inside of the room and of every one of his movements. He lit the two candles which stood upon the mantelpiece, and then he proceeded to turn back the corner of the carpet in the neighbourhood of the door. Presently he stooped and picked out a square piece of board, such as is usually left to enable plumbers to get at the joints of the gas-pipes. This one covered, as a matter of fact, the T joint which gives off the pipe which supplies the kitchen underneath. Out of this hiding-place he drew that little cylinder of paper, pushed down the board, rearranged the carpet, blew out the candles, and walked straight into my arms as I stood waiting for him outside the window.

Vicious Harrison attacked Holmes with his knife, and Holmes grasped him twice and received a cut over the knuckles. Holmes replied by blotting out one of Harrison's eyes, when he listened to Holmes' reasoning, and gave up the little cylinder of blue-grey paper, (the original of the secret naval treaty between England and Italy, and of such importance that the French or Russian Embassy would have paid an enormous sum for it).

Holmes also had some knowledge of baritsu, or the Japanese system of wrestling, which was more than once useful to him, particularly against his arch-enemy.

Holmes was certainly a card player. Did he belong to one of the London card clubs, the Baldwin, Cavendish, Bagatelle, Carlton, Anglo-Indian, Tankerville or the Diogenes? Watson does not enlighten us. In 1890 Holmes, anticipating that there might have been a chance of a game, put a pack of cards in his pocket in the hope of a rubber, knowing that there would be a foursome when he went with Watson, Inspector Jones of Scotland Yard and Mr Merryweather. The latter was the chairman of the directors of the City branch of the City and Suburban Bank; the object was to apprehend John Clay, forger and murderer, late of Eton and Oxford and a royal duke's grandson. The banker was somewhat put out, having to forgo his card game. 'It is the first Saturday night for seven and twenty years that I have not had my rubber.' When they were all assembled in the bank cellar, where thirty thousand French napoleons, (the twenty-franc gold coins issued by Napoleon) were stored, Holmes had to insist upon a dark lantern, much to the chagrin of the banker, who had hoped that he might have had a rubber after all. But it was not to be, for the enemy's preparations had gone too far, and Merryweather had to be content with playing for much higher stakes than in a card-game.

When Mr Henry Baker called at Baker Street, in answer to Holmes' advertisement, he came to claim his hat and his Christmas goose. Holmes told him that he was 'somewhat of a fowl fancier', and that he had seldom seen a better grown goose. Perhaps Holmes advised Mrs Hudson where game and poultry were concerned.

Holmes once described himself as a 'dog-fancier', although it is not known if, like Watson, he ever kept a dog, unless it was in the parental home.[109] While he was staying with Watson at an old-fashioned tavern called the Green Dragon at Crendall, three miles from Shoscombe Park, he spoke to the sporting host, Josiah Barnes. Holmes was duly attracted to the innkeeper's dog: 'By the way, that was a most beautiful spaniel that was whining in the hall… Now, if it is a fair question, what would a prize dog like that cost?' 'More than I could pay, sir.' Being one of the real Shoscombe breed, it was the best in England. Watson already knew about this most exclusive breed of spaniels, the pride of every dog show and of their owner, Lady Beatrice Falder of Shoscombe Old Place, because he once had his summer quarters down there.

Watson was the man who had some knowledge of the 'Turf' and did place bets upon racehorses; perhaps he passed on this information to Holmes. He only recorded one instance of Holmes betting upon the horses – there may have been others – when they both went down to Dartmoor at the invitation of Inspector Gregory and Colonel Ross, the owner of Silver Blaze, a powerful bay horse from the Isonomy stock and favourite for the Wessex Cup. The horse had disappeared and John Straker, the trainer, killed. After the disguised favourite had won and the killer of Straker exposed, Holmes, having a bet upon the next race and hoping to win, deferred his explanation until the return journey to Victoria, when he related the full account to Colonel Ross.

Holmes had a different kind of bet, this time at Covent Garden, with Mr Breckinridge the purveyor of geese: he asked him from whence he obtained the birds he sold to the Alpha Inn near the British Museum. Holmes bet one pound that the geese were country bred, and not town bred; Mr Breckinridge, knowing that he was on to a winner, got his lad to bring out the books, which showed the geese came from the Brixton Road. As Watson recorded: 'Sherlock Holmes looked deeply chagrined. He drew a sovereign from his pocket and threw it down upon the slab, turning away with the air of a man whose disgust is too deep for words.' He had lost one pound purposely, but he had gained the information that he needed.

---

[109]Abercrombie Smith said to Edward Bellingham at Oxford: 'I am a bit of a dog-fancier myself.' ACD, *Lot 249.*

If Holmes wished to prove a theory of his, then he would leave no stone unturned in order to do so. He asked himself the question: did John Hopley Neligan murder Captain Peter Carey, by driving a steel harpoon through his chest and transfixing the body to the wooden wall of the outhouse at Woodman's Lee? Holmes related his personal experience of harpooning to Watson: 'If you could have looked into Allardyce's back shop, you would have seen a dead pig swung from a hook in the ceiling, and a gentleman in his shirt sleeves furiously stabbing at it with this weapon [a barbed-headed spear]. I was that energetic person, and I have satisfied myself that by no exertion of my strength can I transfix the pig with a single blow. This somewhat negative exercise suggested to Holmes that the murderer had to be a strong, practised harpooner.

Holmes was also interested in archaeology, and could quite easily detach himself from a case in hand to discourse to Watson for two hours upon Neolithic man and the Celts, arrowheads and pottery shards in Cornwall. He called himself 'a bit of an archaeologist' when he called upon Nathan Garrideb at Little Ryder Street, off the Edgware Road, for he wanted to see if Nathan was another fraud, as well as the Kansas Garrideb. Immediately he became interested in the house and wondered whether it was Queen Anne or Georgian: Garrideb thought the latter; Holmes the former. He then called upon the house agents, Holloway and Steele, in the Edgware Road, hoping to gather information about the former residents for the last five years, but unfortunately they were closed.

Was Holmes a photographer while at Baker Street, or did he only take up this hobby after his retirement to Sussex? Holmes was present when the local science master, Fitzroy McPherson, died in agony, just after he had been swimming in one of the sea pools; his back was covered with dark red lines as though he had been flogged by a thin wire scourge, the long angry weals curving round his shoulders and ribs. The only clue that Holmes had to go upon were the last rather incoherent words he heard, which rather sounded like 'the lion's mane'. Holmes must have taken photographs, for later on, when Inspector Bardle asked him his opinion, Holmes brought out an enlarged photograph of the curious lines, saying: 'This is my method in such cases', which called forth the inspector's approbation. 'You certainly do things thoroughly, Mr Holmes.' 'I should hardly be what I am if I did not,' replied Holmes.

While Holmes was in Cornwall, he received a consignment of books upon philology, for the ancient Cornish language had arrested his attention; he conceived that it was akin to the Chaldean and had been largely derived from the Phoenician traders in tin.

In 1894 Holmes was deciphering the remains of the original inscription upon a palimpsest, with the aid of his powerful lens, which might have been an old manuscript or a monumental brass from a church.

Holmes was well versed in French, German and Latin, and had a knowledge of Greek and Italian, and possibly some Persian. He particularly needed his German because he had done a good deal of business in the past in Germany. He thought the German language most unmusical but the most expressive. Goethe, he thought, was 'always pithy', and he liked to quote him as well as Gustave Flaubert to Watson. There is no instance of him quoting Greek, but he just touched upon it in the case of handwriting, where it was relevant. His Italian enabled him to decipher the candle message flashed from the red house in Howe Street to the window in Mrs Warren's lodging house, which he read as 'beware danger'. From the upstairs window of the red house, Holmes used the same candle to flash to Mrs Lucca, the lodger, the signal to come to him – *Vieni* – with which she complied, thinking it was her husband, Gennaro's message. In order to illustrate his point to Watson that Miss Sutherland would not believe that her stepfather, James Windibank, was the same as her pretended lover, Hosmer Angel, he quoted the Persian of Hafiz:[110] 'There is danger for him who taketh the tiger cub, and danger also for whoso snatches a delusion from a woman.' (Watson does not record whether this was from the original or a translation.)

Holmes was a keen single-stick expert. (A fighting stick for

---

[110]Mohammed Hafiz, 1310–1389. Poems known as 'The Divan' (Brewer, Rev. E C transl., *Reader's Handbook*, n.d.).

one hand.)[111] He found his skill in this art a great asset to him when he was attacked in London in 1902.

If the London daily newspapers contained no criminal news, upon which Holmes could concentrate all his energy, then he might have been prompted to sally forth on his own to consult a back number of *The Times*, for this newspaper reported so well upon court cases, or make one of his numerous visits to the British Museum. Upon one of these trips he was anxious to consult Eckermann's *Voodooism and the Negroid Religions* to see if he could throw any light upon the doings of Garcia's cook of Wisteria Lodge, who came from the backwoods of San Pedro, and performed such an unusual ritual in the kitchen – a torn bird, a pail of blood and charred bones.

Or his walk might take him to Doctors' Commons, to look up a will in association with his client's work.[112] As he reported to Watson on one occasion: 'I have seen the will of the deceased wife [of Dr Roylott, formerly Mrs Stoner]. To determine its exact meaning I have been obliged to work out the present prices of the investments with which it is concerned.' This told Holmes the revealing information that Dr Roylott would gain financially from the death of his two stepdaughters.

In order to trace the movements of the American ship, the *Lone Star*, and its captain, James Calhoun, the leader of the Ku Klux Klan secret society,[113] Holmes spent a whole day checking over Lloyd's registers and files of old papers. He followed the future career of every vessel which touched at Pondicherry in January and February 1883. He then searched the Dundee records and found that the *Lone Star* was there in January 1885. He then checked the vessels at present in the port of London and found that the ship had been there during the week; at the Albert Dock, Holmes found that the sailing ship had already left for Savannah. He hoped that the American police would apprehend the three

---

[111]Abercrombie Smith kept, 'a couple of single-sticks in his Oxford college room. ACD, *Lot 249*

[112]Doctors' Commons before the establishment of the Divorce Court and Probate Court in 1857, the College of Civil Law in London, incorporated by Royal charter in 1768.

[113]KKK. Secret society in 1868 in Alabama and other southern states of the North American Union. *Haydn's Dictionary of Dates*, 1876.

murderers at Savannah, and thus reward him for all his research work.

Travelling and Modes of Transport

Bad winter weather never deterred Holmes and Watson from following a criminal trail. The evening before, might find them sitting snugly in their chairs, one either side of a blazing log fire, while the London fog in Baker Street – a greasy, heavy, brown swirl drifted past outside, and condensed in oily drops upon the window panes. As they sat, Holmes might dip into an old black leather volume, or some other book, or sit with knitted brows and an air of abstraction, formulating tomorrow's plans, when it would be imperative to make an early start in the cold light of day. By then, Holmes, with a red-hot energy underlying his phlegmatic exterior, now suddenly upon the scent, tense and alert, with shining eyes, set face and limbs quivering with eager activity, would awaken Watson by the light of a candle with a 'Come, Watson, come. The game is afoot. Not a word! Into your clothes and come.' And meek, comradely Watson, willing always to pander to his friend's slightest whim, would be dragged away without breakfast (Holmes never worried over the loss of food at these times), and not until the cab had dropped them at Charing Cross, blurred and indistinct in the opalescent London fog, yellowed by the smoking chimneys, were they both permitted to drink some hot tea before their cold journey. Rather hard luck on Watson's empty stomach, because he could not function on raw energy and nervous force.

Upon such a journey, when a dun-coloured veil hung over the house tops, looking like the reflection of the mud-coloured street beneath, the weather called for warm apparel, so they would don tweed suits – Holmes, a long grey travelling cloak, or an ulster, a close-fitting, ear-flapped, cloth travelling cap; Watson, overcoat and hat. Both wore stockings and boots. They both sometimes wore shoes and presumably spats. (Watson wore them at Stoke Moran, when he took them off in the bedroom of Helen Stonor, and Holmes wore them in the snow at Fairbank, Streatham, the home of Alexander Holder when he was investigating the loss of part of the Beryl Coronet.) Sometimes they would wear cravats. But, rain or shine, winter or summer, Holmes was always well dressed, having a cat-like personal cleanliness, with a certain quiet primness. In London it was usually a frock coat and top hat for Holmes, and Watson when he was on medical work; otherwise a bowler and comfortable coat, waistcoat and trousers.[114]

Sometimes a Gladstone bag was carried if a number of things were required, such as a little pocket lantern which, when the darkening slide was drawn back, shot a long tunnel of vivid yellow light; sometimes only a tiny tunnel of light when Holmes had forgotten to trim the wick and give it a good clean. Other essentials often included a notebook, a pair of night glasses, penknife, tape measure, large round magnifying glass, revolver (sometimes called a pistol), and ammunition; some 'Derbies', steel handcuffs of a new pattern with instantaneous spring locking (these were far in advance of those used by Scotland Yard, but the official police preferred the old pattern); visiting cards, a case of cigars, cigarettes in a silver case, pipes, tobacco pouch and matches, although Watson was rather relied upon for the latter; in the cold weather, a spirit flask. Unless Holmes' coat lining was one capacious pocket like that of H G Wells' tramp, he certainly needed some kind of receptacle for his oft-times assorted paraphernalia. Sometimes Holmes wore a pea-jacket and carried a loaded hunting crop – sometimes a cane. When they were stopping over, they would take things for the night. In April 1891 Holmes carried a handbag when travelling to the Continent.

Once they travelled from King's Cross Station to Cambridge, to help Cyril Overton find his important vanished rugby player, Godfrey Staunton. While there, Holmes rode a bicycle, trying to follow Dr Leslie Armstrong, but seen through the back window of his brougham, his mission was abortive. Watson was also a cyclist, so that they must have owned their machines in earlier days.

When upon a train journey, Holmes was inclined to take with him a number of newspapers, for he had the following daily papers (including extra editions) delivered by his newsagent to

---

[114]The bowler was named after William Bowler, the English hatter who designed it in 1850. *Chambers Dictionary*,1983.

Baker Street: *The Times*, *Daily Telegraph*, *Daily Gazette*, *Morning Post*, *Morning Chronicle*, *Daily News*, *Standard*, and the biweekly, *North Surrey Observer*, and any local newspaper in the area of the crime. Holmes was inclined to unfold his newspaper in a leisurely fashion, then having rummaged, read and inwardly digested, and made notes upon the criminal news and news in the agony columns, he would dispose of the lot by rolling them into one gigantic ball and either throwing it up upon the rack, or under the seat. He was then free to relax and judge the speed of their train. 'We are going well,' said Holmes to Watson as their train sped from Paddington to Exeter. 'Our rate at present is fifty-three and a half miles an hour,' he added as he glanced at his watch. Watson not having observed the quarter-mile posts, wondered how Holmes had arrived at his conclusion. 'The telegraph posts upon this line are sixty yards apart, and the calculation is a simple one.' On other occasions after a discussion, Holmes would immerse himself in his pocket Petrarch,[115] or would sit with his chin upon his breast, his hat drawn over his eyes, deep in thought.

Sometimes they travelled on the main line train from Waterloo, Charing Cross, Paddington, Victoria or Euston; sometimes by the Underground. It seems that Holmes always purchased the tickets, which were first-class. After all, Watson always travelled at the invitation of Holmes, who remembered that Watson only had his army pension, private means never being mentioned, while he lived at Baker Street.

They travelled together from Euston to Mackleton in the Peak District, where they both stayed at Dr Thorneycroft Huxtable's Priory School, in preference to accepting the invitation to stay at Holdernesse Hall, Hallamshire, the home of the late chief secretary of state. The ten-year-old son and heir of the duke had joined the school on 1 May, the beginning of the summer term, and disappeared on 13 May. This was the reason for the doctor calling upon Holmes' unique assistance, hoping that he would succeed where the police had failed and find the missing boy.

In January 1903, Holmes, James M Dodd and Sir James Saunders travelled down by train to Bedford where they took a

[115]Francesco Petrarca or Petrarch. Italian poet 1304–1374.

trap to Tuxbury Old Park, five miles away. Their journey had been taken on behalf of Dodd, who had been in the South African War with Godfrey Emsworth, only son of Colonel Emsworth, the Crimean VC Dodd was worried over the mystery surrounding his friend, for whom he had real affection, for he felt that he was being held some kind of prisoner in his own house. There was good reason for this, as the father thought that he had contracted leprosy; luckily Holmes' friend was the great dermatologist, Sir James Saunders, and he diagnosed the complaint to be ichthyosis, or pseudo-leprosy, a scale-like affection of the skin, unsightly, obstinate, but possibly curable, and certainly non-infective.

Occasionally Holmes and Watson would get away very early upon their travels, like the winter train they caught at 6 a.m. from Charing Cross to Chatham. Detective Stanley Hopkins had asked for their help in unravelling the mystery of the murder of Willoughby Smith (of Uppingham and Cambridge), who had been employed as a secretary by Professor Coram. He had met his death by the severance of the carotid artery.[116]

The usual mode of travel about London for Holmes and Watson was by hansom cab, a light two-wheeled vehicle, with the driver's seat raised behind.[117] Holmes employed his own method of summons, by putting his two forefingers between his teeth, and emitting a shrill whistle. Even to ensure that something was safely delivered in person, and not left to a messenger, a cab would be taken. As, for example, the trip in 1894 to leave a packet at the Russian embassy, containing the diary of Anna, the wife of Sergius the Russian, and letters to her from a close friend, Alexis. It was hoped that the information might help to release Alexis from a Russian salt mine. Sometimes a journey was made easier, by taking a hansom all the way, like the one taken to Kingston to visit Baron Gruner.

Whether Holmes ever 'travelled' on the outside of a hansom goes unrecorded; but there was an instance when he travelled on the outside of a 'growler' – a four-wheeled horse-drawn cab. It arose when 'Mrs Sawyer', a very old and wrinkled woman,

---

[116]Professor Presbury of Camford was attacked by his faithful wolfhound. Roy, whose sharp teeth passed dangerously near the carotid artery. ACD, *Creeping Man*.
[117]Invented by Joseph A Hansom 1803–1882. *Dictionary National Biography*, 1903.

hobbled into the Baker Street flat. She had come in reply to Holmes' advertisement in the evening paper to claim the gold wedding ring found in the Brixton Road, (when in reality of course, it was found under the body of Enoch Drebber, an American of Cleveland, found murdered at 3 Lauriston Gardens, Brixton Road), which belonged to her daughter Sally Dennis. Holmes, thinking that the woman might be an accomplice, decided to follow her to her house at 13 Duncan Street, Houndsditch. The limping and footsore woman eventually hailed a four-wheeler, and as soon as she was inside, Holmes perched himself behind, an art he said at which every detective should be an expert. The cab stopped in Duncan Street, and Holmes really thought that he was on a winner, instead of which it was an empty vehicle that Holmes looked into: Holmes had been outmanoeuvred by an active, young male actor, and he was the old woman!

Sometimes Holmes and Watson used a brougham.[118] Such a conveyance was used one October day, at 7.30 a.m., in the first dim glimmer of daylight, when they travelled to the house of Dr Percy Trevelyan, at 403 Brook Street, where they had been summoned by a scribbled pencil note, to come at once, for Blessington had been murdered.

Watson never recorded that they ever travelled by the horse bus (even when mechanised) of the London General Omnibus Company, which was formed in 1855, whose white, green or chocolate-coloured buses (according to their destination) rumbled through the mist by day and under the blue spluttering arc lamps at night.[119]

Sometimes travel would be by dog cart, and although a slightly unusual one, Holmes was a competent driver.[120]

Such a journey was undertaken to Lee in Kent in a tall dog cart driven by Holmes through the gloom, aided by the two golden tunnels of yellow light from its side lanterns, a distance of some seven miles. He drove to The Cedars, to meet the wife of the

---

[118]A one-horse closed carriage named after the Chancellor, Lord Brougham, 1778–1868. (*Dictionary National Biography*, 1903).
[119]R J Unstead, *Travelling Roads through the Ages*, 1969.
[120]Two-wheeled horse vehicle with seats back-to-back, originally used to carry sporting dogs.

missing person, Neville St Clair, which mystery he hoped to clear up by the morning. The charge for the dog cart, for the return journey, was two shillings and sixpence.

Holmes and Watson travelled down to Charlington Heath, near Farnham in Surrey, in April 1895, to assist Miss Violet Smith, who had sought Holmes' advice concerning a solitary cyclist who appeared to follow her on her journey to and from Farnham Station. Holmes and Watson had to walk from the railway station to the heath and, nearing their destination, they espied coming towards them an empty dog cart, the horse cantering and the reins trailing, and no sign of Miss Smith, who should have been the passenger. Holmes suspected abduction, and wondered if they might be too late to help her. Watson stopped the runaway horse, and they both sprang in. Holmes took the reins and turned the horse round, and giving it a sharp cut with the whip they sped back along the road. They were not in time to stop the phoney wedding between Mr Woodley and Miss Smith, but their intervention culminated in Williamson and Woodley being tried for abduction and assault and getting seven and ten years' jail sentences apiece.

Another form of conveyance used by Holmes and Watson, was the horse drawn trap. They needed to keep a rendezvous with Miss Helen Stoner at Stoke Moran on the western border of Surrey, so they took the train from Waterloo to Leatherhead, where they were able to hire a trap at the station inn, and were driven by a driver for the five-mile journey; thus Holmes was able to sit in the front of the trap, with folded arms, his hat pulled down over his eyes and his chin sunk upon his breast, buried in the deepest thought. They often used a trap to take them from a main line station to their country destination.

Sometimes the escapade demanded that Holmes and Watson travelled on foot, and who better than Holmes as a guide, for his knowledge of the London byways was extraordinary; as he remarked: 'It is a hobby of mine to have an exact knowledge of London.' He would pass rapidly and with an assured step through a network of mews, stables, alleys, courts, passages and narrow streets; this was where Holmes found his large-scale map of the city invaluable. Did he not take Watson from his consulting room upon such a journey, such as he had never experienced before, or believed ever existed, when they walked to Camden House in Baker Street?

For Holmes was an excellent map reader, and could also draw a fair sketch-map: did he not draw such a map of the neighbourhood of the Priory School, Mackleton, so that Watson could become familiar with the geographical features which might well have a good deal to do with their investigation. Any other map needed for a journey he easily acquired from the London suppliers. If the need arose for a foreign map, then he would send for it specially. If urgent, he would send a telegram and receive the map the next day; such Victorian expedition! I wonder if Holmes ever hankered after being the proud owner of a car or motorcycle, so that he would not have to rely upon public transport? It never actually happened, but it was just conceivably possible. After all, Watson owned a car in 1914.

Payments to Sherlock Holmes

Watson remembered the time when Holmes rubbed his thin hands together with an appearance of avidity, which rather surprised him, for he knew Holmes generally to have frugal tastes, content to earn his money from professional detection where the money was not always of paramount importance, he living for art's sake. Wrote Watson:

> So unworldly was he – or so capricious – that he frequently refused his help to the powerful and wealthy where the problem made no appeal to his sympathies, while he would devote weeks of most intense application to the affairs of some humble client whose case presented those strange and dramatic qualities which appealed to his imagination and challenged his ingenuity.

A case which offered neither money nor credit, but which intrigued Holmes, was the mystery hanging over Mrs Warren's lodger in Great Orme Street; Holmes, being of an inquisitive nature, said: 'I have a great fancy to see this lodger of yours, Mrs Warren.' So Holmes and Watson went round to spy out the land at half past twelve. They discovered that a female had been substituted for the original male lodger and that Mr Warren had been attacked. Watson was not impressed with the case. 'Why should you go further in it? What have you got to gain from it?' 'What, indeed? It is art for art's sake, Watson… Education never ends, Watson. It is a series of lessons with the greatest for the last. This is an instructive case. There is neither money nor credit in it, and yet one would wish to tidy up.' Holmes saw the matter to the end, with the murder of Black Gorgiano by Gennaro Lucca; Inspector Gregson wondered how Holmes had been mixed up in this matter. 'Education, Gregson, education. Still seeking knowledge at the old university.'

Another case which brought no financial remuneration to Holmes concerned Mrs Maberley of Harrow Weald; she consulted him over a burglary at her house, although the thieves appeared not to have stolen anything. But Holmes detected that a book, still in manuscript, written by her son Douglas, had been stolen from his trunk: the instigator of the break-in was a Spanish woman, Isadora Klein, a celebrated beauty and wealthy widow, at one time a lover of Douglas. The book, in rather thinly disguised form, told of their love and she could not countenance its publication, which would have a far-reaching effect upon her pending marriage to the Duke of Lomond. Holmes compounded a felony (for he was not the police), but he made sure of obtaining some redress for Mrs Maberley in the shape of a Klein cheque for five thousand pounds. Perhaps Holmes only asked for expenses?

Holmes never took advantage of the wealth of his clients when setting the fee which he considered reasonable, for oft-times he could have received far more than asked.

Take the case of the abduction of Arthur, Lord Saltire, the son of the Duke of Holdernesse, by James Wilder, secretary and illegitimate son of His Grace. Wilder enticed him away from the Priory School, and gave him into the hands of Reuben Hayes (murderer of Heidegger, the German master), who confined him in an upper room at the Fighting Cock Inn. This became known to His Grace, who consented to leave Arthur there for three days, thus aiding and abetting in the escape of Hayes. Holmes claimed the reward of five thousand pounds offered by the Duke in return for knowledge of his son's whereabouts, and asked if the duke would pay him another thousand pounds if he told him the identity of the man or men who took him. The duke tried unsuccessfully to buy Holmes' silence with a cheque for twelve thousand pounds but Holmes could not be bribed. He was content to receive his cheque for six thousand pounds payable to his account in the Capital and Counties Bank in Oxford Street.[121] As Holmes folded up the cheque and placed it carefully in his notebook, he said, 'I am a poor man', as he patted his notebook affectionately.[122]

Mr Alexander Holder, senior partner in the banking firm of Holder & Stevenson of Threadneedle Street, the second largest private banking firm in the City of London, received from a client (one of the highest, noblest, most exalted names in England) as security upon a loan of fifty thousand pounds, paid in one hundred pound notes, the Beryl Coronet, contained in a square black morocco case, 'imbedded in soft, flesh-coloured velvet'. The coronet consisted of thirty-nine enormous beryls, set in gold chasing of incalculable value. The banker knew it to be 'one of the most precious public possessions of the empire'. The total value might have been half a million pounds or more. The coronet was subsequently stolen, then retrieved, but damaged, a piece with three beryls missing. Holmes managed to recover the missing portion from a receiver of stolen goods, who had bought it from the thief, Sir George Burnwell (a man of evil reputation among women) for six hundred pounds. Holmes had to buy back the missing portion for three thousand pounds, (an indication of Holmes' affluent position). The banker's joy was as great as his grief had been. Said Holmes, 'You would not think one thousand pounds a piece an excessive sum for them?' 'I would pay ten.' 'That would be unnecessary. Three thousand will cover the matter. And there is a little reward, I fancy. Have you your chequebook? Here is a pen. Better make it out for four thousand pounds.'

---

[121]Capital and Counties Bank. The same bank for Cadogan West and Neville St Clair.

[122]The prefect of Paris police gave a cheque for five thousand francs to Dupin for the stolen letter from the royal apartments, who put it in his pocket-book Edgar Allan Poe, *The Purloined Letter*.

We get another insight into Holmes' sound financial position at the time that Watson sold his small Kensington practice to a young Dr Verner, and at Holmes' request moved back to the Baker Street flat. Watson had been a little surprised that there had been no demur at the highest price that he had ventured to ask. It was only later on that he learned that Verner was a distant relative of Holmes, and that it was his friend who had actually paid the purchase price.

On the night of 20 March 1888, the King of Bohemia had called upon Holmes, and he, looking out of the window, had seen 'A nice little brougham and a pair of beauties. A hundred and fifty guineas apiece. There's money in this case, Watson, if there is nothing else.' (One must remember that these were early days at Baker Street, and Holmes still had his living to make.)

The king hoped that Holmes would be able to retrieve from Irene Adler a cabinet-sized photograph of the two of them together; other attempts to secure the photograph had failed: Irene would not sell, burglars had failed, her luggage had been diverted and she had been waylaid, with negative results. The king expected threatening blackmail should he go ahead with his intended Scandinavian marriage. Holmes mentioned money and was given carte blanche, even to the extent of receiving one of the Bohemian provinces. For present expenses, the King took a heavy chamois leather bag from under his cloak, containing three hundred pounds in gold and seven hundred pounds in notes; Holmes scribbled a receipt upon a sheet of his notebook. But Irene Adler had been warned against Holmes as a possible king's agent, married the man she really loved, Godfrey Norton (before Holmes came to her house, upon what turned out to be an abortive mission), and escaped, taking the photograph with her as a security against any likely move by the king. So Holmes, outwitted by this woman, failed in his mission to secure the photograph, and was paid one thousand pounds for it. Holmes apologised to the king: 'I am sorry that I have not been able to bring your Majesty's business to a more successful conclusion.' Although Holmes had failed miserably in his mission, the king was still pleased. 'On the contrary, my dear sir... nothing could be more successful. I know that her word is inviolate. The photograph is now as safe as if it were in the fire.' Slipping an emerald snake ring from his finger, he asked Holmes to accept it, which was declined, asking only for the lady's portrait. (Perhaps Holmes thought that he had already been paid munificently.) But later on, Holmes received a snuffbox of old gold, with a great amethyst in the centre of the lid, which caused Holmes to remark to Watson: 'It is a little souvenir from the King of Bohemia, in return for my assistance in the case of the Irene Adler papers.' Did Holmes try again to get Watson to sample snuff?

In 1891 Holmes confided to Watson his sound financial position. 'Between ourselves, the recent cases in which I have been of assistance to the royal family of Scandinavia, and to the French Republic, have left me in such a position that I could continue to live in the quiet fashion which is most congenial to me, and to concentrate my attention upon my chemical researches.'

By 1895 Holmes' increasing fame had brought with it an immense practice. So when he was asked to name his price to take up a case, where money meant nothing to him, he said coldly, that his professional charges were upon a fixed scale. Holmes said this, but his meaning was unknown.

Sir James Damery (a natural diplomat, who had the reputation for arranging delicate matters which needed to be kept out of the newspapers) called at Baker Street at 4.30 p.m. on 4 September 1902.

Sir James was acting on behalf of General de Merville of Khyber fame, who was trying to prevent his daughter Violet from marrying the Austrian Baron Gruner (who had murdered his wife in the Splugen Pass), whom she had met on a Mediterranean yachting voyage. Unfortunately, in spite of, or because of, the baron's evil ways, she simply doted upon this man of complex mind; he had expensive tastes, was a horse-fancier, played polo at Hurlingham, collected books and pictures and was a recognised authority upon Chinese pottery. He was as 'cool as ice, silky voiced… soothing… and poisonous as a cobra'; an 'aristocrat of crime, with a superficial suggestion of afternoon tea and all the cruelty of the grave behind it'. Perhaps the waxed tips of hair under his nose like the short antennae of an insect, added to his attractions for the young girl.

Holmes twice visited the baron at his Kingston home in Surrey, the second time to secure his 'love' diary. This evidence, and Miss Kitty Winter's vitriol attack, helped to secure the renouncement of Miss Violet Merville's marriage. Sir James had promised Holmes that his fees would be assured – Watson never mentioned the amount involved – hopefully it included payment for the damage that Holmes sustained.

In 1903 Holmes received a commission from the Sultan of Turkey, which called for immediate action, as political consequences of the gravest kind might arise from its neglect. This must have been most remunerative, but again Watson leaves no record as to the amount.

When Holmes, disguised as Altamont, the Irish-American, worked for Von Bork before the outbreak of Word War I, he was paid a salary, plus payment for information concerning naval signals. He was paid an extra five hundred pounds for bogus information, said to have been obtained from a gunner at Portsmouth in August 1914. Von Bork wrote a cheque – was this the last money that Holmes received for services rendered – or did the British government amply reward Holmes for his capture of the German spy?

Sherlock Holmes' Other Names

Holmes rarely permitted anyone, except his friend Watson, to call him only by his surname, but there were exceptions, some permitted and some distasteful to Holmes. Of these, there was Victor Trevor (his university friend), Inspector Athelney Jones, Sir Henry Baskerville, Robert Ferguson, Count Negretto Sylvius and Dr Grimesby Roylott.

With Count Negretto Sylvius, Holmes was very much upon his dignity. The count went to Baker Street with the express intention of assaulting Holmes, because he had seemingly gone out of his way to annoy him, by putting his minions upon his back, which of course Holmes denied (he being the perpetrator in disguise). 'Nonsense! I have had them followed. Two can play at that game, Holmes.' (When dealing with an angry man, Holmes would speak in a quiet voice, with a cool assured manner.) 'It is a small point, Count Sylvius, but perhaps you would kindly give me my prefix when you address me. You can understand that, with my routine of work, I should find myself on familiar terms with half the rogues' gallery, and you will agree that exceptions are invidious.' 'Well, *Mr Holmes*, then.'

Dr Roylott spoke most threateningly to Holmes at the flat, as he shook his hunting crop at him, knowing that his stepdaughter had recently visited him. 'I know you, you scoundrel! I have heard of you before. You are Holmes... the meddler... Holmes, the busybody! Holmes the Scotland Yard Jack-in-office!' It was not so much the lack of the use of a prefix to his name, as the parting remark, which cut Holmes to the quick; the fact that the doctor had the insolence to confound him with the official detective force, which must have halted the ready rebuke upon his tongue.

Other names came Holmes' way. He was called 'Mr Theorist', by Thaddeus Sholto, at Pondicherry Lodge; 'this plain clothes copper' and 'Mr Busybody Holmes', by Mr Williamson, the unfrocked clergyman, at Chiltern Grange; 'Mr Cocksure' by Mr Breckinridge at Covent Garden; ' a wizard, a sorcerer' by Trelawney Hope; 'the devil himself ' by Dr Sterndale and Count Sylvius; 'wizard' by James M Dodd; 'This gentleman who seems to have powers of magic', by Mr Ferguson; and 'very intelligent man' by Nathan Garrideb. Dr Leslie Armstrong commented that, not everyone was in favour of private detectives. 'I am familiar with your ignoble profession' said Colonel Emsworth of Tuxbury Old Park, Bedford. Colonel Hayter of Reigate said that he was privileged to see Holmes' methods; Hilton Soames of St Luke's College said that Holmes had discretion as well known as his powers; Percy Phelps called Holmes 'an inscrutable fellow' and 'Watson's celebrated friend'. Holmes sometimes called himself an ass[123]

Sherlock Holmes and Bribery

Holmes placed himself upon a pinnacle where bribery was

---

[123]Mr Losberne called at the wrong house near Chertsey Bridge, and said to Oliver, 'I am an ass!' Charles Dickens, *Oliver Twist*, 1838.

concerned; no one, not even a duke, let alone Killer Evans, was able to deflect him from the path of righteousness, otherwise he could have been a very wealthy man.

Holmes and Watson encountered Evans at Ryder Street, the former home of Roger Prescott, forger and coiner from Chicago. Evans superficially wounded Watson, and Holmes, seeing his friend hurt, in his rage floored Evans with his revolver. They then looked into the cellar under the floor, where lay a mass of rusted machinery, great rolls of paper, a litter of bottles and a number of neat little bundles arranged upon a small table.

> 'A printing press – a counterfeiter's outfit,' said Holmes.
>
> 'Yes, sir,' said our prisoner, staggering slowly to his feet... The greatest counterfeiter London ever saw. That's Prescott's machine, and those bundles on the table are two thousand of Prescott's notes worth a hundred each and fit to pass anywhere. Help yourselves, gentlemen. Call it a deal and let me beat it.' [Holmes only laughed.] 'We don't do things like that, Mr Evans. There is no bolt-hole for you in this country. You shot this man Prescott, did you not?'

Subsequently, as Watson wrote: 'The Killer returned to those shades from which he had just emerged'.

Although Holmes could not be bribed himself, he expected that lesser mortals had their price.

For instance, there was Dawson, head groom to Silas Brown, the horse trainer (a fierce-looking elderly man). Holmes was told that loiterers were not welcome:

> 'I only wished to ask a question,' said Holmes, with his finger and thumb in his waistcoat pocket. 'Should I be too early to see your master, Mr Silas Brown, if I were to call at five o'clock to-morrow morning?'
>
> 'Bless you, sir, if anyone is about he will be, for he is always the first stirring. But here he is sir, to answer your questions for himself. No, sir, no, it is as much as my place is worth to let him see me touch your money. Afterwards, if you like.'

So Holmes replaced the half-crown which he had drawn from his pocket, with which bribe he had hoped to obtain information about the horse, Silver Blaze.

Then there was Constable John Rance, of Audley Court, Kennington Park Gate – 'a narrow slit in the line of dead-coloured brick', an unattractive locality. The narrow passage led to a flag-paved quadrangle, lined by sordid buildings. Here dirty children played, and discoloured linen hung out to dry. Number 46 had a slip of brass upon the door, with the name Rance engraved thereon. The constable was displeased at being disturbed from his slumbers and said somewhat irritably, 'I made my report at the office.' 'We thought that we should like to hear it all from your own lips,' said Holmes, as he took a half-sovereign from his pocket and played with it pensively. Now that money was in the offing, the constable changed his tune, with his eyes upon the small golden disc. 'I shall be happy to tell you anything I can.' 'Just let us hear it all in your own way as it occurred.' Rance was now at ease and, sitting down upon the parlour horsehair sofa, he told his story. The information gained for ten shillings and six pence, did not elevate the man in Holmes' estimation. 'I'm afraid, Rance, that you will never rise in the force. That head of yours should be for use as well as ornament. You might have gained your sergeant's stripes last night.'

In order that Holmes might obtain some information concerning the whereabouts of Mr Mordecai Smith (who hired boats by the hour or by the day, and who kept a steam launch beside a small wooden wharf at the end of Broad Street, on the Thames, opposite Millbank), Holmes tried to win the good graces of Mrs Smith. Fortunately, her son Jack, a little curly-headed lad of six, came running out, followed by his stoutish red-faced mother, who was trying to wash him. Here was Holmes' chance.

'Dear little chap!' cried Holmes strategically. 'What a rosy-cheeked young rascal! Now, Jack, is there anything you would like?'

The youth pondered for a moment.

'I'd like a shillin',' said he.

'Nothing you would like better?'

'I'd like two shillin' better,' the prodigy answered after some thought.

'Here you are, then! Catch! – A fine child, Mrs Smith!'

The mother's heart warmed to Holmes. Soon he learnt that Mr Smith was away in his launch. He was then told of a wooden-legged man – Jonathan Small – and by adroit questioning learnt that the launch was called *Aurora*, black with two red streaks, with a black funnel and white band. Holmes knew that the way to get information was to listen to the speaker as if under protest and then you were likely to gather all the necessary information.

Holmes then consulted his Baker Street Irregulars, the urchin police led by Wiggins. They were asked to find the whereabouts of the *Aurora* and to search both banks of the Thames. 'The old scale of pay,' said Holmes 'and a guinea to the boy who finds the boat. Here's a day in advance. Now off you go!' Each street Arab received one shilling and away they buzzed upon their mission.[124]

Holmes and Watson had recourse to go to Mackleton, to assist Dr Thorneycroft Huxtable in finding the abducted son of the Duke of Holdernesse.

There, Holmes tried to bribe Reuben Hayes, landlord of the forbidding and squalid inn called the Fighting Cock, in order to secure a bicycle. Said Holmes, 'We'll have some food first. Then you can bring round the bicycle.' 'I haven't got a bicycle.' For Holmes was hopeful that here he might get news of the bicycle with the patched Dunlop tyre. Even the bribe of a sovereign failed to produce results. 'I tell you, man, that I haven't got one. I'll let you have two horses as far as the Hall.' This time, even the persuasive powers of Holmes failed.

While Holmes was carrying out investigations for Mrs Maberley at Harrow Weald, he tried to bribe Susan Stockdale, the great gaunt maid, with ten pounds, if she would tell him who was the person behind Barney, her husband, to whom she had spoken over the hedge. But apart from learning that it was a very rich woman, Holmes had to admit defeat.

Miss Dobney, a former governess of Lady Frances Carfax, consulted Holmes over the disappearance of her mistress, for her regular letters to her had ceased, and the 'exceedingly wealthy' family were most anxious as to her whereabouts. Lady Frances always carried with her some very remarkable old Spanish

---

[124]Street Arab. A neglected or homeless child.

jewellery of silver and curiously cut diamonds. She fell into the hands of an Australian rascal call Holy Henry Peters, travelling under the alias of the Reverend Dr Shlessinger from South America.[125] He, with his 'wife', Fraser, an Englishwoman, had a house at 36 Poultney Square, Brixton. Having obtained the jewels, the thieves intended to have a genuine burial of Rose Spender, an aged woman from Brixton Workhouse Infirmary, but including unofficially the body of Lady Frances. On the morning of the funeral, Holmes and Watson went post-haste to Brixton, and persuaded the undertaker's men to take the extra large coffin back inside, saying a warrant was on the way. 'Quick, Watson, quick! Here is a screw-driver! …Here's one for you, my man! A sovereign if the lid comes off in a minute! Ask no questions – work away! That's good! Another! And another! Now pull all together! It's giving! It's giving! Ah, that does it at last.'

The bribe was rewarded with the saving of Lady Frances's life from within the heavily chloroformed coffin.

Holmes wished to get to the Church of St Monica in the Edgware Road in a great hurry and to follow the cab of Godfrey Norton and the neat little landau of Irene Adler. In the character of an out-of-work groom he had been gathering information from the ostlers, in a mews which ran beside Briony Lodge, Serpentine Avenue, St John's Wood, the home of Irene Adler. Holmes hailed a cab, and the driver looked askance at such a shabby fare, but the bribe of half a sovereign settled all his doubts.

Sherlock Holmes' Disbelief in the Supernatural

To the man pursuing an exact scientific approach to crime, there was no room for the supernatural. Holmes certainly did not believe in the legend of the Baskerville hound. When Dr Mortimer had finished reading the early eighteenth century manuscript dealing with the legend, Holmes yawned and, tossing his cigarette into the fire, said, in answer to the doctor's question as to whether he found it interesting, it was only so 'To a collector of fairy tales.' Nor did Holmes give supernatural credence to the

---

[125]Mrs Shlessinger, a nurse from Florence, was a passenger on the sternwheeler *Korosko* on 13 February 1895. ACD, *The tragedy of the Korosko*, 1898.

doctor's seeing the footprints of a gigantic, enormous hound, for he did not believe that there was a diabolical agency abroad on Dartmoor.

When Brenda Tregennis died and her brothers, Owen and George, were taken away insane from their house of Tredannick Wartha, in the hamlet of Tredannick Wollas, in Cornwall, there was no visible explanation of what the horror could have been to have caused such a situation. Holmes merely observed that 'On the face of it, it would appear to be a case of a very exceptional nature... Now, let us calmly define our position, Watson. Let us get a firm grip of the very little which we *do* know, so that when fresh facts arise we may be ready to fit them into their places. I take it, in the first place, that neither of us is prepared to admit diabolical intrusions into the affairs of men. Let us begin by ruling that entirely out of our minds.' Holmes only allowed himself to reason from cold, hard facts, with a calm assurance of power. 'I fear that if the matter is beyond humanity, it is certainly beyond me. Yet we must exhaust all natural explanations before we fall back upon such a theory as this.' For Mortimer Tregennis had thought that the explanation was, 'not of this world'.

Mr Robert Ferguson, of Ferguson and Muirhead, tea brokers of Mincing Lane, thought that his beautiful Peruvian wife might be a vampire, as he had witnessed her in the nursery drawing blood from her child's exposed neck, and having blood all round her lips. He wrote to Holmes imploring his help. Holmes looked up 'vampires' in his great index volume, and read about them in Hungary and Transylvania; he threw the book down 'with a snarl of disappointment'.

'Rubbish, Watson, rubbish! What have we to do with walking corpses who can only be held in their grave by stakes driven through their hearts? It's pure lunacy.'

'But surely,' said I, 'the vampire was not necessarily a dead man? A living person might have the habit. I have read, for example, of the old sucking the blood of the young in order to retain their youth.'

'You are right, Watson. It mentions the legend in one of these references. But are we to give serious attention to such things? This agency stands flat-footed upon the ground, and there it must remain. The world is big enough for us. No ghosts need apply.'

Inspector Hopkins thought Holmes had powers that were not human, and Mr Ferguson credited Holmes with magical powers. The Prime Minister called Holmes a wizard and sorcerer.

Sherlock Holmes' Blunders

Holmes admitted to have been beaten four times – three by men and once by a woman. He admitted that he had been sluggish in his mind and wanting in that mixture of imagination and reality which was the basis of his art. This must have cut him to the quick, for normally he never liked admitting defeat in a case. Where Holmes failed or blundered it happened too often that no one else succeeded, and that the tale was left for ever without a conclusion. Now and again, however, it chanced that even when he erred the truth was still discovered, for his deductions were nearly always founded upon a logical basis.

Holmes blundered in the way he thought that he would be received by Professor Presbury at Camford. He thought that the professor's mind would not be very clear after taking some drug; that he would assume that he had invited Holmes down and had perhaps confused the date. But the professor's mind was abundantly clear. 'Too clear!' Holmes said. 'That was my miscalculation. It is evident that his memory is much more reliable than I had thought.' Had it not been for Bennett's intervention (he being the professor's professional assistant), Holmes no doubt would have been thrown out.

Holmes admitted that sometimes his line of thought was mere imagination, but added 'but how often is imagination the mother of truth.' He admitted that he blundered more often than was generally known to people, who only knew of these happenings through Watson's memoirs. He could always conceive an alternative explanation, but had to beware a premature theory based upon indifferent data, for this might lead to an erroneous conclusion.

When Sir Henry Baskerville was being shadowed by a black-bearded man in a cab from Northumberland Avenue towards Oxford Street, Holmes noticed that the cab had halted on the other side of the street, and then proceeded slowly onward again. 'There's our man, Watson! Come along! We'll have a good look at him, if we can do no more.' Watson then saw a bushy black beard and a pair of piercing eyes looking at them through the side window. Instantly the trapdoor at the top flew up, something was screamed at the driver, and the cab flew madly off down Regent Street. Regardless of the traffic, Holmes dashed in pursuit, hoping to engage an empty cab, but he was out of luck. He returned to Watson 'panting and white with vexation'. 'There now,' he grumbled. 'Was ever such bad luck and such bad management, too? Watson, Watson, if you are an honest man you will record this also and set it against my successes!' For Holmes had expected the stranger to pursue his quarry upon foot! Holmes did at least note the cab's number: 2704.

Holmes had a temporary lapse over solving the disappearance of the handsome forty-year-old Lady Frances Carfax, for he had too easily dismissed the remark of the undertaker's wife.

'Should you care to add the case to your annals, my dear Watson,' said Holmes that evening, 'it can only be as an example of that temporary eclipse to which even the best-balanced mind may be exposed. Such slips are common to all mortals, and the greatest is he who recognise and repair them. To this modified credit I may, perhaps, make some claim. My night was haunted by the thought that somewhere a clue, a strange sentence, a curious observation, had come under my notice and had been too easily dismissed. Then, suddenly, in the grey of the morning, the words came back to me. It was the remark of the undertaker's wife, as reported by Philip Green. She had said, "It should be there before now. It took longer, being out of the ordinary." …That could only mean that it had been made to some special measurement. But why? Why? Then in an instant I remembered the deep sides, and the little wasted figure at the bottom. Why so large a coffin for so small a body? To leave room for another body. Both would be buried under the one certificate. It had all been so clear, if only my own sight had not been dimmed. At eight the Lady Frances would be buried. Our one chance was to stop the coffin before it left the house.

'It was a desperate chance that we might find her alive, but it *was* a chance, as the result showed. A clever device, Watson. It is new to me in the annals of crime.'

While Holmes and Watson were upon the moors of Mackleton, many tracks of cows were noticed, at the morass, on the path and where Heidegger met his death. It was not till later that Holmes suddenly saw a light in the darkness. Marks of cows' feet, and yet not a cow to been seen. 'Strange, Watson, that we should see tracks all along our line, but never a cow on the whole moor. Very strange, Watson, eh?' Then, by the aid of breadcrumbs on the table, Holmes showed Watson the variations in the tracks, indicating a remarkable cow which walked, cantered and galloped. 'What a blind beetle[126] I have been, not to draw my conclusion. By George! Watson, it was no brain of a country publican that thought out such a blind as that.' For Hayes had shod his horses with the mediaeval shoes from the Duke's museum, shaped below with a cloven foot of iron, so as to throw pursuers off the track.

Holmes came to an entirely erroneous conclusion over the death of Julia Stonor, of Stoke Moran in Surrey. Just before her death she had shrieked out: 'Oh, my God! Helen! It was the band, the speckled band!' The presence of gypsies nearby and the word 'band' were sufficient to put Holmes upon an entirely wrong scent, which showed how dangerous it was to reason from insufficient information. When, however, it became clear to Holmes that whatever danger threatened an occupant of the room could not have come either from the window or the door, he then reconsidered his position.

Over the case of the disappearance of Neville St Clair, Holmes was a little slow in unravelling the mystery. 'I think, Watson, that you are now standing in the presence of one of the most absolute fools in Europe. I deserve to be kicked from here to Charing Cross. I confess that I have been as blind as a mole, but it is better to learn wisdom late than never to learn it at all.' Holmes had realised that the crippled, disfigured, professional beggar was none other than the missing man.

Holmes was also a little slow at reading the clue upon the dead body at Birlstone Manor House. The dead man was said to have

---

[126]Jim Browner called himself 'a blind beetle'. (ACD, *The Adventure of the Cardboard Box*.) Mr Hall Pycroft called himself the same name. (ACD, *The Stockbroker's Clerk*, 1892.)

been John Douglas, for he wore his clothes and finger rings, and a piece of sticking plaster covered the cut he had made while shaving. His wedding ring was missing, leading them to deduce that it had been removed, but in fact it had never been on the dead man's finger, for the bodies had been switched. Douglas could not get the ring off, so had to leave that detail to chance. Ted Baldwin from Vermissa Valley had perished by his own sawn-off shotgun. 'You slipped up there, Mr Holmes, clever as you are; for if you had chanced to take off that plaster you would have found no cut underneath it.' John Douglas had the last word.

On a Tuesday evening Holmes received telegrams from Colonel Ross (owner of the racehorse called Silver Blaze) and from Inspector Gregory, inviting his co-operation at King's Pyland, Dartmoor, concerning the mysteries of the missing horse and the murder of John Straker, trainer and retired jockey. But it was not until Thursday morning that Holmes and Watson caught the Paddington train for the West Country. Watson could not understand the delay:

> 'Why didn't you go down yesterday?'
>
> 'Because I made a blunder, my dear Watson – which is, I am afraid, a more common occurrence than anyone would think who only knew me through your memoirs. The fact is that I could not believe it possible that the most remarkable horse in England could long remain concealed, especially in so sparsely inhabited a place as the north of Dartmoor. From hour to hour yesterday I expected to hear that he had been found, and that his abductor was the murderer of John Straker. When, however, another morning had come and I found that beyond the arrest of young Fitzroy Simpson nothing had been done, I felt that it was time for me to take action. Yet in some ways I feel that yesterday has not been wasted.'

'Watson,' said Holmes, 'if it should ever strike you that I am getting a little over-confident in my powers, or giving less pains to a case than it deserves, kindly whisper "Norbury" in my ear, and I shall be infinitely obliged to you.' He was referring to the case he undertook on behalf of Mr Grant Munro, who had been married to Mrs Effie Hebron for three years. Then a secret had grown up between them which was destroying their lives, in their nice eighty pounds a year villa at Norbury, in the country. Holmes thought that it was Mrs Hebron in a nearby cottage, which she had visited in the night. He suspected blackmail, for had not she asked her husband for one hundred pounds! The mystery turned out to be the daughter of John Hebron of Atlanta, a little coal-black Negress, hiding behind a mask of the strangest livid tint.

In the winter of 1897, Holmes and Watson, forgoing breakfast, hastened down to Abbey Grange, Marsham, in Kent, where they found the head of Sir Eustace Brackenstall knocked in with his own poker, and bent into a curve by the blow. Holmes observed at the conclusion of the case to Watson: 'We have got our case – one of the most remarkable in our collection. But dear me, how slow-witted I have been, and how nearly I have committed the blunder of my lifetime!'

While Holmes was engaged upon the case of Professor Presbury, he asked Watson if he had observed the professor's knuckles, to which Watson confessed that he had not.

'Thick and horny,' replied Holmes, 'in a way which is quite new in my experience. Always look at the hands first, Watson. Then cuffs, trouser-knees, and boots. Very curious knuckles which can only be explained by the mode of progression observed by—' Holmes paused and suddenly clapped his hand to his forehead. 'Oh, Watson, Watson, what a fool I have been! It seems incredible, and yet it must be true. All points in one direction. How could I miss seeing the connection of ideas? Those knuckles – how could I have passed those knuckles? And the dog! And the ivy! It's surely time that I disappeared into that little farm of my dreams.'

Gifts to Sherlock Holmes

Holmes did say that his most prized possession was the photograph of Irene Adler, before she became Mrs Norton. This she left behind in her secret cupboard, where formally she kept the photograph of herself and the King of Bohemia, and which the king gave to Holmes as he prized it more than the emerald snake ring from the royal finger. On the evening of 20 March 1888, Holmes had been given one thousand pounds – three hundred pounds in gold and seven hundred pounds in notes – as a retainer fee to secure the cabinet-sized photograph of the king with Irene Adler, currently in the American's possession. Holmes failed dismally in this mission, being outwitted by a woman. As he said to the king, 'I am sorry that I have not been able to bring your Majesty's business to my more successful conclusion.' But the king was happy at the outcome, knowing that Mrs Norton's word was inviolate, and he would be able to proceed with his marriage to the daughter of the King of Scandinavia. So happy was he, that he later sent Holmes an old gold snuffbox with a great amethyst in the centre of the lid.[127] Holmes received from Irene Norton a sovereign (he being in disguise) as her sole witness to her marriage; he wore this gift on his watch-chain, a further reminder of a most beautiful woman. The King of Scandinavia was also a client of Holmes, but alas, there is no record of the munificent present which he no doubt received.

Another present Holmes received was a ring from the reigning family of Holland, but as the circumstances surrounding this gift were of too delicate a nature, Watson never divulged the details of Holmes' work.

In 1894 Holmes received an autographed letter of thanks from the French President and the Order of the Legion of Honour for his work in tracking down and arresting Monsieur Huret, the Boulevard assassin.

Holmes wore a fine emerald tiepin, a present from a certain gracious young lady, after he visited Windsor in November 1895. Watson fancied that he knew the name of that august lady, and that the pin recalled to Holmes the episode of the Bruce-Partington plans.

Another very important possession of Holmes (whether a gift is not known) was his low-power microscope.[128] After Holmes had brought a coiner to justice by the discovery of some zinc and copper filings in the seam of his cuff, Scotland Yard began to realise the great importance of this use of the microscope in the detection of the criminal.

Did Holmes receive a special gift from his Holiness the Pope

---

[127]Dupin purposely left a gold snuffbox when he visited Minister D, Edgar Allan Poe, *The Purloined Letter*.
[128]The prefect of the Paris police used a 'most powerful microscope'. Poe, op. cit.

for his investigation into the sudden death of Cardinal Tosca? We would expect so, but Watson, in his care not to offend Holmes, is silent upon this score. He never recorded the reward from the wealthy family of Lady Frances Carfax.

Sherlock Holmes and Music

Although not a present from a king, Holmes highly prized his violin, a Stradivarius, which he never kept in a case, leaving it lying in the corner of the sitting room; instead the violin was to be found resting upon the table or on a chair, ready to be picked up as the mood came upon him. In the early days Holmes was not too pleased with the tone, for he said to Watson, 'My fiddle would be better for new strings,' but he never seemed to have time to see to this, for he makes no more mention of this matter.

Holmes had purchased this violin for fifty-five shillings from a Jew broker's in the Tottenham Court Road, and he considered it to be worth five hundred guineas. (I wonder to whom Holmes bequeathed this valuable instrument, for its value in 1985 might well have been some four hundred thousand pounds, according to a London sale room, and today, who knows?)

Holmes was an accomplished violinist and composer, although we have no knowledge of his compositions. He had a knowledge of Cremona fiddles and appreciated the difference between an Amati and a Stradivarius; he had a remarkable gift for improvisation. Music affected Holmes; he preferred introspective German music to the Italian and French and when he listened to other players like Norman Neruda and Sarasate, his face gently smiled, and his eyes became languid and dreamy as his long fingers waved in time to the music. The music reflected his thoughts: sonorous, melancholy, fantastic and cheerful.

When Watson listened to a Holmes' recital, it was the difficult pieces that he played at first, finishing with Watson's favourite airs. But when Holmes was on his own, he would close his eyes and scrape carelessly upon the instrument held across his knee – the droning soothing his ruffled nerves. He would even carry the low melancholy wailings far into the night, particularly when his high hopes of a successful venture had not been fulfilled.

Holmes also knew much about Paganini and could recount many anecdotes of that extraordinary man; he also counted Charlie Peace, the violin virtuoso, among his acquaintances.

In the autumn of 1895, Holmes increased his musical knowledge, this time with a study of the music of the Middle Ages.

Did Holmes originally have among his possessions a camera? Did his knowledge of Monsieur Bertillon's use of the camera spur him on to have his own, and eventually to improve upon the known French data at the time? Nothing unfortunately was ever mentioned as in use at Baker Street; but Holmes certainly possessed a camera after his retirement and had equipment and photographic knowledge which enabled him to enlarge a photograph of the dead body of Fitzroy McPherson. This helped him in his diagnosis of the meaning of the queer dark red lines, as if made by a thin wire scourge.

Sherlock Holmes and Dr Watson – Affection for Each Other

There were many instances when both Holmes and Watson showed their understanding and affection for each other. With Holmes, he became in a state of nervous exhalation, when Watson called him 'brilliant', and he liked Watson to accompany him upon his various expeditions, for thereby his dear Watson conferred a great favour upon him. He admitted that Watson had some remarkable characteristics of his own, to which in his modesty he gave little attention amid his exaggerated estimates of his own performances. Watson was Holmes' ideal helpmate, for each development of Holmes' came as a perpetual surprise and the future a closed book. Anything a client wished to say to Holmes, he could also say in front of Watson, his friend and colleague – except in the very early days when Holmes was getting to know Watson. It made a considerable difference to Holmes having someone with him on whom he could thoroughly rely, for a trusty comrade was a great asset and a chronicler still more so. Holmes appreciated Watson's grand gift of silence, so invaluable in a companion to whom he could talk; Holmes was always warmed by Watson's genuine admiration. He thought

Watson was born to be a man of action and to instinctively do something energetic; sometimes Watson was called his 'intimate friend and associate', for he was always willing and keen to share an adventure with Holmes, whatever the task, for there was always something in the ice-cold reasoning of Holmes which made it impossible to resist him.

Watson exulted in danger and being a burglar with Holmes, even defying the law, with perhaps a police cell in sight. That was when Watson said that he 'would see it out', or he would clasp Holmes' hand in silence, 'and the die was cast'. When Watson commiserated with Holmes over a feigned weakness, Holmes felt deeply for his friend, saying: 'I was sorry to cause you the sympathetic pain which I know that you felt.' Watson would tingle with that half-sporting, half-intellectual pleasure which he invariably experienced when he went with Holmes during his investigations; for he had great faith in Holmes' insight and was the very soul of discretion, trusting in Holmes' judgment. When Holmes was ill in France in 1887, Watson was so concerned that he rushed to his sickbed, getting there in twenty-four hours.

Even when Holmes chided Watson, the bond that existed between them still showed, for one needs to know a person exceptionally well before a joke is permitted at the other's expense. Commenting upon the relationship between Selden the convict and the Barrymores, Holmes observed: 'This also you cleared up in a very effective way, though I had already come to the same conclusions from my own observations.' (Just a slight prick to his ego?) Holmes agreed to some extent when Watson said: 'In your own case, from all that you have told me, it seems obvious that your faculty of observation and your peculiar facility of deduction are due to your own systematic training.'

As the case of the Dancing Men entered its final phase Holmes drew his chair up to the table and spread out in front of him the various papers upon which were recorded the antics of the Dancing Men; he then turned to his friend: 'As to you, friend Watson, I owe you every atonement for having allowed your natural curiosity to remain so long unsatisfied.'

As Holmes acted out the part of the dying detective, he spoke with a feverish energy, his long hands twitching and jerking as he motioned Watson away. 'Contagious by touch, Watson – that's it, by touch. Keep your distance and all is well.' 'Good heavens, Holmes! Do you suppose that such a consideration weighs with me for an instant? It would not affect me in the case of a stranger. Do you imagine it would prevent me from doing my duty to so old a friend?' (This was only a 'blind', to ensure that Watson believed that he was really ill and at death's door, so that he would transmit this feeling in his interview with Culverton Smith.) Holmes brushed aside Watson's medical help: 'If I am to have a doctor whether I will or not, let me at least have someone in whom I have confidence.' (Actually Holmes admired Watson's medical attributes and this must have hurt him to say this, just as Watson was bitterly hurt at the time to hear such a comment from his friend.) While Holmes awaited the arrival of the planter from Sumatra – well versed in the Tapanuli fever – his cab drew up at the door. 'There are the wheels, Watson. Quick, man, if you love me! And don't budge, whatever happens – whatever happens, do you hear? Don't speak! Don't move! Just listen with all your ears.' Watson thought that it was possible that Count Sylvius might kill Holmes, and his honest face twitched with anxiety, knowing the immense risk his friend was taking. But he patiently bowed to Holmes' will and hid himself as best he could, behind the head of Holmes' bed.

While they were both down at Poldhu Bay in Cornwall, Holmes experimented with a deadly poisonous powder by placing it above the burning duplicate lamp which he had purchased. Soon a thick musky odour came from the dense black cloud and Holmes' face went white, rigid and drawn with horror, the forerunner of death. Watson only just managed to bestir himself in time and dragged Holmes to safety. 'Upon my word, Watson! …I owe you both my thanks and an apology. It was an unjustifiable experiment even for one's self, and doubly so for a friend. I am really very sorry.' Seeing so much of Holmes' heart, filled Watson with great emotion. 'You know… that it is my greatest joy and privilege to help you.'

When they travelled from Winchester to Thor Place, in a first-class carriage, Holmes seated himself opposite to Watson, laid a hand upon each of his knees, looked into his eyes with a mischievous imp-like gaze, and asked him if he was armed, as was his custom, for Watson liked to feel that he was a protector to his friend.

Watson was always ready and willing to be with Holmes, and to go with him anywhere at a moment's notice, even if his own medical practice suffered or even if there might be great danger. He was willing even to lie about not being busy, although Holmes knew differently and called this adding fibbing to Watson's other vices, although it made him happy to know that he had his trusted comrade and biographer by his side.

Holmes told Watson that he was going to burgle Milverton's house. Watson said: 'When do we start?' When Holmes replied that he was going alone, Watson rebutted him.

> 'Then you are not going,' said I. 'I give you my word of honour – and I never broke it in my life – that I will take a cab straight to the police-station and give you away, unless you let me share this adventure with you.'
>
> 'You can't help me.'
>
> 'How do you know that? You can't tell what may happen. Anyway my resolution is taken. Other people beside you have self-respect, and even reputations.'

And affectionate Watson had his own way. While at Appledore Towers – the house of the king of the blackmailers – inside, in the darkness, Holmes' affection showed itself. 'I felt', said Watson, 'Holmes' hand steal into mine and give me a reassuring shake, as if to say that the situation was within his powers, and that he was easy in his mind.' For Holmes had remarkable powers of seeing in the dark, and Watson knew that Holmes would guide him safely through. Holmes showed his wish to protect Watson, by gripping his wrist with a cold, strong, restraining grip; a tug at his coat sleeve, attracted Watson's attention but forbade speech; a shoulder pressing against a shoulder in the darkness showed their mutual sympathetic observations.

After Holmes explained finally about a case, Watson would say in unfeigned admiration: 'You reasoned it out beautifully. It is so long a chain and yet every link rings true. And you are a benefactor of the race.' This kind of remark would bring something approaching tenderness to the look in Holmes' eyes; sometimes even a friendly slap upon Watson's shoulder. It wasn't that Watson thought himself more dense than his fellow man, but he was always oppressed with a sense of inadequacy in his dealings with Holmes, for they both heard and saw the same things and yet Holmes not only saw clearly what had happened, but what was about to happen, while the whole business was confused to Watson, as it would have been to any other lesser intelligence than Holmes, who only admitted to one man being his equal.

A pity that Watson never published the shocking affair of the Dutch steamship *Friesland* which nearly cost them their lives, for it might well have revealed another facet of their mutual affection.[129] Why did Holmes refuse Watson permission to publish this case? Perhaps some high-ranking person was involved who wished anonymity.

Holmes was very concerned about sending Watson to Devon with Sir Henry Baskerville, and he was by no means easy in his mind about it. 'It's an ugly business, Watson, an ugly, dangerous business, and the more I see of it the less I like it. Yes, my dear fellow, you may laugh, but I give you my word that I shall be very glad to have you back safe and sound in Baker Street once more. At the station he asked Watson: 'You have arms, I suppose?' 'Yes, I thought it as well to take them.' 'Most certainly. Keep your revolver near you night and day, and never relax your precautions.' Holmes showed that he had great confidence in Watson while he was in Devon, asking him to open all notes and telegrams and to act upon his own judgment if any news came.

If there was any possibility of danger upon an expedition, then Holmes preferred to have Watson with him. While Holmes was investigating the case of the missing Norwood builder, he told Watson that he must go to Blackheath. Watson wished to go too. 'No, my dear fellow,' said Holmes, 'I don't think you can help me. There is no prospect of danger, or I should not dream of stirring out without you.'

When Holmes returned from Briarbrae, (where he was endeavouring to help Percy Phelps find the lost naval treaty) to

---

[129]The Dutch–American liner, SS *Friesland* saw the pterodactyl released by Professor Challenger. ACD, *The Lost World*, 1912.

Baker Street with his left hand swathed in a bandage, and his face grim and pale, Watson was immediately very concerned for his friend's health. 'You are not wounded, Holmes?' said a worried Watson. 'Tut, it is only a scratch through my own clumsiness.' 'That bandage tells of adventures. Won't you tell us what has happened?' Holmes then explained how he had fought with Joseph Harrison for the little cylinder of paper, and found him more vicious than he had expected, and armed with a knife from which he had received a cut over the knuckles, but not before he had given Harrison a black eye.

The immense exertions of Holmes on the Continent, in the spring of 1887, over the question of the Netherlands–Sumatra Company, and the schemes of Baron Maupertuis, considerably undermined his health. The extent of his exertions was reflected in the praise he received. Watson commented that 'his room was literally ankle-deep with congratulatory telegrams.' Watson thought that a week of springtime in the country, away from his work at Baker Street, was just what his friend needed. No case to solve, no Lestrade to worry him. How well Watson convinced him that he needed a holiday, for Holmes did not take too kindly to an aimless period away from London.

So, in April, they travelled down to Reigate in Surrey, to the home of Colonel Hayter, a friend of Watson's, who had come under his professional care in Afghanistan. But, even here, Holmes became involved in a local murder. With Watson, he visited the home of the Cunninghams hoping to find the murderer of William Kirwan. While there, the father and son tried to murder Holmes, who had discovered the missing part of the torn note in the pocket of a dressing gown hanging up behind the door. When he called out, 'Help! Help! Murder!' Watson, recognising with a thrill, the voice of his friend, rushed madly from the room, onto the landing and into the bedroom and dressing room beyond to help his friend; he got there just in time to save Holmes from possible death, for the Cunninghams were bending over the prostrate figure, the younger clutching Holmes' throat with both hands, while the father twisted a wrist, trying to reclaim the little crumpled piece of paper. In an instant, Watson, the colonel and Inspector Forrester had torn Holmes free, and he staggered to his feet, very pale and greatly exhausted.

In order to keep himself informed upon the happenings at Baskerville Hall and the people in the vicinity, Holmes, unbeknown to Watson, made his temporary abode in a Neolithic hut upon the moor. There, Watson chanced to track him down, which surprised Holmes, who had no idea that his temporary retreat was no longer a secret. As Watson met his friend under such strange and unusual circumstances, he cried, 'Holmes! Holmes!' for he was never more astonished and glad to find his friend safe and well as he wrung his hand.

Watson came to be superficially wounded in the thigh by the Chicago killer, James Winter, alias Morecroft, alias Killer Evans. It happened in the curious museum room of Nathan Garrideb; Evans took them by surprise as he unexpectedly whipped out a revolver from his breast pocket and fired two shots. Watson felt a sudden hot sear as if a red-hot iron had been pressed against his thigh. Holmes floored Evans with his revolver, giving him a bloody face. With his wiry arms Holmes led Watson to a chair. 'You're not hurt, Watson? For God's sake, say that you are not hurt!' 'It's nothing, Holmes. It's a mere scratch.' As Holmes ripped up Watson's trousers with his pocket knife, he cried with an immense sigh of relief, 'You are right… It is quite superficial.' At Evans he glared, his face set like flint. 'By the Lord, it is as well for you. If you had killed Watson, you would not have got out of this room alive.' Watson saw the usual cold mask of Holmes fall away, saw his eyes dim for a moment and the firm lips shake. A great heart and brain had suddenly opened to him. All Watson's years of humble but single-minded purpose culminated in that great moment of revelation.

Holmes, in his more intense moments, would permit himself no food, not being able to spare energy and nerve force for digestion. So often he dragged Watson away from his food to accompany him upon an expedition, but not always. There were times when he was able to consider that perhaps his friend needed sustenance, even if he didn't. 'Take your breakfast, Watson, and we will go out together and see what we can do. I feel as if I shall need your company and your moral support today.'

In 1883 Holmes and Watson travelled to Stoke Moran, to

unravel the cause of the death of Julia, sister to Helen Stonor. They stayed at the Crown Inn, and intended to visit the house of the Roylotts in the night. 'Do you know, Watson, I really have some scruples as to taking you to-night. There is a distinct element of danger.' This was no deterrent to faithful Watson. 'Can I be of any assistance?' 'Your presence might be invaluable.' 'Then I shall certainly come.' 'It is very kind of you.' For as Holmes said of Watson: 'there is no man who is better worth having at your side, when you are in a tight place.'

When Holmes and Watson stayed at the Westfield Arms, Birlstone, on the northern border of the county of Sussex, they slept in a double-bedded room. It seemed to be their custom to engage not only a hotel bedroom – where Holmes liked his bed linen to be above reproach – but a sitting room as well. They again shared a similar room at The Cedars, while investigating the disappearance of Neville St Clair, although here Holmes had no sleep during his night vigil. Holmes whispered to Watson, 'I say, Watson... would you be afraid to sleep in the same room with a lunatic, a man with softening of the brain, an idiot whose mind has lost its grip?' Kindly Watson answered in astonishment, having full faith in Holmes and all his doings: 'Not in the least.' 'Ah, that's lucky,' these were Holmes' last words that night.

In 1891 Holmes deemed it advisable to leave England during the time that the police would be able to arrest Moriarty and his minions. He called upon Watson, but refused the invitation to stay the night, not wishing to jeopardise his friend's safety. 'No, my friend, you might find me a dangerous guest'; but he desired nothing better than Watson's presence with him. 'It would be a great pleasure to me, therefore, if you could come on to the Continent with me.' Kindly Watson instantly agreed, and the next day saw both of them together on their journey. At Strasbourg, Holmes received a telegram from the London police, informing him that Moriarty had escaped their clutches; whereupon Holmes said, thinking of Watson's safety: 'I think that you had better return to England, Watson... you will find me a dangerous companion now. I should certainly recommend you to return to your practice.'

Holmes knew that now London was denied to Moriarty, he

would devote all his energies towards taking revenge upon him. They argued the question for half an hour, until Watson's affection won the day. They continued their journey together. At the Reichenbach Falls, Watson received a bogus letter, purporting to have come from a dying Englishwoman at Meiringen, and as a doctor felt that he could not refuse this call for help, so left Holmes alone, although something told him that perhaps he was doing the wrong thing. 'Yet', said Watson, 'I had my scruples about leaving Holmes', for he feared for his safety. Even when Holmes looked death in the face, as Moriarty bided his time, while he wrote a letter to Watson, perhaps his last, he thought of the great affection which existed between them. 'I am pleased to think that I shall be able to free society from any further effects of his presence, though I fear that it is at a cost which will give pain to my friends, and especially, my dear Watson, to you.'

After Holmes returned to England, following the death of Moriarty, he visited Watson in his Kensington consulting room in April 1894 in the disguise of an elderly, deformed bookseller. (Holmes was interested in early publications, having at one time picked up from a bookstall, *De Jure inter Gentes*, published in Latin at Liége in the Lowlands, in 1642.) Said Holmes, 'Well, sir, if it isn't too great a liberty, I am a neighbour of yours, for you'll find my little bookshop at the corner of Church Street, and very happy to see you, I am sure. Maybe you collect yourself, sir. Here's *British Birds* and *Catullus*, and, *The Holy War* – a bargain, every one of them. With five volumes you could just fill that gap on that second shelf. It looks untidy, does it not, sir?'

Watson turned his head to look at the cabinet behind him and when he turned round again, there stood Sherlock Holmes, smiling at him across the table. (Watson had presumed his friend to be dead.) Watson rose to his feet, stared at Holmes in utter amazement, and then fainted. When he came round, having been revived with brandy, he found his collar-ends undone, and Holmes bending over him.

> 'My dear Watson,' said the well remembered voice, 'I owe you a thousand apologies. I had no idea that you would be so affected.'
> I gripped him by the arms.
> 'Holmes,' I cried. 'Is it really you? Can it indeed be that you

are alive? Is it possible that you succeeded in climbing out of that awful abyss? I can hardly believe my eyes. Good heavens! to think that you – you of all men – should be standing in my study… Well, you're not a spirit, anyhow,' said I.

'My dear chap, I'm overjoyed to see you. Sit down, and tell me how you came alive out of that dreadful chasm.'

Holmes explained that he had no difficulty in getting out of the chasm, for the very simple reason that he was never in it; he then told all that had happened during the last three years. 'Several times during the last three years I have taken up my pen to write to you, but always I feared lest your affectionate regard for me should tempt you to some indiscretion which would betray my secret.' Holmes then asked for Watson's co-operation in a hard and dangerous night's work ahead. 'You'll come with me to-night?' 'When you like, and where you like,' replied Watson. 'This is, indeed, like the old days. We shall have time for a mouthful of dinner before we go.'

Their journey led them to an empty house in Baker Street, opposite their own flat. Holmes anticipated the capture of Colonel Sebastian Moran, one of Moriarty's still free men, by Inspector Lestrade and 'his merry men', who were stationed in the street. Holmes had not expected Moran to operate from Camden House, and use the convenient front window. Watson recorded:

All was still and dark, save only that brilliant yellow screen in front of us with the black figure outlined upon its centre. Again in the utter silence I heard that thin, sibilant note which spoke of intense suppressed excitement. An instant later he pulled me back into the blackest corner of the room, and I felt his warning hand upon my lips. The fingers which clutched me were quivering. Never had I known my friend more moved, and yet the dark street still stretched lonely and motionless before us.

After the capture of Colonel Moran, Holmes invited Watson back to the flat, where he was pleased to see his 'stormy petrel of crime' once more in his old seat contentedly smoking one of his cigars.

In November 1895 the masterful, practical Holmes again showed some emotion. Holmes considered that it was absolutely imperative that they should both go to Hugo Oberstein's house, while on a case dealing with lost secret submarine plans, in order not to let down his brother Mycroft, the Admiralty, the Cabinet and a very exalted person. There was great danger in going. Said Watson:

'Could we not get a warrant and legalise it?'
'Hardly on the evidence.'
'What can we hope to do?'
'We cannot tell what correspondence may be there.'
'I don't like it, Holmes.'
'My dear fellow, you shall keep watch in the street. I'll do the criminal part. It's not a time to stick at trifles… We are bound to go.' My answer was to rise from the table.
'You are right, Holmes. We are bound to go.' Holmes sprang up and shook me by the hand.
'I knew you would not shrink at the last.'

And for a moment, there was something in Holmes' eyes which was nearer to tenderness than Watson had ever seen.

During the time that Watson lived away from Baker Street, he was missed so much that Holmes would only venture out upon professional business, for he missed their conversations, and the long London walks that they had shared together, in silence when necessary, each pleasantly aware of the other's company.

Sherlock Holmes and Women

Watson, in the early days at Baker Street, spoke of Holmes' aversion to women as being typical of his unemotional character, for he had said that he disliked and distrusted the other sex, and that their motives were so inscrutable. Sometimes he spoke of the softer passions with a gibe or a sneer; he admitted that a woman's heart and mind were insoluble puzzles to a man. Subsequently, Watson thought that all emotions and love particularly were abhorrent to his cold, precise but admirably balanced mind; for a trained reasoner to admit such intrusions into his delicate and finely adjusted temperament, would introduce a distracting factor, which could possibly throw a doubt upon his mental results: in a nature such as his, strong emotions would have been too disturbing. Perhaps Watson may have misconstrued what Holmes actually said. Certainly, over the years, Watson came to realise that he must change his preconceived views relating to Holmes and women.

Later on Watson recorded Holmes as saying: 'I have seen too much not to know that the impression of a woman may be more valuable than the conclusion of an analytical reasoner.'

For Holmes placed true cold reason above all emotional things, which precluded him from serious affairs of the heart. At times he might have wished it but had to forbear. As he observed to Watson: 'I have never loved, Watson, but if I did and if the woman I loved had met such an end, I might act even as our lawless lion-hunter has done. Who knows?' I should never marry myself lest I bias my judgment.' Perhaps it might have been more truthful if Holmes had said that he never permitted himself to love, for such a thing as an affair of the heart would have run counter to all that he held dear.

Holmes did once allude to his deeper unexhibited emotions and his thoughts of marriage and family, when he spoke to Mr Alexander Holder, a banker of Threadneedle Street, over the return of the missing piece of the Beryl Coronet. He told him that he owed his son a humble apology, having wrongfully accused him of theft, and that his son had 'carried himself in this matter as I should be proud to see my own son do, should I ever chance to have one.' In fact, Holmes never married, although he became engaged, but only to suit his own purpose.

This was to Agatha, the maid of Charles Augustus Milverton of Appledore Towers, Hampstead, where he used the peculiarly ingratiating ways he had with women, thus establishing a cordial relationship.

You would not call me a marrying man, Watson?'
    'No indeed!'
    'You'll be interested to hear that I'm engaged.'
    'My dear fellow! I congrat—'
    'To Milverton's housemaid.
    'Good Heavens, Holmes!'
    'I wanted information, Watson.'
    'Surely you have gone too far?'

'It was a most necessary step. I am a plumber with a rising business, Escott, by name. I have walked out with her each evening, and I have talked with her. Good heavens, those talks! However, I have got all I wanted. I know Milverton's house as I know the palm of my hand.'

'But the girl, Holmes?' [This was not at all to Watson's liking].

Holmes shrugged his shoulders. 'You can't help it, my dear Watson. You must play your cards as best you can when such a stake is on the table. However, I rejoice to say that I have a hated rival, who will certainly cut me out the instant that my back is turned.'

Hardly the act of a gentleman, to philander with the affections of a lady!

Among all the women whom Holmes ever encountered, there was, to his way of thinking, only one woman. Indeed, he always referred to her under the honourable title of *the* woman.[130] This was Miss Irene Adler. Her life history was to be found in Holmes' index, where he had a system of docketing all paragraphs concerning all men and things. Her biography was 'sandwiched in between that of a Hebrew rabbi and that of a staff-commander who had written a monograph upon the deep-sea fishes'. She was an American, born in New Jersey in 1858; she was a contralto at La Scala, prima donna in the Imperial Opera of Warsaw, after which she retired from the operatic stage and came to live in London.

She came to know the King of Bohemia in Warsaw, when he was still the Crown prince. He wrote some compromising letters to her and allowed a cabinet-sized photograph to be taken of them together. She had the face of the most beautiful of women, and the mind of the most resolute of men, and lived at Briony Lodge, Serpentine Avenue, St John's Wood. The king told Holmes: 'Five attempts have been made. Twice burglars in my pay ransacked her house. Once we diverted her luggage when she travelled. Twice

---

[130]Holmes also called Isadora Klein '...*the* celebrated beauty.' ACD, *The Adventure of the Three Gables.*

she has been waylaid.'[131] But all attempts to retrieve the photograph were negative. 'What a woman – oh, what a woman!' cried the king to Holmes. 'Would she not have made an admirable queen? Is it not a pity that she was not on my level?' Later, after Holmes knew more about her, and how she was one of the few women who had got the better of him, he was inclined to think that Irene seemed to be on a very different level to the king, in fact upon a higher one. Holmes thought of her as the daintiest woman under a bonnet, and cherished her photograph in evening dress, above all his possessions.

Mrs Norton, née Adler, before she left for the Continent, found time to write Holmes a letter, which she left in the secret hiding place in her drawing room. It was addressed to 'Sherlock Holmes, Esq. To be left till called for'.

> My dear Mr Sherlock Holmes,
>
> You really did it very well. You took me in completely. Until after the alarm of fire, I had not a suspicion. But then, when I found how I had betrayed myself, I began to think. I had been warned against you months ago. I had been told that if the king employed an agent it would certainly be you. And your address had been given me. Yet, with all this, you made me reveal what you wanted to know. Even after I became suspicious, I found it hard to think evil of such a dear, kind old gentleman. But, you know, I have been trained as an actress myself. Male costume is nothing new to me. I often take advantage of the freedom which it gives. I sent John, the coachman, to watch you, ran upstairs, got into my walking-clothes, as I call them, and came down just as you departed. Well, I followed you to your door, and so made sure that I was really an object of interest to the celebrated Mr Sherlock Holmes. Then I, rather imprudently, wished you goodnight, and started for the Temple to see my husband.
>
> We both thought the best resource was flight, when pursued by so formidable an antagonist; so you will find the nest empty when you call to-morrow. As to the photograph, your client may rest in peace. I love and am loved by a better man than he. The king may do what he will without hindrance from one whom he

---

[131]The prefect of Paris police said of the thief, the Minister D, 'He has been twice waylaid as if by footpads and his person vigorously searched under my own inspection. Edgar Allan Poe, *The Purloined Letter*.

has cruelly wronged. I keep it only to safeguard myself, and to preserve a weapon which will always secure me from any steps which he might take in the future. I leave a photograph which he might care to possess; and I remain, dear Mr Sherlock Holmes,

Very truly yours,

Irene Norton, neé Adler.

Perhaps it was the Bohemian affair which made Holmes see the cleverness of women in a new light, for up until that time he used to make merry over the cleverness of women. But there was another time when Holmes was outwitted by a woman, or more truly by a male impersonation, and yet Holmes always prided himself upon being able to see through a disguise.

This person was 'Mrs Sawyer', who came to Baker Street to claim the gold wedding ring, advertised by Holmes as found in the Brixton Road; he hoped that perhaps his ruse might bring along someone connected with the murder of the American, Enoch J Drebber of Cleveland, Ohio. He was to find himself up against a most astute brain.

'Mrs Sawyer' was a very old and wrinkled woman who hobbled into the flat, her bleared eyes dazzled by the sudden blaze of light as she dropped Holmes a curtsey. 'It's this as has brought me, good gentlemen... a gold wedding-ring in the Brixton Road. It belongs to my girl Sally...' She was most pleased to recover the ring, saying she lived in Houndsditch. Holmes thought that he had caught her out: 'The Brixton Road does not lie between any circus and Houndsditch,' he said sharply. But the old woman was not put out of countenance. 'The gentleman asked me for *my* address... Sally lives in lodgings at 3 Mayfield Place, Peckham.'

With mumbled blessings and protestations, she pocketed the ring and shuffled off downstairs. 'I'll follow her... she must be an accomplice and will lead me to him,' said Holmes as he left the flat, to dog the feeble footsteps of the old woman; but she made a fool of Holmes with her disappearing act, and it was Holmes who was the 'old woman'.

When dealing with women, Holmes was most courteous and gentle and had a peculiarly ingratiating way with them and very readily established terms of confidence with them. Even when he was immersed in a very abstruse and complicated problem and wished no interruption, he would lay aside his work when a young lady implored his assistance, irrespective of whether she was beautiful or not. Helen Stonor was one visitor in the latter category, who came into Holmes' presence shivering with fear; she was some thirty years old, with early greying hair, her face weary and haggard looking. 'You must not fear… We shall soon set matters right, I have no doubt,' said Holmes soothingly, bending forward and patting her forearm.

Holmes could not bear to see a woman imposed upon or unjustly treated; he took up the case of the missing bridegroom on behalf of Miss Mary Sutherland. Her stepfather, Mr Windibank, posed as Hosmer Angel, a suitor for Mary's hand and her money, for he didn't wish another to benefit from her nest egg of two thousand five hundred pounds in New Zealand stock; so, having proposed marriage, he then disappeared upon the wedding day, the marriage to have been at St Saviour's near King's Cross. Mary was left to mope for and to be true to her lover and to marry no other. After Holmes had solved the mystery, he invited Windibank to Baker Street for a 'showdown', explaining who Mr Angel really was. Holmes wished to punish this blackguard but was not quite sure what to do. 'The law', said Holmes, 'cannot, as you say, touch you… yet there never was a man who deserved punishment more. If the young lady has a brother or a friend, he ought to lay a whip across your shoulders. By Jove! …It is not part of my duties to my client, but there's a hunting crop handy, and I think I shall just treat myself to—' Exit hurriedly the villain, and a fleeting glance at the softer side of Holmes.

Annie Harrison, fiancé, of Percy Phelps of Woking, wrote a letter to Watson on behalf of Phelps, who was recovering from nine weeks of brain fever, following a most horrible misfortune which had happened to him, namely the theft of the original naval treaty between England and Italy. The letter ran:

My Dear Watson,
    I have no doubt that you can remember 'Tadpole' Phelps, who was in the fifth form when you were in the third. It is possible even that you may have heard that through my uncle's influence I obtained a good appointment at the Foreign Office, and that I was in a situa-

tion of trust and honour until a horrible misfortune came suddenly to blast my career.

There is no use writing the details of that dreadful event. In the event of your acceding to my request it is probable that I shall have to narrate them to you… Do you think that you could bring your friend Mr Holmes down to see me? …I am still so weak that I have to write, as you see, by dictating. Do try to bring him.

Your old school-fellow,
Percy Phelps

Within the hour, Watson had left Kensington and shown Holmes the letter at Baker Street, which caused his observation: 'It does not tell us very much does it? …And yet the writing is of interest.' 'But the writing is not his own.' 'Precisely. It is a woman's.' Watson thought that it was a man's. 'No, a woman's,' said Holmes, 'and a woman of rare character. You see, at the commencement of an investigation it is something to know that your client is in close contact with someone who, for good or evil, has an exceptional nature. My interest is already awakened in the case.'

They travelled to Woking and saw the young couple. Holmes advised Miss Harrison that he must not make the mistake of coming to a conclusion too rapidly. When she told him to go to London to test his conclusions, he told her that her advice was excellent. Later she helped Holmes considerably, by falling in with his wishes to stay where she was all day, as it was of the utmost importance to Holmes. She promised that when she went to bed, she would lock the door on the outside and keep the key. She certainly complied with all Holmes wishes to the letter, and without her co-operation, Phelps would never have again seen the stolen naval treaty.

Lady Hilda Trelawney Hope, wife of the Right Honourable Trelawney Hope, and youngest daughter of the Duke of Belminster, was the most lovely woman in London, with a 'subtle, delicate charm', with a 'beautiful colouring' of an 'exquisite head'. She called to see Holmes, hoping to extract information concerning her husband's visit over the loss of a letter from a foreign potentate, in a long, thin, pale blue envelope, which had been kept in a locked despatch box in their bedroom.

But now her lovely cheek was pale with emotion, her eyes bright with fever or terror, her sensitive mouth 'tight and drawn in an effort after self-command', her body restless with suppressed excitement, and she asked question after question with a great tenacity of purpose. Her tall, graceful, intensely womanly presence was not so queenly as usual, and she sat with her back to the light so that her expression could not be read. She failed to get any assurance from Holmes that he would not tell her husband, and she departed, leaving behind an impression of a beautiful haunted face. Lovely as she was, Holmes knew that she was not to be entirely trusted. As with all women, her most trivial action might mean volumes or her extraordinary conduct might depend upon a hairpin or curling tongs.

Holmes knew that he must now play his trump card, and so confronted Lady Hope at her residence in Whitehall Terrace; here Holmes came straight to the point and asked her to give him the letter, knowing full well that she herself had stolen it. She, with astonishment and indignation, told Holmes that he insulted her. 'If you work with me I can arrange everything. If you work against me I must expose you,' said Holmes. She tried to browbeat Holmes by pretending to press the bell for the butler, but failed in her endeavour. She realised that she had met her match and, throwing caution to the wind, she was suddenly down on her knees at Holmes' feet, her hands outstretched in supplication, her beautiful face upturned and wet with tears. Such a situation affected even Holmes, and together they connived that Holmes would screen her, as the letter was replaced, never apparently having ever been absent.

Mrs Marker was the housekeeper at Yoxley Old Place, where Holmes and Watson went to unravel the mystery over the death of Willoughby Smith, secretary to Professor Coram. There, Holmes said to Watson, 'Ah, here is the good Mrs Marker! Let us enjoy five minutes of instructive conversation with her.' Holmes' peculiarly ingratiating way with women had, within half the time that he named, established terms of confidence with her. He soon captured her goodwill, and chatted to her as if he had known her for years. He soon learnt that Professor Coram was a heavy smoker, which possibly spoilt his appetite, thought Holmes. But no, if anything, he was eating more than ever, in spite of death in the house. Such information gave Holmes the clue that he was looking for – why food more than enough for two – to back up and perhaps to confirm his suspicions.

Was Lady Frances Carfax (the sole survivor of the direct family of the late Earl of Rufton) dead or alive? That was the question Holmes put to Watson, as he explained:

> 'The estates went, as you may remember, in the male line. She was left with limited means, but with some very remarkable old Spanish jewellery of silver and curiously cut diamonds to which she was fondly attached – too attached, for she refused to leave them with her banker and always carried them about with her. A rather pathetic figure, the Lady Frances, a beautiful woman, still in fresh middle age, and yet, by a strange chance, the last derelict of what only twenty years ago was a goodly fleet…
>
> 'She is a lady of precise habits, and for four years it has been her invariable custom to write every second week to Miss Dobney, her old governess, who has long retired and lives in Camberwell. It is this Miss Dobney who has consulted me. Nearly five weeks have passed without a word. The last letter was from the Hôtel National at Lausanne. Lady Frances seems to have left there and given no address. The family are anxious, and as they are exceedingly wealthy no sum will be spared if we can clear the matter up.'

To Watson's query as to whether there were other correspondents, Holmes replied: 'There is one correspondent who is a sure draw, Watson. That is the bank. Single ladies must live, and their passbooks are compressed diaries. She banks at Silvester's. I have glanced over her account.[132] The last cheque but one paid her bill at Lausanne, but it was a large one and probably left her with cash in hand. Only one cheque has been drawn since.' This was to her maid, Miss Marie Devine, for fifty pounds cashed at Montpellier.

Watson set out upon her trail to Lausanne and Baden. He learnt that she had met a Dr Shlessinger and his wife, and that the three of them had returned to London. The Honourable Philip Green, a former lover of Lady Frances, tracked the couple to

---

[132]Was not a private bank account sacrosanct?

Brixton; Holmes here discovered the lady, chloroformed, in a coffin, containing also another body, so that the crime could pass unnoticed. Holmes stopped the funeral in time, and the life of Lady Frances was saved.

Holmes became involved in the Harrow Weald case following a letter from Mrs Maberley:

> Dear Mr Sherlock Holmes,
>
> I have had a succession of strange incidents occur to me in connection with this house, and I should much value your advice. You would find me at home any time to-morrow. The house is within a short walk of the Weald Station. I believe that my late husband, Mortimer Maberley, was one of your clients.
>
> Yours faithfully,
> Mary Maberley

Holmes knew that Mary's son, Douglas, had been a lover of Isadora Klein, and from the one sheet of paper which Mrs Maberley tore from one of the burglars in her house, he sensed that Isadora was at the root of the evil. He told Watson:

> 'There was never a woman to touch her. She is pure Spanish, the real blood of the masterful Conquistadors, and her people have been leaders in Pernambuco for generations. She married the aged German sugar king, Klein, and presently found herself the richest as well as the most lovely widow upon earth. Then there was an interval of adventure when she pleased her own tastes. She had several lovers, and Douglas Maberley, one of the most striking men in London, was one of them. It was by all accounts more than an adventure with him. He was not a society butterfly but a strong proud man who gave and expected all. But she is the *belle dame sans merci* of fiction. When her caprice is satisfied the matter is ended, and if the other party in the matter can't take her word for it she knows how to bring it home to him.'

The story Douglas wrote was their story. She wished to marry into the aristocracy, the Duke of Lomond, many years her junior, a fact which a wise mother could overlook, but a scandal would be a different matter.

Holmes and Watson visited her address in Grosvenor Square,

a fine corner house in the West End of London. His note, written against the wishes of an opposing footman, simply said: 'Shall it be the police, then?' and passed them in with amazing clarity into an 'Arabian Nights drawing room, vast and wonderful, in a half gloom, picked out with an occasional pink electric light', the most welcome for a proud beauty, now not so young. A tall, queenly, perfect figure, with a lovely mask-like face, and two wonderful Spanish eyes met them. Her steely attitude soon changed to velvet as Holmes showed that he had no alternative but to go to Scotland Yard.

'Come and sit down, gentlemen. Let us talk this matter over. I feel that I may be frank with you, Mr Holmes. You have the feelings of a gentleman. How quick a woman's instinct is to find it out. I will treat you as a friend.' Holmes did not promise to reciprocate. 'No doubt,' said Isadora, 'it was foolish of me to threaten a brave man like yourself.' She was not foolish enough to let a band of ruffians blackmail her – they were her paid servants – and she smiled and nodded with a charming coquettish intimacy. Holmes suggested that he might bring her into the burglary charge. 'No, no, you would not. You are a gentleman. It is a woman's secret.'

She was told that the manuscript must be given back. This provoked her ripple of laughter. Pointing to a calcined mass in the fireplace, she said: 'Shall I give this back?' as she challenged Holmes with a roguish and exquisite smile. But Holmes was like Victoria with Palmerston: he was certainly not amused. 'That seals your fate… You are very prompt in your actions, madam, but you have overdone it on this occasion.' 'How hard you are!' she cried. 'Well, well,' said Holmes, 'I suppose I shall have to compound a felony as usual,' but not before he made her pay up five thousand pounds as retribution for damages done to Mrs Maberley.

It was on a cold, early spring morning, with a thick fog outside in Baker Street, and the gas lit within, that Holmes and Watson sat on either side of a cheery fire, leaving the breakfast table uncleared. Holmes' mood was in no way in sympathy with the fire as he tossed a crumpled letter across to Watson to read; for it concerned Miss Violet Hunter – a governess of five years – of Montague Place, who simply desired to consult Holmes as to whether she should accept a new similar situation. Holmes thought that this really was the last straw – whatever was his profession coming to!

As Miss Hunter entered, a plain but neatly dressed young lady, with a 'bright, quick face, freckled like a plover's egg', and with the brisk manner of a woman (without parents or relations to advise her) having to make her own way in the world, Holmes rose to greet her. His previous attitude thawed somewhat, for he was immediately favourably impressed by the manner and speech of his new client; he looked her over in his searching fashion, with his eyelids drooping and his fingertips together, waiting for her story.

She told Holmes that her previous salary had been only forty-eight pounds and that she was now offered one hundred and twenty pounds per annum. Holmes thought that the pay was too good and that the request to cut her luxuriant hair (of a rather peculiar tint of chestnut) quite short was a most odd one. Added to which was the odd request for her to wear any dress that might be given to her. 'I thought that if I told you the circumstances you would understand afterwards if I wanted your help,' said Miss Hunter. 'I should feel so much stronger if I felt that you were at the back of me.' Holmes endeavoured to reassure her. 'Oh, you may carry that feeling away with you. I assure you that your little problem promises to be the most interesting which has come my way for some months. There is something distinctly novel about some of the features. If you should find yourself in… danger… at any time, day or night, a telegram would bring me down to your help.' Two weeks later came the telegram which Holmes had expected:

> PLEASE BE AT THE BLACK SWAN HOTEL AT WINCHESTER AT MIDDAY TO-MORROW. DO COME! I AM AT MY WIT'S END.

Certainly Holmes was intrigued, although there would be no pecuniary gain; with a damsel in distress his heart softened.

Later on, at The Copper Beeches, near Winchester, she carried out Holmes' wishes in inveigling Mrs Toller into the wine cellar, and securing a duplicate set of Mr Rucastle's keys, held by the drunken Toller. 'You have done well indeed!' cried Holmes with enthusiasm, and thought her a very brave and a quite exceptional woman. Watson was rather disappointed that once Miss Hunter had ceased to be the centre of one of his problems, he manifested no further interest in her, was not even interested in the fact that she became the headmistress of a private school in Walsall.

Late in 1896 Watson called at Baker Street in response to a note from Holmes, where he was introduced to Mrs Merrilow, an elderly, waddling, motherly woman of the buxom landlady type, from South Brixton. Her only lodger of the last seven years was Mrs Eugenia Ronder (late of Ronder's wild beast show at Abbas Parva),[133] who always kept her face veiled in the greatest privacy. She wished someone to know the truth about her and why she was veiled. Mrs Merrilow suggested Holmes to her: 'this detective man what we read about'. (Ronder and Holmes already knew each other.)

Mrs Ronder called Holmes a 'man of judgment', for she knew his character and methods, having followed his work for some years, reading being the only pleasure left to her. She told Holmes her story, how a lion had torn away the beauty of her face, and how she felt like a poor wounded beast that had crawled into its hole to die. After a long silence, Holmes stretched out his long arm and patted her hand with such a show of sympathy as Watson had seldom seen Holmes show. 'Poor girl! Poor girl!' said Holmes. 'The ways of fate are indeed hard to understand. If there is not some compensation hereafter, then the world is a cruel jest.' Before Holmes departed, he warned Mrs Ronder not to take her life, but she lifted her veil and said, 'I wonder if you would bear it.' For the sight was horrible to behold. Two living and beautiful brown eyes looked sadly out from a face that was only a grisly ruin. All Holmes could do was to hold up his hand in a gesture of pity and protest, and take his leave.

It was the winter of 1897 that Inspector Stanley Hopkins sent a note to Holmes, asking for his advice and immediate assistance at the Abbey Grange, Marsham in Kent, where Sir Eustace Brackenstall had been murdered. Holmes, needing as much

---

[133]Mr Harding, ex-Warden of Hiram's Hospital was expected to be the Vicar of Crabtree Parva. Anthony Trollope, *The Warden*, 1855.

information as possible, decided to question Lady Brackenstall's nurse, Theresa Wright, from Australia. This was not going to be easy, for the woman was a stern, taciturn, suspicious and ungracious person, who loved her mistress and was willing to protect her. Holmes assumed his most pleasant manner; he listened quietly, and frankly accepted all that she told him about the master; under such kind behaviour she gradually thawed into a corresponding amiability and poured out all the information that Holmes required. Holmes was also struck with her mistress, and Watson had seldom seen 'so graceful a figure so womanly a presence, so beautiful a face, blonde, golden-haired, and blue-eyed...'

Holmes was asked to act on behalf of the most beautiful débutante of the previous season, none other than Lady Eva Blackwell, fiancée of the Earl of Dovercourt. His business was to try and buy back some imprudent letters, written to an impecunious young squire in the country, for they would be sufficient to prevent the wedding taking place. Charles Augustus Milverton, a professional blackmailer called the letters 'very sprightly', and the correspondent, 'charming' and for the return of the letters, his price was seven thousand pounds. Holmes offered two thousand pounds, which was refused, for Milverton knew that the exposure of one client would bring pressure to bear upon similar cases maturing, and make them more open to reason.

Holmes went with Watson to Milverton's house, hoping to retrieve the letters and save a marriage, but before he could do this Milverton was killed by an unexpected female visitor. Holmes decided that the murder was no concern of his, that the blackmailer was one of the most dangerous men in London; that this was one of the crimes which the law could not touch, and so to some extent justified private revenge. He had no sympathy with this criminal. After all incriminating letters in the safe had been burnt, Holmes and Watson beat a hasty retreat on foot.

Holmes was greatly accessible 'upon the side of flattery, and... upon the side of kindliness'. This is where Mrs Warren of Great Orme Street scored, for Holmes had said to her, 'I cannot see that you have any particular cause for uneasiness, not do I understand why I, whose time is of some value, should interfere in the matter.' His great scrapbook, in which he was arranging and indexing some of his recent material, he thought was more important. However, the landlady had the 'pertinacity and also the cunning of her sex'; she was not going to be sidetracked, and she let drop that Holmes had helped Mr Fairdale Hobbs, a lodger of hers. Hobbs had applauded the way in which Holmes had brought light into his darkness. 'Well, well, Mrs Warren, let us hear about it, then… You are uneasy, as I understand, because your new lodger remains in his room and you cannot see him. Why, bless you, Mrs Warren, if I were your lodger you often would not see me for weeks on end.' But this did not satisfy Mrs Warren, for she was frightened, always hearing footsteps, but never seeing her lodger; her nerves could stand it no longer. Holmes was touched. He 'leaned forward and laid his long, thin fingers upon the woman's shoulder. He had an almost hypnotic power of soothing when he wished. The scared look faded from her eyes, and her agitated features smoothed into their usual commonplace, as Holmes seated her in a chair, and she recounted her story.

Holmes expounded upon women and love to Watson at Birlstone Manor House, where Mrs Douglas appeared to be taking her husband's murder too lightly. 'She does not shine as a wife even in her own account of what occurred. I am not a whole-souled admirer of womankind, as you are aware, Watson, but my experience of life has taught me that there are few wives, having any regards for their husbands, who would let any man's spoken work stand between them and that husband's dead body. Should I ever marry, Watson, I should hope to inspire my wife with some feeling which would prevent her from being walked off by a housekeeper, when my corpse was lying within a few yards of her.' (Holmes did not totally discard the idea of marriage, should the time come when he no longer gave priority to his detective work.)

Watson understood only too well Holmes' feelings as he took a stroll in the curious old-world garden which flanked Birlstone Manor House. Here he became aware of voices behind the yew trees including a ripple of feminine laughter, which came from Mrs Douglas as she talked to Barker, a friend of her husband's. 'In the dining room she had been demure and discreet. Now all pretence of grief had passed away from her. Her eyes shone with the joy of living, and her face still quivered with amusement at some remark of her companion. He sat forward, his hands clasped and his forearms on his knees, with an answering smile upon his bold, handsome face.' As Watson came into view, the pair resumed their solemn masks, hoping that their levity had not been noticed.

Holmes was quite capable, if the situation warranted it, to speak eloquently from the heart, and not with his head, as was usual. When he spoke to Miss Violet de Merville, (daughter of General de Merville), young, rich, beautiful, accomplished and a wonder woman in every way, 'with the ethereal other-world beauty of some fanatic whose thoughts are set on high', Holmes thought that he had seen such faces in the pictures of the old masters of the Middle Ages; he wondered how such a woman could fall in love with such a vile monster as Baron Gruner – perhaps a case of extremes calling to each other. When Holmes spoke to her, he thought of her as if she were his daughter, and pleaded with her with great warmth of words; but no colour came to her ivory cheeks, no gleam of emotion to her abstracted eyes, as if she lived in some ecstatic dream. She loved the baron, and was adamant that he returned her love. But Holmes, (who was only trying to help her, was furious at being outmanoeuvred by her calm aloofness and supreme self-complaisance. As he remarked to Watson, 'Woman's heart and mind are insoluble puzzles to the male.'

Among the women who affected Holmes was Miss Maud Bellamy of Fulworth, Sussex, daughter of Tom Bellamy, fisherman and boat owner, who lived at The Haven, a house with a corner tower and a slate roof. 'There was no gainsaying', wrote Holmes, 'that she would have graced any assembly in the world. Who could have imagined that so rare a flower would grow from such a root and in such an atmosphere? Women have seldom been an attraction to me, for my brain has always governed my heart, but I could not look upon her perfect clear-cut face, with all the soft freshness of the downlands in her delicate colouring, without realising that no young man would cross her path unscathed.' So even as late as 1907, when Holmes was fifty-three or fifty-four, his heart could still flutter at the sight of a pretty girl.

Writings of Sherlock Holmes

Sherlock Holmes wrote several monographs upon different subjects before he met Dr Watson, and accumulated information upon many more, which alas were never published.

One monograph was upon 'The Distinction between the Ashes of the Various Tobaccos', wherein Holmes enumerated one hundred and forty forms of ash, from cigarette, cigar and pipe tobaccos; for Holmes flattered himself that he could distinguish at a glance the ash of any known brand of tobacco. The monograph was printed with coloured plates, illustrating the differences in the ash.

This knowledge he applied to an early case, at No. 3 Lauriston Gardens, off the Brixton Road, and it helped him to unravel the mystery of the murder of Enoch J Drebber of Cleveland, Ohio, USA, by poison, by a man smoking a Trichinopoly cigar. For Holmes had found upon the floor a little pile of grey dust, dark in colour and flaky which corresponded to that particular Indian cigar.

Holmes explained to Watson how tobacco ash often turned up in criminal trials, as a clue of supreme importance. 'If you can say definitely, for example, that some murder had been done by a man who was smoking an Indian *lunkah*, it obviously narrows your field of search. To the trained eye there is as much difference between the black ash of a Trichinopoly and the white fluff of bird's-eye as there is between a cabbage and a potato.'[134]

Charles McCarthy, an Australian, was murdered by Boscombe Pool, in Boscombe Valley, not far from Ross in Herefordshire. There Holmes carried out his investigations and found traces of cigar ash upon the ground behind a tree, and the cigar stump among the moss, where it had been tossed. He was able to declare that it was an Indian cigar, rolled in Rotterdam, the tip having

[134]Abercrombie Smith smoked bird's eye tobacco in 1884. ACD, *Lot 249*. Robert Montgomery bought his bird's eye from a little tobacco shop at the corner of the street. ACD, 'The Croxley Master', *Strand Magazine*, October 1888.

been cut off by a blunt penknife, and had been smoked in a cigar-holder. This knowledge, together with other evidence, led Holmes to John Turner, the murderer.

Dr Percy Trevelyan was set up in practice in Brook Street by a Mr Blessington who came to live there also as the doctor's resident patient. He said that he had a weak heart and needed constant attention, which was purely an excuse. Later, Blessington was found hanging in his room, his death thought to have been suicide. Inspector Lanner found four cigar ends in the fireplace, and a cigar case in the dead man's coat pocket. Holmes smelt the single cigar that it contained. 'Oh, this is a Havana, and these others are cigars of the peculiar sort which are imported by the Dutch from their East Indian colonies. They are usually wrapped in straw, you know, and are thinner for their length than any other brand.' Holmes examined the cigar ends with his pocket lens: 'Two of these have been smoked from a holder and two without… Two have been cut by a not very sharp knife, and two have had the ends bitten off by a set of excellent teeth. This is no suicide, Mr Lanner. It is a very deeply planned and cold-blooded murder.'

When Dr Grant Munro visited Baker Street, he left behind his pipe; Holmes knocked a little ash from the bowl onto his hand and examined it, and pronounced the tobacco to have been 'Grosvenor mixture at eightpence an ounce', a fairly expensive tobacco. 'As he might get an excellent smoke for half the price, he had no need to practise economy.'

I wonder if Dr Mortimer was familiar with Holmes' monograph on tobacco ash? While he was at Baskerville Hall in Devon, he deduced from the ash dropped twice from the cigar of Sir Charles Baskerville that he had stood for five to ten minutes by the wicket-gate. And yet he seemed to only smoke his own hand-twirled cigarettes.

Another of Holmes' monographs was 'Upon the Tracing of Footsteps'. 'There is no branch of detective science which is so important and so much neglected as the art of tracing footsteps', said Holmes. Here he showed the invaluable use of plaster of Paris (a gypsum which is a soft mineral found near Paris, partially dehydrated by heat, which, when mixed with water, dries into a hard white substance, which was ideal as a preserver of impresses).

When Watson saw the round, well defined muddy disks upon the floor in Bartholomew Sholto's chamber, he said, 'That is not a footmark.' Replied Holmes, 'It is something much more valuable to us. It is the impression of a wooden stump, worn away upon the inner side. You see here on the sill is the boot-mark with a square-toed sole of a heavy boot, with a broad metal heel, and beside it is the mark of the timber-toe.'

In the garret above, there were footsteps in the dust, and Holmes asked Watson to notice them particularly. 'Do you observe anything noteworthy about them?' Watson said that they belonged to a child or small woman. 'Apart from their size, though, is there nothing else?' Watson saw nothing particular in them. 'Look here! This is a print of a right foot in the dust. Now I make one with my naked foot beside it. What is the chief difference?' 'Your toes are all cramped together. The other print has each toe distinctly divided.' 'Quite so. That is the point' said Holmes. The diminutive footmarks, Holmes later discovered, belonged to Tonga, an Andaman islander. As Holmes explained: 'Some of the inhabitants of the Indian Peninsula are small men, but none could have left such marks as that. The Hindoo proper has long and thin feet. The sandal-wearing Mohammedan has the great toe well separated from the others because the thong is commonly passed between. These little darts, too, could only be shot in one way. They are from a blow-pipe. Now then, where are we to find our savage?' Holmes took down a bulky volume from the shelf – the first volume of a gazetteer then being published – and found his answer to be the 'Andaman Islands, situated three hundred and forty miles to the north of Sumatra, in the Bay of Bengal.' Here the aborigines were 'the smallest race upon the earth… Their feet and hands, however, are remarkably small.'

When Holmes visited 3 Lauriston Gardens off the Brixton Road, to check the death of Enoch J Drebber of Cleveland, he noticed outside the wheel-marks of a four-wheeled cab and the hoof marks of the horse; these were of three old shoes and one new shoe on the off foreleg. There were many marks of footsteps upon the wet clayey soil; these showed that there were two men involved. One was 'Patent-leather boots' who took short strides and the other, 'Square-toes', the murderer, who wore small square-toed boots. He was six feet tall as was shown by his four and a half foot stride over a puddle, and by the writing upon the wall.

Holmes explained to Watson how he calculated the height of a man:

'Why, the height of a man, in nine cases out of ten, can be told by the length of his stride. It is a simple calculation enough, though there is no use my boring you with figures. I had this fellow's stride both on the clay outside and on the dust within. Then I had a way of checking my calculation. When a man writes on a wall, his instinct leads him to write above the level of his own eyes. Now that writing was just over six feet from the ground. It was child's play… I'll tell you one other thing,' he said. 'Patent-leathers and square toes came in the same cab, and they walked down the pathway together as friendly as possible – arm-in-arm, in all probability. When they got inside, they walked up and down the room – or rather, Patent-leathers stood still while Square-toes walked up and down. I could read all that in the dust; and I could read that as he walked he grew more and more excited. That is shown by the increased length of his strides. He was talking all the while, and working himself up no doubt, into a fury. Then the tragedy occurred.'

While working on the case called 'The Crooked Man' at Aldershot, Holmes explained to Watson his discovery of some unusual foot impressions: 'There had been a man in the room, and he had crossed the lawn coming from the road. I was able to obtain five very clear impressions of his footmarks: one in the roadway itself, at the point where he had climbed the low wall, two on the lawn, and two very faint ones upon the stained boards near the window where he had entered. He had apparently rushed across the lawn, for his toe-marks were very much deeper than his heels. But it was not the man that surprised me. It was his companion.' Holmes made tracings upon a large sheet of tissue paper, showing five well marked footpads, an indication of long nails, and the whole print nearly as large as a dessert spoon.

Holmes diagnosed that the unknown animal was some fifteen inches from forefoot to hind and possibly some two feet long. The length of stride was indicated as three inches. Later, Holmes learned that these impressions belonged to a mongoose, a thin, lithe reddish-brown creature, with fine red eyes.

Holmes explained to Alexander Holder, banker of Threadneedle Street, (who received the Beryl Coronet as security upon a loan of fifty thousand pounds) that by his observations of the impressions of footsteps, his son Arthur was not the thief who has stolen the coronet.

'When I arrived at the house... I at once went very carefully round it to observe if there were any traces in the snow which might help me. I knew that none had fallen since the evening before, and also that there had been a strong frost to preserve impressions. I passed along the tradesmen's path, but found it all trampled down and indistinguishable. Just beyond it, however, at the far side of the kitchen door, a woman had stood and talked with a man, whose round impressions on one side showed that he had a wooden leg. I could even tell that they had been disturbed, for the woman had run back swiftly to the door, as was shown by the deep toe and light heel marks, while Wooden-leg had waited a little, and then had gone away. I thought at the time that this might be the maid and her sweetheart, of whom you had already spoken to me, and inquiry showed it was so. I passed round the garden without seeing anything more than random tracks, which I took to be the police; but when I got into the stable lane a very long and complex story was written in the snow in front of me.

'There was a double line of tracks of a booted man, and a second double line which I saw with delight belonged to a man with naked feet. I was at once convinced from what you told me that the latter was your son. The first had walked both ways, but the other had run swiftly, and as his tread was marked in places over the depression of the boot, it was obvious that he had passed after the other. I followed them up and found they led to the hall window, where Boots had worn all the snow away while waiting. Then I walked to the other end, which was a hundred yards or more down the lane. I saw where Boots had faced round, where the snow was cut up as though there had been a struggle, and, finally, where a few drops of blood had fallen, to show me that I was not mistaken. Boots had then run down the lane, and another little smudge of blood showed that it was he who had been hurt. When he came to the highroad at the other end, I found that the pavement had been cleared, so there was an end to that clue.

'On entering the house, however, I examined, as you remember, the sill and framework of the hall window with my lens, and I could at once see that someone had passed out. I could distinguish the outline of an instep where the wet foot had been placed in coming in. I was then beginning to be able to form an opinion as to what had occurred. A man had waited outside the window; someone had brought the gems; the deed had been overseen by your son; he had pursued the thief; had struggled with him; they had each tugged at the coronet, their united strength causing injuries which neither alone could have effected. He had returned with the prize, but had left a fragment in the grasp of his opponent. So far I was clear. The question now was, who was the man and who was it brought him the coronet?'

Holmes enquiries then led him to Sir George Burnwell, gambler, villain and of evil reputation among women, who had an understanding with Mary, Mrs Holder's niece; she stole the coronet for him and he sold the three gems for six hundred pounds and then they fled away together.

While Holmes was investigating the disappearance of Mr Jonas Oldacre, who lived in Deep Dene House, Lower Norwood, and endeavouring to show that John Hector McFarlane was not a murderer, he examined the bedroom; there he found footmarks of both these men upon the carpet, but not any impressions of a third person, which evidence tended rather to go against his client. So Holmes this time had to rely upon other detective work to winkle out Oldacre; he found that the upper corridor was six feet shorter than the one below, suggesting a hiding place, which turned out to be the truth.

While at Boscombe, Holmes called at Hatherley Farm,[135] the rented home of McCarthy the murdered man; there the maid showed him a pair of her master's boots, worn at the time of his death, and a pair of the son's. He measured these very carefully

---

[135]Victor Hatherley, hydraulic engineer. ACD, *The Adventure of the Engineer's Thumb*.

from seven or eight different points. He then went on to Boscombe Pool, where the marks of many feet, upon the path and short grass, showed in the damp marshy ground, including, unfortunately, many of Lestrade's left foot, with its inward twist, making identification more difficult. 'Here is where the party with the lodge-keeper came, and they have covered all tracks for six or eight feet round the body. But here are three separate tracks of the same feet.' After a closer inspection Holmes said: 'These are young McCarthy's feet. Twice he was walking, and once he ran swiftly, so that the soles are deeply marked and the heels hardly visible. That bears out his story. He ran when he saw his father on the ground. Then here are the father's feet as he paced up and down. What is this, then? It is the butt-end of the gun as the son stood listening. And this? Ha, ha! What have we here? Tiptoes! tiptoes! Square, too, quite unusual boots! They come, they go, they come again – of course that was for the cloak. Now where did they come from?'

Holmes found a jagged stone, and knew it to be the murder weapon, because the grass had been growing under it for the past few days. From all the signs, Holmes knew the murderer to be 'a tall man, left-handed, limps with the right leg, wears thick-soled shooting-boots and a grey cloak, smokes Indian cigars, uses a cigar-holder and carries a blunt pen knife in his pocket'.

Lestrade could not be bothered to follow Holmes' valuable clues, otherwise he could have had the credit of arresting John Turner, dying of diabetes.

After the murder of Aloysius Garcia, of Wisteria Lodge, two miles from Esher, in March 1892, whose body was found upon Oxshott Common, Holmes and Watson went down to investigate.

They were told by PC Walters that he had seen a queer face looking through the lower pane of the window. 'It wasn't black, sir, nor was it white, nor any colour that I know, but a kind of queer shade like clay with a splash of milk in it. Then there was the size of it…' It looked twice the size of Inspector Baynes' face. Holmes went outside and examined with his little pocket lantern the grass bed for footprints, and found them to correspond to a number twelve shoe and thought that the owner might well be a giant. The impressions turned out to belong to the hideous mulatto cook from San Pedro, but Holmes was not convinced that he was the murderer.

Another case of Holmes' observations upon footsteps, took place at 403 Brook Street, where Dr Trevelyan's resident patient, Mr Blessington, was murdered by hanging in his bedroom. Holmes observed of the pseudo-cataleptic Russian's son: 'This young man has left prints upon the stair-carpet which made it quite superfluous for me to ask to see those which he had made in the room. When I tell you that his shoes were square-toed instead of being pointed like Blessington's, and were quite an inch and a third longer than the doctor's, you will acknowledge that there can be no doubt as to his individuality.'

Holmes said that there were three conspirators: 'There were three of them in it: the young man, the old man, and a third, to whose identity I have no clue... The three men having ascended the stairs, which they did on tiptoe, the elder man first, the younger man second, and the unknown man in the rear—' To Watson's surprised ejaculation, Holmes said, 'Oh, there could be no question as to the superimposing of the footmarks. I had the advantage of learning which was which last night.' But, for all the sleuth work, the murderers were never caught.

When Holmes was in one of the rooms at Birlstone Manor House, Sussex, he went to the window and examined the blood mark upon the sill. 'It is clearly the tread of a shoe. It is remarkably broad; a splay-foot, one would say. Curious, because, so far as one can trace any footmark in this mud-stained corner, one would say it was a more shapely sole. However, they are certainly very indistinct.'

Holmes had another opportunity to examine footmarks at Riding Thorpe Manor, Norfolk, the home of Hilton Cubitt. He took Inspector Martin into the garden to look for further evidence. 'A flower-bed extended up to the study window, and we all broke into an exclamation as we approached it. The flowers were trampled down and the soft soil was imprinted all over with footmarks. Large masculine feet they were, with peculiarly long, sharp toes. Holmes hunted about among the grass and leaves like a retriever after a wounded bird. Then, with a cry of satisfaction, he bent forward and picked up a little brazen cylinder. This was the third revolver cartridge.

While Holmes was investigating the murder of John Straker and the mystery of the missing racehorse, Silver Blaze, he inspected a hollow upon the moor and the trampled mud there. Inspector Gregson gave him a boot of the dead man, a shoe of Fitzroy Simpson and a cast horseshoe of Silver Blaze. He then compared the impressions of each of them with the marks upon the ground. Further on, they came upon the track of a horse in the soft earth, and the shoe of the racehorse fitted the impression exactly. Holmes told Watson that Silas Brown, the trainer, was the abductor. 'He tried to bluster out of it, but I described to him so exactly what his actions had been upon that morning that he was convinced that I was watching him. Of course you observed the peculiarly square toes in the impressions, and that his own boots exactly corresponded to them.'

The year 1897 found Holmes down in Cornwall, inspecting a strange case at Tredannick Wartha and as he explained to Watson: 'Our next obvious step is to check, so far as we can, the movements of Mortimer Tregennis after he left the room. In this there is no difficulty, and they seem to be above suspicion. Knowing my methods as you do, you were, of course, conscious of the somewhat clumsy water-pot expedient by which I obtained a clearer impress of his foot than might otherwise have been possible. The wet, sandy path took it admirably. Last night was also wet, you will remember, and it was not difficult – having obtained a sample print – to pick out his track among others and to follow his movements.'

When Holmes, Watson and Bob Carruthers were approaching the shrubbery at Charlington Hall, in their attempt to rescue Violet Smith from the clutches of Mr Woodley, Holmes pulled up. 'They didn't go to the house. Here are their marks on the left – here, beside the laurel bushes. Ah! I said so.' So the signs diverted them to the bowling alley where they found their quarry.

A few months after Watson's marriage, upon a summer night at a quarter to twelve, Holmes rang the doctor's bell, hoping that he could be put up for the night. 'Sorry to see that you've had the British workman in the house. He's a token of evil. Not the drains, I hope?' Watson said it was the gas. Holmes knew there had been a stranger in the house, for the workman had left two nail marks from his boot upon the linoleum, where the light picked them out.

Of all foot impressions, surely the most familiar ones to Holmes were those of his companion, and yet he failed to recognise them upon the Devon moor. It was while Holmes was in hiding and returning to his Neolithic hut dwelling (where Watson was hiding), and when he was still within twenty paces of the door, that he knew the interloper to be his old friend. Watson thought that his foot impressions had given him away. 'No, Watson; I fear that I could not undertake to recognise your footprint amid all the footprints of the world.' And yet the only other likely footprints which might have been seen would have been those left by the boy Cartwright.

Holmes not only made deductions from footsteps, but, just as important, from the lack of them when they might have been expected to be visible. For someone stole the naval treaty left lying unattended for a short while upon the desk of Percy Phelps in the Foreign Office. Holmes advertised in every London evening paper as follows:

£10 REWARD. THE NUMBER OF THE CAB WHICH DROPPED A FARE AT OR ABOUT THE DOOR OF THE FOREIGN OFFICE IN CHARLES STREET AT A QUARTER TO TEN IN THE EVENING OF MAY 23RD. APPLY 221B. BAKER STREET.

Watson queried this. 'You are confident that the thief came in a cab?' 'If not, there is no harm done. But if Mr Phelps is correct in stating that there is no hiding-place either in the room or the corridors, then the person must have come from outside. If he came from outside on so wet a night, and yet left no trace of damp upon the linoleum, which was examined within a few minutes of his passing, then it is exceedingly probable that he came in a cab. Yes, I think that we may safely deduce a cab.'

Holmes had little success down at Briarbrae, Woking, where he was working upon the case of Percy Phelps. He made an inspection outside the house, accompanied by Watson, Phelps and Harrison, whose sister Annie was to become the future Mrs

Phelps. They passed round the lawn to the outside of the young diplomat's window. Holmes examined some marks upon the flower bed, hopelessly blurred and vague. Holmes stooped over them for an instant and then rose, shrugging his shoulders. 'I don't think anyone could make much of this,' he said.

After Holmes' final victory over Professor Moriarty at the Reichenbach Falls, he wondered how he could deceive his pursuers. Should he reverse his boots as he had done on similar occasions?[136] But the sight of three sets of tracks in one direction would certainly have suggested a deception, so Holmes did not resort to this subterfuge.

Not all of Holmes' observations upon footsteps were human. During his investigation into the disappearance of Lord Saltire, the ten-year-old son and heir of the Duke of Holdernesse, he pondered over the many tracks of cows, for never a cow did he see upon the moor. 'What a blind beetle I have been,' said Holmes, not for the first time, 'not to draw my conclusion.' 'And what is your conclusion?' queried Watson. 'Only that it is a remarkable cow which walks, canters and gallops.' Reuben Hayes had shod his horses with shoes which counterfeited the tracks of cows; the scheming brain behind the operation was that of James Wilder, the illegitimate son of the duke, who hated the rightful heir. The duke showed Holmes into his museum and pointed to an inscription in a glass case. 'These shoes were dug up in the moat of Holdernesse hall. They are for the use of horses, but they are shaped below with a cloven foot of iron, so as to throw pursuers off the track. They are supposed to have belonged to some of the marauding Barons of Holdernesse in the Middle Ages.' A thin film of mud upon the shoes showed that they had been recently used.

Wheel marks, just as much as footsteps, told their story to the observant Holmes. While Holmes was at The Myrtles, Beckenham, the house of the Greek lady called Sophy, and having arrived there late, owing to his having to obtain a warrant from Inspector Gregson, the house was found in darkness and the 'birds' flown. They had departed during the past hour in a

---

[136]Watson never published a case of Holmes using this subterfuge.

carriage heavily loaded with luggage. Holmes deduced this from the two sets of wheel tracts – the inward ones having light tracks, and the outward ones being much deeper. Gregson was duly impressed, for he had seen the wheel tracks in the light of the gate lamp, but could make nothing of them. He shrugged his shoulders as he admitted that Holmes was a trifle beyond him.

Holmes was also well informed upon the wheel marks left by a cab. While he was examining the cause of the death of Enoch Drebber, at Brixton, he observed to Watson that the murderer had arrived in a four-wheeled cab, which 'had made two ruts with its wheels close to the kerb. Now, up to last night, we have had no rain for a week, so that those wheels which left such a deep impression must have been there during the night... Since the cab was there after the rain began, and was not there at any time during the morning – I have Gregson's word for that – it follows that it must have been there during the night, and therefore, that it brought those two individuals to the house... I satisfied myself that it was a cab and not a private carriage by the narrow gauge of the wheels. The ordinary London growler is considerably less wide than a gentleman's brougham.'[137]

Holmes was familiar with forty-two different impressions left by the tyres of bicycles. Whether this information remained in note form or was published as a monograph is not quite clear.

While Holmes and Watson were investigating the disappearance of Lord Saltire from the Priory School at Mackleton, they found tyre marks upon the moor. 'This, as you perceive, is a Dunlop, with a patch upon the outer cover. Heidegger's tyres were Palmer's, leaving longitudinal stripes. Aveling, the mathematical master, was sure upon the point. Therefore, it is not Heidegger's track.' Watson thought that perhaps they were those of the boy. 'Possibly, if we could prove a bicycle to have been in his possession. But this we have utterly failed to do. This track, as you perceive, was made by a rider who was going from the direction of the school.' Watson thought that the rider might have been going towards the school. 'No, no, my dear Watson. The more deeply sunk impression is, of course, the hind wheel, upon

---

[137]London growler was a four-wheeled horse-drawn cab.

which the weight rests. You perceive several places where it has passed across and obliterated the more shallow mark of the front one. It was undoubtedly heading away from the school. It may or may not be connected with our inquiry, but we will follow it backwards before we go any further.'

They continued their search. 'It is, of course, possible that a cunning man might change the tyres of his bicycle in order to leave unfamiliar tracks. A criminal who was capable of such a thought is a man whom I should be proud to do business with.' Further along on the sodden portion of the moor they came to a miry path. Here Holmes was delighted to find an impression like a fine bundle of telegraph wires running down the centre of it; the marks of Palmer tyres. 'Here is Herr Heidegger, sure enough!' exclaimed Holmes exultantly. 'My reasoning seems to have been pretty sound, Watson.'

Further tracks showed that the rider was throwing all his weight forward as if he were sprinting. Some of the tracks were smudged; there were some footmarks and further tyre impressions, and then dark stains of clotted blood. The rider had fallen wounded – then stood up and remounted and cycled on. They came upon the Palmer-tyred bicycle in the gorse bushes, horribly smeared with blood and one pedal bent; then the body of the murdered German master, with a crushed skull.

Perhaps Holmes might well have added to a monograph the marks made by a tyre of a Rudge-Whitworth bicycle, for he had the opportunity to examine one at Birlstone Manor House. This was found concealed in a clump of evergreens, and was thought by the police to have some connection with the murder of Mr Douglas. Inspector MacDonald's comment was that bicycles should be numbered like other wheeled traffic and registered, thus helping the police.

Another of Holmes' monographs was entitled 'Influence of a Trade upon the Form of the Hand'. This was a matter of great practical interest to the scientific detective, especially in cases of unclaimed bodies, or in discovering the antecedents of criminals. Included were lithotype illustrations of the hands of compositors, cork cutters, diamond polishers, sailors, slaters and weavers.

Holmes surprised Jabez Wilson, pawnbroker of Coburg

Square, when he explained to him that he had at one time done manual labour, which was quite true, for he had been at one time a ship's carpenter. 'Your hands, my dear sir. Your right hand is quite a size larger than your left. You have worked with it, and the muscles are more developed.'

The hands of Mycroft, Sherlock's brother, were broad and fat, like a seal's flippers. I wonder what the detective would have deduced from those hands, had he not known their owner.

A retired sergeant of marines, employed as a commissionaire, called at Baker Street to deliver a letter from Tobias Gregson. Holmes noticed him walking down the other side of the street, and, even at that distance, discerned 'a great blue anchor tattooed on the back of the fellow's hand' and knew thereby that he had been connected with the sea. Watson thought it all 'Brag and bounce', but afterwards had to concede that it was wonderful; Holmes' expression showed that he was pleased at the doctor's surprise and admiration.

Steve Dixie was sent by Barney Stockdale to Baker Street to endeavour to intimidate Holmes, by telling him that his life would not be safe if he went down Harrow way. 'See here, Masser Holmes, you keep your hands out of other folks' business. Leave folks to manage their own affairs. Got that, Masser Holmes?' And the huge Negro swung a huge knotted lump of a fist under Holmes' nose. It was the type of fist which stamped Dixie as a bruiser and Holmes told him so.

Dr Mortimer called to see Holmes concerning Sir Henry Baskerville and the eighteenth century legend of the family hound of the Devon moor. Holmes noticed his long quivering fingers 'as agile and restless as the antennae of an insect and commented, 'I observe from your forefinger that you make your own cigarettes. Have no hesitation in lighting one.' Whereupon the visitor proceeded to produce paper and tobacco and twirled the one up in the other with surprising dexterity.

'Mrs Sawyer' visited Holmes to collect her daughter's lost wedding ring. In effect, it was a young male actor, impersonating a very old and wrinkled woman with a hobble. One thing which might well have given the young man away would have been his masculine hands, but as Holmes made no observation upon this point, 'she' no doubt wore gloves, and so gave Holmes no chance of breaking through the very efficient disguise.

When Miss Violet Smith called to seek Holmes' advice, he knew by her 'spatulate finger-ends' that she was either a typist or a musician, but taking also into account the spirituality of the face, he knew it was the latter.[138]

Did Holmes, I wonder, include in his monograph the unique impressions from hands and fingers? For Holmes was very alive to their potential as an aid to detection. As Holmes, Watson and the dog Toby followed the creosote trail towards the Thames, along by the boundary wall of Pondicherry Lodge, the home of Bartholomew Sholto, they came to a corner where the two walls joined. There Holmes observed: 'There's the print of Wooden-leg's hand. You see the slight smudge of blood upon the white plaster. What a lucky thing it is that we have had no very heavy rain since yesterday! The scent will lie upon the road in spite of their eight-and-twenty hours' start.'

Holmes had devoted some time to the study of the typewriter, and its relation to crime. He thought that some day, when he had some spare time, he would write a little monograph upon the subject.

He was able to utilise this knowledge to outwit Mr Windibank, the stepfather of Miss Mary Sutherland, who also impersonated the rôle of her lover, Hosmer Angel, to whom she became engaged, but who vanished before the wedding ceremony could take place. Thus he hoped that he would not lose the benefit of her income of one hundred pounds, since in future she would stay at home, awaiting Mr Angel, who would never materialise.

> 'It is a curious thing,' remarked Holmes [to Mr Windibank], 'that a typewriter has really quite as much individuality as a man's handwriting. Unless they are quite new, no two of them write exactly alike. Some letters get more worn than others, and some wear only on one side. Now, you remark in this note of yours,

---

[138]At Lady Windermere's reception at Bentinck House, Lady Flora held out a long, bony hand with spatulate fingers for Mr Podgers, chiromantist, to examine. 'Ah a pianist! I see,' he said. Oscar Wilde, *Lord Arthur Saville's Crime*, 1891. ACD, *The Adventures of the Solitary Cyclist*, 1903.

Mr Windibank, that in every case there is some little slurring over of the "e", and a slight defect in the tail of the "r". There are fourteen other characteristics, but those are the more obvious... And now I will show you what is really a very interesting study, Mr Windibank... I have here four letters which purport to come from the missing man. They are all typewritten. In each case not only are the "e's" slurred and the "r's" tailless, but you will observe, if you care to use my magnifying lens, that the fourteen other characteristics to which I have alluded are there as well.'

So the impostor was exposed, although, unfortunately, the case was not actionable.

Perhaps Holmes might have added to the foregoing the type used in watermarks. For Holmes commented to Watson upon this matter, after receiving on 20 March 1888 a letter, written upon thick pink-tinted notepaper, from the King of Bohemia. Said Holmes, 'It is not an English paper at all. Hold it up to the light.' Watson did so and saw a large 'E' with a small 'g', a 'P', and a large 'G' with a small 't'. Holmes explained: 'The "G" with the small "t" stands for 'Gesellschaft', which is the German for "Company". It is a customary contraction like our "Co", "P" of course, stands for "Papier". Now for the "Eg". Let us glance at our Continental Gazetteer.' From the heavy brown volume he read out: 'Eglow, Eglonitz – here we are, Egria. It is in a German-speaking country – in Bohemia, not far from Carlsbad. "Remarkable as being the scene of the death of Wallenstein, and for its numerous glass factories and paper mills." Ha, ha, my boy, what do you make of that?'

Another monograph might well have been written upon the type used in newspapers, another of Holmes' special hobbies. 'There is as much difference to my eyes between the leaded bourgeois type of a *Times* article and the slovenly print of an evening half-penny paper... The detection of types is one of the most elementary branches of knowledge to the special expert in crime, though I confess that once when I was very young I confused the *Leeds Mercury* with the *Western Morning News*. But a *Times* leader is entirely distinctive, and these words could have been taken from nothing else.' Holmes was explaining to Sir Henry Baskerville the origin of the message he had received: 'As you value your life or your reason keep away from the moor'. All the words, except the last one, had been cut from the previous day's leading article in *The Times*, on free trade, with short-bladed scissors, and gummed onto a half sheet of foolscap paper.

Holmes wrote two short monographs upon the human ear, for the *Anthropological Journal*. He said that there was no part of the body which varied so much as the human ear. Each ear was as a rule quite distinctive and different from all the other ones.

Thus was Holmes able to apply this knowledge when he travelled down to Croydon, with Watson to interview Miss Susan Cushing, a maiden lady of fifty, and examine the most macabre postal package that she had received. Holmes had been invited down by Inspector Lestrade, for he found it rather difficult to get anything to work upon; the two human ears mystified him. The package was addressed to 'Miss S Cushing'. Her other sisters were Sarah and Mary; the yellow cardboard box, with two distinctive thumb marks at the bottom left corner, had originally contained half a pound of honeydew tobacco, but now had been filled with coarse salt and contained two human ears, which were not a pair, and had been cut off with a blunt instrument. One ear was that of a woman, small, finely formed and pierced for an earring. The other was that of a man, sunburned, discoloured, and also pierced for an earring.

Holmes noted the anatomical peculiarities of the ears and was surprised to see that Sarah Cushing's ear corresponded exactly with the ear in the box. Said Holmes, 'The matter was entirely beyond coincidence. There was the same shortening of the pinna, the same broad curve of the upper lobe, the same convolution of the inner cartilage. In all essentials it was the same ear.' This showed Holmes that the victim was a close blood relation. And so it turned out. The ear belonged to Mary Cushing, youngest of the three sisters.

It was the tarred twine round the box which led Holmes towards the owner of the male ear. It was similar to that used by sailmakers aboard ship, and the knot used was a popular sailor's knot; the pierced ear indicated a sailor more than a landsman.[139]

---

[139]Marie Roget was murdered and her body thrown into the River Seine and was then found by some fishermen. The strings of her bonnet were found round her

Mary Cushing married James Browner, a sailor, but took a lover, Alec Fairbairn, another sailor. Browner exacted revenge upon the two of them, and sent the ears to Susan, intending them for her sister Sarah, because of her hate for him as he refused her love.

There was also a monograph upon the Polyphonic Motets of Lassus.[140] This was printed for private circulation and was said by the experts to have been the final word upon the subject.

Holmes told Watson that he intended to write a monograph upon Malingering, for Holmes could feign death only too well, as he did so convincingly when he set himself to catch the criminal Culverton Smith.

Holmes was most intrigued by handwriting, ciphers and codes, and what might be deduced from their study. He was fairly familiar with all forms of secret writings and wrote a trifling monograph upon the subject, in which he analysed one hundred and sixty separate ciphers. Holmes read many ciphers as easily as reading the apocrypha of the agony column.

But when Holmes was confronted with some chalk drawings, which looked like a child's conception of 'dancing' men, which had appeared upon the black wooden door of the tool house, at the home of Hilton Cubitt, seven miles from north Walsham in Norfolk, he confessed that they were entirely new to him.

Holmes observed to Inspector Martin from Norwich, after finding that Hilton Cubitt had been shot through the heart and his wife severely injured, that he had anticipated the crime, but had hoped that he would have arrived in time to prevent it, for the evidence of the dancing men, had put him upon the scent, although the object of those who had invented the system, was to conceal that the characters contained a message. Holmes started with the most common symbol used and called it E, this being the most common letter used in the English alphabet. As he acquired new groups of pictographs, so he gradually arrived at other letters, until he had eighteen letters for eighteen different symbols; he

---

neck. The knot by which the strings were fastened was a sailor's knot. Edgar Allan Poe, *Mystery of Marie Roget*.
[140]Polyphonic choral composition usually unaccompanied – anthem or church cantata.

eventually revealed the full messages: 'AM HERE ABE SLANEY'; 'AT ELRIDGE'S; 'ELSIE PREPARE TO MEET THY GOD'. Holmes presumed that the man was an American, as indicated by his first name; he had this confirmed by William Hargreave of the New York Police Bureau and was told that this man was the most dangerous crook in Chicago. Holmes wrote a note to Slaney, at Elridge's Farm, using the same cipher, purporting to come from Elsie Cubitt, (the American wife of Hilton Cubitt), simply saying, 'COME HERE AT ONCE'. The bait was taken, and he came to the house expecting to see the woman he loved. Instead, handcuffs were snapped upon his wrists by the inspector. Slaney was absolutely dumbfounded to think that Holmes had been able to decode the cipher, invented by Elsie's father, Patrick, for as he said, 'There was no one on earth outside the Joint, [the Chicago gang of seven], who knew the secret of the Dancing Men. How came you to write it?' Said Holmes, 'What one man can invent another can discover.'

In the late 1880s Holmes received a cipher message from his agent, Fred Porlock; the key to it should have been sent separately, but with the matter becoming dangerous – there was a chance of Moriarty finding out – Porlock decided not to send it, and asked Holmes to burn the message which ran as follow:

534 C2 13 127 36 31 4 17 21 41
DOUGLAS 109 293 5 37 BIRLSTONE
26 BIRLSTONE 9 13 171

Holmes was not daunted by not having the key. Together with Watson, he thought over the matter. 'It is clearly a reference to the words in a page of some book. Until I am told which page and which book I am powerless.' The words 'Douglas' and 'Birlstone', being unique, had to be written in plain language. Holmes, summing up, indicated a large, standardised common book, printed in lengthy double columns, a book he would be expected to own. Watson suggested the Bible, *Bradshaw* and then an almanac. 'Excellent, Watson! I am very much mistaken if you have not touched the spot.' So *Whitaker's Almanac* was tried, but being 7 January the new almanac was tried without success. 'It is more likely that Porlock took his message from the old one'; and

Holmes found in the cupboard last year's large, standardised, yellow-covered volume, one which Porlock would have expected Holmes to have. Holmes turned to page 534 with the double columns. The numbers revealed the following message:

> There is danger – may – come – very – soon – one… Douglas – rich – country – now – at – Birlstone – House – Birlstone – confidence – is – pressing.

It had not been possible for Porlock to find a faultless message; but Holmes understood that some devilry was afoot against one Douglas, a rich country gentleman, and that 'confidence' was as near as he could get to 'confident'. This was subsequently confirmed by the arrival of Inspector MacDonald, who said that Mr Douglas of Birlstone Manor had been murdered; he was much surprised to find that Holmes already had some information upon the subject.[141]

When Holmes paid his second visit to Victor Trevor, at Donnithorpe, towards the end of his autumn college vacation, he was shown the coded message sent to Mr Trevor before his death. It was scribbled upon a single sheet of grey paper, as follows:

> The supply of game for London is going steadily up. Head-keeper Hudson, we believe, has been now told to receive all orders for fly-paper, and for preservation of your hen-pheasant's life.

At first Holmes was truly bewildered, but upon further careful consideration, he thought that a secret meaning lay buried in the

---

[141]Edgar Allan Poe in his short story, 'The Gold Buy', used a cipher, presumably by Captain Kidd, to denote where he had hidden his treasure. William Legrand, when asked if he had solved it said:

> Readily; I have solved others of an abstruseness ten thousand times greater. Circumstances, and a certain basis of mind, have led me to take interest in such riddles, and it may well be doubted whether human ingenuity can construct an enigma of the kind which human ingenuity may not, by proper application, resolve. In fact having once established connected and legible characters, I scarcely gave a thought to the mere difficulty of developing their impact.

It could have been Sherlock Holmes speaking.

strange combination of the words. Holmes tried it backward, and used alternate words, but without success; then he hit upon using every third word, which gave a short, terse warning message: 'The game is up. Hudson has told all. Fly for your life.' This message had been the death knell for Trevor senior.

Miss Mary Morstan (later to become Mrs John Watson) visited Baker Street. She showed Holmes six very large and lustrous pearls, (originally belonging to a chaplet,) of a rare variety and of considerable value, from an unknown donor and a letter, unsigned, asking her to be outside the Lyceum Theatre to meet an unknown friend. Miss Morstan was worried over these mysteries. Holmes examined the envelope and letter and the pearl box address. 'They are disguised hands, except the letter... but there can be no question as to the authorship. See how the irrepressible Greek *e* will break out and see the twirl of the final *s*. They are undoubtedly by the same person.'

When Miss Morstan had departed, Holmes asked Watson to look at the writing of the letter and to see if he could define the character of the sender from the scribbled handwriting. Watson thought that the writing, being legible and regular, indicated: 'A man of business habits and some form of character.' Holmes was disappointed with this diagnosis. 'Look at his long letters. They hardly rise above the common herd. That "d" might be an "a", and that "l" an "e". Men of character always differentiate their long letters, however illegibly they may write. There is vacillation in his "k's" and self-esteem in his capitals.'

Holmes observed to Jabez Wilson, the pawnbroker of Coburg Square, that he had done a considerable amount of writing recently. 'What else can be indicated by that right cuff, so very shiny for five inches, and the left one with the smooth patch near the elbow where you rest it upon the desk?' Which was perfectly true, for Mr Wilson had copied out everything beginning with the letter A from the *Encyclopaedia Britannica* for his employer, Mr Duncan Ross, of the Red-Headed League, thereby earning thirty-two pounds, minus the cost of finding his own ink, pens, foolscap and blotting papers.

When Holmes and Watson visited Mrs St Clair at The Cedars, they were shown a letter from her husband, Neville. The coarse envelope was stamped with the Gravesend postmark and written in coarse writing which Holmes thought was certainly not that of St Clair, and that whoever addressed the envelope had to first ascertain the address. To Mrs St Clair's query, Holmes replied: 'The name, you see, is in perfectly black ink, which has dried itself. The rest is of the greyish colour, which shows that blotting paper had been used. If it had been written straight off, and then blotted, none would be of a deep black shade. This man has written the name and there has then been a pause before he wrote the address, which can only mean that he was not familiar with it. It is, of course, a trifle, but there is nothing so important as trifles.' The writing on the note inside, Mrs St Clair knew to be her husband's, his hand when he wrote hurriedly, as also was the signet ring:

> Dearest do not be frightened. All will come well. There is a huge error which it may take some little time to rectify. Wait in patience.
> Neville

Holmes observed that the note was 'Written in pencil upon the fly-leaf of a book, octavo size, no water-mark. Hum! Posted to-day in Gravesend by a man with a dirty thumb. Ha! And the flap has been gummed, if I am not very much in error, by a person who had been chewing tobacco.' Mrs St Clair was adamant that the writing was her husband's. Watson could not see that all this information was relevant to solving the mystery; it took Holmes, after Watson went to sleep, until 4.25 a.m. to reach a conclusion. (Rather strange that Holmes never informed his kind hostess of his early start for Bow Street!)

Holmes stayed at Reigate, in Surrey, in 1887, as a guest of Colonel Hayter. He explained why he thought that the letter written to the murdered coachman, William Kirwan, had been written by two people, the Cunninghams, father and son. There was not the least doubt that it had been written by two people writing alternate words. 'When I draw your attention to the strong "t's" of "at" and "to", and ask you to compare them with the weak ones of "quarter" and "twelve" you will instantly recognise the fact. A very brief analysis of these four words would enable you to say with the utmost confidence that the "learn" and the "maybe" are written in the stronger hand, and the "what" in the weaker.' To the question why two men should write the letter together, Holmes replied: 'Obviously the business was a bad one, and one of the men who distrusted the other was determined that, whatever was done, each should have an equal hand in it. Now, of the two men, it is clear that the one who wrote the "at" and "to" was the ringleader.' This Holmes deduced 'from the mere character of the one hand as compared with the other. But we have more assured reasons than that for supposing it. If you examine this scrap with attention you will come to the conclusion that the man with the stronger hand wrote all his words first, leaving blanks for the other to fill up. These blanks were not always sufficient, and you can see that the second man had a squeeze to fit his "quarter" in between the "at" and the "to", showing that the latter were already written. The man who wrote all his words first is undoubtedly the man who planned the affair.'

Holmes presented further proof: 'You may not be aware that the deduction of a man's age from his writing is one which has been brought to considerable accuracy by experts. In normal cases one can place a man in his true decade with tolerable confidence. I say normal cases, because ill-health and physical weakness reproduce the signs of old age, even when the invalid is a youth. In this case looking at the bold, strong hand of the one, and the rather broken-backed appearance of the other, which still retains its legibility although the "t's" have begun to lose their crossing, we can say that the one was a young man and the other was advanced in years without being positively decrepit.'

Holmes further pointed out the common factor in the hand-writing, showing that they were blood relations. There were twenty-three other deductions (only understood by the expert), which pointed to the Cunninghams, father and son, having written the letter. 'I am sure that you cannot fail to be delighted with the traces of heredity shown in the "p's" and in the tail of the "g's". The absence of the "i"-dots in the old man's writing is also most characteristic.'

Inspector Lestrade, while at Lauriston Gardens, Brixton, dis-covered the word 'Rache' written in blood-red letters, and thought that a woman called Rachel had something to do with the crime. Holmes laughed. 'You may be very smart and clever,' said Lestrade, 'but the old hound is the best, when all is said and done.' Holmes apologised. He knew that it was the German word for 'revenge', and had been a blind to suggest to the police, American Socialism, (for they had branches in the USA), and secret societies. 'It was not done by a German. The A, if you noticed, was printed somewhat after the German fashion. Now, a real German invariably prints in the Latin character, so that we may safely say that this was not written by one, but by a clumsy imitator who overdid his part.' So he told the inspector not to lose his time looking for Miss Rachel.

There was the case where John Hector McFarlane, solicitor, expected to be arrested for the murder of Jonas Oldacre, the builder, of Deep Dene House, Lower Norwood. Holmes examined the rough draft of Oldacre's will and told Lestrade that it was written on a train, which suggested that the writer did not expect that it would be of any practical importance. Said Holmes: 'The good writing represents stations, the bad writing movement, and the very bad writing passing over points. A scientific expert would pronounce at once that this was drawn up on a suburban line, since nowhere save in the immediate vicinity of a great city could there be so quick a succession of points. Granting that his whole journey was occupied in drawing up the will, then the train was an express, only stopping once between Norwood and London Bridge.' This corroborated McFarlane's story to the extent that the will had been drawn up by Oldacre on his journey.

Upon the few occasions that Holmes wrote a letter, it was in a most precise hand; when he wished anonymity, as he did when he sent a note, in dancing men code to Abe Slaney, he addressed the outside of the note, in straggling, irregular characters, very much unlike his usual hand.

Holmes was most conversant with the styles and shapes of pen nibs, quill pens and pencils, which knowledge he no doubt intended for a monograph.

While he was investigating the murder of Mr Douglas of Birlstone Manor House, he observed to Inspector MacDonald – commenting upon a queer card presumably left behind by the murderer whereon was written, 'V V 341', that it was not printed in that room (for when Holmes asked Ames the butler if there was any of this rough cardboard in the house, he replied that he did not think so). Holmes dabbed a little ink from each bottle on the desk upon blotting paper. 'This is black ink and the other purplish. It was done by a thick pen, and these are fine. No, it was done elsewhere…'

During the case which Watson recorded as *The Adventure of the Red Circle*, Mrs Warren, a landlady with a yellow-brick house in Great Orme Street, near the British Museum, came to see Holmes being frightened by the behaviour of her lodger; for he was never to be disturbed in his rooms at the top of the house; his meals were to be left and collected upon a chair outside his door. Anything else he needed he printed upon a slip of paper and left it on the chair. This intrigued Holmes. 'Yes, sir; prints it in pencil. Just the word, nothing more.' She showed Holmes some examples – SOAP and MATCH, the latest being, DAILY GAZETTE printed on slips of foolscap. 'This is certainly a little unusual,' said Holmes. 'Seclusion I can understand; but why print? Printing is a clumsy process. Why not write?' Watson suggested that he desired to conceal his handwriting. 'It opens a pleasing field for intelligent speculation. The words are written with a broad-pointed, violet-tinted pencil of a not unusual pattern. You will observe that the paper is torn away at the side here after the printing was done, so that the "s" of SOAP is partly gone.' Holmes thought that there had been a switch of lodgers, for the original man who took the rooms spoke good English with a foreign accent, and the word 'match' should have been 'matches', so perhaps a wish to conceal a knowledge of English. Holmes had originally said to Mrs Warren that she had no particular cause for uneasiness, but the evident change of lodger alerted Holmes' interest.

Holmes became most interested in the pencil chips and the remainder of a pencil which were found in the room of Mr Hilton Soames, tutor and lecturer at the College of Saint Luke's in one of the great university towns. Soames was the examiner of a large passage of Greek translation, part of the Fortescue Scholarship; he had left the proofs upon his table unattended, and during his absence someone had been able to study them, thus

322

gaining an unscrupulous advantage over his fellow contestants. Holmes observed: 'Well, he wrote so furiously that he broke his pencil, and had, as you observe, to sharpen it again. This is of interest, Watson. The pencil was not an ordinary one. It was above the usual size, with a soft lead, the outer colour was dark blue, the maker's name was printed in silver lettering, and the piece remaining is only about an inch and a half long.' Looking at one of the chips with the letters NN upon it, Holmes diagnosed that the maker's name was possibly that of Johann Faber, a common maker's name. When Holmes visited the four stationers in the town, he was told that it was not a usual size of pencil, was seldom kept in stock, but could be ordered. 'Look for such a pencil, Mr Soames, and you have got your man. When I add that he possesses a large and very blunt knife, you have an additional aid.'

When Holmes looked at the blotting paper copy of the telegram which Godfrey Staunton sent while he was staying at Bentley's private hotel in London, he observed, 'It is a pity he did not write in pencil… As you have no doubt frequently observed, Watson, the impression usually goes through – a fact which has dissolved many a happy marriage. However, I can find no trace here. I rejoice, however, to perceive that he wrote with a broad-pointed quill pen, and I can hardly doubt that we will find some impression upon this blotting-pad.' Holmes tore off a strip of the blotting paper, and the paper being thin, he reversed the writing and read the tail end of the message: 'Stand by us for God's sake', proving that the sender saw danger approaching him.

Holmes made a further observation upon pens, when he examined the note sent to Sir Henry Baskerville, at the Northumberland Hotel, London, and thought that the envelope address had been written in a hotel. He explained his methods to Dr Mortimer:

'If you examine it carefully you will see that both the pen and the ink have given the writer trouble. The pen has spluttered twice in a single word and has run dry three times in a short address, showing that there was very little ink in the bottle. Now, a private pen or ink-bottle is seldom allowed to be in such a state, and the combination of the two must be quite rare. But you know the hotel ink and the hotel pen, where it is rare to get anything else. Yes, I have very little hesitation in saying that could we examine the waste-paper baskets of the hotels around Charing Cross until we found the remains of the mutilated *Times* leader we could lay our hands straight upon the person who sent this singular message.'

Holmes explained to Inspector Lestrade, while they were at the house of Miss Susan Cushing, of Cross Street, Croydon, during his examination of the wrapper of the cardboard box: 'Address printed in rather straggling characters: "Miss S Cushing, Cross Street, Croydon." Done with a broad-pointed pen, probably a J, and with very inferior ink. The word "Croydon" has been spelt originally with an "i" which has been changed to "y". The parcel was directed, then, by a man – the printing is distinctly masculine – of limited education and unacquainted with the town of Croydon. So far, so good!'

Holmes wrote a little monograph upon old manuscripts. It was this particular study which enabled him to date to within twelve years a manuscript dated 1742, which Dr James Mortimer carried sticking out of his pocket when he visited Holmes at Baker Street. Although only an inch or so was showing, Holmes was able to say immediately that it was: 'Early eighteenth century, unless it is a forgery… It would be a poor expert who could not give the date of a document within a decade or so… You will observe, Watson, the alternative use of the long "s" and the short. It is one of several indications which enabled me to fix the date.' The manuscript recounted the Baskerville legend of how Hugo Baskerville had had his throat torn out by a foul, great, black beast, shaped like, yet larger, than a hound.

Holmes made a small study of tattoo marks and made a contribution to the literature upon the subject. He was able to inform Jabez Wilson, pawnbroker of Coburg Square, that he had been in China, having observed the fish tattooed above his right wrist, whose scales were of a delicate pink, and quite peculiar to that country. 'When, in addition,' said Holmes, 'I see a Chinese coin hanging from your watch-chain, the matter becomes even more simple.'

When Holmes was invited to stay at the little hamlet of

Donnithorpe, the home of Mr Trevor senior, in Norfolk, he was asked to see what he could deduce from his host. Holmes told him that he had been intimately associated with someone whose initials were J A and whom he was afterwards eager to forget; this observation caused his host to have a short fainting fit, and then he said: 'Might I ask how you know, and how much you know?' Holmes said that it was a simple matter. 'When you bared your arm to draw that fish into the boat I saw that J A had been tattooed in the bend of the elbow. Those letters were still legible, but it was perfectly clear from their blurred appearance, and from the staining of the skin round them, that efforts had been made to obliterate them. It was obvious, then, that those initials had once been very familiar to you, and that you had afterwards wished to forget them.' Holmes from his Baker Street flat window noticed a large blue anchor on the back of the hand of a retired sergeant of the marines.

Did Holmes write a monograph upon perfumes? There certainly should have been one. As Holmes recounted to Watson: 'There are seventy-five perfumes, which it is very necessary that a criminal expert should be able to distinguish from each other, and cases have more than once within my own experience depended upon their prompt recognition.' When Holmes made a close inspection of the letter to Sir Charles Baskerville (sent by Mrs Laura Lyons) he looked for a watermark and, holding it close to his eyes, detected a faint smell of white jessamine scent. This suggested the presence of a lady. It subsequently transpires that Mrs Lyons had written to Sir Charles at Stapleton's dictation, as as to lure him from the house (and ths be at the hound's mercy), and she was then persuaded not to keep the appointment, so giving the murderer a clear field.

Even as late as 1903, Holmes seriously thought of writing a monograph upon the uses of dogs in the work of the detective. Not bloodhounds because this line of thought was obvious. No, far more devious observations. He highlighted this train of thought in *The Adventure of the Copper Beeches*. There he was able, by watching the mind of a child, to form a deduction as to the criminal habits of the very smug and respectable father, Jephro Rucastle. 'My line of thought about dogs,' he said to his friend, 'is analogous. A dog reflects the family life. Whoever saw a frisky dog in a gloomy family, or a sad dog in a happy one? Snarling people have snarling dogs dangerous people have dangerous dogs. And their passing moods may reflect the passing moods of others. The practical application of what I have said is very close to the problem which I am investigating. It is a tangled skein, you understand, and I am looking for a loose end. One possible loose end lies in the question; why does Professor Presbury's wolf-hound, Roy, endeavour to bite him?' For the devoted dog had twice attacked the professor, but no one else. As Holmes discovered later on, it was not the professor the dog attacked and tore his throat, but the pseudo great black-faced monkey of the Himalayas, the form of which the sixty-one-year-old professor had assumed after taking the monkey serum, which he had hoped would give rejuvenescence, and the elixir of life. Thus he had hoped to attain the love of Alice Morphy.

In 1895, Holmes being in one of the university towns, made some laborious researches into the early English charters which led to some most striking results. But Watson records no monograph.

It was in 1897 while Holmes, was having a complete rest from detective work with Watson down in Cornwall, that he became interested in the ancient Cornish language; he thought that it might have been akin to the Chaldean and derived largely from the Phoenician traders in tin. A number of books upon philology were sent down to him (no doubt by his brother Mycroft), and he became deeply immersed in his subject. The result of his studies was never completed, being interrupted at the time by what he called 'The Cornish Horror', to be published by Watson in 1910 and called, 'The Adventure of the Devil's Foot'; otherwise there would surely have been a monograph.

Among his other writings were a magazine article, called the 'Book of Life' which discussed the science of deduction and analysis; *Sigerson's Norwegian and Tibetan Explorations*; an account of a visit to the Khalifa of Khartoum; researches into coal-tar derivatives; *The Practical Handbook of Bee Culture*; *The Adventure of the Blanched Soldier*, and *The Adventure of the Lion's Mane*.

Visitors to Baker Street

There must have been so very many visitors to Baker Street over the years that Dr Watson worked with Holmes, and yet not all visits were reported, for as Watson recorded: 'I should be guilty of an indiscretion if I were even to hint at the identity of some of the illustrious clients who crossed our humble threshold in Baker Street.' He referred to these visits as some 'dramatic entrances and exits upon our small stage at Baker Street'.

Some of the clients initially sent telegrams, or wrote a letter, and these varied from the nobleman with crest and monogram upon his notepaper, to the humbler sort, a fishmonger or a tidewaiter. The humbler were usually the more interesting to Holmes who thought that 'the simple case was usually the most difficult. The more featureless and commonplace a crime is, the more difficult it is to bring it home', for 'circumstantial evidence is a very tricky thing'. Holmes, when interrupted in one of his problems by a visitor, would still see them, but with 'a resigned air and a somewhat weary smile'. But he was a past master in the art of putting a humble witness at his ease.

Holmes generally never assisted his clients to speak, for he said that he found it wise to impress his clients with a sense of his power. It was one of the peculiarities of his proud, self-contained nature, although there was no harshness there, that though he documented any fresh information from his client very quickly and accurately in his brain, he seldom made any acknowledgement to the giver; but if his client happened to be deranged, he would then turn on his charm and chat in an easy and soothing tone.

Fortunately, we know the names of some of the clients who came to Baker Street, apart from the American visitors.

Josiah Amberley called twice in 1899, a miserly man with few outward graces; a pathetic, futile, broken-looking man, his curved back bowed down by care, although with the chest and shoulders of a giant, and with the strength of a lion; he had an artificial limb, with the right shoe smooth and the left shoe wrinkled; snaky locks of grizzled hair curled from under a straw hat; his face had a fierce eager expression with deeply lined features.

He had retired in 1896, at the age of sixty-one, having made a fortune with the firm of Brickfall and Amberley, manufacturers of artistic materials. The next year he married a woman of forty-one and lived at The Haven, Lewisham. He excelled at chess, and invited another keen player into his house, one Dr Ray Ernest; he became a frequent visitor and an intimacy between him and Mrs Amberley was a natural sequence, for she was twenty years younger than her husband.

Amberley told Holmes that the couple went off together the previous week, their destination untraced. Added to which, they had taken his deed-box, with a good part of his life's savings within. Could Holmes find the lady? Could he find the money? Both things were vital for Josiah Amberley. He had only come to Holmes because Scotland Yard were unable to help. As Holmes was to find out later, during his investigations, the whole story was false. Amberley had become suspicious of his wife and the doctor, and, being determined upon revenge, had planned his scheme with diabolical cleverness. When Amberley was confronted by Holmes with the murders of his wife and her lover by gas poisoning in the strongroom of his own house, and their concealment in a disused well, cleverly hidden by a dog kennel, he became 'a misshapen demon with a soul as distorted as his body,' as he clawed the air with his bony hands, and with open mouth, looked like a horrible bird of prey. He then tried to commit suicide, but Holmes forestalled him, twisting his face towards the ground as a white pellet fell from his gasping lips; he was then taken to the police station.

A little after half past six in the evening of 27 December, Mr Henry Baker called at the flat, hoping that he would retrieve his goose and his hat, which he had lost on Christmas morning. He came following Holmes advertisement in the evening papers. He was a large, tall, middle-aged man, with a comical pomposity of manner, who perspired freely and wore a Scotch bonnet, which fitted neither his years nor his gravity. His coat was buttoned up to the chin and he had round shoulders with a massive head. His grizzled hair was anointed with lime-cream and he had a broad, intelligent face which sloped down to a pointed brown grizzled beard; there was a touch of red upon his nose and cheeks. He was dressed in a rusty black frock coat with a turned-up collar, his lank wrists protruding from the sleeves, without a sign of shirt or cuff. Although hard up for a shilling, he gave the impression of a man of learning, with his slow staccato speech; his once best quality, round, three-year-old, cracked, exceedingly dusty, black, tallow-stained billycock hat, with a discoloured red silk lining, looked much the worse for wear.[142] The initials H B were scrawled upon one side, but there was no maker's name. (But the small card tied to the bird's left leg said 'For Mr Henry Baker', which gave Holmes his necessary information.) It was pierced in the brim for a hat securer, with the elastic missing, and had several discoloured patches smeared with ink to disguise them. Mr Baker was totally unaware that his goose (which cost wholesale seven and six and retail twelve shillings) had contained the Countess of Morcar's blue carbuncle: 'a brilliantly scintillating blue stone, rather smaller than a bean in size, but of such purity and radiance that it twinkled like an electric point'. About twenty years old, the stone had been found on the banks of the Amoy River in southern China and was unique, as the usual carbuncle was red.

Mr Baker was more than glad to have back his hat and a substitute goose, the original one having been eaten on Christmas Day. Did Peterson, the commissionaire, who discovered the gem, receive the one thousand pounds reward for the gem which had caused two murders, a vitriol throwing, a suicide and several robberies?

Cecil James Barker visited Holmes late at night. A tall, loose-jointed figure of forty-five years, of Hales Lodge, Hampstead, he was reputably a wealthy English bachelor; broad-chested, with a clean-shaven prizefighter face, and thick, strong, black eyebrows overhanging masterful black eyes. He was also a pipe smoker. He had been a friend of John Douglas in America and a frequent and welcome visitor to the ancient moated Birlstone Manor House, in Sussex, where the butler, Ames, had called him, 'An easygoing free-handed gentleman'. Barker told Holmes that John and Ivy Douglas had taken his advice and left England, travelling on the

---

[142]A hard felt hat, originally from the nineteenth century, made by a Cornish hatter, William Cock.

Palmyra to Cape Town, but had been swept overboard in a gale off St Helena. Holmes knew it was murder, not an accident. 'There is a master hand here. It is no case of sawed-off shotguns and clumsy six-shooters. You can tell an old master by the sweep of his brush. I can tell a Moriarty when I see one. This crime is from London, not from America.'

Sir Henry Baskerville, nephew of the late Sir Charles Baskerville, and now heir to the family estate in Devon, called at Baker Street with Dr Mortimer at ten in the morning.

Sir Henry was a 'small, alert, dark-eyed, man about thirty years of age, very sturdily built', who showed pride, valour, and strength in a pugnacious, strong dark and expressive face; he had large hazel eyes and sensitive nostrils. He had, according to Dr Mortimer, 'the rounded head of the Celt, which carries inside it the Celtic enthusiasm and power of attachment.' He wore a ruddy-tinted tweed suit and had the weather-beaten appearance of one who has spent most of his time in the open air, and yet there was something in his steady eye and the quiet assurance of his bearing which indicated the gentleman. Truly a comrade to share any risk.

He had previously farmed in Canada, and had purchased his black boots from Meyers of Toronto; he had acquired an American accent, and when he became furious, so as to be hardly articulate, he spoke in a much broader and more Western dialect.

The story of the fearsome hound upon Dartmoor did not frighten Sir Henry – he made his position clear: 'There is no devil in hell, Mr Holmes and there is no man upon earth who can prevent me from going to the house of my own people, and you may take that to be my final answer.'[143]

Sir Henry was in his teens at the time of his father's death and had never seen Baskerville Hall, having lived in a little cottage on the south coast, and thence been taken to a friend in America. He

---

[143]On Thursday, 28 December 1989, ITV showed on television *The Hound of the Baskervilles*, directed by Douglas Hickox, with Ian Richardson as Holmes, Donald Churchill as Watson and Martin Shaw as Sir Henry Baskerville. Sir Henry was allowed to say, erroneously, that he had no intention of going to the Devon moor, for he was back to America just as soon as his attorney had settled the estate affairs. Many other liberties were taken with the story. Why oh why?

showed Holmes a note he had received on half a sheet of foolscap paper, folded into four. Across the middle of it a single sentence had been formed by the expedient of pasting printed newspaper words upon it, except for the word 'moor', which was printed in ink: 'As you value your life or your reason keep away from the moor.' This heightened Holmes' interest in Sir Henry, and decided that he must visit Devon and scotch this legend of the family hound.

When all was over and sorted out at Baskerville Hall, Sir Henry and Dr Mortimer called for the last time, on a raw November afternoon, to see Holmes and Watson again, before beginning their long voyage together, which had been recommended for the restoration of Sir Henry's nerves.

Marlow Bates was a thin, nervous wisp of a man with frightened eyes and a twitching, hesitant manner. Watson thought that he was upon the verge of a nervous breakdown. He was employed as a manager by the American millionaire, J Neil Gibson, of Thor Place, in Hampshire, whose Brazilian wife had been killed at Thor Bridge. Bates, knowing through Mr Ferguson, Gibson's secretary, that his employer was coming to Baker Street, thought that he should warn Holmes that he was plausible and cunning, an infernal villain. 'I have to be emphatic, Mr Holmes, for the time is so limited. I would not have him find me here for the world... I have given him notice. In a couple of weeks I shall have shaken off his accursed slavery. A hard man, Mr Holmes, hard to all about him. Those public charities are a screen to cover his private iniquities. But his wife was his chief victim. He was brutal to her – yes, sir, brutal! How she came by her death I do not know, but I am sure that he had made her life a misery to her... Don't take him at his face value. There is more behind.' With a frightened look at the clock, Bates literally ran to the door and disappeared.

Inspector Baynes of the Surrey Constabulary called, in the company of Inspector Gregson of Scotland Yard, towards the end of March 1892; a gross, stout, puffy, red-faced man, with small, extraordinary bright eyes, almost hidden behind the heavy creases of his cheek and brow. Both inspectors were on the trail of John Scott Eccles, suspected of the murder of Aloysius Garcia of

Wisteria Lodge, for in the dead man's pocket was a letter from Scott Eccles, accepting an invitation to stay there for a few days. Baynes told Holmes how he had found the note to Garcia, overpitched into the back of the dog grate and unburnt. Holmes complimented Baynes upon his attention to detail in his examination of it, and exclaimed that he must have examined the house very carefully to find a single pellet of paper. 'I did, Mr Holmes. It's my way.' Scott Eccles was taken to the police station for questioning. Later Holmes and Watson went down to Esher to investigate; there Baynes gave Holmes more information concerning the finds in the kitchen – a white cock, torn savagely to pieces, a quantity of blood in a zinc pail and charred non-human bones. 'I must congratulate you, Inspector, on handling so distinctive and instructive a case. Your powers, if I may say so without offence, seem superior to your opportunities', which made the inspector's eyes twinkle with pleasure.

Lord Bellinger had been twice prime minister of England; he had an austere, gaunt, ascetic face, 'high-nosed, eagle-eyed, and dominant'. His thin blue veined hands gripped an ivory-headed umbrella. With him came the Right Honourable Trelawney Hope, the Secretary for European Affairs. He was of a dark complexion, clear-cut, elegant, and still to reach middle age. He was nervous, pulling at his moustache and the seals of his watch-chain, as they both arrived one Tuesday morning in autumn. They sat side by side upon the paper-littered settee, their worn and anxious faces indicating business of the most pressing importance.

At eight o'clock in the morning, Trelawney Hope discovered the loss of a document of such immense importance that its publication would probably lead to European complications of the utmost moment – peace or war might well hang upon the issue. It was vitally necessary that utmost secrecy attended the document's recovery. The letter from a foreign potentate was received six days ago, and the secretary had kept it in its long, thin, pale blue envelope, stamped upon a seal of red wax with a crouching lion, in a locked despatch box in his bedroom in Whitehall Terrace. Last night it was there, but this morning it was gone. He and his wife were adamant that no one could have entered the room during the night; his wife had no knowledge of the document before its loss was known, the secretary informed Holmes. The thief would be likely to take the letter to one of the known international spies, Holmes informed the PM, who concurred with him. Holmes said that he would check upon three of the foremost names, and if one was missing this might well give him a lead. With this the two visitors left.

A little later, Holmes had another visitor, Lady Hilda Trelawney Hope, wife of the Secretary for European Affairs, and daughter of the Duke of Belminster, known as the most lovely woman in London. As Watson recorded:

> I had often heard of the beauty of the youngest daughter of the Duke of Belminster, but no description of it, and no contemplation of colourless photographs, had prepared me for the subtle, delicate charm and the beautiful colouring of that exquisite head. And yet as we saw it that autumn morning, it was not its beauty which would be the first thing to impress the observer. The cheek was lovely but it was paled with emotion, the eyes were bright, but it was the brightness of fever, the sensitive mouth was tight and drawn in an effort after self-command. Terror – not beauty – was what sprang first to the eye as our fair visitor stood framed for an instant in the open door.

She wondered if her husband had called and what was the nature of the stolen paper, but Holmes maintained secrecy. Was her husband's career likely to be affected? 'Well, madam,' answered Holmes, 'unless it is set right, it may certainly have a very unfortunate effect.' Lady Hope, unable to open the clam-like Holmes, took her departure, looking back at Holmes and Watson from the doorway with her beautiful haunted face, startled eyes and drawn mouth. Then she was gone.

Trevor Bennett, thirty years old, tall, handsome, elegant and well dressed, was assistant to Professor Presbury, the sixty-one-year- old physiologist. He was very worried over the behaviour of the professor and his dog at Camford. The professor, despite his age, was engaged to the daughter of Professor Morphy; after his visit to Prague he became a changed man, becoming furtive, sly and rather sinister; at times irascible and violent.

Bennett was followed to Baker Street by his fiancée, Edith Presbury, a 'bright, handsome girl of a conventional English type'. She said her father lived as in a strange dream, 'his outward shell was there, but it was not really he. But, oh, Mr Holmes, can you do nothing for my poor father?' Holmes told the couple that he would go down to Camford the next day.

The King of Bohemia, Wilhelm Gottsreich Sigismond von Ormstein, Grand Duke of Cassel-Felstein, from Prague, thirty years old, called at 7.45 p.m. on 20 March 1888. He was about to be married to Clotilde Lothman von Saxe-Meningen, second daughter of the King of Scandinavia; he was six inches taller than Holmes and a veritable Hercules with broad shoulders; his forehead was white and high, his dress so rich that it was almost in bad taste. His double-breasted coat was slashed with astrakhan and his deep blue cloak, lined with flame-coloured silk, was secured at the neck with a brooch of a single beryl; his half-boots were trimmed at the top with rich brown fur and he carried a broad-brimmed hat. He was a man of strong character, with a thick hanging lip and a long straight chin; he wore a black vizard mask across the upper part of his face, extending down past the cheekbones. He spoke with a deep harsh voice and strangely marked German accent. He called himself Count Von Kramm, a Bohemian nobleman, which title, he confessed, was not his own; he queried Watson's presence, the matter being of extreme importance, so the doctor rose to go, but Holmes held him back by the wrist. 'It is both, or none. You may say before this gentleman anything which you may say to me.'

The count bound them both to secrecy for two years – both Holmes and Watson agreed. The count continued to emphasise his incognito – to excuse his mask – for the matter implicated the great House of Ormstein, hereditary kings of Bohemia. Holmes murmured that he was aware of these things, as he settled himself down in his armchair and closed his eyes, which rather surprised the visitor. Holmes was just a little nettled at all this pretence: 'If your Majesty would condescend to state your case, I should be better able to advise you.' This surprised the king. 'Some five years ago,' said the king, 'during a lengthy visit to Warsaw, I made the acquaintance of the well known adventuress, Irene Adler.' He wrote some compromising letters and allowed the two of them to be photographed together; this photograph Miss Adler threatened to send to the King of Scandinavia which would have put paid to the marriage with his daughter. It was expedient that Holmes recover the letters and photographs within the next three days, in which matter Holmes failed dismally, being outmanoeuvred by the lady herself.

Holmes did say to Von Bork in 1914 that 'It was I who brought about the separation between Irene Adler and the late King of Bohemia, when your cousin Heinrich was the Imperial Envoy.' Holmes had apparently forgotten by then that there was no case of 'separation', as the two of them were friends only, and Irene wished to and did marry Godfrey Norton of whom she had said, 'I love and am loved by a better man than he'; and she retained the cabinet-sized photo of herself and the king, Holmes failing dismally to retrieve it.

Lord Cantlemere looked in to see how Holmes' self-appointed task was going – what progress he was making towards the recovery of the Mazarin stone, the Crown yellow diamond. He was 'a thin, austere figure with a hatchet face and drooping mid-Victorian whiskers of a glossy blackness which hardly corresponded with the rounded shoulders and feeble gait'. Billy the page had already expressed his personal feelings to Watson about Cantlemere. 'He's a stiff 'un, sir, if I may say so. I can get along with the Prime Minister, and I've nothing against the Home Secretary, who seemed a civil, obliging sort of man, but I can't stand his Lordship. Neither can Mr Holmes, sir. You see, he don't believe in Mr Holmes and he was against employing him. He'd *rather* he failed.' Which was perhaps a good enough reason for Holmes to have a joke at his Lordship's expense, the eminent peer who represented the very highest interests. 'He is an excellent and loyal person,' said Holmes to Watson, 'but rather of the old régime. Shall we make him unbend? Dare we venture upon a slight liberty?' For his Lordship knew not that the stone was recovered.

Cantlemere sneered as he said that he feared Holmes' task would be a difficult one. 'Every man finds his limitations, Mr Holmes, but at least it cures us of the weakness of self-satisfaction.' Holmes knew that he must really cut this old courtier down to size, 'Now, what would you regard as final evidence against the receiver?' 'The actual possession of the stone,' he replied. 'You would arrest him upon that?' 'Most undoubtedly.' 'In that case, my dear sir, I shall be under the painful necessity of advising your arrest.' (For Holmes had put the diamond into Lord Cantlemere's pocket at the beginning of the interview.) Cantlemere was not amused, indeed he was very angry at what appeared to be a foolish joke, and said he had never believed in Holmes' detective powers. Holmes prevented him from making a hasty exit. 'To actually go off with the Mazarin stone would be a more serious offence than to be found in temporary possession of it.' Holmes still blocked the door. He said, 'Put your hand in the right-hand pocket of your overcoat', which irritated his visitor. 'Come – come, do what I ask.' An instant later the yellow stone appeared upon his shaking palm. Holmes smiled at the peer's shattered hauteur. 'Sir, I am bewildered. But – yes – it is indeed the Mazarin stone. We are greatly your debtors, Mr Holmes. Your sense of humour may, as you admit, be somewhat perverted, and its exhibition remarkably untimely, but at least I withdraw any reflection I have made upon your amazing professional powers.' Holmes, surely, must have allowed himself a little inward laugh!

Holmes was anxious to arrest Patrick Cairns for the murder of Peter Carey, who retired as captain of the steam sealer, *Sea Unicorn* in 1884; he retired to Woodman's Lee, near Forest Row, in Sussex. There he built himself a wooden outhouse, a ship's cabin to him, some sixteen feet by ten; there, six years later, he met his death with a steel harpoon driven so hard through his broad breast, that it sank deep into the wood of the wall behind him. 'He was pinned like a beetle on a card' – so said Inspector Stanley Hopkins.

Holmes asked Watson to send two telegraphs, the first to 'Sumner, Shipping Agent, Ratcliff Highway. Send three men on, to arrive ten to-morrow morning. Basil.' (Captain Basil was Holmes latest alias.) The second was to 'Inspector Stanley Hopkins, 46 Lord Street, Brixton. Come breakfast to-morrow at nine thirty. Important. Wire if unable to come. Sherlock Holmes.' The case had haunted Holmes for ten days and now he felt it drawing to a close. Breakfast over, the three men waited. At last Mrs Hudson opened the door to say that three men desired to see him – she let them in, one at a time. The first was James Lancaster,[144] a 'little Ribston pippin of a man, with ruddy cheeks and fluffy white side-whiskers'; Holmes knew this was not his man and he was given half a sovereign and told to wait in the bedroom. The second man, Hugh Pattins, a 'long, dried-up creature, with lank hair and sallow cheeks', received similar treatment.

The third man, Patrick Cairns, was a man of remarkable appearance. 'A fierce bull-dog face was framed in a tangle of hair and beard, and two bold, dark eyes gleamed behind the cover of thick, tufted, overhung eyebrows. He saluted and stood sailor fashion, turning his cap round in his hands.' He told Holmes that he had been a harpooner for twenty-six voyages, out from Dundee. Holmes knew that he now had his man, as Cairns stooped over the table to sign the papers. As Watson wrote:

> I heard a click of steel and a bellow like an enraged bull. The next instant Holmes and the seaman were rolling on the ground together. He was a man of such gigantic strength that, even with the handcuffs which Holmes had so deftly fastened upon his wrists, he would have very quickly overpowered my friend had Hopkins and I not rushed to his rescue. Only when I pressed the cold muzzle of the revolver to his temple did he at last understand that resistance was in vain. We lashed his ankles with cord, and rose breathless from the struggle.

A surprised Hopkins took his prisoner away in the waiting cab.

John Clayton called in answer to Holmes' telegram to the Official Registry, thinking that Holmes had something against him. He was a rough-looking fellow, cabman No. 2704 for seven years, who lived at 3 Turpey Street, the Borough, his cab out of Shipley's Yard near Waterloo Station. 'I have nothing in the world against you, my good man. On the contrary, I have half a sovereign for you if you will give me a clear answer to my questions… Now, Clayton, tell me all about the fare who came

---

[144]Perhaps suggested by Sir James Lancaster, who took part in the Armada, 1588. *Dictionary National Biography*, 1903.

and watched this house at ten o'clock this morning and afterwards followed the two gentlemen down Regent Street.' 'He hailed me at half past nine in Trafalgar Square. He said that he was a detective, and he offered two guineas if I would do exactly what he wanted all day and ask no questions,' replied Clayton. When they had driven down Regent Street some way, the 'fare' cried out that he should be taken to Waterloo Station quickly, which Clayton managed in ten minutes. He was then told that he had been driving Mr Sherlock Holmes. After the cabby had departed, Holmes observed, 'I tell you, Watson, this time we have got a foeman who is worthy of our steel. I've been checkmated in London. I can only wish you better luck in Devonshire… It's an ugly business, Watson, an ugly, dangerous business.'

It was in the early days at Baker Street that a commissionaire called. Watson had spotted him walking slowly down the other side of the street, looking anxiously at the numbers, and when he spotted 221B, he ran rapidly across the road, knocked and entered. Then a deep voice was heard below, followed by heavy steps ascending the stairs. He proved to be an ex-sergeant in the Royal Marine Light Infantry, dressed in 'civvies' as his uniform was away for repairs. Thus Holmes' diagnosis was verified and Watson's respect for Holmes' powers of analysis increased wondrously. He handed Holmes a large blue envelope, which contained a letter from Tobias Gregson, regarding the death of Enoch J Drebber of Cleveland, Ohio.

Captain Crocker called towards the end of the winter of 1897. He was 'a very tall young man, golden-moustached, blue-eyed, with a skin that had been burned by tropical suns, and a springy step, which showed that the huge frame was as active as it was strong.' Jack Crocker was in charge of a new ship, the *Bass Rock* due to sail from Southampton in two days' time; his home was in Sydenham. He was said to be reliable on duty, but a wild, desperate fellow off the deck of his ship – hot-headed, excitable, but loyal, honest and kind-hearted.

Crocker had been involved in a fight with Sir Eustace Brackenstall at the Abbey Grange, Marsham in Kent – a poker against a blackthorn cudgel – and he had killed him, for Brackenstall was a brute who had hurt his wife, and her marriage of a year had not been a happy one. Formerly she was Mary Fraser, whom Crocker had loved. Holmes felt that Crocker was sincere in all his actions, as, having suggested that Crocker should disappear and no one would hinder him, Crocker said, 'What sort of proposal is that to make to a man? I know enough of law to understand that Mary would be held as accomplice. Do you think I would leave her alone to face the music while I slunk away? No, sir, let them do their worst upon me, but for heaven's sake, Mr Holmes, find some way of keeping my poor Mary out of the courts.'

Holmes knew that he must protect him from a police warrant, for if that happened, nothing would save him; after all, Holmes was not the law. When Holmes asked Watson his opinion as a 'British jury', he said to Holmes as the 'judge', 'Not guilty, my lord.' Added Holmes, 'You are acquitted, Captain Crocker. So long as the law does not find some other victim you are safe from me. Come back to this lady in a year, and may her future and yours justify us in the judgment which we have pronounced this night!'

Hilton Cubitt of Riding Thorpe, Norfolk, called, a 'tall, ruddy, clean-shaven gentleman', with clear eyes and florid cheeks; a man of the open-air life. He had married an American girl, Elsie Patrick, who had become frightened to death by the conundrum of what appeared to look like drawings of childish little 'match-stick' figures, drawn in pencil on a page torn from a notebook. Mr Cubitt had sent the drawings on ahead of his visit so that Holmes could study them. 'Well, Mr Holmes, what do you make of these?. They told me that you were fond of queer mysteries, and I don't think you can find a queerer one than that.' 'It is certainly rather a curious production. At first sight it would appear to be some childish prank. It consists of a number of absurd little figures dancing across the paper upon which they are drawn. Why should you attribute any importance to so grotesque an object?'

Mr Cubitt was not affected, but he had seen the terror in his wife's eyes, and that was why he wanted to sift the matter to the bottom. He could not make a direct appeal to his wife and ask to share her secret, for he had promised her never to allude to her past. If Elsie wished to tell him she would, he would not force her confidence. But that didn't prevent him from making his own investigations. Said Holmes, 'Then I will help you with all my heart.'

Two weeks or so later, following upon his telegram to Holmes, Cubitt called again, having come from Liverpool Street as fast as a hansom could bring him, a worried and depressed man, with tired eyes and a lined forehead. 'It's getting on my nerves, this business, Mr Holmes. It's bad enough to feel that you are surrounded by unseen, unknown folk, who have some kind of design upon you, but when, in addition to that, you know that it is just killing your wife by inches, then it becomes as much as flesh and blood can endure. She's wearing away under it – just wearing away before my eyes.'

He told Holmes that fresh chalk drawings of the 'men' had appeared upon the black wooden door of the tool house. After making a copy of the drawings he rubbed them out; two mornings later a fresh inscription appeared which he copied. Three days later another message was left, scrawled upon paper and placed under a pebble upon the sundial. It was time, Cubitt thought, to sit up, with his pistol, and see if the intruder came again, and he was fortunate enough to see a dark, creeping figure which crawled round the corner of the tool house, and squatted in front of the door. He prepared to rush out, but was restrained by his wife, which gave the intruder the chance to escape, having first left another message upon the door. He gave Holmes copies of all the messages. Holmes would have liked Cubitt to have stayed in London for a few days, but this was declined: 'I must go back to-day. I would not leave my wife alone all night for anything. She is very nervous, and begged me to come back.'

Holmes promised to study the drawings, and shortly to travel down to Norfolk, which he subsequently did; he was too late to prevent a murder, but helped to apprehend the killer, one Abe Slaney, a Chicago gangster.

Before calling, Colonel Sir James Damery, sent Holmes a note from the Carlton Club, dated 2 September 1902:

Sir James Damery presents his compliments to Mr Sherlock Holmes and will call upon him at 4.30 to-morrow. Sir James begs to say that the matter upon which he desires to consult Mr

Holmes is very delicate and also very important. He trusts, therefore, that Mr Holmes will make every effort to grant this interview, and that he will confirm it over the telephone to the Carlton Club.'

Sir James was an aristocratic, large, bluff, honest-looking man with a broad, clean-shaven face, grey Irish eyes, smiling lips and a pleasant mellow voice. His dress was a dark frock coat, a shiny top hat, a pearl pin in a black satin cravat, kid-gloves and lavender spats, worn over varnished shoes. He was the intermediary for General de Merville, on behalf of his daughter Violet, whom he did not wish to marry Baron Adelbert Gruner, the Austrian murderer of Kingston, Surrey. Could Holmes help where Scotland Yard were unable to act? With help from 'Dr Hill Barton' (Watson's alias), Shinwell Johnson, (Holmes' underworld spy), and Kitty Winter, the baron's last mistress, Holmes brought about the prevention of the intended marriage, which notice was in the *Morning Post*, three days later.

James M Dodd called in January 1903; a big, fresh sunburned, virile man, with a short beard, blue eyes and a square jaw, who carried his handkerchief in the sleeve of his coat. In 1901 he had joined the army and served in South Africa with the Imperial Yeomanry, Middlesex Corps. Now he was a stockbroker in Throgmorton Street. He was worried about his army mate, Godfrey Emsworth, who had been hit with a bullet from an elephant gun in the action near Diamond Hill outside Pretoria.[145] Since then, he had only two letters, one from the Cape Town hospital and the other from Southampton. When Colonel Emsworth tried to fob him off with some made-up story as to his son's absence from his Tuxbury Old Park home, near Bedford, five miles from anywhere, Dodd thought the whole affair seemed 'fishy'; after all, Godfrey had saved his life from the rifles of the Boers, and, meaning to get to the bottom of things, he went down to the ancestral home. There he luckily had a glimpse of his old friend, looking through his window. The face horrified him; it was ghastly, 'glimmering as white as cheese in the darkness', something slinking, something furtive, something guilty, but the

---

[145]ACD, *The Adventure of the Blanched Soldier*.

eyes were those of a living man. But he had seen more than Colonel Emsworth liked, who sent his guest packing on the eight thirty morning train to London.

Dodd told Holmes that he thought his friend was being concealed from the world and that he was no longer a free agent; he was therefore determined to get to the bottom of the mystery, and hoped that Holmes would offer advice and assistance. Holmes could see that there was a very limited choice of alternatives in getting to the root of the matter and few difficulties in the solution. Elementary as it appeared to Holmes, there were points of interest and novelty about it which intrigued him. He decided therefore that he would go with Dodd to Tuxbury Old Park, but the journey had to wait until the beginning of the next week, as Holmes was involved in clearing up the case concerning the Duke of Greyminster, and executing a commission from the Sultan of Turkey. At Euston, Sir James Saunders, the noted dermatologist, joined Holmes and Dodd on the journey to Bedford. Sifting through all the evidence, and the fact that Godfrey Emsworth had been in South Africa where leprosy was not uncommon, suggested to Holmes the third possibility that by some extraordinary chance the young soldier might have contracted this disease. Sir James was able to define Godfrey's case as one of pseudo-leprosy, which was possibly curable, and certainly non-infective.

Scott Eccles arrived at Baker Street to see Holmes just before the arrival of the police who suspected the visitor of murder. Eccles of Popham House, Lee, was a man of very conventional British respectability; a tall, stout, pompous, grey-whiskered person of heavy features, with unbrushed, bristling and unkempt hair; gold-rimmed spectacles, dress boots and spats. His waistcoat was buttoned awry; his cheeks were flushed and angry, his chin unshaven; his manner flurried and excited; he was a Conservative and a churchman. He was an acquaintance of Aloysius Garcia of Wisteria Lodge, Esher, where he had stayed the night, only to find when he awakened in the morning that the house was empty. His host, footman and cook had vanished. Mr Eccles's telegram preceded him:

HAVE JUST HAD MOST INCREDIBLE AND GROTESQUE EXPERIENCE.

'I have had a most singular and unpleasant experience, Mr Holmes. Never in my life have I been placed in such a situation. It is most improper – most outrageous. I must insist upon some explanation.' Holmes wondered why he came to him at all. 'Well, sir, it did not appear to be a matter which concerned the police, and yet, when you have heard the facts, you must admit that I could not leave it where it was. Private detectives are a class with whom I have absolutely no sympathy, but none the less, having heard your name—' (This must have annoyed Holmes inwardly.) Inspector Gregson and Baynes called to arrest Scott Eccles of the suspected murder of Garcia, but before he was taken away by them, he implored Holmes to help him. 'I retain your services, Mr Holmes. I desire you to spare no expense and no pains to get at the truth.'

Mr Edmunds, a young constable of the Berkshire Constabulary, a thin, yellow-haired man, called in 1889. He smoked a few pipes with Holmes while they discussed certain points concerning the mauling by a lion of Mrs Ronder, of Ronder's wild beast show at Abbas Parva in Berkshire. For there were one or two points which still worried him, and being an inexperienced policeman, he was glad of Holmes' superior knowledge.

Robert Ferguson, of Ferguson and Muirhead, tea brokers of Mincing Lane, called at ten o'clock in the morning, having previously written Holmes a very lengthy letter. He had known Watson during their rugby days, when he was a three-quarter for Richmond and Watson played for Blackheath.[146]

The once fine athlete was now a wreck of a man. He thought that his Peruvian-born wife might be a vampire, although he thought that such a happening was a wild tale from foreign places. The nurse had seen the mother apparently biting the neck of her baby son. Then he and the nurse one day, called by cries into the nursery, had seen Mrs Ferguson, rise from a kneeling position beside the cot and saw blood upon the child's exposed neck and

[146]Name of Ferguson used in ACD, *The Adventure of the Three Gables*' and *The Adventure of the Engineer's Thumb*.

343

upon the sheet. There was blood all round her lips, suggesting that she had drunk the baby's blood.

As Ferguson gave Holmes all the relative information, he made notes; then he said, 'I fancy that I may be of more use at Lamberley than here. It is eminently a case for personal investigation. If the lady remains in her room, our presence could not annoy or inconvenience her. Of course, we would stay at the inn.' Ferguson was relieved. 'It is what I hoped, Mr Holmes. There is an excellent train at two from Victoria if you would come.' 'Of course we could come. There is a lull at present. I can give you my undivided energies. Watson of course, comes with us.'

Holmes did not think the problem was insoluble, and the three travelled down to Cheeseman's, Lamberley, in Sussex, Holmes and Watson staying at the Chequers Inn. Holmes was able to inform Ferguson that his wife was only sucking out a poison from the baby, caused by a prick from a poisoned South American arrow, shot from a small bird-bow by Jack, the son of fifteen, who was suffering from a weak spine and was jealous of the baby.

The Honourable Philip Green (son of Admiral Green, commander of the Sea of Azof fleet in the Crimean War) called in relation to the disappearance of Lady Frances Carfax, with whom he had been in love in younger days, before he went to South Africa. He was a huge, swarthy man with a bristling black beard, a grip of iron and the fury of a fiend; he was staying at the Langham Hotel in London. He called four times at Baker Street. On the evening of his third visit he rushed into the sitting room, pale, trembling, with every muscle of his powerful frame quivering with excitement. He had observed the 'wife' of Shlessinger in Bovington's in the Westminster Road, pawning another of Lady Frances Carfax's pendants. When she left, Green followed her up the Kennington Road and into an undertaker's shop. She spoke to a woman behind the counter, saying 'It is late,' getting the reply, 'It should be there before now. It took longer, being out of the ordinary.' When the woman left the shop, Philip Green followed her in another cab, her cab setting her down at No. 36 Poultney Square, Brixton. He then watched the house, and after a while a covered van drove up with two men in it, who delivered a coffin to the hall door, and were admitted by the same woman. Holmes congratulated Green on his excellent work, for he now had a clue as to the mystery. But he knew that he could do nothing without a warrant, and so sent Green with a note to Lestrade to obtain one. It was the unusually large coffin which aroused Holmes' interest, and his surmise that it might contain the body of Lady Frances proved to be correct.

Inspector Gregson called, a robust, energetic, gallant, official-looking and quite a capable officer, for Holmes thought that he was 'the smartest of the Scotland Yarders'; he told Holmes that he had the murderer of Enoch J Drebber, one Arthur Charpentier, sub lieutenant in Her Majesty's navy, at which news Holmes 'gave a sigh of relief and relaxed into a smile', for he knew otherwise. He went on to tell Holmes how he went to John Underwood and Sons, hatters of 129 Camberwell Road, having seen the name in the hat beside the dead man. He was told that a hat of the given description had been sold to Mr Drebber, residing at Charpentier's Boarding Establishment, Torquay Terrace. Gregson then had questioned Mrs Charpentier and her daughter Alice, who both admitted that Drebber had returned again after missing his train. Drebber tried to take Alice away by force, just as her brother Arthur had come in, holding a stick; he had had violent words with Drebber, who then had left. 'I don't think that fine fellow will trouble us again. I will just go after him and see what he does with himself.' Arthur was away some four or five hours, and Drebber being found dead was sufficient for Arthur's arrest. 'I suppose you are arresting me for being concerned in the death of that scoundrel Drebber,' said Arthur. To all this explanation by Gregson, Holmes merely yawned and said, 'It's quite exciting.'

The inspector called again in 1892, to arrest Mr Eccles for the murder of Aloysius Garcia, of Esher, Surrey.

Victor Hatherley, an hydraulic engineer of 16A Victoria Street, called in the summer of 1889; he was twenty-five years of age and dressed in a suit of heather tweed, with a soft cloth cap. He came with Watson, who had just received him as a patient, he had been brought to his surgery by his friend, a guard at Paddington Station. Hatherley was in a hysterical state, for his thumb had been hacked off by a butcher's cleaver by a Colonel Lysander Stark, leaving a horrid, red spongy surface. He told Holmes how he had accepted a job of secrecy from Colonel Stark concerning a hydraulic stamping machine needing repair, for which he would be paid fifty guineas for his opinion, which was most acceptable to him. He told of his visit to inspect the machine, his suspicions that it had no connection with fuller's earth, how the German had tried to murder him, his escape, minus his thumb and his return to London.

This led Holmes, Watson, Hatherley and Inspector Bradstreet of the Yard to travel down to Eyford in Berkshire upon the trail of counterfeit coiners, who were turning out half-crowns by the thousand. They arrived at the house, only to find it ablaze and the beautiful woman, the sinister German and the morose English-man, departed, and not all Holmes ingenuity could discover a clue as to their whereabouts; the engineer lost not only his thumb but his fifty-guinea fee.

Alexander Holder came to Baker Street by the Underground and thence upon foot, knowing how slowly the cabs went through the snow, and, hurrying, arrived breathless. He was a fifty-year-old banker of the firm of Holder & Stevenson of Threadneedle Street; a tall, portly, imposing, massive and commanding figure, with a strongly marked face, dressed in a 'sombre yet rich style, in a black frock coat, shining hat, neat brown gaiters and well-cut pearl-grey trousers'; a look of grief and despair was in his eyes. The Beryl Coronet, 'one of the most priceless public possessions of the empire', had been placed in his hands as security against a loan of fifty thousand pounds, paid to the borrower ('one of the highest, noblest, most exalted names in England') in thousand-pound notes.

He wanted Holmes to find the stolen missing piece of the coronet, which he was able to do when the banker called again, giving him the missing little triangular piece of gold, with the three beryls. 'I am saved! I am saved!' gasped Mr Holder, as he wrote out a cheque for four thousand pounds, a quarter of this being Holmes reward.

Mycroft Holmes visited his brother Sherlock at Baker Street twice in 1895. To visit at all was unique – to visit twice was out of this world. For Mycroft to deviate from his restricted course of travel was a phenomenal occurrence, and the business needed to be of prime importance, which it was. This was during the Bruce-Partington submarine plans scare. As Mycroft said to his brother, 'A most annoying business, Sherlock... I extremely dislike altering my habits but the powers that be would take no denial. In the present state of Siam it is most awkward that I should be away from the office. But it is a real crisis. I have never seen the Prime Minister so upset. As to the Admiralty – it is buzzing like an overturned bee-hive.'

So important were these plans that Mycroft later wrote to Sherlock: 'The Cabinet awaits your final report with the utmost anxiety. Urgent representations have arrived from the very highest quarter. The whole force of the State is at your back if you should need it.' Earlier he stressed: 'You must drop everything, Sherlock. Never mind your usual petty puzzles of the police court. It's a vital international problem that you have to solve.' Should Holmes succeed, there appeared to be a high reward for him, as Mycroft thought him the one man who would clear up the matter. 'If you have a fancy to see your name in the next honours list—' This only made Sherlock smile as he remarked, 'I play the game for the game's own sake.'

Sherlock, Mycroft, Watson and Lestrade visited the house of Hugo Oberstein, a top international spy and secret agent. Instead of the spy, they caught Colonel Valentine Walter of the Submarine Department, who had stolen the plans and given three of the essential ones to Oberstein, who then disappeared to Paris. He was lured to London by the offer of a fictitious tracing from the plans, and was duly caught in the smoking room of the Charing Cross Hotel. His over-optimism led to his imprisonment for fifteen years.

Mycroft Holmes made another of his most unusual visits to Baker Street, when he wished to see Sherlock over the case of Mr Melas, the Greek interpreter, who lodged on the floor above Mycroft; they were known slightly to each other, so Melas sought his aid, in his perplexity. Mycroft was already ensconced in an armchair, smoking, as Holmes and Watson returned home. 'Come in, Sherlock! Come in, sir. You don't expect such energy from me, do you, Sherlock?' he said as he smiled at the look in his brother's face.

Mycroft showed Sherlock a letter he had received from a man of Lower Brixton, in answer to his advertisement concerning Sophy Kratides, who knew the lady very well. So it was that Mycroft, Sherlock, Watson and Inspector Gregson travelled by train to The Myrtles, Beckenham, where they were able to rescue Melas from approaching death.

Inspector Stanley Hopkins first called upon Holmes upon a wild tempestuous night in November 1894. He sought his help to unravel the cause of the death of Willoughby Smith, secretary to Professor Coram of Yoxley Old Place, a country house situated on the London to Chatham road. Smith had died by a very small but very deep wound in the neck, which had divided the carotid artery, and Hopkins was by no means clear about the case. 'It means that I can make neither head nor tail of it. So far as I can see, it is just as tangled a business as ever I handled, and yet at first it seemed so simple that one couldn't go wrong. There's no motive, Mr Holmes. That's what bothers me – I can't put my hand on a motive. Here's a man dead – there's no denying that – but, so far as I can see, no reason on earth why anyone should wish him harm.' Hopkins thought that here was an excellent chance for Holmes to put his theories into practice; which of course he did, and soon diagnosed that Smith had been stabbed accidentally, while trying to seize a woman intruder, (Anna, the Russian wife of the professor), who was subsequently discovered when she came from her secret hiding place behind the movable bookcase in the professor's bedroom. She evaded arrest by taking poison from a small phial.

Inspector Hopkins called again at Baker Street in July 1895, and towards the end of the winter of 1897.

Miss Violet Hunter wrote to Holmes from Montague Place.

I am very anxious to consult you as to whether I should or should not accept a situation which has been offered to me as a governess. I shall call at half-past ten to-morrow, if I do not inconvenience you.

Holmes considered this note to be upon the very lowest rung ever of his detective work, but Watson soothed him by saying: 'It may turn out to be of more interest than you think. You remember that the affair of the blue carbuncle, which appeared to be a mere whim at first, developed into a serious investigation. It may be so in this case, also.'

It was on a cold, early spring morning with thick fog that Miss Hunter, with a quick firm step, entered the sitting room, warmed by a cheery fire. She was plainly but neatly dressed, 'with a bright, quick face, freckled like a plover's egg'. Her manner was brisk; her hair a wonderful luxuriant tint of chestnut; she was an orphan, and needed Holmes' advice concerning a very strange experience she had had lately. 'I shall be happy to do anything that I can to serve you,' said Holmes, being favourably impressed by the manner and speech of his new client. He looked her over in his searching fashion, then composed himself, with drooping eyelids and fingertips together, to listen to her story.

'I have been a governess for five years, in the family of Colonel Spence Munro, but two months ago the colonel received an appointment at Halifax, in Nova Scotia, and took his children over to America with him, so that I found myself without a situation. I advertised, and I answered advertisements, but without success. At last the little money which I had saved began to run short, and I was at my wit's end as to what I should do.' She called at Westaway's, a West End agency for governesses run by a Miss Stoper, once a week. With her last visit to the little office, she found a man there as well; a 'prodigiously stout man with a very smiling face and a great heavy chin which rolled down in fold upon fold over his throat', and who wore spectacles. She thought him a comfortable-looking man, and pleasurable in her eyes. Mr Jephro Rucastle, for such was his name (of The Copper Beeches, a Hampshire house five miles from Winchester), became most enthusiastic when he saw the colour of Miss Hunter's hair. He offered a salary of one hundred pounds a year – a vast increase over her previous salary of forty eight pounds a year. But acceptance of the post, meant that she would have to cut her hair short, which she refused to do, and so declined the situation. Two days later she received a letter from Mr Rucastle offering her one hundred and twenty pounds a year, to recompense her for any inconvenience caused by his fads. Miss Hunter wished to accept, being in financial difficulties, but Holmes thought that it did not seem to be a nice household for a young lady. He was uneasy over the salary – it was too good, especially when Mr Rucastle could have his pick for forty pounds; there must be a very strong reason behind it, and Holmes sensed some danger. He promised Miss Hunter that he would hurry to Winchester to assist her in any way, upon receipt of a telegram, at any time, day or night.

Two weeks later came a late-night telegram:

PLEASE BE AT THE BLACK SWAN HOTEL AT WINCHESTER AT MIDDAY TO-MORROW. DO COME! I AM AT MY WIT'S END. HUNTER.

Holmes and Watson hurried down to Winchester, on the 9.30 a.m. train. It eventually transpired that Mr Rucastle's daughter Alice, instead of going to Philadelphia, had been imprisoned in the house in order to prevent her marrying a Mr Fowler; Miss Hunter was used purely as a substitute in order to quieten any fears that her lover might have. She later became head of a private school in Walsall. Alice Rucastle and Mr Fowler married by a special licence in Southampton.

Dr Thorneycroft Huxtable, MA PhD, of the Priory School near Mackleton, in the north of England, called in person, fearing that no telegram would convince Holmes of the urgency of his case. He was a large, pompous, dignified man, with a white face seamed with lines of trouble and hanging pouches under his eyes; he had a loose mouth an unshaven chin with three days' growth, a dirty collar and shirt, and a well shaped head, covered with bristly, unkempt hair. Exhausted with fatigue and hunger, he slumped down upon the bearskin hearthrug, and a glass of milk and a biscuit revived him.

'Forgive this weakness, Mr Holmes, I have been a little over-wrought.' Which was not surprising, since one of his pupils, the only son of the late Cabinet minister, the Duke of Holdernesse had been abducted. When asked to go to Mackleton by the next train, Holmes demurred, saying that he had two cases on hand, and only something of extreme importance could take him from

London. When told that His Grace would willingly pay six thousand pounds to be told where his son was and the name of his abductor, Holmes commented: 'it is a princely offer. Watson, I think that we shall accompany Dr Huxtable back to the north of England.' (The pending cases, then, were apparently not quite so important, and not so pecuniary.)

Shinwell Johnson was originally a very dangerous person and served two terms at Parkhurst Prison. 'Finally he repented and allied himself to Holmes, acting as his agent in the huge criminal underworld of London, and obtaining information which often proved to be of vital importance.' He was; a 'huge, coarse, red-faced, scorbutic man, with a pair of vivid black eyes which were the only external sign of the very cunning mind within.'

He brought with him Miss Kitty Winter, whom he introduced with a wave of his fat hand. 'What she don't know – well, there, she'll speak for herself. Put my hand right on her, Mr Holmes, within an hour of your message.' Miss Winter was a 'slim, flame-like young woman with a pale, intense face, youthful, and yet so worn with sin and sorrow that one read the terrible years which had left their leprous mark upon her'.

'I'm easy to find,' said Miss Winter. 'Hell, London, gets me every time. Same address for Porky Shinwell. We're old mates, Porky, you and I. But, by Cripes! there is another who ought to be down in a lower Hell than we if there was any justice in the world! That is the man you are after, Mr Holmes… If I can help to put him where he belongs, I'm yours to the rattle… You needn't go into my past, Mr Holmes. That's neither here not there. But what I am Adelbert Gruner made me. If I could pull him down! …Oh, if I could only pull him into the pit where he has pushed so many!'

Her reward was not money, all she wanted was to see Gruner in the mud with her foot on his cursed face. She agreed to go with Holmes to see Miss Violet de Merville, to try to persuade her to cancel her marriage to the baron.

She called at Baker Street the following evening at five, and journeyed with Holmes by cab to 104 Berkeley Square, the residence of General de Merville; they were there received by the daughter in a great yellow-curtained drawing room. Miss Winter tried to make Miss de Merville change her views about the baron as she explained:

'I am his last mistress. I am one of a hundred that he has tempted and used and ruined and thrown into the refuse heap, as he will you also. *Your* refuse heap is more likely to be a grave, and maybe that's the best. I tell you, you foolish woman, if you marry this man he'll be the death of you. It may be a broken heart or it may be a broken neck, but he'll have you one way or the other. It's not out of love for you I'm speaking. I don't care a tinker's curse whether you live or die. It's out of hate for him and to spite him and to get back on him for what he did to me. But it's all the same, and you needn't look at me like that, my fine lady, for you may be lower than I am before you are through with it.'

By this time Miss Winter had become hysterical and tried to clutch this maddening woman by the hair, who was only saved by Holmes' quick intervention in getting Kitty away and into a cab. Eventually Miss Winter reaped her revenge by splashing vitriol over the baron's face at Kingston; between his screams the victim raved against her as the vitriol ate into his face. 'It was that hell-cat, Kitty Winter!' This, and the exposure of the baron's lust diary, persuaded Miss de Merville to cancel the wedding.

Inspector Athelney Jones of Scotland Yard called at three o'clock one afternoon, when only Watson was at home; the visit, in reply to Holmes' telegram, dated from Poplar at twelve o'clock which said:

GO TO BAKER STREET AT ONCE. IF I HAVE NOT RETURNED, WAIT FOR ME. I AM CLOSE ON THE TRACK OF THE SHOLTO GANG. YOU CAN COME WITH US TO-NIGHT IF YOU WANT TO BE IN AT THE FINISH.

No longer was the inspector the brusque and masterful professor of common sense who had taken over the case so confidently at Upper Norwood. His expression was downcast, and his bearing meek and even apologetic. Watson waved him to a chair, gave him a cigar and a half glass of whisky and soda, which allowed him to collect himself and cool down. He said that he had been obliged to reconsider the Norwood case. 'I had my net drawn tightly round Mr Sholto, sir, when pop he went through a hole in the middle of it. He was able to prove an alibi which could not be shaken. From the time that he left his brother's room he was never out of sight of someone or other. So it could not be he who climbed over roofs and through trapdoors. It's a very dark case, and my professional credit is at stake. I should be very glad of a little assistance.' The telegram seemed to show that Holmes had picked up the scent again, which rather pleased the inspector to think that he wasn't the only one at fault. 'Even the best of us are thrown off sometimes. Of course this may prove to be a false alarm, but it is my duty as an officer of the law to allow no chance to slip.'

Holmes eventually came home in the disguise of an aged seafaring man, and was complimented by Jones upon his acting ability. He insisted upon Jones staying to dinner, which was oysters and grouse. About seven o'clock, the trio sallied forth upon the trail of the murderer.

Peter Jones was a bulky official police agent of Scotland Yard. Holmes referred to him as an absolute imbecile in his profession, although as brave as a bulldog and tenacious as a lobster; a man with deep and heavy breathing.

Another man also arrived at the same time; this was Mr Merryweather, banker of the Coburg branch of the City and Suburban Bank; a 'long, thin, sad-faced man, with a very shiny hat and oppressively respectable frock coat'. Both men arrived by cab; Watson arrived at ten o'clock, having walked from his house in Kensington, via the Park and Oxford Street. 'We're hunting in couples again, Doctor,' said Jones. 'Our friend here is a wonderful man for starting a chase. All he wants is an old dog to help him to do the running down.' Mr Merryweather gloomily observed, 'I hope a wild goose may not prove to be the end of our chase.'

The four men were on the trail of John Clay, alias Vincent Spaulding, a small, stoutly built, clean-shaven man of some thirty years, with a white splash of acid upon his forehead, who had become an employee of Mr Jabez Wilson, pawnbroker of Coburg Square. Holmes thought he knew this man, a murderer, thief, smasher, and forger, although he was well connected – his grandfather being a royal duke – and well educated at Eton and Oxford; he was also known to have raised money to build an orphanage. Clay was intending to steal the thirty thousand gold napoleons borrowed by the bank from the Bank of France. It was past ten o'clock when the foursome left Baker Street; one to safeguard his gold, one to collar his man, Holmes to be saved from ennui, and Watson to assist as usual.

Smart-looking Inspector Lanner called at three o'clock upon an October day, in response to an invitation from Holmes; this followed upon their meeting in the bedroom of 'Mr Blessington', where the previous police informer had been hanged by Biddle, Haywood and Moffat, all members of the Worthingdon bank gang. But he had to wait until three forty-five, when Holmes arrived back home and gave Lanner a full explanation of the case.

Inspector Lestrade was well known to Holmes from the early days, when he used to call three or four times a week at Baker Street, and became a regular visitor over the years of Holmes' tenancy. Two columns in a newspaper, reporting upon the case of the Six Napoleons, may serve to illustrate the working of the two men together, as seen through the eyes of the Press:

> It is satisfactory to know that there can be no difference of opinion upon this case, since Mr Lestrade, one of the most experienced members of the official force, and Mr Sherlock Holmes, the well-known consulting expert, have each come to the conclusion that the grotesque series of incidents, which have ended in so tragic a fashion, arise from lunacy rather than from deliberate crime. No explanation save mental aberration can cover the facts.

Holmes chuckled over the report, for he was after a particular bust, while Lestrade was after the murderer of Pietro Venucci, one Beppo of hideous sallow face and writhing furious features. Lestrade called twice over this case. Usually, as Lestrade made his departure, Holmes would say: 'If any little problem comes your way, I shall be happy, if I can, to give you a hint or two as to its solution.' (Lestrade actually asked Watson's opinion over the Napoleon busts!)

Lestrade called to see Holmes over the Drebber case, and told him that Joseph Stangerson had been murdered at Halliday's Private Hotel. As the years went by, Holmes reached the opinion that perhaps Lestrade was the best of the professionals.

Inspector MacDonald called at Baker Street towards the end of the 1880s, rather early, for Holmes had left his breakfast untasted, preferring to flatten out upon his unused plate the coded message received from Porlock. Before the inspector arrived, Holmes, with Watson's assistance, had decoded the message, which indicated that some devilry was intended against someone called Douglas, living at Birlstone House. As Holmes chuckled over his success at decoding, Billy the pageboy opened the door and ushered in the Scotland Yard inspector. 'You are an early bird, Mr Mac. I wish you luck with your worm. I fear this means that there is some mischief afoot.' 'If you said "hope" instead of "fear", it would be nearer the truth, I'm thinking, Mr Holmes.' He accepted Holmes' offer of a wee nip, to keep out the raw morning chill, but declined a cigar; he was in a hurry to get to Birlstone to investigate a murder – that of Mr Douglas – and hoped that Holmes and Watson would go with him. Then the inspector noticed the paper upon the table, whereon Watson had scrawled the enigmatic message as dictated by Holmes; he thought it was witchcraft that a man in London could prophesise a crime before it had been committed. Holmes told the inspector that at the moment they must not form premature theories based upon insufficient information; he could see only two things for certain – a great brain in London and a dead man in Sussex – and he had to trace the chain between. Holmes was too fast a thinker for the inspector: 'You leave out a link or two, and I can't get over the gap.'

John Mason sent a letter to Holmes one bright May day, advising him of his intention to call upon him, but it did not explain anything to Holmes. Later Mason explained: 'It was too delicate a thing for me to put the details on paper. And too complicated. It was only face to face I could do it… I think that my employer, Sir Robert, has gone mad.' Holmes wondered why he said so. 'Well, sir, when a man does one queer thing, or two queer things, there may be a meaning to it, but when everything he does is queer, then you begin to wonder. I believe Shoscombe Prince and the

Derby have turned his brain.' Thus spoke the tall, clean-shaven man, with a firm austere expression – the look of a man who either controlled boys or horses – the head trainer at the stables of Sir Robert Norberton at Shoscombe Old Place, Berkshire.

He went on to tell Holmes that Sir Robert had given away his sister's pet spaniel to Barnes, mine host of the Green Dragon, at Crendall, three miles away. He now never went near her; instead he visited the old church crypt at night, and had even dug up a dead body. Lady Beatrice was no longer interested in the race-horse, and was drinking like a fish. 'I am not clear yet what you want me to do in this matter, Mr Mason. Can't you make it more definite?' Mason then showed a charred fragment of bone, taken from the central heating furnace in the cellar under Lady Beatrice's room, part of a human femur.

Immediately Holmes became very serious. 'These are deep waters, Mr Mason; deep and rather dirty... You may address us in future at the Green Dragon. We should reach it to-night. I need not say that we don't want to see you, Mr Mason, but a note will reach us, and no doubt I could find you if I want you. When we have gone a little further into the matter I will let you have a considered opinion.'

The usual morning quiet of the sitting room was shattered by the wild entry of John Hector McFarlane, a wild eyed frantic young man, pale, perspiring and dishevelled, flaxen-haired and handsome, with frightened blue eyes and a clean-shaven face with a rather weak, sensitive mouth. He was a gentleman perhaps of some twenty-seven years. He apologised for his unceremonious entry. 'I'm sorry, Mr Holmes. You mustn't blame me. I am nearly mad.'

Holmes immediately deduced that he was a bachelor, solicitor, Freemason and an asthmatic; McFarlane expected to be arrested upon the charge of murdering Mr Jonas Oldacre, a bachelor and builder, fifty-two years of age, who lived in Deep Dene House, Sydenham Road, Lower Norwood. For McFarlane had left his oak walking stick there, when he called late at night with Oldacre's will. Thus he was able to be traced to the London office of Graham and McFarlane of 426 Gresham Buildings, London, EC. The police were soon upon his trail, and, in the shape of

Inspector Lestrade and two uniformed policemen came to Baker Street to arrest him. Lestrade gave his prisoner half an hour to explain, in which time he protested his innocence and was then taken in a four-wheeler to the police station, with the knowledge that Holmes would be moving heaven and earth in order to prove his innocence, which Holmes was able to do.

Mrs Merrilow, of South Brixton, an elderly motherly woman of the buxom landlady type, waddled into the sitting room one morning, late in 1896. She was worried over Mrs Ronder, her lodger, who had kept her face veiled, throughout her seven year sojourn. Only once had the veil been raised, and the landlady wished that she had never looked, for it was hardly a face at all, so badly was it mutilated. She had come on behalf of Mrs Ronder, who requested that Holmes should come to see her. 'Bring him here, Mrs Merrilow, and if he won't come, tell him that I am the wife of Ronder's wild beast show. Say that, and give him the name Abbas Parva... That will bring him if he's the man I think he is.' And it did, for Holmes and Watson arrived at South Brixton at three o'clock the same afternoon.

Sam Merton was a heavily built young prizefighter; large and ugly, his hair cropped short, with a stupid, obstinate, slab-sided face – Holmes called him 'a great big silly bull-headed gudgeon, not a shark'. He was a minion of Count Negretto Sylvius, a vile and dangerous forger and robber. Holmes asked Billy, the pageboy, to bring him up, for he was standing guard outside the front door; he wished Merton to be alone with the count in the room, for he thought that he might get some information concerning the Crown diamond this way while they talked together during Holmes' absence.

Charles Augustus Milverton called on a cold frosty winter's evening. He was the king of the blackmailers, fifty, and as slippery as a serpent; a small stout man in a shaggy astrakhan coat with a large intellectual, broad, grizzled head, a round, plump, hairless face with a perpetual frozen smile; keen, grey, restless penetrating eyes, with broad gold-rimmed glasses and plump little hands. He smoked a long black cigar. In the inside pocket of his coat, he carried a revolver. He was in possession of some 'imprudent' letters written by Lady Eva Blackwell to a country squire, which

Milverton called 'very sprightly', adding that the lady was a 'charming correspondent'. Lady Eva was to be married in two weeks time to the Earl of Dovercourt and, if he received the letters, they would be sufficient to break off the marriage. Holmes had been commissioned by Lady Eva to meet Milverton and obtain the best terms he could for the return of the letters. The blackmailer demanded seven thousand pounds to be paid on the fourteenth, otherwise there would be no marriage of the eighteenth. Holmes assured Milverton that Lady Eva was not a wealthy woman and even two thousand pounds would be a drain upon her resources. Milverton, knowing that he held all the trump cards, considered the offer as unfortunate and was surprised that Holmes should haggle over the terms; for if he made an example of Lady Eva, some ten similar cases maturing would be more open to reason, not wishing exposure. Holmes saw now what a vile blackmailer he was, who would stop at nothing so long as he received the price asked. Holmes sprang from his chair with the intention of preventing Milverton's exit. 'Get behind him, Watson! Don't let him out!' Watson picked up a chair to attack but was restrained by Holmes, for Milverton had glided as quick as a rat across the room and stood with his back to the wall. They were no match against a large revolver, seen poking out from an inside pocket. With a bow, a smile, and a twinkle the repulsive man made a quick exit and the rattle of his carriage wheels were heard as he drove away.

Professor Moriarty, the 'Napoleon of crime', and the king of the underworld, visited Holmes upon the morning of 24 April 1891. He said that he would no longer tolerate Holmes forever being upon his trail; either Holmes desisted, or he would be destroyed.

Miss Mary Morstan (later Mrs John Watson) called to see Holmes in 1888. She was the daughter of a senior captain in an Indian regiment, in charge of a convict guard in the Andaman Islands. She had been sent home to England as a child, motherless and without relatives; she was then educated in Edinburgh until she was seventeen years of age. Her father, home on leave, arranged a meeting at the Langham Hotel, but failed to keep the appointment upon 3 December 1878. His only known friend was

Major Sholto of the thirty-fourth Bombay Infantry, living at Norwood. Every year for the last six years there had arrived through the post, in a small cardboard box, one very large and lustrous pearl of a rare variety, and valuable, but no word of explanation. She kept the pearls in a flat box in her bosom. Now she had received an unsigned letter asking for a meeting. Mrs Cecil Forrester of Lower Camberwell had advised Miss Morton to seek Holmes' assistance.

Dr James Mortimer, MRCS of Grimpen, Dartmoor, Devon, who preferred to be called a humble 'Mister' was another visitor.'[147] He was the medical officer for the parishes of Grimpen, Thorsley and High Barrow. He had been house surgeon at Charing Cross Hospital from 1882 to 1884. His usual visit to London often took him to the Museum of the College of Surgeons; he was also an amateur archaeologist and had excavated a barrow at Long Down.

The first time that he called at Baker Street, he inadvertently left behind his stick, a fine, thick piece of wood, bulbous-headed, known as a 'Penang lawyer',[148] with a broad silver band, whereon was engraved, 'To James Mortimer, MRCS from his friends of the CCH 1884.' A dignified stick, solid and reassuring, a friend that he would not wish to lose; he had sought it first in the Shipping Office.

The next morning he called again, hoping to find his stick. He was a very tall, thin man, with a long nose like a beak, which jutted out between two keen, grey eyes, set closely together and sparkling brightly from behind a pair of gold-rimmed spectacles. He was clad in a professional but rather slovenly fashion, for his frock coat was dingy and his trousers frayed. His young long back was bowed as he walked with a forward thrust of the head, and he had a general air of peering benevolence, 'long, quivering fingers as agile and restless as the antennae of an insect,' and he spoke in a

---

[147]Mr Mortimer Maberley was an early client of Sherlock Holmes. ACD, *The Adventure of the Three Gables*.
[148]Walking stick made from the stem of a prickly dwarf palm, *Licuala acutifida*, from Penang. Dr Grimstone, was recommended by Marmaduke Paradine, to use a Penang-lawyer for educational purposes at his school. F Anstey, *Vice Versa*, 1882. Fitzroy Simpson, suspected of the death of John Straker, carried a Penang-lawyer, weighted with lead. ACD, *Silver Blaze*'.

high cackling voice. He was most adept at making his own cigarettes, as Holmes observed by the nature of his forefinger.

He wished to consult Holmes upon the recent sudden death of Sir Charles Baskerville of Baskerville Hall in Devon. He showed Holmes a yellow manuscript with faded script, dated 1742, and read to him the story of the curse of the Baskerville family and the legend of the large black hound which killed Hugo Baskerville. Dr Mortimer had done a little detection work himself regarding the death of Sir Charles, who had gone out for his usual nocturnal walk, smoking a cigar; from the two droppings of cigar ash, he deduced that Sir Charles had stood by the wicket-gate, for five or ten minutes. More important still, the doctor observed some fresh and clear footprints of a gigantic hound, some twenty yards from the body. Dr Mortimer then asked Holmes what he should do with Sir Henry Baskerville, the new heir, due to arrive shortly at Waterloo Station, for every Baskerville who took up residence at the family home met with an evil fate.

Dr Mortimer called a third time the next morning, at ten o'clock, with Sir Henry Baskerville. So that Sir Henry would not be alone at Baskerville Hall in Devon, Dr Watson accompanied him thither, travelling down with Dr Mortimer on the train from Paddington Station, the following Saturday.

It was during an afternoon at the end of November that Dr Mortimer paid his fourth visit to Baker Street, accompanied by Sir Henry; they were about to commence a long voyage, which had been recommended for the restoration of Sir Henry's shattered nerves.

Mr Grant Munro (whose step daughter was Lucy Hebron, a coal-black Negress) was a hop merchant of Norbury, who always wrote his name upon the lining of his hat. He called one early spring day while Holmes and Watson were walking in the park. But having waited half an hour, restlessly walking and stamping up and down, he left, saying he would be back before long, wishing to wait in the open air for he felt half choked in the sitting room.

Holmes was somewhat put out, for he was badly in need of a case, and this one, by the man's impatience, seemed important; he was also much intrigued by the man's pipe left behind.

Later on, Munro returned to Baker Street; he was a tall young man, looking like thirty years old, but actually older. He entered the sitting room without knocking. He was quietly dressed in a dark grey suit and carrying a brown wideawake hat. He apologised. 'I beg your pardon, I suppose I should have knocked. Yes, of course I should have knocked. The fact is that I am a little upset, and you must put it down to that.' He seemed somewhat dazed and slumped down upon a chair. 'I can see that you have not slept for a night or two… That tries a man's nerves more than work, and more even than pleasure,' said Holmes, in his 'easy, genial way'. 'May I ask how I can help you?' Munro spoke in little, sharp, jerky outbursts, that of a reserved and self-contained man with some pride. 'I wanted your advice, sir. I don't know what to do, and my whole life seems to have gone to pieces.' 'You wish to employ me as a consulting detective?' 'Not that only,' said Munro. 'I want your opinion as a judicious man – as a man of the world. I want to know what I ought to do next.'

He had been married for three years to the widow of an American Negro lawyer, one Mrs Effie Hebron, twenty-five years old. Their only child, Lucy, had died like her father of yellow fever in Atlanta. The Munros lived happily together until recently, when some inexplicable barrier had grown up between them. His wife had gone out at three in the morning, with no very good reason for being absent. He was mystified. Holmes wanted a little time to think things over. 'Let me advise you, then, to return to Norbury and to examine the windows of the cottage again. If you have reason to believe that it is inhabited, do not force your way in, but send a wire to my friend and me. We shall be with you within an hour of receiving it, and we shall then very soon get to the bottom of the business.' If it was still empty, Holmes said, 'I shall come out to-morrow and talk it over with you. Goodbye, and, above all, do not fret until you know that you really have a cause for it.' For at the back of Holmes' mind was the thought that there was blackmail in the case.

Sir Leslie Oakshott, the famous surgeon, called to see Holmes after he had been attacked by two men with sticks in Regent Street, where he sustained two lacerated scalp wounds and considerable bruises. Several stitches were necessary. He received an injection of morphine, and had to be kept very quiet, Watson only being allowed a few minutes to see his friend.

John Openshaw (his father had patented the Openshaw unbreakable tyre at Coventry) called upon a late, stormy September evening in 1887, having travelled up from the south-west from Horsham. Holmes guessed as much as he remarked, 'That clay and chalk mixture which I see upon your toe caps is quite distinctive.'[149]

Cyril Overton of Trinity College, Cambridge, called on a gloomy February morning, following his somewhat weird telegram, with a Strand postmark, which had been dispatched at 10.36 a.m. and read as follows:

> PLEASE AWAIT ME. TERRIBLE MISFORTUNE. RIGHT-WING THREE-QUARTER MISSING, INDISPENSABLE TO-MORROW.

He was an enormous young man, 'sixteen stone of solid bone and muscle', who spanned the doorway with his broad shoulders. His comely face was haggard with anxiety. He had been sent on from Scotland Yard, by Inspector Stanley Hopkins, who thought that such a case was not in his line of business. When Holmes admitted that he knew neither Cyril Overton nor Godfrey Staunton, the Cambridge rugby Captain, Overton was absolutely flabbergasted. Holmes did not retain such data in his attic room of knowledge. With the match against Oxford on the morrow, Overton was most worried over the disappearance of Staunton, his most valuable three-quarter. He had last been seen leaving Bentley's private hotel and running down the street in the direction of the Strand. Overton could make nothing of it. Holmes agreed to help. 'Well, well, I have a clear day, and I shall be happy to look into the matter. I should strongly recommend you to make your preparations for your match without reference to this young gentleman... It must, as you say, have been an overpowering necessity which tore him away in such a fashion, and the same necessity is likely to hold him away. Let us step

---

[149]Charles Dickens made a similar observation in *Oliver Twist*, 1838. Fagin: 'From the country, I see, sir?' Noah Claypole: 'How do yer see that?' Fagin 'We have not so much dust as that in London' pointing to Noah and Charlotte's shoes.

round together to the hotel, and see if the porter can throw any fresh light upon the matter.'

It was the second morning after Christmas, and Watson called at Baker Street to wish Holmes the compliments of the season; while there, Peterson the commissionaire burst into the room with flushed cheeks and a dazed look in his eyes. 'The goose, Mr Holmes! See here, sir! See what my wife found in its crop!' (For about four o'clock on Christmas morning, Peterson was making his way homeward down Tottenham Court Road, when he encountered a tall man carrying a white goose slung over his shoulder, and being attacked by a little knot of roughs. Peterson rushed forward to protect the stranger and the roughs fled. The man, seeing an official-looking person in uniform rushing towards him, took to his heels – for he had accidentally smashed a shop window with his stick – leaving his hat and goose behind.) He showed Holmes a brilliantly scintillating blue stone, 'smaller than a bean in size, but of such purity and radiance that it twinkled like an electric point in the dark hollow of his hand'. This made Holmes sit up on the sofa with a whistle. 'By Jove, Peterson! This is treasure trove indeed. I suppose you know what you have got?' Peterson thought that it was just another very precious diamond. 'It's more than a precious stone. It is *the* precious stone.' In fact it was the unique blue carbuncle belonging to the Countess of Morcar, lost in the Hotel Cosmopolitan, for the safe return of which she would no doubt be willing to part with half her fortune. Holmes told Peterson that a reward of one thousand pounds was offered to the finder at which Peterson exclaimed, 'A thousand pounds! Great Lord of mercy!' and he plumped down into a chair, utterly amazed. Strangely, Watson does not record that Peterson received his reward.

Percy Phelps arrived at Baker Street in July 1887 with Watson, having travelled up from Woking; he was put into the spare bedroom. Phelps had written to his old school friend, Watson, asking him to bring his friend Holmes down to Woking if possible, for a horrible misfortune had overtaken him at the Foreign Office and he much desired the opinion of the notable detective in relation to the disappearance of a secret naval treaty, written upon a grey or blue-grey roll of paper, between England

and Italy. So important was it, that the French or Russian embassies would pay any price to learn the content. Phelps had been asked by his uncle, Lord Holdhurst, the foreign minister, to make a copy of the treaty, written in French and containing twenty-six separate articles.

Phelps related the story of his distress to Holmes, how he had gone downstairs at the office to see why the commissionaire had not brought up his coffee, and, returning, had found the secret document stolen. Watson saw that the tangled problem interested Holmes intensely, as he sat up in his chair and rubbed his hands. 'Do you see any prospect of solving this mystery, Mr Holmes?' asked Miss Harrison, Phelps's fiancée, with a touch of asperity in her voice. 'Well, it would be absurd to deny that the case is a very abstruse and complicated one, but I can promise you that I will look into the matter and let you know any points which may strike me,' replied Holmes. So Holmes sent Phelps with Watson to London, for his own safety, while he stayed at Woking, surmising, correctly as it happened, that it was there that he would find the answer.

Holmes subsequently recovered the secret treaty from Joseph Harrison, at Woking, about two in the morning, but not before he received a vicious knife cut over the knuckles. Holmes arrived at Baker Street in a hansom, shortly after eight, and sat down to breakfast with Phelps and Watson. Mrs Hudson brought in three covered dishes, one of curried chicken, another of ham and eggs and the third containing the cylinder of blue-grey paper. Phelps having no stomach for breakfast was asked by ravenous Holmes, to serve him from the third dish. Phelps raised the cover and screamed, his face turning white as he saw the cylinder. So great was his emotion, that he was given brandy to save him fainting. Holmes' love of the dramatic could have had serious consequences.

Colonel Ross was a small, alert, well known sportsman, with trim little side-whiskers and an eyeglass; very neat and dapper in a frock coat, gaiters and a top hat. He kept a stable at King's Pyland, Dartmoor, and was the owner of the missing race horse, Silver Blaze, due to run in the Wessex Cup. His trainer, John Straker, had been murdered. These two facts were the one topic of conversation though the length and breadth of England.

Holmes was asked by telegrams from Colonel Ross and Inspector Gregory to help solve the mysteries, and as he said to Watson, 'I am afraid, Watson, that I shall have to go.' To Watson's query, he replied: 'To Dartmoor; to King's Pyland.' So they both travelled down.

The manner of Colonel Ross to Holmes was just a trifle cavalier as he said: 'So you despair of arresting the murderer of poor Straker.' Holmes repaid in kind; after Holmes had discovered the lost horse, which went on to win the Wessex Cup, he played a little joke upon the colonel when he told him that he had discovered the murderer. The powerful bay horse with the black and red colours of the colonel had certainly won, but the colonel was flabbergasted, for the horse had not a white hair upon its body like the true Silver Blaze. But Holmes told the colonel that he had only to wash the face and leg in spirits of wine and the true identity would be revealed. Colonel Ross apologised for doubting Holmes' ability, and added that he would be rendered a great service if Holmes could find the murderer. 'I have done so,' responded Holmes quietly. 'He is here. In my company at the present moment.' The Colonel was angry, thinking that this was a bad joke, or an insult. 'The real murderer is standing immediately behind you.' Which, of course, was Silver Blaze himself, who had lashed out early in defence against the cataract knife of John Straker, and the steel shoe had struck Straker full on the forehead.

Colonel Ross travelled back with the detective duo to Victoria Station, and he was then invited back to Baker Street to smoke a cigar and hear further details of the Devon affair.

It was early April in the year 1883 when Dr Grimesby Roylott dashed open the sitting room door at Baker Street, unannounced, which caused Holmes to exclaim, 'But what in the name of the devil!' as he beheld a huge man framed in the doorway.

The doctor was the last survivor of one of the oldest Saxon families, of Stoke Moran, western Surrey. He had previously had a medical practice in Calcutta, served a long term of imprisonment for beating his native butler to death, and then returned, disappointed and morose, to the family seat in England. He had married Mrs Stonor, the young widow of Major General Stonor of the Bengal Artillery, who had twin daughters, Helen and Julia. As Watson recorded:

> His costume was a peculiar mixture of the professional and of the agricultural, having a black top-hat, a long frock coat, and a pair of high gaiters, with a hunting-crop swinging in his hand. So tall was he, that his hat actually brushed the cross bar of the doorway, and his breadth seemed to span it across from side to side. A large face, seared with a thousand wrinkles, burned yellow with the sun, and marked with every evil passion, was turned from one to the other of us, while his deep-set, bile-shot eyes, and his high, thin, fleshless nose, gave him somewhat the resemblance to a fierce old bird of prey.

The doctor, having traced his stepdaughter Helen Stonor to Baker Street, wanted to know what she had said to Holmes. He told Holmes not to meddle with his affairs, for he was a dangerous man to fall foul of. Holmes parried all his violent questions in his imperturbable way, much to the anger of his visitor. He refused Holmes' offer of a seat. Holmes observed that it was cold for the time of year and that the crocuses promised well. 'Your conversation is most entertaining. When you go out, close the door, for there is a decided draught,' said Holmes. In a rage, the doctor stepped swiftly forward, seized the poker, and bent it into a curve with his huge brown hands. 'See that you keep yourself out of my grip,' he snarled, and hurling the twisted poker into the fireplace he strode out of the room. Holmes laughed. 'He seems a very amiable person. I am not quite so bulky, but if he had remained I might have shown him that my grip was not much more feeble than his own.' Wherewith he picked up the steel poker and, with a sudden effort, straightened it out again, which of course required even greater strength than the original bending.

James Ryder, head attendant at the Hotel Cosmopolitan, stole the Countess of Morcar's blue carbuncle from her jewel case and allowed suspicion to fall upon a plumber named Horner, who was duly arrested by the police.

Holmes picked Ryder up in Covent Garden Market, as he overheard him asking Mr Breckinridge, the salesman, about a goose, a white one with a black bar across the tail, wherein he had concealed the jewel. (Only, of course, there were two geese with similar markings, which foxed him.) Ryder, a little rat-faced, cringing shrimp of a man, was taken by Holmes in a cab back to Baker Street, where he could be questioned in the warmth of the sitting room about the jewel theft. A very frightened man begged for mercy, and as it was the Christmas season of forgiveness, and as Holmes was not retained by the police to supply their deficiencies, he did not see why he should not commute a felony, perhaps even save a soul. Holmes pondered, breathed heavily, tapped his fingertips upon the edge of the table, then rose up and opened the door. 'Get out!' 'What, sir! Oh, Heaven bless you!' 'No more words. Get out!' Ryder needed no further bidding – a rush, a clatter upon the stairs, the bang of a door and he was away down the street. 'This fellow will not go wrong again; he is too terribly frightened. Send him to jail now, and you make him a jail-bird for life,' observed Holmes to Watson as he reached up for his clay pipe.

Mr Sandeford of Reading travelled up to Baker Street after he had received a letter from Holmes which read:

> I desire to possess a copy of Devine's Napoleon, and am prepared to pay you ten pounds for the one which is in your possession.

He was an elderly red-faced man, with grizzled side-whiskers; he carried an old-fashioned carpet bag in his right hand, which contained the sixth and last plaster copy of the bust, made by Gelder & Co of Stepney. He had purchased the bust from Harding Brothers for fifteen shillings, and told Holmes so, not wishing to take advantage of Holmes' generous offer. 'I am sure the scruple does you honour, Mr Sandeford. But I have named that price, so I intend to stick to it.' He laid a ten-pound note upon the table. 'You will kindly sign that paper, Mr Sandeford, in the presence of these witnesses. It is simply to say that you transfer every possible right that you ever had in the bust to me. I am a methodical man, you see, and you never know what turn events might take afterwards. Thank you, Mr Sandeford; here is your money, and I wish you a very good evening.'

After the visitor had departed, Holmes placed the bust in the centre of a clean white cloth he had taken from the drawer, and picking up his hunting crop, struck Napoleon a sharp head blow, shattering the bust. From one of the fragments came a round dark object, 'like a plum in a pudding'. 'Gentlemen, let me introduce you to the famous black pearl of the Borgias.' Lestrade and Watson both spontaneously broke out clapping. Watson recorded:

> A flush of colour sprang to Holmes' pale cheeks, and he bowed to us like the master dramatist who receives the homage of his audience. It was at such moments that for an instant he ceased to be a reasoning machine, and betrayed his human love for admiration and applause. The same singularly proud and reserved nature which turned away with disdain from popular notoriety was capable of being moved to its depths by spontaneous wonder and praise from a friend.

'Mrs Sawyer,' a very old and wrinkled woman – in effect, a young actor friend of the murderer, Jefferson Hope – came to retrieve a gold wedding ring, advertised by Holmes in the 'Found' column of all the newspapers: Holmes, thinking that Mrs Sawyer must be an accomplice, followed her, only to find that he had followed a wild goose chase, and had been 'taken in' by an actor as good as himself. He later on agreed heartily with Jefferson Hope that he had been duped.

Lord Robert St Simon, having written a letter to Holmes, advising him that he would call at four o'clock in the afternoon, and hoping that he would be at home, as the matter he wished to discuss was of paramount importance, arrived a few minutes after the appointed time.

Holmes rose from his chair, and bowed. Strange perhaps, as he already had had three kings as his clients! He waved his visitor to the basket chair. St Simon thought that he was conferring an honour upon Holmes in coming to see him, presuming that Holmes' clients were usually of the humbler sort. Rather an aristocratic snob! But Holmes put him in his place by telling him that in seeing him, he was descending in rank, as his last client was the King of Scandinavia, upon which subject he would not enlarge, as he extended 'to the affairs of my other clients the same secrecy which I promise to you in yours'. At which a little of the hauteur disappeared, as he begged Holmes' pardon.

St Simon was a man with a 'pleasant, cultured face, high-nosed and pale, with something perhaps of petulance about the mouth, and with the steady well-opened eye of a man whose pleasant lot it had ever been to command and to be obeyed'. He had a brisk manner, and yet his general appearance gave an undue impression of age, for he had a slight forward stoop and a little bend of the knees as he walked; his hair was grizzled round the edges and thin on top; he wore a very curly-brimmed hat; his dress was rather foppish, with high collar, black frock coat, white waistcoat, yellow gloves, patent-leather shoes and light-coloured gaiters; his golden eyeglasses swung from a cord in his right hand.

He wished to consult Holmes regarding a painful happening in connection with his marriage to Miss Hatty Doran of America, who had vanished at the wedding breakfast; he even placed Holmes on a par with the aristocracy, by putting both their heads on the same level: 'I am afraid that it will take wiser heads than yours or mine,' he remarked, and bowing in a stately, old-fashioned manner he departed. Lord Robert called a second time at Baker Street, in order to meet Mr and Mrs Francis Hay Moulton.

After the chase by the police, Holmes and Watson of the *Aurora* upon the Thames, and the final capture of Jonathan Small, the prisoner was brought to Baker Street. Small was a Worcestershire man, born near Pershore. 'He was a sunburned reckless-eyed fellow, with a network of lines and wrinkles all over his mahogany features'; aged about fifty, with black curly hair streaked with grey, heavy eyebrows and an aggressive bearded chin; a good deal of skin missing from the palm of his hand. Mrs Mordecai Smith described his wrinkled, brown monkey face as ugly, his voice thick and foggy, his talk outlandish. His right leg was off from the thigh downwards, the substitute, a wooden stump, was worn away on the inner side; his left boot had a coarse square-toed sole with a band round the heel.

Small had been a soldier with the Third Buffs in India, and while swimming in the Ganges had his right leg nipped off just above the knee by a crocodile; he was saved from death by his company sergeant, John Holder; then he was invalided out of the army, and became an overseer for Abel White, an indigo planter. Then the Indian mutiny had broken out. Small was arrested for murder and condemned to penal servitude on Blair Island in the Andamans. From here he escaped with the help of the native Tonga and eventually returned to England to track down Major Sholto, who had broken his trust and stolen the Agra Treasure. He only wanted his rightful share of the treasure, being one of the 'four', the others, being Abdullah Khan, Dost Akbar and Mahomet Singh. There was really no case against Small, as Bartholomew Sholto was killed by Tonga with one of his poisoned darts.

Mr Culverton Smith arrived on a foggy November day at Baker Street after a most pressing summons from Watson; he came hoping to see the slow death of Holmes from poisoning, for he had sent Holmes a small black and white ivory box with a sliding lid, which contained death within to the person who opened it. They were not absolute strangers, having met before through business deals.

He was a man with a high snarling voice, a great coarse-grained and greasy yellow face, with a heavy double chin and two sullen menacing grey eyes under tufted sandy brows; he had a high bald head of enormous capacity, although he was a small and frail figure twisted in the shoulders. He was a planter in Sumatra – an authority upon tropical diseases, but now upon a visit to London.

Instead of a dying man, Smith found that Holmes was more than his equal when it came to strategy; for the foul disease was a sham, just a decoy to get Smith back to Baker Street.

So Holmes outwitted Smith, and got him to confess to the poisoning of Victor Savage. Inspector Mortan, following the pre-arranged signal of the turning up of the gas, arrived at the right moment to secure his prisoner upon a charge of murdering Savage. 'And you might add', said Holmes, 'of the attempted murder of one Sherlock Holmes.'

Miss Violet Smith from Farnham, Surrey, called late in the evening of Saturday, 23 April 1895. Her visit was somewhat unwelcome to Holmes, for he was very busy with the abstruse and complicated problem concerning the peculiar persecution to which John Vincent Harden, the tobacco millionaire, had been subjected. He explained that he was very fully occupied just at that moment; but when a young and beautiful woman, tall graceful, and queenly, implored his assistance and advice and was determined to stay and tell her story – nothing short of force would have got her out of the room – what could Holmes do? He just resigned himself with a somewhat weary smile and begged Miss Smith to take a seat and tell him of her troubles.

She was a keen and energetic cyclist, as evidenced by the slight roughening of the side of the sole caused by the friction of the edge of the pedal; and cycling had a lot to do with her visit. Holmes took her ungloved hand and examined it carefully, her 'spatulate finger-ends' coupled with the spirituality about her face, told Holmes she was a musician. Her dead father had conducted the orchestra at the old Imperial Theatre, and the family had been left very poor. She eventually took a post as music teacher to the ten-year-old daughter of Mr Carruthers of Chiltern Grange, about six miles from Farnham, at an annual salary of one hundred pounds.

She was engaged to be married to Cyril Morton, an electrical engineer, so she found rather repulsive the love advances made to her by Mr Woodley, a visitor to the Grange.

Every Saturday morning, Miss Smith cycled to Farnham Station to catch the 12.22 to London; near Crooksbury Hill she found she was being followed by a stranger, a middle-aged cyclist with a short dark beard; this was repeated every Saturday and on her return journey on Monday.

Holmes chuckled and rubbed his hands as he listened to her story. 'This case certainly presents some features of its own... You will let me know any fresh development, Miss Smith. I am very busy just now, but I will find time to make some inquiries into your case. In the meantime, take no step without letting me know. Goodbye, and I trust that we shall have nothing but good news from you.' Holmes and Watson travelled down the following Saturday morning to investigate, after receiving a note from Miss Smith saying that her employer had proposed marriage to her, and had taken her refusal seriously but very gently.

Miss Helen Stonor – according to Watson – called in early

April 1883, at a quarter past seven in the morning.

She had made an early start for her journey to London, leaving before six o'clock in a dog cart from The Crown Inn, Stoke Moran in Surrey; she had caught the first train to Waterloo from Leatherhead at six twenty, and thus was a very early caller.

Thirty years old and dressed in black and heavily veiled the sleeve of her dress was fringed with black lace at the wrist, hiding five little livid spots, the marks of four fingers and a thumb. Her face was drawn and grey, with restless frightened eyes, like those of some hunted animal; her hair prematurely turning grey, her expression weary and haggard. Her left arm was splattered with mud from the dog cart. She shivered with fear and terror and was worried over her sister Julia's death, possibly, she thought, from shock.

By the time Watson joined Holmes downstairs, Mrs Hudson had a bright fire going to warm the visitor, and Watson heard Miss Stonor's story, how her sister Julia's hair had begun to whiten at the time of her death, two years ago, although only thirty. Julia had met a half-pay major of marines while spending Christmas with Helen at the house of her aunt, Miss Honoria Westphail, near Harrow. Their stepfather offered no objection to the marriage, but within a fortnight of the wedding day, Julia died, and the coroner could find no cause of death; her last words to her twin sister were: 'Oh, my God! Helen! It was the band! The speckled band!' Now Helen was to be married to an old friend, Percy Armitage, of Crane Water, near Reading. She told Holmes that she too had heard the low whistle in the night, the same as her sister had heard prior to her death; she had lit the lamp, but nothing was visible to account for the sound. Being too shaken to go back to sleep, she had waited for daylight, and then made her early trip to Baker Street.

'This is a very deep business,' said Holmes. 'There are a thousand details which I should desire to know before I decide upon our course of action. Yet we have not a moment to lose.' She was told to expect Holmes and Watson early in the afternoon. Her heart had been lightened since confiding her troubles to Holmes, and, dropping her thick black veil over her face, she glided from the room. A most dark and sinister business now lay before Holmes, and he wondered whether he might have to take Miss Stonor to her aunt's home for safety.

Miss Mary Sutherland was the daughter of a deceased plumber in the Tottenham Court Road, whose business at Camberwell had been sold somewhat untimely for four thousand, seven hundred pounds by her stepfather, Mr Windibank. Her 'own little income' of one hundred pounds per annum was derived from two thousand, five hundred pounds in New Zealand Stock left to her by Uncle Ned in Auckland.

Holmes had seen her between the parted blinds as he gazed down into the dull neutral-tinted London street, standing on the opposite pavement, peeping up in a nervous hesitating fashion at his window; her body oscillated backward and forward, while her fingers fidgeted with her glove buttons. Having made up her mind, she suddenly crossed the road and rang the bell. 'I have seen those symptoms before... Oscillation upon the pavement always means an *affaire de coeur*. She would like advice, but is not sure that the matter is not too delicate for communication. And yet even here we may discriminate. When a woman has been seriously wronged by a man she no longer oscillates, and the usual symptom is a broken bell wire. Here we may take it that there is a love matter, but that the maiden is not so much angry as perplexed, or grieved.' Holmes just had time to make this observation to Watson before the boy in buttons announced the visitor, Miss Mary Sutherland, looming 'behind his small black figure like a full-sailed merchantman behind a tiny pilot boat.' Holmes welcomed her with his natural courtesy and bowed her into an armchair, looking her over in his minute, peculiar yet abstracted fashion.

She was a large woman, with a broad, vacuous, good-humoured face, a heavy boa round her neck and a large, red curling feather in her broad-brimmed, slate-coloured straw hat, 'which was tilted in a coquettish Duchess-of-Devonshire fashion over the ear'. Black beads were sewn upon her black jacket, with a fringe of little black jet ornaments. 'Her dress was brown, rather darker than coffee colour, with a little purple plush at the neck and sleeves. Her gloves were greyish, and were worn through at the right forefinger... She had small round hanging gold earrings, and a general air of being fairly well-to-do in a vulgar, comfortable, easygoing way.' She wore odd boots, the toecap of one slightly decorated, the other plain; one was buttoned only in the two lower buttons out of five and the other at the first, second and fifth buttons. All these signs told Holmes that she had left home in a hurry. The dint of a pince-nez at either side of her nose indicated her short sight, and the tell-tale marks in a double line a little above the wrist suggested the use of a typewriter; she was able to earn some three shillings and fourpence a day.

Miss Sutherland had heard of Holmes through Mrs Etheridge, whose husband he found after the police had given him up for dead. Could he find Mr Hosmer Angel, her husband-to-be? He was a cashier in an office in Leadenhall Street, and they had met at a gasfitter's ball. The wedding 'was to be at St Saviour's, near King's Cross, and we were to have breakfast afterwards at the St Pancras Hotel. Hosmer came for us in a hansom, but as there were two of us he put us both into it and stepped himself into a four-wheeler, which happened to be the only other cab in the street. We got to the church first, and when the four-wheeler drove up we waited for him to step out, but he never did, and when the cabman got down from the box and looked inside, there was no one there! The cabman said that he could not imagine what had become of him, for he had seen him get in with his own eyes. That was last Friday, Mr Holmes, and I have never seen or heard anything since then to throw any light upon what became of him.'

Her stepfather, Mr Windibank, made light of the whole matter. He was only five years and two months her senior and some fifteen years younger than her mother. He travelled for Westhouse & Marbank, claret importers of Fenchurch Street.

Before Miss Sutherland departed, she left with Holmes a slip from the *Chronicle*, and four typed letters, including the signatures, which were most significant. 'Let the weight of the matter rest upon me now,' said Holmes, 'and do not let your mind dwell upon it further. Above all, try to let Mr Hosmer Angel vanish from your memory, as he has done from your life.'

Holmes told Watson that the actual problem was rather a trite one and that there were parallel cases in Andover in 1877, and something similar at The Hague. The idea of impersonation was an old one.

Count Negretto Sylvius called some time after 13 February 1892, (upon which date he was robbing the Riviera train). He was half Italian, with dark hairy hands; he sometimes showed the southern graces of good manners and at other times, he was a veritable devil. Watson described him as: 'The famous game-shot, sportsman and man-about-town… a big, swarthy fellow, with a formidable dark moustache shading a cruel, thin-lipped mouth, and surmounted by a long, curved nose like the beak of an eagle. He was well dressed, but his brilliant necktie, shining pin, and glittering rings were flamboyant in their effect.' He intended to kill Holmes.

It was a close, rainy October day, with the sitting room blinds half-drawn, when Holmes and Watson returned home after a three-hour walk, only to find a brougham outside their front door. Inside their room, sitting by the fire, was the owner, a Dr Percy Trevelyan of London University, who lived at 403 Brook Street, a sombre flat-faced house associated with a West End practice. Fortunately he had only been waiting a few minutes. His own hobby was nervous disease, and Watson knew that he had written upon obscure nervous lesions, which surprised and pleased the visitor.

The doctor was a 'pale, taper-faced man with sandy whiskers'; thirty-three or -four years old, unhealthy looking, with a haggard expression and an unhealthy hue, which told of a life which had sapped his strength and robbed him of his youth. He had a nervous and shy manner like that of a sensitive gentleman; he wore a black frock coat, dark trousers and a touch of colour about his necktie, and had the thin and white hands of an artist rather than a surgeon.

'The fact is,' said the doctor, 'that a very singular train of events has occurred recently at my house in Brook Street, and to-night they came to such a head that I felt it was quite impossible for me to wait another hour before asking for your advice and assistance.'

His financial position had prohibited him from taking a house in the Cavendish Square quarter, which would have entailed enormous expenses in rent, furnishings, upkeep, and a horse and carriage. Then a stranger arrived, a Mr Blessington, who offered to set him up in Brook Street and pay all expenses, mostly for his own sake, for he wished to make a good investment with his money. All the doctor had to do was to receive his patients in his consulting room and to retain a quarter of his earnings, plus pocket money. Thus Blessington became his resident patient, as his heart was weak and he needed constant medical supervision. The arrangement was a financial success.

After two visits from a Russian nobleman and his son to see the doctor, Blessington, returning from his walk, was surprised to see strange large footprints upon his light carpet, whose appearance he appeared to overrate. So Holmes and Watson accompanied Trevelyan to see Blessington. Later Trevelyan told Holmes that Blessington had committed suicide by hanging. Trevelyan called again at Baker Street with Inspector Lanner at Holmes' invitation, and were told that the three intruders were the Worthingdon bank robbers, who, having served time, had taken revenge upon Blessington, the police informer.

Mrs Warren, a neighbouring landlady of Great Orme Street, called to see Holmes, as a previous lodger of hers, Mr Fairdale Hobbs, had recommended him to her, and could not praise him enough; she knew that if anyone could help her, Holmes could.

Mrs Warren was worried over her new lodger – a middle-sized man, dark, bearded, not over thirty, who spoke good English but with a foreign accent; he was smartly dressed in dark clothes. He kept to his rooms, and paid her extra in rent – five pounds a week, so as not to be disturbed, and had free entry with his own door key; he had only been out once, on the first night. He rang for his meal, which was left upon an outside chair. Anything else required was printed in pencil on a slip of foolscap paper and left on the chair; so far there was, DAILY GAZETTE, SOAP and MATCH. Mrs Warren showed Holmes two burnt matches and a cigarette-end. The end was matted, so it wasn't smoked in a holder, so it could hardly have been smoked by a man with a beard and moustache. This suggested to Holmes a clean-shaven smoker and perhaps no longer an English person as suggested by the word 'Match' and not matches. And why the *Daily Gazette*? Holmes consulted his great day book, where he found the *Daily Gazette* extracts for the last two weeks, and found in the agony columns suggestive messages, signed 'G'. The latest message said: 'High red house with white stone facings. Third floor. Second window left. After dusk. G'. In the previous message was an agreed code: 'One A, two B, and so on.'

The next morning Mrs Warren suddenly burst into the room with an explosive energy. 'It's a police matter, Mr Holmes! I'll have no more of it! He shall pack out of there with his baggage. I would have gone straight up and told him so, only I thought it was but fair to you to take your opinion first. But I'm at the end of my patience, and when it comes to knocking my old man about…' Apparently, earlier in the morning, as Mr Warren walked down the road towards the Tottenham Court Road, where he worked as timekeeper at Morton and Wright's, two men threw a coat over his head and bundled him into a cab, which drove about for an hour, and then they bundled him out on Hampstead Heath.

Holmes told Mrs Warren that he had a great fancy to see the lodger. She thought that she could arrange a viewing if Holmes went into the boxroom opposite. There hiding behind the door, he would be able to see a reflection in a looking glass.

So Holmes and Watson called round at the landlady's high, thin, yellow-brick edifice at half past twelve, so as to be in position before the lodger's lunch at one o'clock.

Wiggins was the leader of the Baker Street Irregulars, taller and older than the other six to twelve boys. He called when he had information for Holmes, whom he called the 'guv'nor'; Holmes called him 'my dirty little lieutenant'.

Jabez Wilson, a widower, called upon a June Saturday in 1890. A very stout, florid-faced elderly gentleman, his fiery red hair was his most striking attribute. He was addicted to taking snuff, and was pompous and slow. 'He wore rather baggy grey shepherd's check trousers, a not over-clean black frock coat, unbuttoned in the front, and a drab waistcoat with a heavy brassy Albert chain,[150] and a square pierced bit of metal dangling down as an ornament.

---

[150]Short kind of watch chain, named after the Prince Consort, Albert of Saxe-Coburg, husband of Queen Victoria.

A frayed top hat and a faded brown overcoat with a wrinkled velvet collar lay upon a chair beside him. Watson also noticed his small, fat-encircled eyes and red thick fingers.

Holmes went further: 'Beyond the obvious facts that he has at some time done manual labour, that he takes snuff, that he is a Freemason, that he has been in China, and that he has done a considerable amount of writing lately, I can deduce nothing else.'

Wilson had been a ship's carpenter, wore an arc-and-compass breast-pin, was tattooed above the right wrist with a Chinese fish, and had a right shiny cuff and a smooth patch near the left elbow. Wilson thought all this very clever at first, but, after Holmes' explanation, saw that there was really nothing in it after all!

Wilson kept a small pawnbroker's business at the faded and stagnant Saxe-Coburg Square, Aldersgate, near the City – a 'poky, little, shabby-genteel place, where four lines of dingy two-storeyed brick houses looked out into a small railed-in enclosure, where a lawn of weedy grass and a few clumps of faded laurel bushes made a hard fight against a smoke-laden and uncongenial atmosphere.' Originally employing two assistants, he only now had one, Vincent Spaulding, who had a white splash of acid upon his forehead and was small, stoutly built with a hairless face, about thirty and quick in his movements; a gypsy had pierced his ears when he was a lad. He was willing to work for half wages.

It was Spaulding who pointed out to Wilson the following advertisement in the *Morning Chronicle* of 27 April 1890:

To the Red-Headed League:
On account of the bequest of the late Ezekiah Hopkins, of Lebanon, Pennsylvania, USA, there is now another vacancy open which entitles a member of the League to a salary of £4 a week for purely nominal services. All red-headed men who are sound in body and mind, and above the age of twenty-one years, are eligible. Apply in person on Monday, at eleven o'clock, to Duncan Ross, at the offices of the League, 7 Pope's Court, Fleet Street.

The fact that Wilson got the job over the multitude of red-headed folk who choked Pope's Court seeking to be employed, plus Spaulding's unusual cheapness and the fact that his ears were pierced, and that the League was dissolved within five months, excited Holmes considerably, for he thought he knew this man, whose name was John Clay, a bank-robber among other things. For when Holmes had knocked on the door of the pawnbroker's and spoken to Spaulding, he noticed the knees of his trousers. He had fooled Wilson into believing that he was developing photographs in the cellar, when in reality he was tunnelling beneath the adjacent City and Suburban Bank, after the French gold. He had not fooled Holmes, who had noted that the bank premises backed on to Mr Wilson's shop.

Mr James Windibank, stepfather of Miss Mary Sutherland, called at Baker Street at six o'clock in the evening to see Holmes concerning the disappearance of Hosmer Angel, in reply to Holmes' letter.

James Windibank was a traveller for Westhouse and Marbank, claret importers of Fenchurch Street; 'a sturdy, middle-sized fellow, some thirty years of age, clean-shaven, and sallow-skinned, with a bland, insinuating manner, and a pair of wonderfully sharp and penetrating grey eyes'. He wore a shiny top hat. His letter to Holmes and the four letters from 'Mr Angel', were all typed upon the same typewriter, as evidenced by the slurred 'e's' and the tailless 'r's' and fourteen other similar characteristics. Thus it was that Holmes knew that he had solved the mystery of the missing bridegroom.

Holmes knew that Windibank's scoundrelly action was not outside the law, even if he did pose as Hosmer Angel. 'The law cannot, as you say, touch you... yet there never was a man who deserved punishment more. If the young lady has a brother or a friend, he ought to lay a whip across your shoulders. By Jove!' he continued, flushing up at the sight of a bitter sneer upon the man's face, 'it is not part of my duties to my client, but here's a hunting crop handy and I think I shall just treat myself to—' But before Holmes could grip the crop, the visitor had disappeared through the open door, down the stairs, banged the hall door and was away running at top speed down Baker Street.

Sherlock Holmes and the Americans

Sherlock Holmes came to know many Americans during his life

at the Baker Street flat. Watson records a few of the names of those who actually visited Baker Street. There are possibly others, who go unrecorded – perhaps their mission was of too delicate a nature and Holmes forbade publication, for Holmes was very pro-American and would not have wished any indiscretion to occur.

There was John Garrideb, Counsellor at Law, Moorville, Kansas, USA. He called at Baker Street in June 1902. Watson described him as a ' short, powerful man with the round, fresh, clean-shaven face, characteristic of so many American men of affairs. The general effect was chubby and rather child-like, so that one received the impression of quite a young man with a broad set smile upon his face. His eyes, however, were arresting. Seldom in any human head have I seen a pair which bespoke a more intense inward life, so bright were they, so alert, so responsive to every change of thought. His accent was American, but was not accompanied by any eccentricity of speech.'

Holmes deduced that he had been in England some time, as his clothes were 'nearly all London', from the shoulder cut of his coat to the toes of his boots, and his accent had worn thin with time. After he had said he was in law at Topeka, Holmes observed that he knew Dr Lysander Starr, mayor in 1890 there. His visitor neatly fell into the trap as he said, 'His name is still honoured', for Holmes had fabricated the name. When Garrideb showed Holmes an advertisement in a Birmingham newspaper with the name of Howard Garrideb, constructor of agricultural machinery – the word 'plows' being spelt the American way – Holmes became suspicious of his whole story, of the true existence of A H Garrideb, his will, and the necessity to find two more Garridebs to share the fifteen million dollars.

Holmes consulted Lestrade, and among the rogues' portrait gallery was found James Winter, alias Morecroft, alias Killer Evans. He was aged forty-four years and a native of Chicago, and was known to have shot three men in the States. Having escaped from prison, he came to London in 1893 and shot Roger Prescott (Chicago forger and coiner) in January 1895 in a nightclub in the Waterloo Road. Evans was released in 1901. He was a dangerous, usually armed, man. Holmes sensed that the home of Nathan

Garrideb – a beneficiary-to-be – was formerly that of Prescott. There, Holmes and Watson confronted Evans, who fired two shots, missing Holmes but wounding Watson. Both could easily have been killed. The law saw to it that Evans was again put safely behind prison bars.

Upon a wild October morning, after a month of trivialities and stagnation, Holmes' depressed spirits took a bright and joyous turn, when he received a letter from the American, Neil Gibson, the Gold King, former senator for a Western state, and now living at Thor Place in Hampshire. The letter, from Claridge's Hotel, London, (passionate, unconventional, unbusinesslike), ran as follows:

Dear Mr Sherlock Holmes,
        I can't see the best woman God ever made go to her death without doing all that is possible to save her. I can't explain things – I can't even try to explain them, but I know beyond all doubt that Miss Dunbar is innocent. You know the facts – who doesn't? It has been the gossip of the country. And never a voice raised for her! It's the damned injustice of it all that makes me crazy. That woman has a heart that wouldn't let her kill a fly. Well, I'll come at eleven to-morrow and see if you can get some ray of light in the dark. Maybe I have a clue and don't know it. Anyhow, all I know and all I have and all I am are for your use if only you can save her. If ever in your life you showed your powers, put them now into this case.

Mr Gibson ascended the stairs with a heavy step and was shown into the room; Watson recorded his impression of the millionaire:

As I looked upon him I understood not only the fears and dislike of his manager [Marlow Bates] but also the execrations which so many business rivals have heaped upon his head. If I were a sculptor and desired to idealise the successful man of affairs, iron of nerve and leathery of conscience, I should choose Mr Neil Gibson as my model. His tall, gaunt, craggy figure had a suggestion of hunger and rapacity. An Abraham Lincoln keyed to base uses instead of high ones would give some idea of the man. His face might have been chiselled in granite, hard-set, craggy, remorseless, with deep lines upon it, the scars of many a crisis. Cold grey eyes looking shrewdly out from under bristling brows, surveyed us each in turn. He bowed in perfunctory fashion as Holmes mentioned my name, and then with a masterful air of possession he drew a chair up to my companion and seated himself with his bony knees almost touching him.

Holmes was six feet tall, but Gibson's great loose figure towered above him.

His Brazilian wife, clad in a dinner-dress with a shawl over her shoulders, was found at Thor Bridge, with a revolver bullet through her brain, about eleven at night. A note clutched very tightly in her left hand, from Miss Dunbar, cast suspicion upon the governess as being the murderess. The short note said:

I will be at Thor Bridge at nine o'clock. G Dunbar.

Could Neil Gibson have been connected with the murder? Holmes had to consider all the options; the manager had called Gibson a villain, a man of violence who overawed his staff, slept with a loaded revolver to hand and used words of cold, cutting contempt to his wife in front of the servants. 'Our millionaire does not seem to shine in private life,' said Holmes; but, by bringing a little imagination to reality and the use of Watson's revolver, he was able to vindicate Miss Dunbar and show how perverted love had caused a suicide.

Jefferson Hope, an American from Salt Lake City, 'visited' the Baker Street flat, brought there by young Wiggins, in his own cab, thinking he had a legitimate passenger; but it was a ruse by Holmes to capture the murderer of two American Mormons in London, Enoch J Drebber from Cleveland, Ohio, (found in the front room of 3 Lauriston Gardens, Brixton, with two letters upon his body, one addressed to the American Exchange, Strand, London, and the other to his secretary, Joseph Stangerson), and Stangerson.

Hope was tall with gaunt hands, his original black hair of twenty years ago now grizzled, his face weather-beaten and sunburnt. He had been in turn a pioneer in California, a Washoe hunter, scout trapper, ranchman and silver prospector in the Nevada mountains. He had occasion to save Lucy Ferrier from being trampled and crushed to death by a drive of fierce-eyed, long-horned bullocks. They both fell in love and she became the happiest girl in all Utah. Both Drebber and Stangerson wanted Lucy for another of their wives; they killed Lucy's adopted father and Drebber married the girl, but she only lived for a month. Hope vowed vengeance upon the Mormons and, after snatching Lucy's wedding ring from her dead finger, travelled for five years upon the Mormons' trail, through the United States across to Europe, on to St Petersburg, Paris, Copenhagen and eventually to London. Drebber, Hope poisoned; Stangerson, he stabbed in the heart. He thought that Holmes deserved to be a chief of police.

The next night, before sentence could be passed, Hope died from a bust aneurism and he was found in the morning 'stretched upon the floor of his cell, with a placid smile upon his face, as though he had been able in his dying moments to look back upon a useful life, and on work well done'.

John Openshaw of Horsham called upon Holmes in 1887. He claimed an American connection though his uncle, Elias, who had emigrated to America as a young man and became a planter in Florida. He fought under Jackson and Hood, reaching the rank of colonel. He later returned to England, buying a Horsham estate in Sussex. Elias, Holmes was told, was found dead in a little green-scummed pool in the garden, on the night of 2 May 1883. His father, who inherited the estate, was murdered in one of the deep chalk pits near one of the forts upon Portsdown Hill in January 1885. Both men had previously received through the post an envelope containing five dried orange pips, the death sign from the Ku Klux Klan, for upon the inner flap just above the gum were the letters KKK scrawled in red ink. This was the terrible secret society formed by ex-Confederate soldiers in the Southern states after the Civil War. Now John Openshaw showed Holmes a similar envelope containing five little dried orange pips, with a repeated instruction to 'Put the papers on the sundial.' Holmes advised him to accede to instructions, and put the remaining pieces of paper – the others having been burnt – in a brass box and place it upon the sundial. (The papers belonged to the society and were taken by Elias upon the break-up of the KKK when he disappeared from America.) But Openshaw never reached home; he was murdered near Waterloo Bridge. At the news, Holmes felt depressed, for he had not been able to forestall the last death. But he would seek revenge; he studied the Lloyd's ship registers and files of old papers and, with other information, he finally tracked down a Captain Calhoun of the *Lone Star*, an American ship, as the leader of the gang. The ship was homeward bound for Savannah, Georgia, but foundered in the equinoctial gales, so that Holmes' plan, contained in a letter to the Savannah police – to arrest the captain and his two mates for murder – was unnecessary.

Two Americans, Mr and Mrs Francis Hay Moulton, were invited by Holmes to Baker Street after he had cleared up the mystery of Lord St Simon's missing wife.

Francis Hay came originally from the Rockies, and his wife (daughter of Aloysius Doran, a rich gold miner) from San Francisco. They met at McQuire's Camp near the Rockies in 1884, where Doran was working a claim. The lovers became engaged and married in secret, against her father's wishes. Francis sought his fortune in Montana, Arizona and New Mexico, where he was reported killed by Apache Indians who raided the miners' camp. But he had escaped, and came to England hoping to find his wife.

Lord St Simon met Mrs Moulton at 'Frisco', and she, thinking herself to be a widow, allowed herself to be brought to London and married to her lord. As Lady Simon, she fully intended to be a true wife to him, but when she saw her husband, Francis, in the church, she knew what her first duty should be, after receiving his note asking her to join him in the park. For Francis had seen the wedding announcement and the name of the church in the newspaper. He disposed of the wedding clothes to cover up their escape, and together they took lodgings at 226 Gordon Square, intending to return to America without giving an explanation to His Lordship.

In the pocket of the discarded wedding dress, Lestrade found a note:

You will see me when all is ready. Come at once. F H M.

It had been written on the reverse side of a hotel bill, whose prices indicated a most select establishment of which there were not many in London. Holmes traced the hotel down to the one in Northumberland Avenue, whose register showed Moulton as a visitor; he had asked that any letters should be forwarded to 226 Gordon Square. Thus Holmes was able to find them, and he showed them that it was wrong to be so secretive and cajoled them into coming round to Baker Street. There they met Lord St Simon, who rather coldly acknowledged the loss of his 'wife', and departed, the happy couple staying to supper.

Another visitor to Baker Street was Steve Dixie, a Negro bruiser and one of the Spencer John gang, who possibly may have hailed from America. He burst into the room and began to threaten Holmes with his huge knotted fist. 'Well, I've given you fair warnin'… I've a friend that's interested out Harrow way – you know what I'm meaning – and he don't intend to have no buttin' in by you. Got that? You ain't the law, and I ain't the law either, and if you come in I'll be on hand also. Don't you forget it.' But Holmes parried the threat by reminding the Negro of a certain killing outside the Holborn Bar, which was enough to create a hasty exit by Dixie.

Some Americans Holmes met away from Baker Street, in the course of his investigations. He met the American woman, Irene Adler, at her home, Briony Lodge, Serpentine Avenue, St John's Wood, and although acting the part of a Nonconformist minister, never deceived the astute woman.

Holmes met Abe Slaney, an American, at Riding Thorpe Manor, the home of Hilton Cubitt and his people for the last five hundred years. Slaney was tall, handsome and swarthy, with blazing black eyes, a bristling black beard, a great aggressive hooked nose, who wore a panama hat[151] and flourished a cane as he swaggered up the path to the manor house. He had known Mrs Elsie Cubitt as the daughter of Mr Patrick, the gang boss of seven men. He became engaged to Elsie, but marriage was forbidden. Elsie came to London staying at a boarding house in Russell Square. There, too, came Hilton Cubitt (upon his vicar's recommendation), who falling in love with the young American

---

[151]Hand-plaited hat made in Ecuador, from the leaves of a South American cyclanthaceous plant, *Carludorica palmata*.

girl married her quickly at a registry office, before returning to Norfolk. Slaney followed Elsie to England and eventually to Norfolk, staying at Elridge's Farm, East Ruston, where, occupying a downstairs room, he was able to go out at night without causing suspicion and leave a coded message for Elsie upon the pedestal of the sundial. Later Slaney came to the house and shot Cubitt, and nearly drove Elsie to death's door. Holmes was able to bring the gangster to the Manor House by using the gangster's code, and there he clapped a pistol to his head and Inspector Martin slipped the handcuffs over his wrists. Slaney was condemned to death, but later the sentence was commuted to penal servitude.

Mr Grant Munro, a hop merchant of Norbury, who had married a widow called Mrs Effie Hebron, came to see Holmes at Baker Street because after three blissful married years an unknown barrier had recently sprung up between them. Upon marriage, his wife's income of four thousand, five hundred pounds, invested at seven per cent, was made over to her husband, with the proviso that if she ever needed money, her 'banker' would give it to her. One day she asked for one hundred pounds, which surprised her husband, as she would concede no reason for wanting such a sum. Then Mr Munro, taking a local walk, noticed that a lone empty cottage was now let, for furnishings were being taken inside, and he was mildly interested, wondering who the new people were. As he looked, he saw a face at the window and he gained the impression that the features were unnatural and inhuman, which sent a chill down his back, for they were of a livid chalky white. Knocking at the door, just to be neighbourly, he asked if, as he lived nearby, he could be of any help. But he was rebuffed by a tall, gaunt woman with a harsh face and a Northern accent, who shut the door in his face. He told Holmes of his wife's furtive movements and her visits to the cottage, which aroused his suspicions. Together with Holmes and Watson, the trio forced an entry into the cottage in spite of his wife's entreaties not to do so. Rushing upstairs, they found a young girl in the bedroom, dressed in a red frock and white gloves, her face of the strangest livid tint. Holmes soon exposed the mystery by pulling off a mask, exposing a coal-black Negress, Lucy Hebron. When Mr Munro saw the child he stared and clutched at his throat in utter disbelief for ten minutes; then reaching a magnanimous decision, he lifted the child up, kissed her, and taking his wife's hand, they returned happily home.

Among the Americans Holmes met away from Baker Street was Mr Leverton, a detective of Pinkerton's American Agency; although Holmes never met William Hargreave of the New York Police Bureau, they did correspond by cable.

Birdy Edwards was an American detective of Pinkerton's American Agency in Chicago; he used two aliases, John McMurdo and Edward John Douglas, as he travelled to Vermissa Valley and Benito Canyon. He was said to have made his money in the California goldfields, and wore a gold ring with a nugget on it. Halfway up his right forearm was a curious brown design – a triangle within a circle, the brandmark of Lodge 341, Vermissa Valley; this penance he had been forced to undergo as part of his 'cover' while on the trail of the McGinty gang of murderers, whom he eventually cornered. He came to England, bought Birlstone Manor House in Sussex and married an English girl, Ivy, after their meeting in a London boarding house. [152]

But Edwards was pursued by one of the gang, an American called Ted Baldwin, who came to England under the alias of Hargrave, and stayed at the Eagle Commercial in Tunbridge Wells; from here he used a Rudge-Whitworth bicycle to travel to Birlstone Manor House. In a scuffle between Edwards and Baldwin, the latter was killed by his own American sawn-off shotgun.

Holmes received information from Porlock from the crowded underworld, contained in a code, which, when deciphered, told him that there was pressing danger at Birlstone House, against a man called Douglas. Within the hour, Inspector MacDonald of Scotland Yard called and told Holmes that Mr Douglas of Birlstone Manor House had been murdered; MacDonald asked them both to go with him to Birlstone. There, Holmes read a local compilation which described the concealment in the Birlstone Manor House of King Charles, and this together with his other detection work, made Holmes convinced that he would

---

[152]Hilton Cubitt met Elsie Patrick in a London boarding house. ACD, *The Adventure of the Dancing Men*.

find Mr Douglas in the house, which proved to be true as the American eventually came out from the secret hiding place.

After John Douglas was acquitted of murder at the Quarter Sessions, Holmes advised him to leave England and to live in South Africa, but the mighty hand of Moriarty struck him down while still at sea.[153]

Sherlock Holmes had a vision of a future American entente with England, for he believed 'that the folly of a monarch and a blundering of a minister in far-gone years will not prevent our children from being some day citizens of the same worldwide country under a flag which shall be a quartering of the Union Jack with the Stars and Stripes'. (Holmes must have envisaged the future Communist menace.)

American visitors to London collected their letters from home at the American Exchange in the Strand, as did the two Mormons from Salt Lake City, Drebber and Stangerson.

The Americans appreciated intelligence, and paid for it accordingly, which Holmes called the American principle. He thought that American slang was sometimes very expressive, and among his valuable books of reference was an American encyclopaedia; he had a knowledge of American guns. American clients consulted him at and away from Baker Street, and he exchanged criminal information by cable with his American friend, William Hargreave of the New York Police Bureau. In 1914, Holmes played his finest rôle, that of Mr Altamont, an Irish-American from Chicago, with a goatee beard (like the caricatures of Uncle Sam), and a half-smoked cigar hanging from the corner of his mouth – perhaps the American accent came half naturally to him? Holmes noticed very particularly that Beddington the forger stole one hundred thousand pounds worth of American railway bonds. Certainly, Holmes had a great warmth of feeling for America and its people. As he said: 'It is always a joy to meet an American.'

Sherlock Holmes' Retirement

Watson recorded that Holmes was in active practice for twenty-three years, and that, during seventeen of these years, he co-

---

[153]A large proportion of *The Valley of Fear* by ACD takes place in America.

operated with him and kept notes of his cases. Watson's marriages and his return to general medical practice thus kept him from living at Baker Street for some years.

Watson did not always find it easy to determine which cases of Holmes to publish; for some, he had to wait for special permission from Holmes after his retirement before he committed them to print for the public so that it is from these messages that it is possible to arrive at a possible retirement date, for Watson never mentioned the precise date of Holmes leaving Baker Street.

'The Adventure of the Creeping Man,' Watson recorded as taking place in September 1903, the facts of which he said 'formed one of the very last cases handled by Holmes before his retirement from practice'.

It was after the Spring of 1904, that Watson was allowed to publish 'The Adventure of the Empty House,' which had taken place in the Spring of 1894.

As Watson recorded:

> Let me say to that public, which has shown some interest in those glimpses which I have occasionally given them of the thoughts and actions of a very remarkable man, that they are not to blame me if I have not shared my knowledge with them, for I should have considered it my first duty to have done so, had I not been barred by a positive prohibition from his own lips, which was only withdrawn upon the third of last month.

It must have hurt Watson considerably to record that Holmes had 'definitely retired from London'.

So we may surmise Holmes' departure from Baker Street, for the country life, as taking place sometime between September 1903 and early 1904. We know that in 1907 he discovered the murderer of Fitzroy McPherson, in the Sussex countryside.

Obeying at last nature's call, and being in a very sound financial position, Holmes packed his bags, and, saying goodbye to Mrs Hudson, Baker Street and London, retired to a small lonely farmhouse, five miles from Eastbourne. As Holmes recounted:

> My villa is situated upon the southern slopes of the downs, commanding a great view of the Channel. At this point, the coastline

is entirely of chalk cliffs, which can only be descended by a single, long, tortuous path, which is steep and slippery. At the bottom of the path lie a hundred yards of pebble and shingle, even when the tide is at full. Here and there, however, there are curves and hollows which make splendid swimming-pools filled afresh with each flow. This admirable beach extends for some miles in each direction, save only at one point where the little cave and village of Fulworth break the line.

Here it was that Holmes often went swimming with Fitzroy McPherson.[154]

'Towards the end of July 1907, there was a severe gale, the wind blowing up-channel, heaping the seas to the base of the cliffs and leaving a lagoon at the turn of the tide.' It was this freak of nature, that was to call the recluse back to his life's profession. From being a lover of the teeming life of the metropolis, Holmes was at last permitted to appreciate the calm of the countryside, to philosophise, keep bees – his *Practical Handbook of Bee Culture, with Some Observations upon the Segregation of the Queen*, became the apiarist's textbook; the bees had the estate all to themselves. Only his old housekeeper lived with him. His large store of books he kept in the garret. No princely sums of money, often offered to him since his retirement, had as yet tempted him back to his former study. He was determined that his retirement should be a permanent one. He became a little crippled by odd bouts of rheumatism, and, excepting for the rare weekend visit, he saw very little of Watson.

But, even here, in the quiet Sussex countryside, eventually in late 1907, Holmes unwittingly found himself involved in a most obscure and strange death. It was while Holmes was taking a pre-breakfast stroll along the cliff path, which led to the steep descent to the beach, that he met his friend, Harold Stackhurst – a former rowing blue, who lived half a mile away at a large house called The Gables, a coaching establishment for some twenty young men of different professions. There was a staff of several masters, of whom Fitzroy McPherson took science. Holmes and

[154]The name Fitzroy used in *Silver Blaze* – Fitzroy Simpson. Lord Charles Fitzroy was in command of the ship HMS *Beagle*, with Charles Darwin, 1831–1836 *Dictionary of National Biography,* 1903.

Stackhurst suddenly came upon McPherson, who was staggering like a drunken man, and obviously dying. He shrieked out some slurred and indistinct words, which Holmes could only twist into 'the lion's mane'. He died in agony, a reticulated pattern of red inflamed lines across his back. Both Anderson, the village constable (slow of Sussex speech, with a big ginger moustache), and Inspector Bardle of the Sussex Constabulary (a staid, solid bovine man), asked for the great detective's assistance in solving this death. 'I know your immense experience, sir… This is quite unofficial, of course, and need go no further. But I am fairly up against it in this McPherson case. The question is, shall I make an arrest, or shall I not?' He continued: ' What would my position be if I let him [Ian Murdock] slip away with all this evidence against him?' Holmes went through all the known evidence with Bardle, and assured him that his case was far too weak for an arrest; the last word of the dying man was certainly not Murdock, far more likely to have been 'mane'.

Then came the death of McPherson's dog. The news told to Holmes by his old housekeeper; it had died of grief, down on the beach, at the very place where his master had been attacked by something as yet unknown. It was the phrase 'at the very place' which aroused something in Holmes' memory. When he was told the Airedale terrier had been found on the very edge of the pool, his crowded boxroom mind told him that there was something there which related to the present mystery. He then knew it to be a book, so he rummaged for an hour among his books stored in the garret of his house, until he found a small chocolate and silver coloured volume called *Out of Doors* by J G Wood, telling how he very nearly died from the stings of *Cyanea capillata*.

Holmes made an enlarged photograph of the marks upon the back, and through his lens could see that the weal, which extended round the right shoulder, was unequal in its intensity and showed dots of extravasated blood.[155] Holmes reasoned that what made the marks would bring him a long way towards finding the criminal.

Then Ian Murdock, the mathematics master who had also

---

[155]Watson never mentioned that Holmes was interested in photography at Baker Street. It must have only started in Sussex when Holmes had leisure.

been swimming in the natural sea pool, received similar marks across his back, but not fatal ones. So Holmes led Stackhurst and the inspector to the lagoon and there upon a rocky shelf, some three feet under the water, they saw the murderer of McPherson: *Cyanea capillata*, the fearful stinger, more deadly than the bite of the cobra. Holmes observed that it, 'did indeed look like a tangled mass torn from the mane of a lion... a curious waving, vibrating, hairy creature with streaks of silver among its yellow tresses. It pulsated with a slow, heavy dilation and contraction.' Holmes cried, with a shout of triumph, 'Cyanea! ...Behold the Lion's Mane!' To his friend he exclaimed: 'Help me, Stackhurst! Let us end the murderer for ever.' And together they pushed a big boulder over the ledge, down upon the creature, which ended its poisonous life. All that could be seen was one flapping edge of yellow membrane; a thick oily scum oozed out, staining the water, rising slowly to the surface.

For the next five years, Holmes continued to live an Arcadian existence, deep in the Sussex countryside, until 1912. At this time the British government knew that members of the German secret service were at work in England, supplying the Kaiser with England's most vital secrets. But there was no one astute enough to catch the master spy who worked under their very noses, except, of course, one particular man, and he had unfortunately retired to Sussex. If the prophet will not go to the mountain, then the mountain must bestir itself and go to the prophet.

And so a harassed and very worried government, first in the shape of the Foreign Minister, called upon Holmes and pleaded for help, all to no avail. The matter being of first importance called for the head of the government to climb down from his London pinnacle, and to deign to visit the humble farmhouse roof – in short, the Prime Minister himself, who brought strong pressure to bear upon the world's most renowned detective. Holmes eventually succumbed to such high adulation, even if his exterior frame concealed his innermost joy at being once again in the throes of his second love; he was ready to lay his remarkable combination of intellectual and practical activity at the disposal of the British government, which was to uproot him from Sussex for the next two years.

Sherlock Holmes' War Service

So from 1912 to 1914 Holmes assumed a new identity, coupled with perhaps his finest acting of his career, that of Mr Altamont of Chicago, a real bitter, anti-English, Irish-American; a tall, gaunt man with clear-cut features and a small goatee beard which gave him a general resemblance to the caricatures of Uncle Sam. A partially smoked sodden cigar usually hung from the corner of his mouth, and so difficult was he to understand, that it would appear that he had 'declared war upon the King's English'. He graduated in an Irish secret society at Buffalo, seriously troubled the constabulary at Skibbareen, and so eventually caught the attention of a subordinate agent of Von Bork of the German secret service. Thinking that Altamont was just the man to probe into and obtain useful information concerning English naval secrets, Von Bork took Holmes into his confidence. This did not prevent Holmes feeding the Germans with bogus information and ensuring that Jack James, an American, Hollis, Steiner and two other German agents finished up in a Portsmouth jail, not forgetting of course, Holmes' ultimate plan to secure the Kaiser's most devoted agent, who since 1910 had lived in a quiet country house at Harwich, posing as a hard-drinking, hard-riding county squire.

In order to have his ear nearer to the ground regarding naval activities, Holmes took lodgings at Fratton near Portsmouth; he also ensured that Von Bork's only servant was Martha – a dear old ruddy-faced woman in a country cap. On the night of Von Bork's downfall she knitted, stopping occasionally to stroke a large black cat upon a stool beside her. She sat at a table in the window whereon was a lamp, which was later to play a very important rôle in the life of Von Bork. He had spoken of Martha to his friend Baron Von Herling (chief secretary of the legation, and owner of a large 100-horsepower Benz car) as the woman who 'might almost personify Britannia… with her complete self-absorption and general air of comfortable somnolence'; this was the woman who had been personally chosen by Holmes to work for Von Bork and to be in his own private pay.

Holmes was responsible to Von Bork for naval signals; he posed as a motor expert, and the German kept a full garage –

everything likely to arise being named after a spare part. Hence sparking plugs were naval signals, a radiator a battleship, an oil pump a cruiser and so on, including semaphore, lamp code and Marconi. All documents were as Holmes said, only copies, his excuse being that bringing originals was far too dangerous.

Came the night of 2 August 1914, when Holmes would rise to the zenith of his powers and land the chief German spy in his net. Von Bork was looking forward to the welcome he would receive in Berlin for the admirable spy network he had controlled in England; he did not rate the English very highly, referring to them as a 'docile, simple folk'. Holmes had sent Watson a telegram, asking him to bring his Ford car and meet him in Harwich. This request had brought the doctor great happiness and he felt twenty years younger, being, once again, after so long an interval, an associate of Holmes, in whatever devilry was afoot. Together they arrived at the German's residence, where Holmes alighted at the gate and went inside, leaving Watson (now a heavily built elderly man with a grey moustache) in the car.

Holmes entered the German's study. 'You can give me the glad hand to-night, mister… I'm bringing home the bacon at last.' 'The signals?' 'Same as I said in my cable. Every last one of them…' The 'Irish-American' was now a tall gaunt man of sixty, and he sat down in the armchair, stretching his long limbs. He looked around the room. 'Making ready for a move?' he said as his eyes fell upon the open safe. 'Say, mister… you don't tell me you keep your papers in that?' 'Why not?' said Von Bork. 'Gosh, in a wide-open contraption like that! And they reckon you to be some spy. Why, a Yankee crook would be into that with a can-opener. If I'd known that any letter of mine was going to lie loose in a thing like that I'd have been a mug to write to you at all.' 'It would puzzle any crook to force that safe…. It's a double combination lock.' Holmes pretended ignorance of such things. 'Well, you need a word as well as a set of figures before you can get the lock to work.' He indicated a double-radiating disc round the keyhole, the outer one for letters, the inner one for figures. 'So it's not quite as simple as you thought. It was four years ago that I had it made, and what do you think I chose for the word and figures?' Again Holmes pleaded ignorance. 'Well, I chose

August for the word, and 1914 for the figures.' Holmes expressed surprise and admiration, to think that the Germans knew in advance when they would make their final move, even to closing down the next day. Holmes was worried over the fact of a stool pigeon somewhere, and planned a hurried escape to little Holland. Von Bork concurred and told Holmes that a Dutch boat to New York would be the only safe escape within the week.

Holmes handed over the bogus parcel of Signals, and as the German opened it, he was surprised as he read the title of the small blue book, printed in golden letters: *Practical Handbook of Bee Culture, with Some Observations upon the Segregation of the Queen*, by Sherlock Holmes. In an instant, the master spy had gripped Von Bork at the back of the neck by a grasp of iron, and a chloro-formed sponge was held in front of his writhing face. His upper arms and legs were then strapped, and he was placed upon the sofa, sleeping soundly. Meanwhile, Martha had put out her lamp as a signal to Watson that all had gone according to plan.

Together, Holmes and Watson then celebrated their victory with a few glasses of Imperial Tokay, from the Schoenbrun Palace cellar of Franz Josef. (Holmes, like Thaddeus Sholto, appreciated Tokay wine; even Von Bork appreciated that Holmes had a discerning taste in wines.) 'It is a good wine, Holmes.' 'A remarkable wine, Watson.'

From the safe, Holmes removed many dossiers and packed them into the German's valise; Martha was told to report to him the next day at Claridge's Hotel in London. As Von Bork came to from the effects of the drug, he looked at Holmes in amazement and hatred. 'I shall get level with you, Altamont... If it takes me all my life I shall get level with you!' His captor spoke to him as a sportsman: 'Besides ...it is better than to fall before some more ignoble foe.' Other people had tried to get even with Holmes, but he still lived, and now kept bees upon the South Downs – as he said: 'The old sweet song.'

The two friends, holding Von Bork's arms, walked him slowly down the garden walk. After a short final struggle – for the German was a strong and desperate man – bound hand and foot he was hoisted into the spare seat of the little Ford car; he refused Holmes' offer of a cigar. As a private individual, Holmes was proceeding in an absolutely illegal and outrageous way, having no warrant for his arrest, said the German. 'Well, you realise your position, you and your accomplice here. If I were to shout for help as we pass through the village—'

'My dear sir,' said Holmes, 'if you did anything so foolish you would probably enlarge the two limited titles of our village inns by giving us "The Dangling Prussian" as a signpost. The Englishman is a patient creature, but at present his temper is a little inflamed, and it would be as well not to try him too far. No, Mr Von Bork, you will go with us in a quiet, sensible fashion to Scotland Yard, whence you can send for your friend, Baron Von Herling, and see if even now you may not fill that place which he has reserved for you in the ambassadorial suite.'

Holmes explained to Watson how he came to be involved in counter-espionage work. He took his old friend by the shoulders. 'I've hardly seen you in the light yet. How have the years used you? You look the same blithe boy as ever.' Watson was never so happy. 'But you Holmes – you have changed very little – save for that horrible goatee.' 'These are the sacrifices one makes for one's country Watson… To-morrow it will be but a dreadful memory. With my hair cut and a few superficial changes, I shall no doubt reappear at Claridge's to-morrow, as I was before this American stunt – I beg your pardon, Watson, my well of English seems to be permanently defiled – before this American job came my way.' (Good old Watson had thought of Holmes as still being tucked away in the Sussex countryside, living a hermit's life on his South Downs farm. But it does show that Holmes kept in touch with Watson, and knew his address in 1914 which enabled him to communicate quickly by telegram.)

The two friends chatted intimately for a few minutes, before they set off to take their prisoner to Scotland Yard. Holmes pointed to the moonlit sea. 'There's an east wind coming Watson.' 'I think not Holmes. It is very warm.' 'Good old Watson! You are the one fixed point in a changing age. There's an east wind coming all the same, such a wind as never blew on England yet. It will be cold and bitter, Watson, and a good many of us may wither before its blast. But it's God's own wind none the less, and a cleaner, better, stronger land will lie in the sunshine when the storm has cleared.'

Before Holmes returned to the peace of the Sussex countryside, it is pleasant to think that he visited his previous landlady,
Mrs Hudson, for she had been very fond of her tenant, if at times
a little overawed, but she had never interfered with him, however
outrageous his proceedings. She had tolerated the invasion of her
'castle', by undesirable people, Holmes' eccentricity, his irregularity, his untidiness, his music at unseemly hours – sometimes
far into the night, his revolver practice and malodorous scientific
experiments, which, all in all, had made him the worst tenant in
London. Perhaps she had been mollified by the princely payments
she had received, for Watson said that they were sufficient to have
even bought the house.

Sherlock Holmes had been, in turn, a Victorian, an Edwardian
and a Georgian, the most scientific master consulting detective of
all time. No other detective had, or would ever have such world
renown. The body may have died in a Sussex farmhouse,
although there is no record of his death; perhaps he acquired the
elixir of life, and is still alive. Perhaps we may leave his friend
Watson to have the final word, for he thought Holmes 'the best
and wisest man whom I have ever known'.

Index

C

Cabinet, the, 124, 146

Café Royal, 180

Cairns, Patrick, 121, 161, 336, 337

Calhoun, Captain James, 246, 384

Camberwell, 66, 80, 178, 290

Cambridge, 24, 123, 129, 145, 192, 248

Camden House, 51, 88, 117, 196, 213, 225, 253, 281

Camford, 199

Campden Mansions, 124

Canada, 140, 330

Candahar, 25

Canterbury, 186, 198

Cantlemere, Lord, 45, 335

Cape Town, 330, 341

Capital and Counties Bank, 255

Caratal, Louis, 185

Cardboard Box, The Adventure of the, 267

Carey, Captain Peter, 121, 160, 208, 244, 336

Carfax, Lady Frances, 74, 83, 122, 200, 232, 262, 266, 271, 290, 344

Carina (singer), 137

Carlton Club, 130, 340

Carlyle, Thomas, 78, 79

Carruthers, Bob, 205, 306

Cartwright, 121, 175, 211, 307

Catullus, Gaius Valerius, 78, 138, 139

Caulfield Gardens, 124

Cavendish Square, 117

Cavendish tobacco, 235

Cedars, The, 236

Chaldean, 245, 326

Challenger, Professor, 276

Charing Cross, 50, 92, 102, 110, 111, 122, 127, 175, 180, 247

Charles I, King of Great Britain, 20, 128, 156, 387

Charles Street, 122, 169, 307

Charlington Hall, 205, 240, 306

Charlington Heath, 80, 208

Charpentier, Arthur, 345

Charpentier, Mrs, 103

Charron, Pierre, 30

Chatham, 110, 134, 250

Chertsey Bridge, 259

Chilton Grange, 205

China, 110, 324, 329

Chiswick, 126

Chopin, Frédéric François, 136

Church Street, 78, 233, 280

ciphers and codes, 315

City and Suburban Bank, 213, 353

Claridge's Hotel, 171, 381, 395

Clay, John, 171, 212, 213, 236, 242, 353

Clayton, John, 189, 337

Coburg Square, 311, 318

Cock, William, 329

Cold Harbour Lane, 64

Colonna, Prince of, 110

COMMERCIAL ROAD, 125

Conduit Street, 116

Constant, Benjamin, 147

Continental Gazetteer, 138, 313

Coombe Tracey, 83, 86

Copenhagen, 383

Copernicus, Nicolaus, 33

Copper Beeches, The Adventure of the, 325

Coram, Professor, 128, 238, 250, 289, 348

Cornwall, 36, 76, 94, 160, 179, 208, 220, 244, 245, 264, 274, 306, 326

Cosmopolitan, Hotel, 132
Court of Queen's Bench, 85
Covent Garden, 137, 191, 203, 243, 259, 366
Coventry, Sergeant, 171, 201
Cox & Co, 102
Crabtree Parva, 294
Crédit Lyonnais, 119, 183
Creeping Man, The Adventure of the, 389
Cremona violins, 271
Crendall, 243, 356
Criterion Bar, 27
Crocker, Captain, 36, 205, 338
Crockford's Clerical Directory, 121
Crooked Man, The, 301
Croxley Master, The, 240, 298
Croydon, 43, 149, 164
Cubitt, Elsie, 316
Cubitt, Hilton, 47, 162, 305, 315, 339
Cunninghams, 54, 231, 277, 319, 320
Cushing, Miss Mary, 152, 164
Cushing, Miss Sarah, 135, 164
Cushing, Miss Susan, 43, 164
Cuvier, George, 18
Cyanea capillata, 166, 391, 392

D

Dacre Hotel, 110
Dacre, Lionel, 42
Daily Press, 70
Damery, Sir James, 22, 130, 257, 340
Dancing Men, The Adventure of the, 47, 162, 273, 315
Dantzig, 173
Dartmoor, 33, 50, 73, 91, 96, 155, 190, 221, 243, 264, 268
Darwin, Charles, 390

Davenport, J, 142
Dawson (groom), 260
De Quincey, Thomas, 56
De Reszkes, 137
Defoe, Daniel, 13
Dennis, Sally, 251, 286
Derby, the, 224
Deutsche Bank, 183
Devil's Foot, The Adventure of the, 93, 179, 326
Devine, Marie, 83
Devon, 50, 73, 80, 83, 85, 86, 98, 121, 155, 175, 179, 211
Dickens, Charles, 68, 104, 109, 123, 236, 259, 362
Diogenes Club, 141
Dixie, Steve, 311
Dixon, Jeremy, 130
Dobney, Miss, 232, 262
Doctors' Commons, 246
Dodd, Dr James M, 249, 259, 341
dog cart, 167
dogs, 60, 115, 130, 144, 145, 146, 325
Donnithorpe, 15
Dorak, A, 125, 176
Doran, Hatty, 369
Douglas, John, 268, 329, 387, 388
Douglas, Sir John Sholto, 124
Dovercourt, Earl of, 217, 232, 295, 358
Downing, Constable, 167
Dowson, Baron, 226
Drebber, Enoch, 23, 57, 60, 103, 116, 132, 143, 200, 251, 286, 298, 300, 309, 338, 345, 354, 382, 383, 388
Dublin, 152
Dubugue, Monsieur, 173
Dulong, Hôtel, 54

Dunbar, Miss, 37, 94, 128, 171, 201
Duncan Street, 251
Dundee, 84, 160, 246, 337
Dupin, Auguste, 18, 31, 38, 39, 40, 44, 201, 229, 255

E

East London, 84
Eccles, Scott, 82, 122, 207, 331, 342
Edgware Road, 94, 213, 244
Edmunds, Constable, 343
Edwards, Birdy, 387
Elman, Reverend, 121, 210
Elridge's Farm, 386
Emsworth, Colonel, 49, 250, 259
Emsworth, Godfrey, 49, 250, 341
Encyclopaedia Britannica, 318
English Channel, 389
Ernest, Dr Ray, 163, 172, 223, 224
Esher, 80, 122, 166, 207, 304, 332, 342, 345
Essex, 121, 210, 224
Etheridge, Mrs, 374
Euclid, 39
Euston Station, 249
Evans, Killer, 213, 278
Exeter, 249
Eyford, 78, 346

F

Fagin, 144, 362
Fairbairn, Alec, 152, 164
Falder, Lady Beatrice, 87, 224, 243
Falder, Sir Denis, 225

Falder, Sir William, 225
Family Herald (ladies magazine), 137
Farnham, 80, 205, 213, 252, 370
Farquhar, Dr, 69
Ferguson, R, 24, 37, 73, 130, 258, 264, 331
Ferrier, Lucy, 74
FFOLLIOTT, SIR GEORGE, 123
Fighting Cock Inn, 88, 194, 254
Flaubert, Gustave, 245
Fleet Street, 80, 217
Florence, 82
Fool's cap and bells, 57
Forbes, Detective, 168, 169
Fordingham, 17
Foreign Affairs, Secretary for, 85
Foreign Office, 98, 122, 168, 188, 287, 307
Forest Row, 160, 336
Forrester, Inspector, 54, 162, 194, 231
Forrester, Mrs, 22, 62, 66, 171
Fowler, Mr, 220
Franco–Midland Hardware Company, 75
Frankland, Mr, 85
Fratton, 125
French Embassy, 242
French President, 270
French Republic, 257
Fresno Street, 229
Friesland (Dutch steamship), 276
Frinton, 210
Fulham Road, 221
Fulworth, 211, 297, 390

G

Gaboriau, Emile, 38, 199

Garcia, Aloysius, 122, 166, 207, 304, 331, 342, 343
Garrideb, John, 85, 108
Garrideb, Nathan, 94, 108, 213, 244, 259
Gelder & Co, 110
Gemmi Pass, 186
Genoa, 132
German agents, 393
German secret service, 392
Ghazis, 26
Gibson, Neil, 37, 94, 171
Gladstone, William Ewart, 159
Glasshouse Street, 181
Gloucester Road, 100, 137
Godolphin Street, 85, 150
Goethe, Johann Wolfgang von, 245
Goldini's Restaurant, 100, 137
GOODGE STREET, 132
Gordon Square, 384, 385
Gordon, General, 109, 203
Gorgiano, Giuseppe, 154, 173, 254
Goring, Septimus, 196
Gorot (clerk), 169
Grafenstein, Count, 21
Grand Hotel, 180
Gravesend, 319
Great Expectations, 109
Great Orme Street, 253, 295, 322, 376
Great Winglebury, 123
Green Dragon (tavern), 210
Green, Philip, 200, 266, 290, 344
Gregory, Inspector, 155, 243, 268, 365
Gregson, Inspector, 35, 58, 62, 72, 114, 119, 132, 148, 154, 173, 174, 200, 254, 306, 308, 311, 331, 338, 343
Grenoble, 116

Greuze, Jean Baptiste, 183, 215
Greyminster, Duke of, 342
Grimesby, Dr, 239, 258, 365
Grimpen Mire, 179, 221
Gross, Hans, 38
Grosvenor Mansions, 45
Grosvenor Square, 22, 291
Grosvenor tobacco, 238
Gruner, Baron Adelbert, 76, 93, 98, 126, 130, 176, 181, 225, 250, 257, 297, 341
Guildford Assizes, 123
Guion Steamship Company, 60

H

Hafiz, Mohammed, 245
Half Moon Street, 76
Hallamshire, 249
Halliday's Private Hotel, 61, 74, 115, 153, 355
Hampshire, 36, 94, 129, 171, 209
Hampstead, 72, 80, 95, 217
Harding Brothers, 126, 148
Hardy, Thomas, 239
Hargreave, William, 174, 316
Harker, Horace, 148
Harley Street, 33, 82, 208
Harold, Mrs, 119
HARRINGBY, LORD, 123
Harrison, Joseph, 169, 241, 242, 277
Harrow, 165, 254, 262
Harwich, 101, 126
Hatherley, Victor, 26, 68, 77, 345, 346
Hayes, Reuben, 230, 254, 262, 308
Haymarket Theatre, 83
Hayter, Colonel, 51, 54, 162, 194, 197, 231, 259, 277, 319

L

M

Palmerston, Lord Henry John, 292

Paris, 55, 127, 173, 186, 201, 383

Park Lane, 92

Parker (garrotter), 116, 187

Parkhurst Prison, 176, 351

Patrick, Elsie, 339, 387

Patterson, Inspector, 100, 187

Pattins, Hugh, 337

Peace, Charlie, 272

Peak District, 249

Peckham, 286

Penang lawyer, 359

Pennsylvania Small Arms Company, 33

Persia, 188

Persian slipper, 235

Peshawar, 26

Peters, Holy, 74, 84, 200

Peterson (commissionaire), 329, 363

Petrarch, Francesco, 249

Phelps, Percy, 24, 27, 55, 98, 99, 112, 122, 134, 135, 169, 205, 206, 207, 218, 241, 259, 276, 287, 288, 307, 308, 363, 364

Pie, Sir Omicron, 185

Pike, Landale, 177

Pinkerton's American Agency, 154, 173, 387

Pinner, Arthur Harry, 75, 234

Pinto, Maria, 94

Pitman, Sir Isaac, 149

Pitt Street, 111

Podgers, Mr, 312

Poe, Edgar Allan, 21, 38, 39, 40, 42, 44, 181, 193, 201, 229, 255, 270, 315, 317

Poldhu Bay, 94, 111, 179, 208, 274

Polyphonic Motets of Lassus, 315

Pondicherry, 24, 65, 80, 84, 144, 169, 188, 240, 246, 259, 312

Pope, Alexander, 30

Pope, the, 270

Poplar, 124, 352

Porlock, Fred, 177, 178, 181, 198, 316, 317, 355, 387

Portsdown Hill, 383

Portsmouth, 26, 125, 258, 393

Poultney Square, 200

Prague, 125, 176, 333, 334

Prendergast, Jack, 23

Prendergast, Major, 23

Presbury, Professor, 70, 101, 102, 125, 176, 199, 250, 265, 269, 326, 333, 334

Prescott, Roger, 260, 380

Pretoria, 341

Prime Minister, 265, 332

Priory School, 135

Proudie, Dr, 185

Purloined Letter, The, 21, 40, 181, 229, 255, 270

Pycroft, Hall, 75, 234, 267

Q

Quarter Sessions, 388

Queen Anne Street, 70

Queer Street, 87

R

Radix pedis diaboli, 76

Railway Timetables, 138

Ralph (butler), 49

Rance, Constable, 261

Randall gang, 162

Reade, Winwood, 63, 78